Internatio ... ›ol (IMPRS)
... ime Affairs
... f Hamburg

Hamburg Studies on Maritime Affairs
Volume 11

Philipp Wendel

State Responsibility for Interferences with the Freedom of Navigation in Public International Law

Springer

Dr. Philipp Wendel
Akademie Auswärtiger Dienst
Schwarzer Weg 45
13505 Berlin
philipp.wendel@gmx.de

Library of Congress Control Number: 2007934272

ISSN 1614-2462

ISBN 978-3-540-74332-3 Springer Berlin Heidelberg New York

Springer is a part of Springer Science+Business Media

springer.com

Production: LE-TEX Jelonek, Schmidt & Vöckler GbR, Leipzig
Cover-design: WMX Design GmbH, Heidelberg

SPIN 12110667 64/3180YL - 5 4 3 2 1 0 Printed on acid-free paper

Preface

No dissertation without a decent preface – and no legal dissertation without an elaborated structure, particularly if an author with a German background bears responsibility for it. Thus, even this preface will need to carry some structure. This study could not have been accomplished without three kinds of support: institutional, academic and personal.

As far as it concerns the institutional support, the International Max Planck Research School for Maritime Affairs deserves first-hand mentioning since it provided a scholarship and excellent research opportunities at the Max Planck Institute in Hamburg. Furthermore, the libraries at the University of Miami, the University of Hamburg, the International Tribunal for the Law of the Sea and the International Maritime Organization contributed significantly to the research for this study.

The academic support consisted mainly in the intensive dialogue with the author's teachers and colleagues. First of all, the supervisor of this thesis, Professor Dr. Rainer Lagoni inspired the author to choose this topic and by critically, but constructively questioning main arguments increased their respective strength. Both Professor Dr. Lagoni and the second reviewer, Professor Dr. Peter Ehlers were particularly helpful by speedily reviewing the thesis. Earlier teachers of the author such as Professor Dr. Wolfgang Graf Vitzthum, Judge Hugo Caminos of the International Tribunal for the Law of the Sea and Professor Bernard H. Oxman also provided some substantial input. Furthermore, the presentation of some of the thesis' arguments in discussions within the Research School led to new ideas, some of them central to the main results of the thesis. Finally, stimulating and witty conversations with Mr. Jens Bopp, a fellow Ph.D. student with a similar subject, reciprocally benefited the respective studies.

Thirdly, the author could rely on constant personal support by his parents Anke and Wolfgang and by Franziska Geibel.

The author would like to use this occasion to convey his most profound gratitude to the afore-mentioned persons because of their important contribution toward this study.

Hamburg, June 2007 Philipp Wendel

Contents

Abbreviations

A.C.	Law Reports: Appeal Cases
ADM	Annuaire du droit de la mer
ADMO	Annuaire de droit maritime et océanique
AFDI	Annuaire français de droit international
A.F. L. Rev.	Air Force Law Review
AJIL	American Journal of International Law
Asian Yb. Int'l L.	Asian Yearbook of International Law
ASIL	American Society of International Law
ASR	Articles on State Responsibility
ATS	Amphetamine-type stimulants
AVR	Archiv des Völkerrechts
Barn. & Ald.	Barnewall and Alderson
BGBl.	Bundesgesetzblatt
BGHZ	Entscheidungen des Bundesgerichtshofs in Zivilsachen
BVerfG	Bundesverfassungsgericht
BYIL	British Yearbook of International Law
Can. Yb. Int'l L.	Canadian Yearbook of International Law
CFR	Code of Federal Regulations
Chinese J. of Int'l L.	Chinese Journal of International Law
Ch. Rob.	Christopher Robinson's Admiralty Reports
CHS	Convention on the High Seas
Colum. J. Transnat'l L.	Columbia Journal of Transnational Law
CSI	Container Security Initiative
CSO	Company Security Officer
CSR	Continuous Synopsis Record
Ct.Cl.	Court of Claims
C-TPAT	Customs-Trade Partnership against Terrorism
DADP	Draft Articles on Diplomatic Protection
Dods.	Dodson's Admiralty Reports
EC	European Community
ECJ	European Court of Justice
ECOMOG	Economic Monitoring Group
ECOWAS	Economic Community of West African States
E.C.R.	European Court Reports
ECT	Treaty Establishing the European Community
EEZ	Exclusive Economic Zone

Emory Int'l L. Rev.	Emory International Law Review
Eng. Rep.	English Reports
ETS	European Treaty Series
EU	European Union
EUV	Vertrag über die Europäische Union
FAO	Food and Agricultural Organization
FBI	Federal Bureau of Investigation
F.Cas.	Federal Cases
F.Supp.	Federal Supplement
FTCA	Federal Tort Claims Act
GYIL	German Yearbook of International Law
Harv. Int'l L. J.	Harvard International Law Journal
Hofstra L. Rev.	Hofstra Law Review
HVR	Humanitäres Völkerrecht
ICCPR	International Covenant on Civil and Political Rights
ICFTU	International Confederation of Free Trade Unions
ICJ	International Court of Justice
ICLQ	International and Comparative Law Quarterly
ICS	International Chamber of Shipping
ICSID	International Centre for the Settlement of Investment Disputes
ILA	International Law Association
ILC	International Law Commission
ILM	International Legal Materials
ILR	International Law Reports
IMB	International Maritime Bureau
IMCO	Inter-Governmental Maritime Consultative Organization
IMO	International Maritime Organization
Ind. Int'l & Comp. L. Rev.	Indiana International and Comparative Law Review
Int'l J. Estuarine & Coast. L.	International Journal of Estuarine and Coastal Law
Int'l J. Mar. & Coast. L.	International Journal of Marine and Coastal Law
Iran-U.S.C.T.R.	Iran-United States Claims Tribunal Reports
ISPS	International Ship and Port Security
ISF	International Shipping Federation
ISSC	International Ship Security Certificate
Italian Yb. of Int'l L.	Italian Yearbook of International Law
ITF	International Transport Workers' Federation
ITLOS	International Tribunal for the Law of the Sea
ITLOS Pleadings	International Tribunal for the Law of the Sea, Pleadings, Minutes of Public Sittings and Documents
J. Int'l L. & Politics	Journal of International Law and Politics
J. Int'l Maritime L.	Journal of International Maritime Law

J. Mar. L. & Com.	Journal of Maritime Law and Commerce
LLP	Lloyd's of London Press
LNTS	League of Nations Treaty Series
LOSC	Law of the Sea Convention
LRAD	Long Range Acoustic Device
MARPOL	International Convention for the Prevention of Pollution from Ships
MOU	Memorandum of Understanding
MT	Motor Tanker
MV	Motor Vessel
NATO	North-Atlantic Treaty Organization
Naval L. Rev.	Naval Law Review
Netherlands Ybk. Int'l L.	Netherlands Yearbook of International Law
ODIL	Ocean Development and International Law
OECD	Organisation for Economic Cooperation and Development
OJ	Official Journal of the European Communities
OPGE	Entscheidungen des Oberprisengerichts
P.	Probate Division (Law Reports)
PCA	Permanent Court of Arbitration
PCIJ	Permanent Court of International Justice
PSC	Port State Control
PSI	Proliferation Security Initiative
RdC	Recueil des Cours de l'Académie de Droit International
REDI	Revista española de derecho internacional
Rev. Gén. Dr. Int'l Publ.	Revue Générale de Droit International Public
RFO	Regional Fisheries Organization
RGZ	Entscheidungen des Reichsgerichts in Zivilsachen
RIAA	Reports of International Arbitral Awards
SDN	Société des Nations
SODA	Status of Force Agreement
SOLAS	International Convention on Safety of Life at Sea
SS	steamer
SSO	Ship Security Officer
SSP	Ship Security Plan
SUA Convention	Convention for the Suppression of Unlawful Acts Against the Safety of Maritime Navigation
Sydney L. Rev.	Sydney Law Review
Syracuse J. Int'l L. & Com.	Syracuse Journal of International Law and Commerce
TEU	Twenty foot equivalent unit
Tex. Int'l L. J.	Texas International Law Journal
Tul. Mar. L. J.	Tulane Maritime Law Journal
U.K.T.S.	United Kingdom Treaty Series
U. Miami Int.-Am. L. Rev.	University of Miami Inter-American Law Review

U. Miami L. Rev.	University of Miami Law Review
UN	United Nations Organization
UNCLOS	United Nations Conference on the Law of the Sea
UNCTAD	United Nations Conference on Trade and Development
UNTS	United Nations Treaty Series
U.S.	United States
U.S.C.	United States Code
USCG	United States Coast Guard
USD	United States Dollar
Va. J. Int'l L.	Virginia Journal of International Law
VCLT	Vienna Convention on the Law of Treaties
VN	Vereinte Nationen
WEU	Western European Union
Wm. & Mary L. Rev.	William and Mary Law Review
WMD	Weapons of Mass Destruction
WMU	World Maritime University
WMU J. of Maritime Affairs	WMU Journal of Maritime Affairs
WTO	World Trade Organization
Yale J. Int'l L.	Yale Journal of International Law
ZaöRV	Zeitschrift für ausländisches öffentliches Recht und Völkerrecht
ZeuS	Zeitschrift für europarechtliche Studien

Introduction

In August 2005, the Pacific Area commander of the U.S. Coast Guard on a maritime security conference in Copenhagen proclaimed that the United States intended to push back its sea borders for searches as much as possible, maybe even by 2,000 nautical miles.[1] According to him, such a step would significantly limit the terror threat the United States is facing. This statement is characteristic for a new attitude concerning the policing of the oceans, an attitude not only of the United States, but also of many of its partners.

The traditional Law of the Sea with its principles of freedom of navigation and exclusive flag State jurisdiction is increasingly considered to be an obstacle for the fight against terror and other security concerns. Consequently, interferences on the high seas have within recent years become quite common.

The maritime industry was confronted with similar scenarios in the past when States tried to combat international crimes like piracy, slave trading, drug smuggling or pirate broadcasting. In fact, the United Kingdom and the United States even faced the so-called "visitation crisis" in the 1850's when the United Kingdom asserted a right to check the papers of foreign vessels in order to prevent the trade of slaves. At the time, the United Kingdom backed down due to U.S. diplomatic pressure. But today, the multipolar system seems to have faded and unilateral abuse of power meets little control mechanisms.

While sometimes, interferences can lead to greater security for navigation as in the prosecution of pirate ships, other interferences may expose shipowners and their partners to new risks and make them incur severe damages. The challenge for States policing the oceans is therefore to find an equitable balance between the need to prevent and repress international crimes and the protection of maritime trade.

The Law of the Sea is a part of public international law which disposes of a particularly sophisticated regulation by international conventions in comparison to some other areas. The Law of the Sea Convention, deemed to be the "Constitution of the Oceans", represents the cornerstone of the whole Law of the Sea, even though it has not yet been ratified by the whole international community. The United Nations and the International Maritime Organization have developed further important treaties for the Law of the Sea. Many of these conventions permit interferences on the high seas by a State other than the flag State. A great part of them attempts to balance the introduction of new boarding authorizations by provisions on the issue of compensation.

---

1 Reuters, 12 October 2005.

However, these provisions have rarely ever been applied in a dispute between the interested States and/or private individuals. An analysis what the reasons for this omission are is not exempt from speculation. It is nevertheless submitted that most States know very little about the relevant provisions. Sometimes, they do not know about their mere existence, but more often they are unsure about the requirements for an obligation to compensate to arise and the exact contents of such an obligation. Among the shipowners and other private actors in maritime trade, knowledge of public international law is even less prevalent. In fact, many of them rely exclusively on maritime law in any dispute. This body of law will definitely predominate in relations between private actors, but in order to complain against the conduct of a State and to find redress in this respect, reliance on public and in particular public international law is essential. While traditionally, public international law only assigned an almost negligible role to the individual, its relevance has recently gained importance. This study will show that this is particularly true for the compensation provisions of the Law of the Sea.

The ignorance about the relevant law on State responsibility may also be due to the fact that most compensation provisions differ from each other slightly or even profoundly in their wording. Furthermore, there has been an extensive and very controversial debate for decades about the general law on State responsibility during the work of the International Law Commission on the topic which only recently led to the adoption the "Articles on Responsibility of States for Internationally Wrongful Acts" (Articles on State Responsibility). A certain degree of uncertainty concerning the applicable rules of State responsibility remains even after the adoption of these articles.

One also has to admit that the lack of application of the relevant compensation provisions was partially due to the fact that States generally show a great reluctance to submit a dispute to the jurisdiction of an international tribunal. They are even more unwilling if these disputes concern some questions of state responsibility. A State simply would not like to be held "responsible" and often regards an obligation to compensate as a kind of humiliation. Reasons of diplomacy have even led States to waive their rights to claim compensation.[2] As far as it concerns domestic remedies, public international law grants immunity to States from the national jurisdiction of any other States.

Hence, there are many obstacles for a compensation provision to find application. This thesis intends to bring these provisions to light from their so far idle and stagnant existence. In a first and less legal chapter, the importance of unhindered maritime trade will be contrasted to the relevance of international crimes in international waters and the measures to combat them. Then, in the main part of this thesis (Chapter II), the existing material public international law on compensation for interferences on the high seas will be analyzed. The analysis will focus on an interpretation of the relevant provisions in international treaties, but it will also include some remarks on the state of the customary international law on state

---

2 *Cf. Nakatani*, Kazuhiro, "Diplomacy and State Responsibility", in *Ragazzi*, Maurizio (ed.), "International Responsibility Today – Essays in Memory of Oscar Schachter" (Leiden: Nijhoff, 2005), pp. 36 *et seq.*, at 42-46.

responsibility. In a third chapter, the U.S. strategy concerning interdictions on the high seas will be analyzed in particular regarding a potential liability of the United States for these interdictions. Finally, this study will deal with the rather unregulated cases where States interfere with the navigation of foreign vessels in situations of war or under a mandate of the United Nations Security Council (Chapter IV).

The insights gained from these studies will enable the author and the reader to estimate whether the international legal system is able to strike a fair balance between freedom of navigation and the combat against international crimes. This may also lead to some modest suggestions of how to improve the existing material international law on the issue in the future.

Chapter I: The perpetual conflict between freedom and security in the Law of the Sea

Research in the existent public international law cannot and must not be isolated from factual matters and policy concerns. In fact, it is very likely that respect of public international law will increase if international lawyers are well aware of these factual matters while applying international law. Furthermore, public international law seems to be more flexible than other legal systems because custom plays a great role as one of its sources and because the analysis of State practice constitutes a major part of the interpretation of treaties.

This thesis will therefore start by confronting the two overriding concerns involved in any interference on the seas. First, the freedom of navigation and its importance for the modern, world-wide economy will be presented. Secondly, this thesis will analyze all major security concerns and outline in how far interferences with navigation on the high seas would be able to alleviate these concerns. As one can presume, the management of these contradicting goals cannot be "sink or swim", but instead a reasonable balance between them should be the goal. Therefore, in a third part, potential legal limits to abusive interferences including an efficient liability[1] regime will be presented.

A. The freedom of navigation – cornerstone of the Law of the Sea

The freedom of navigation represents the overriding principle of the Law of the Sea and has traditionally been one of the most important principles in the law of the sea and in public international law in general. Its content can be described in two parts. First, the freedom of navigation includes the right to enter upon the oceans and to pass them unhindered by efforts of other states or entities to prohibit that use or to subject it to regulations unsupported by a general consensus among

---

1 The terms liability and responsibility, generally and for the sake of this study, have the same meaning, the former rather used in domestic legal systems, the latter for the regime of State responsibility under public international law, *cf.* *Amerasinghe*, Chittharanjan F., "The Essence of the Structure of International Responsibility", in *Ragazzi*, Maurizio (ed.), "International Responsibility Today – Essays in Memory of Oscar Schachter" (Leiden: Nijhoff, 2005), pp. 3 *et seq.*, at 4.

states.[2] Early authors called this aspect *ius communicationis.*[3] The freedom of navigation in this sense found codification in Art. 87, para. 1, lit. (a) of the 1982 United Nations Convention on the Law of the Sea[4] and in Art. 2, para. 1 of the 1958 Convention on the High Seas.[5]

The other aspect of freedom of navigation is the exclusive jurisdiction of the flag State as laid down in Art. 92, para. 1 LOSC and Art. 6, para. 1 CHS and even before declared to be customary international law.[6] According to these provisions, only the flag State may exercise jurisdiction over a certain vessel of its nationality on the high seas.

Both aspects are linked in a resolution of the Institut de droit international which stipulated that "[t]he principle of the freedom of the sea implies specially the following consequences: (i) freedom of navigation on the high seas, subject to the exclusive control, in the absence of a convention to the contrary, of the State whose flag is carried by the vessel…"[7]

Any interference on the high seas is an intrusion into these principles. However, in order to adequately balance security concerns with the freedom of navigation, it seems important to assess the reasoning behind these principles and their economic importance.

I. Freedom of navigation – an instrument of common sense rather than a legal argument

The freedom of navigation has always been attributed to the great works of *Hugo Grotius*[8] who relied on predominantly legal arguments, which were later questioned by English scholars, particularly *John Selden.*[9] The freedom of navigation had even before been advocated by *de Vitoria* in 1509 and by *Vasquez de Menchaca* in 1564.[10] The main issues at the time were whether the sea is the property of States, *res communis* or *res nullius*. These questions depended on whether

2 *McDougal*, Myres Smith/*Burke*, William T., "The Public Order of the Oceans" (New Haven: Yale University Press, 1962), at 763.

3 *de Ferron*, Olivier, "Le droit international de la mer", Vol. 1 (Geneva: Droz, 1958), at 76.

4 United Nations Convention on the Law of the Sea, adopted on 10 December 1982, UNTS, Vol. 1833, pp. 3 *et seq.* [hereinafter "Law of the Sea Convention" or "LOSC"].

5 Convention on the High Seas, adopted on 29 April 1958, UNTS, Vol. 450, pp. 11 *et seq.* [hereinafter CHS].

6 *S.S. Lotus Case (France v. Turkey)*, Judgment of 7 September 1927, (1927) PCIJ Ser. A No. 10, pp. 4 *et seq.*, at 25.

7 (1927) Annuaire de l'Institut de Droit International, Vol. 33, p. 339.

8 See *Grotius*, Hugo, "The Freedom of the Seas or the Right which belongs to the Dutch to take part in the East Indian Trade" (Translated with a revision of the Latin text of 1633 by Ralph van Deman Magoffin) (New York: Oxford University Press, 1916).

9 See *Seldeni*, Ioannis, "Mare clausum seu de Dominio Maris", Libri Duo (London, 1636).

10 *de la Pradelle*, Albert, "Maîtres et Doctrines du Droit des Gens" (1939), at 25-40.

States could exploit, delimit and occupy the sea and one of *Grotius'* main arguments was that one cannot effectively occupy the sea and that therefore all claims of sovereignty over the seas were void.[11]

There are many examples of such claims: In the 10th century, *Edgar the Peaceful* claimed to be the "sovereign of the Britannic Ocean".[12] In the fifteenth century, the kingdoms of Sweden and Denmark, the city-states of Venice, Genoa and Pisa, the United Kingdom and the Pope designated large areas of the sea to be under sovereign control. Quite often, these states levied tolls on foreign ships in order to guarantee passage through these waters.[13] The cost and delay associated with such tolls became an impediment to the growing importance of maritime commerce and exploration.[14]

Spain claimed absolute sovereignty over the entire Pacific Ocean and the Gulf of Mexico, Portugal claimed all of the Indian Ocean, England claimed undefined areas to the north and west and some seas to the south and east.[15] Furthermore, Spain and Portugal divided the Atlantic Ocean in the Treaty of Tordesillas of 7 June 1494 in order to prevent navigation by other States on this ocean.[16]

Norway prohibited other states to sail north of Bergen in the 13th century. When Denmark acquired Norway, it maintained this monopoly north of the Iceland-Faeroes-Shetlands-Bergen line.[17] This Danish *mare clausum* regime was only abandoned by 1600.[18]

It may be right that all these States could not effectively control the large areas they claimed. However, States do nowadays claim large areas of uninhabitable areas like deserts or arctic territories and their sovereignty over these areas is widely recognized without requiring a considerable degree of control. Furthermore, modern navies enable States to control large areas of the ocean. In fact, the British navy had acquired supremacy of the oceans by 1805 and thereby gained a

---

11 Cf. also *Hall*, William Edward, "A Treatise on International Law" (Oxford: Clarendon, 1924), at 189; *Fauchille*, Paul, "Traité de droit international public", Vol I, part II (Paris: Rousseau, 1925), at 11.

12 *de Cussy*, Ferdinand, "Phases et Causes Célèbres du Droit Maritime des Nations", Vol. 1 (Leipzig: Bockhaus, 1856), at 8.

13 *Churchill*, Robin R./*Lowe*, Alan Vaughan: "The Law of the Sea" (3rd ed., Manchester: Juris Publications, 1999), at 204.

14 *Barry*, Ian Patrick, "The Right of Visit, Search and Seizure of Foreign Flagged Vessels on the High Seas Pursuant to Customary International Law: a Defense of the Proliferation Security Initiative", 33 Hofstra L. Rev. (2004), pp. 299 *et seq.*, at 306.

15 *Scott*, James Brown, "Introduction", in *Grotius*, Hugo, "The Freedom of the Seas or the Right which belongs to the Dutch to take part in the East Indian Trade" (Translated with a revision of the Latin text of 1633 by Ralph van Deman Magoffin) (New York: Oxford University Press, 1916) at vii-viii.

16 See *Graf Vitzthum*, Wolfgang, "Geschichte des Seerechts", in *Graf Vitzthum*, Wolfgang (ed.), "Handbuch des Seerechts" (München: Beck, 2006), pp. 1 *et seq.*, at 31.

17 *Alexander*, Lewis M., "The Changing Nature of the High Seas", in *Crickard*, Frew W. *at al.* (eds.), "Multinational Naval Cooperation and Foreign Policy into the 21st century" (Aldershot: Ashgate, 1998), pp. 30 *et seq.*, at 31.

18 *Ibid.*

monopoly in the trade of steam coal.[19] The argument of effective occupation therefore does not convince any more today.[20]

Why did *Grotius'* theory then prevail in spite of the weakness of the legal arguments? The main reason was probably political and economic necessity.[21] The benefit to all States gained by unhindered navigation clearly outweighs the benefit of one State excluding all others from using the ocean or the benefit of a few States barring access to certain parts of the ocean. *Myres Smith Mc Dougal* and *William T. Burke* have brilliantly described these benefits in the following words: "If each state could at its discretion determine the scope of its exclusive access and competence, the result could only be the chaotic frustration of any realistic possibility of the cooperative enjoyment of the oceans. A policy of virtually unrestricted access to the oceans for certain consequential purposes, such as transport and communication, is to be preferred because these purposes involve only the largely noncompetitive use of the positional and spatial characteristics of the sea. The greatest net gain accrues to all participants from permitting the utmost free access for navigation, subject only to imperative demands for protecting common exclusive interests."[22]

Even English scholars admitted that a certain degree of freedom was necessary on the seas. *John Selden, e.g.*, stated that a State could not forbid the navigation of its seas by other people without being wanting in its duties to humanity.[23] Even more explicit was *Sir Philip Medows* who wrote that "[t]he sea is the public property of the Crown of England, but as it is a way, it is common to the peaceable traders of all nations. And this is far from being a damage to any, that it is highly beneficial to all, for as there is no man so self-sufficient as not to need the continual help of another, so neither is there any country which does not at some time or other need the growth and productions of another."[24]

Hence, as early as in the 17th century, there seemed to be common persuasion of the benefits of free trade, at least as far as it concerns the high seas.

The political rather than legal background of *Grotius'* convincing power is furthermore underlined by the fact that *Grotius' mare liberum* originally was an opinion delivered as legal counsel for the Dutch East India Company on their right of access to the trade of the Indies after Portugal had opposed the Dutch commer-

---

19 *Colombos*, Constantin John, "The International Law of the Sea" (6th ed., London: Longmans, 1967), at 56.

20 *Dupuy*, René-Jean/*Vignes*, Daniel, "Traité du nouveau droit de la mer" (Paris: Economica, 1985), at 342.

21 *von Glahn*, Gerhard, "Law Among Nations" (New York: MacMillan, 1992), at 479; *Cavaré*, Louis, "Le droit international public positif", Vol. 2, (Paris: Pedone, 1962), at 624.

22 *McDougal*, Myres Smith/*Burke*, William T., "The Public Order of the Oceans" (New Haven: Yale University Press, 1962), at 748. Cf. also *Kröger*, Herbert, "Die Freiheit der Schiffahrt" (1959), at 3-4; *Friedheim*, Robert L. "Negotiating the New Ocean Regime" (Columbia: University of South Carolina Press, 1993), at 285.

23 *Selden*, John, "Mare clausum, seu de dominio maris", lib. 1, c. 20 (1636).

24 *Medows*, Sir Philip, "Observations concerning the dominion and sovereignty of the seas" (1689), at 6-7.

cial activities in the region.[25] The Dutch were concerned with Portuguese pretensions to sovereignty in East Indian waters; the British had expanding commerce and navigation and supported the Dutch argument.[26]

The Dutch also wanted to fish in the North Sea, despite opposition from *King James VI of Scotland* who had just become *King James I of England* as well.[27] However, within the next centuries, the importance of free navigation in the service of overseas and colonial trade came to overshadow coastal fisheries and the development of real naval power displaced notional claims to sovereignty over the seas."[28]

Since then, great authorities of international law have always in strong terms defended the freedom of navigation, referring particularly to its importance to international trade.[29] *Gidel* realized the factual, instead of legal importance of the freedom of navigation when he wrote that: "Ce que nous appelons le principe de la liberté de la haute mer reste, comme beaucoup d'autres principes juridiques, une de ces hypothèses que nous n'avons pas de raisons de tenir pour vraies, mais que nous avons des motifs de prendre pour règles."[30]

II. Exclusive Flag State Jurisdiction – from an instrument to maintain maritime power to a key to liberalize maritime transport

If the rationale behind the first aspect of free navigation has thus been almost purely political, may it be true to the second aspect, the exclusive flag State jurisdiction, as well? Again, one might put forward legal reasons to defend this exclusivity, such as the vessel being part of the territory of the flag State[31] or the neces-

---

25 *O'Connell,* Daniel P./*Shearer*, Ivan Anthony, „The International Law of the Sea", Vol. 1 (Oxford: Clarendon Press, 1982), at 9; *Wolfrum*, Rüdiger, "Die Internationalisierung staatsfreier Räume: Die Entwicklung einer internationalen Verwaltung für Antarktis, Weltraum, Hohe See und Meeresboden" (Berlin: Springer, 1984), at 125.

26 *Fulton*, Thomas Wemyss, "The Sovereignty of the Sea" (Edinburgh: Blackwood, 1911), at 523.

27 *Johnson*, D.H.N., "Freedom of Navigation", in *Bernhardt*, Rudolf, "Encyclopedia of Public International Law", Vol. 3 (Amsterdam: Elsevier, 1997), pp. 528 *et seq.*, at 529.

28 *Churchill*, Robin R./*Lowe*, Alan V., "The Law of the Sea" (3rd ed., Manchester: Juris Publications, 1999), at 204-5.

29 Cf., *e.g.*, *Colombos*, Constantin John, "The International Law of the Sea" (6th ed., London: Longman, 1967), at 47-8; *de Burgh*, W., "The Elements of Maritime International Law" (1868), at 1; Lord Stowell in *Le Louis*, [1817] 2 Dods. 210, 243; Justice Story in *The Marianna Flora*, 1 Wheaton 1, 43 (1826); recently *Parameswaran*, Benjamin, "The liberalization of maritime transport services: with special reference to the WTO/GATS framework", (Berlin: Springer, 2004), at 83-100.

30 *Gidel*, Gilbert, "Le droit international de la mer", Vol. 1 (Paris-Châteauroux: Mellottée, 1932), at 208.

31 This theory had some exponents in the 19th century. *Hautefeuille*, Laurent Basile, "Des droits et des devoirs des nations neutres en temps de guerre maritime", Vol. 1 (2nd ed., Paris, 1858), at 257; *Harburger*, Heinrich, "Der strafrechtliche Begriff Inland und seine Beziehungen zum Völkerrecht und Staatsrecht" (Nördlingen: Beck, 1882), at 107;

sity of a certain degree of jurisdiction to prevent lawlessness and anarchy on the high seas.

History however shows that until World War II, maritime nations have been able to largely maintain or even extend their dominance in maritime trade by offering exclusive protection and hereby gaining exclusive control over vessels flying their flags. England, for example, restricted the import of goods from Asia, Africa and America to British vessels. Cabotage and fisheries were also reserved to national vessels. It was only after England had acquired a particularly strong position in maritime trade that it opened its ports to vessels of other nationalities, presumably to gain access to continental ports.[32] France also had a trade monopoly to its colonies in place until 1869.[33] Furthermore, the protection by naval vessels of the flag State was a considerable factor for a shipowner choosing his registry in times when pirates and privateers were roaming in many parts of the ocean. Some States like France also offered financial support to have a bigger merchant fleet such as subsidies to the shipbuilding industry.[34]

In return to these at the time very important offers of protection, flag States established very harsh requirements for shipowners in order to have their ships registered. The shipowners had to be nationals of the flag State,[35] have the vessel constructed in the flag State[36] or were not allowed to sell the vessel if it would then fly the flag of another State.[37] In addition, there were requirements concerning the nationality of crew members.[38]

The merchant fleet used to play a considerable role in times of war. Flag States could order their vessels to cease commerce with their enemies.[39] The merchant fleet was even considered to be the fourth arm of the national fleet[40] because the flag State could order its merchant vessels to provide services like the transport of troops or even to be transformed to a naval vessel.

---

von Bar, "Theorie und Praxis des Internationalen Privatrechts", Vol. 2 (Hannover: Hahn, 1899), at 613.

32 *Cantillon de Tramont*, Paul, "De la nationalité des navires" (Montauban, 1907), at 94-96.

33 *Ibid.*, at 98.

34 *Gidel*, Gilbert, "Le droit international de la mer", Vol. 1 (Paris-Châteauroux: Mellottée, 1932), at 75.

35 *Coulter*, Daniel Y./*Goldman*, Alan, "Global Shipping Trends and Implications for Navies", in *Crickard*, Fred W. *et al.* (eds.), "Multinational naval cooperation and foreign policy into the 21st century" (Aldershot: Ashgate, 1998), pp. 46 *et seq.*, at 48.

36 The United States had this requirement in place as late as 1907. Cf. *Cantillon de Tramont*, Paul, "De la nationalité des navires" (Montauban, 1907), at 33.

37 "Un bâtiment d'origine française devait vivre et mourir français". *Ibid.*, at 58.

38 *Ibid.*, at 40-53.

39 In the French-Germany war of 1870/1871, the French *ministre de la marine* ordered all French vessels to cease any commerce with Germany. If they violated this order, they would be confiscated. *Ibid.*, at 26.

40 *Coulter*, Daniel Y./*Goldman*, Alan, "Global Shipping Trends and Implications for Navies", in *Crickard*, Fred W. *et al.* (eds.), "Multinational naval cooperation and foreign policy into the 21st century" (Aldershot: Ashgate, 1998), pp. 46 *et seq.*, at 64.

In the beginning of the 20th century, the flag of an "uncivilized" country was still considered to offer little protection to shipowners and was thus not attractive to them.[41] Therefore, a few maritime powers acting as economic plenipotentiaries were able to practically control international commerce through their merchant vessels.[42]

All States were legally free to use the sea for navigation, but only few were able to assemble the sufficient capital, naval protection and trade connection to really profit from this freedom.

However, this situation changed after World War II when shipowners realized that the obligations imposed by their flag States by far outweighed the benefits offered by them.[43] First, shipowners were no more willing to have their vessels removed from a trade for national security reasons (*e.g.*, transport of troops, military equipment), because these vessels would have found it exceedingly difficult, if not impossible, to re-enter the trade.[44]

Secondly, even though the traditional maritime States mitigated their previous harsh requirements, new flag States with open registers started to offer significant further advantages to shipowners leading them to outflag their vessels. These advantages include largely anonymous ownership (which makes it less likely for the owner to be sued for damages), lower crew costs because of no nationality requirements and the inapplicability of wage agreements with trade unions,[45] simple and flexible registration procedures and little corporations taxes. On the other hand, insurance premiums for vessels under these open registers are not significantly higher than if the vessel was registered in a developed market economy. Finally, less stringent environmental and security regulation and enforcement may save the shipowner between USD 85,000 and USD 273,700 per year[46] or between USD 500 and USD 650 per day[47] for an average vessel.

---

41 Cf. *Cantillon de Tramont*, Paul, "De la nationalité des navires" (Montauban, 1907), at 17.

42 Cf. *Mahalu*, Costa Ricky, "Public international law and shipping practices: the east african aspirations" (Nomos: Baden-Baden, 1984) at 9; *Coulter*, Daniel Y./*Goldman*, Alan, "Global Shipping Trends and Implications for Navies", in *Crickard*, Fred W. *et al.* (eds.), "Multinational naval cooperation and foreign policy into the 21st century" (Aldershot: Ashgate, 1998), pp. 46 *et seq.*, at 48.

43 There were some similar tendencies in the early 20th century. Cf. *Ready*, Nigel P., "Ship Registration" (3rd ed., London: LLP, 1998), at 21.

44 *Coulter*, Daniel Y./*Goldman*, Alan, "Global Shipping Trends and Implications for Navies", in *Crickard*, Fred W. *et al.* (eds.), "Multinational naval cooperation and foreign policy into the 21st century" (Aldershot: Ashgate, 1998), pp. 46 *et seq.*, at 65.

45 For an extensive, but partly outdated study see *Bergstrand*, S.J., "Buy the flag – Developments in the Open Registry Debate" (London: Polytechnic of Central London, 1983), at 49-72.

46 *OECD*, "Cost Savings Stemming from Non-Compliance with International Environmental Regulations in the Maritime Sector" (2003), at 5, available at <www.oecd.org/dataoecd/4/26/2496757.pdf.

47 *OECD* Doc. GF(96)4, "Competitive Advantages obtained by some shipowners as a result of non-observance of applicable international rules and standards" (1996), at 26-7, available at <www.oecd.org/dataoecd/10/10/2754615.pdf>.

As a consequence, the share of open registers in the world dead tonnage rose from 21.6 percent in 1970 to 48.5 percent in 2000 while the share of developed market economies dropped from 65 percent in 1970 to 25.2 percent in 2000.[48] At the same time, the beneficial owners of the majority of the world fleet remain to be nationals from developed market economies like Greece, Japan, Norway and Germany.[49]

Due to the exclusive flag State jurisdiction, traditional maritime States no more exercise legislative control over a very large portion of the world fleet. This development may have had unfortunate consequences such as the exploitation of seafarers from developing States and the frequency of sub-standard, dangerous shipping, but it definitely also helped liberalize maritime transport and thereby worldwide trade because transport costs decreased and worldwide competition between flag States led to less government intervention in maritime transport. Since maritime transport carries 80-90 percent of world-wide trade, this development has had a considerable influence on the liberalization of world-wide trade. There are some efforts to combat open registers,[50] but the most likely means to decrease the share of open registers will be to further liberalize the registers of developed market economies by reducing taxes imposed on shipowners[51] and by abating crewing requirements.[52]

Globalization is definitely not due to one cause only, but it is submitted that the fact that flag States exercise exclusive jurisdiction over their vessels has enabled competition between these States for shipowners, reduced transport costs and significantly contributed to the globalization phenomenon.

III. Free navigation for worldwide economic growth and development

The previous elaborations have only indicated how interrelated the liberal aspects of the Law of the Sea and worldwide economics really are. In fact, the freedom of navigation in its entirety has since long been recognized as a major contributor to economic wealth.

---

48 *UNCTAD*, Review of Maritime Transport (2004), at 29.

49 *UNCTAD*, Review of Maritime Transport (2004), at 33.

50 Argentina, for example, obliges Argentinean shipowners who had flagged out to open register to re-register with the national flag. ITF Seafarer's Bulletin, no. 19 (2005), at 9.

51 Some European Union members States have started to apply tonnage taxes instead of standard tax rules to vessels registered in the country. *UNCTAD*, Review of Maritime Transport (2004), at 26.

52 The European Court of Justice has done a careful step in this direction when it held that a member State of the European Union may only reserve a post on a vessel flying its flag to its national as opposed to nationals of other member States "if the rights under powers conferred by public law granted to masters of such vessels are in fact exercised on a regular basis and do not represent a very minor part of their activities." ECJ Case C-47/02, *Anker and others v. Germany* (30 September 2003), OJ C 275/17 (15 November 2003).

David Ricardo in his treatise "On the principles of political economy and theory" demonstrated how the export of goods pays if the exported goods can be produced at lower costs in the exporting country than they could in the importing country and how all States would benefit if they could use their "comparative advantages" in the production and export of certain goods.[53] However, such an export only remunerates if the transport costs do not exceed this margin between two countries.

Seaborne trade represents the most important means of transport because, contrary to transport on land, it is able to bridge the usually long distances between areas of the world where production costs differ significantly. Furthermore, contrary to air transport, its energy efficiency and thereby low costs even render the transport of bulk articles profitable. That is why seaborne trade has become the "lifeblood of the international economic system and the source of its wealth."[54] Seaborne trade also opens much wider markets for export goods and thereby enables higher degrees of specialization, lower costs for these products and thus the potential for more wealth.[55] Nowadays, between 90 and 95 percent of international merchandise trade by volume is carried on the oceans.[56] The great bulk of the exchange of goods among nations, about 80 to 90 per cent, still depends upon ocean-going vessels.[57]

Basically, it is fair to say that the higher the degree of freedom of navigation, the lower the costs for maritime transport. Any interference on the seas which causes the merest delay also produces extra costs for maritime transport. The bigger the vessel with whose navigation a State interferes, the higher such extra costs. As international marine commerce has grown, ships have grown in size to accommodate increased amounts of cargo. The container ships of the 1960s could carry only a few hundred containers (commonly measured in 20-foot equivalent units, or TEUs). Today, 5,000 TEU vessels are quite common, and the largest container vessels can carry more than 13,500 TEUs, requiring navigation channels of 15 meters depth. Bulk cargo ships are also increasing in size. For example, ultra-large crude oil carriers, known as super tankers, are approaching lengths of 450 meters and widths of 90 meters, requiring channels deeper than 27 meters.[58]

The European Union and the United States seem to have recognized this overwhelming importance of free navigation in their outlines of a future maritime

---

53 See generally *Ricardo*, David, "On the Principles of Political Economy and Taxation" (3rd ed., London, 1817), at 89-91.

54 *Eberle*, Sir James, "Global Maritime Security: What does it mean?", in *Crickard*, Fred W. *et al.* (eds.), "Multinational naval cooperation and foreign policy into the 21st century" (Aldershot: Ashgate, 1998), pp. 21 *et seq.*, at 23-4.

55 *Smith*, Adam, "The Wealth of Nations", Vol. 1 (Rev. ed. 1937), at 18-9.

56 *Coulter*, Daniel Y./*Goldman*, Alan, "Global Shipping Trends and Implications for Navies", in *Crickard*, Fred W. *et al.* (eds.), "Multinational naval cooperation and foreign policy into the 21st century" (Aldershot: Ashgate, 1998), pp. 46 *et seq.*, at 46.

57 *Woytinski*, W.S./*Woytinski*, E.S., "World Commerce and Governments" (New York: The Twentieth Century Fund, 1955) at 429.

58 Hofstra University, available at <http://people.hofstra.edu/geotrans/eng/ch5en/appl5en/tankers.html>.

policy.[59] In the United States, waterborne commerce in 2001 accounted for 78 percent of total U.S. international trade by weight and 38 percent by value.[60] U.S. international and domestic marine cargo is projected to double over the next twenty years.[61] More than thirteen million jobs are related to trade transported by the network of inland waterways and ports that support U.S. waterborne commerce.[62] U.S. marine import-export trade accounts for nearly 7 percent of the nation's gross domestic product.[63]

As far as it concerns the European Union, more than 90 percent of its external trade and some 43 percent of its domestic trade move by sea; more than 1 billion tonnes of freight are unloaded and loaded annually in Union ports.[64] Recognition of the environmental costs of road transport and the relocation of manufacturing services outside Europe have further raised the importance of maritime transport and of intermodality in the transport chain.[65]

However, not only the developed market economies have profited from unhindered navigation in the past. Due to the opportunities of maritime transport, some Asian States have experienced a tremendous development in the last decades. The high growth rates of Japan (1960's until early 1990's), of the Asian Tiger States (1990's) and recently of China have only been possible because they were able to export products to developed States by maritime transport.[66] These numbers have led to a continuing shift in the volume of world trade from the Atlantic and Western Hemisphere to the Pacific and Far East. Asia has become the continent with the largest share of the world tonnage of seaborne loaded goods (38.4 percent).[67]

Nowadays, Asian countries account for 35.8 percent of beneficial containership ownership, 45.7 percent of containership operation, 60.4 percent of seamen, 62.3

---

59 *U.S. Commission on Ocean Policy*, "An Ocean Blueprint for the 21st Century" (20 September 2004); *European Commission* Doc. COM(2006) 275 final, "Green Paper: Towards a future Maritime Policy for the Union: A European vision for the oceans and seas" (7 June 2006).

60 *U.S. Department of Transportation, Bureau of Transportation*, "U.S. International Trade and Freight Transportation Trends 2003" (2003), available at <www.bts.gov/publications/us_international_trade_and_freight_transportation_trends/2003/index.html>.

61 *U.S. Commission on Ocean Policy*, "An Ocean Blueprint for the 21st Century-Final Report" (2004), at 193.

62 *Ibid.*, at 31.

63 *Marine Transportation System National Advisory Council*, "U.S. Economic Growth and the Marine Transportation System" (2000).

64 *European Commission*, Directorate-General for Transport, Maritime Transport, available at <http://europa.eu.int/comm/transport/maritime/index_en.htm>.

65 *Borg*, Joe/*Barroso*, José Manuel, "Toward a Maritime Policy for the Union: A European Vision for the Oceans and Seas", Communication to the Commission from the President and Mr. Borg (2 March 2005), at 4.

66 *Coulter*, Daniel Y./*Goldman*, Alan, "Global Shipping Trends and Implications for Navies", in *Crickard*, Fred W. *et al.* (eds.), "Multinational naval cooperation and foreign policy into the 21st century" (Aldershot: Ashgate, 1998), pp. 46 *et seq.*, at 51-52.

67 *UNCTAD*, Review of Maritime Transport 2005, at 4.

percent of container port throughput, 64.7 percent of container port operators, 83.2 percent of containership shipbuilding and 99 percent of ship demolition.[68] Furthermore, 20 of the world's top 30 container ports are located in Asia, with Singapore and Hong Kong being the largest by far,[69] and sixteen of the world's top 25 liner shipping companies are based in Asia.[70]

Bernard Fensterwald, Jr., member of the office of the legal advisor of the Department of State, recognized the importance of freedom of navigation for developing States when he stated in 1956 that "[i]f the doctrine of freedom of the seas is allowed to die or whither on the vine, it seems certain that the big naval, commercial, and fishing nations will once again get the lion's share, and, as a result, all of the nations of the world, but especially the smaller and less powerful ones, will suffer."[71] The same, though to a lesser degree, is probably true if the freedom of the seas were maintained, but the frequency of interferences with navigation increased.

However, not all developing States have been able to profit from the combination of free navigation and the liberalization of global trade. In Asia, for example, the landlocked States likes Laos, Nepal, Bhutan and Mongolia did not share the economic growth rates of their neighbours. Barred from access to the sea, they faced abnormal transport costs due to border crossings and empty back hauling of trucks.[72]

In Africa, the States with access to the sea, experienced a better development than their landlocked neighbours, but their development was nevertheless significantly behind the development of most Asian States. Why could these African States not adequately profit from the opportunities of maritime transport and the freedom of navigation? Most of their economies heavily rely on the export of goods, particularly raw materials. For example, exports of a state like Kenya depend on the world (extra-African) market for more than 78 percent and Tanzania's export dependency is about 80 percent.[73] Both the infrastructure and the administrative management of the existing facilities in most African States, however, heavily increase transport costs[74] and thereby impede an inexpensive export by maritime transport.

For example, in May 2003, there were average waiting times of 37 hours in the port of Durban.[75] Cameroun's port of Douala is reported not to manage economic growth due to administrative mismanagement.[76]

---

68 *UNCTAD*, Review of Maritime Transport 2004, at 105.
69 *Ibid.*, at 100-101.
70 *Ibid.*, at 104.
71 50 ASIL Proceedings (1956), at 150.
72 *UNCTAD*, Review of Maritime Transport 2004, at 116-118.
73 *Mahalu*, Costa Ricky, "Public international law and shipping practices: the east african aspirations" (Baden-Baden: Nomos, 1984), at 45.
74 For the importance of these costs for economic development see *Parameswaran*, Benjamin, "The Liberalization of Maritime Transport Services" (Berlin: Springer, 2004), at 51-54.
75 *UNCTAD*, Review of Maritime Transport 2004, 77.
76 Schiff & Hafen, Vol. 57, No. 6 (2005), at 28.

The Europe West Africa Trade Agreement, a liner conference operating under EU Regulation 4056/86, in 2004 applied congestion surcharges to a number of ports in West Africa such as Luanda (Angola), Tema (Ghana), Cotonou (Benin), Lagos (Nigeria), Dakar (Senegal) and Malabo (Equatorial Guinea).[77] Furthermore, the liner conferences apply surcharges for extra risks or emergencies (*e.g.*, Liberia, Sierra Leone, Côte d'Ivoire) and for freight taxes (*e.g.*, Nigeria, Benin, Gabon, Ghana). All these charges render maritime transport unnecessarily expensive and impede the development of West African States. The obstacles to development are thus largely internal, while the Law of the Sea with its freedom of navigation offers tremendous opportunities to developing States.

Congestion has become a problem in developed market economies as well, but there, economic wealth has already reached a considerable level, while in African States, any development and catch-up to developed market economies is impeded by congestion and unnecessary costs for maritime transport.

The secretary general of the International Maritime Organisation (IMO) has underlined that developing States may also profit from the ancillary businesses of maritime trade, such as the registration of ships, the supply of sea-going manpower and ship recycling and that maritime trade therefore plays a key role in achieving the United Nations Millenium Goals.[78] However, if one looks at Liberia, the second biggest flag State, one must seriously question whether the registration of ships alone may represent a significant factor in the development of States.

The economic impact of seafarers sending their wages to their families and of ship recycling seems to be more profound. However, it is the maritime trade in general which such developing States really rely on for either the export of their raw materials or of the products of their specialization.

This outline has indicated how important the freedom of navigation is both for developed market economies and (even more) for developing States. Its overwhelming economic importance therefore needs to be taken into consideration by any State which aims to interfere with navigation, whether it is a mere boarding, an inspection, a diversion or even the seizure of a vessel.

B. Security concerns brought forward to interfere with navigation

Even though the freedom of navigation has since *Hugo Grotius* held a very prominent place in public international law, it never enjoyed absolute force. In fact, States have always demanded or even claimed rights to interfere with navigation and some of these rights have been expressly recognized and codified in international conventions.

---

77 *UNCTAD*, Review of Maritime Transport 2004, 77.

78 *IMO* Doc. A 24/INF.7, "Opening Address by Mr. Efthimios E. Mitropoulos, Secretary General., to the Twenty-Fourth Regular Session of the Assembly of the International Maritime Organization" (21 November 2005), at 4.

Common to all these grounds has been the concern that States were afraid that freedom might lead to lawlessness and insecurity. From the beginning of the Law of the Sea it was recognized that piracy and ships without nationality constitute grounds for interferences. However, in the course of centuries, more and more interference rights were demanded. Examples might today seem exotic such as unauthorized broadcasting from the high seas or the slave trade, but they might also be "hot" issues like terrorism, the related transport of weapons of mass destruction, undocumented migration, the transport of drugs or illegal fishing.

At first sight, this multitude of potential grounds for interferences seems substantial, even as compared with the freedom of navigation. This section will nevertheless try to assess the real scope of these concerns and analyze in how far a right to interfere with navigation is reasonable and necessary. Particularly, other measures than interferences with navigation on the high seas might be more efficient, less harmful and thus preferable.

I. Piracy – an ancient, but persistent business

The oldest of all international crimes leading to interferences on the high seas[79] is the crime of piracy.[80] It may seem to be an archaic business, but it has not yet died out. In fact, the crime remains a fairly common phenomenon in some regions of the world.

While the issue of piracy enjoys wide popular attention, the international lawyer needs to be careful not to exaggerate the scope of the problem since most crimes commonly understood to constitute piracy do not fall under the definition of piracy *iure gentium* and thus also not under the provisions of the Law of the Sea Convention which will be discussed in this study.

Piracy *iure gentium* is defined as "any illegal acts of violence or detention, or any act of depredation, committed for private ends by the crew or the passengers of a private ship or a private aircraft, and directed on the high seas, against another ship or aircraft, or against persons or property on board such ship or aircraft" (Art. 101, para. 1, lit. a LOSC)[81]. Three requirements significantly restrict the importance of piracy *iure gentium*. First, such piracy must have occurred in a maritime zone outside the jurisdiction of any State such as the high seas. This excludes, *e.g.*, all crimes committed in the territorial seas, internal and archipelagic waters. As far as it concerns the exclusive economic zone, Art. 101 LOSC is applicable as long as it is not incompatible with Part V of the Law of the Sea Convention. Therefore,

---

79 *Cf. Sunga*, Lyal S., "The Emerging System of International Criminal Law" (The Hague: Kluwer Law International, 1997), at 3, 253, 338.

80 On its origins see *Rubin*, Alfred P., "The Law of Piracy" (2nd ed., Irvington-on-Hudson: Transnational Publishers, 1998) at 6-42; *Lagoni*, Rainer, "Piraterie und widerrechtliche Handlungen gegen die Sicherheit der Seeschiffahrt", in *Ipsen*, Jörn (ed.), "Recht – Staat – Gemeinwohl: Festschrift für Dietrich Rauschning" (Köln: Heymann, 2001), pp. 501 *et seq.*, at 501-505.

81 Other forms of piracy under Art. 101 LOSC such as participation, incitation or facilitation of piracy are not relevant here.

if the sovereign rights of a coastal State in its exclusive economic zone are concerned (*e.g.*, a tussle between two fishing vessels about their catch), the universal jurisdiction to combat piracy does not apply, but instead the criminal jurisdiction of the coastal State.[82] Secondly, piracy must have been committed for private ends. This criterion distinguishes the pirate from the terrorist who commits his crime for political rather than private reasons. Thirdly, two ships are required: the pirate ship and the target vessel. A mutiny by the crew or a hijacking by passengers thus also does not constitute piracy *iure gentium*.

What is thus the relevance of piracy *iure gentium* and consequently of the compensation provisions in Art. 106 and Art. 110, para. 3 LOSC if the seizure, visit or search of a ship suspected of piracy is in question? Both the International Maritime Bureau (IMB) of the International Chamber of Commerce and the International Maritime Organization (IMO) collect reports of piracy around the world. The definitions of piracy underlying these reports, however, are very different from Art. 101 LOSC. Thus, the IMB defines piracy as "an act of boarding any vessel with the intent to commit theft or any other crime and with the intent or capability to use force in the furtherance of that act." Contrary to Art. 101 LOSC, this definition also covers crimes committed inside the territorial sea and inside internal waters. Presumably, the IMB considered it too difficult to clearly locate the commission of the crime based on notices by crew members or shipowers and on radio calls.[83] Furthermore, according to the IMB, piracy does not necessarily need to be undertaken from another vessel or aircraft. Contrary to the LOSC, the IMB thus would consider an armed diver to be a pirate. Finally, the definition of the IMB does not require the conduct of a pirate to be for "private ends" as in Art. 101 LOSC. Therefore, only a few of the incidents reported by the IMB would fall under the piracy provisions of the LOSC including its compensation provisions in Art. 106 and 110, para. 3 LOSC.

Nevertheless, the numbers collected by the IMB together with the description of the individual cases might reveal the scope of piracy *iure gentium*. The IMB reported 276 actual and attempted acts of piracy and armed robbery during 2005, which constitutes a significant decrease from the 325 incidents in 2004 and the 445 incidents during 2003.[84] What is even more fortunate is that in 2005, no seaman was killed in an act of piracy, while in 2004, acts of piracy were accountable for the deaths of 32 seafarers.[85] In the first half of 2006 though, this decline in

---

[82] *Cf. Lagoni*, Rainer, "Piraterie und widerrechtliche Handlungen gegen die Sicherheit der Seeschiffahrt", in *Ipsen*, Jörn *et al.* (eds.), "Recht – Staat – Gemeinwohl: Festschrift für Dietrich Rauschning" (Köln: Heymann, 2001), pp. 501 *et seq.*, at 515 (with further examples).

[83] *Ibid.*, at 510.

[84] *IMB*, "Piracy and Armed Robbery against Ships, Annual Report 2005" (31 January 2006), at 5.

[85] *Ibid.*, at 10.

numbers has slowed down with 127 incidents worldwide.[86] Most attacks in 2005 occurred in Indonesian (79 incidents) and Somalian (35 incidents) waters.[87]

While piracy is on strong retreat in the Malacca Straits[88] and in Western Africa, both Somalia and Iraq appeared to be new breeding grounds for pirates.[89] Between 15 March and 20 October 2005 alone, there were 23 attacks against vessels off the southern and eastern coast of Somalia.[90]

All of these numbers are probably a vast underestimate since many shipowners hesitate to report piracy incidents because they are afraid of higher insurance premiums and their reputation and because they are very reluctant to involve the ship in costly delays.[91] Furthermore, some criminal acts against small local craft may not be reported for fear of reprisal.[92]

It seems necessary to describe some typical scenarios of piracy by referring to recent cases in order to ascertain how relevant the compensation provisions of the LOSC really are. Probably the most common scenario, particularly in the Straits of Malacca, is that small groups of pirates armed with knives or guns board slow moving vessels in areas close to shore by using grappling hooks. The boats used by the pirates are usually small high-speed vessels without lights and without a national flag. In the Malacca Straits, pirates have become well organized and often attack in flotillas of up to seven rather small boats.

After the pirates have boarded the vessel, they will usually choose between three options. They may rob the ship's safe, stores or valuable equipment. They may also highjack the whole ship and/or her crew and demand a ransom for the release. There seems to be a certain trend toward the hijacking of crew members.[93] More rarely, pirates sell the ship's cargo or change the ship's name and sell it as a "phantom ship" to a new owner.

One example of the first scenario occurred on 1 April 2005 when three armed pirates attacked a Japanese-owned bulk carrier in the Malacca Straits off Kuala

---

86 "Decline in pirate attacks slows up", Lloyd's List, 26 July 2006, p. 3.

87 *IMB*, "Piracy and Armed Robbery against Ships, Annual Report 2005" (31 January 2006), at 5.

88 There was only one incident of piracy in the Malacca Straits in the first quarter of 2006. *Cf.* "Malacca Strait shows signs of improvement", Lloyd's List, 4 April 2006, p. 4.

89 *IMB*, "Piracy and Armed Robbery against Ships, Annual Report 2005" (31 January 2006), at 16.

90 "Unprecedented increase in piracy attacks off Somalia", available at <www.icc-ccs.org/main/news.php?newsid=57>.

91 *National Union of Marine, Aviation and Shipping Transport Officers*, "In the firing line" (2004), at 2; *cf. Diaz*, Leticia/*Dubner*, Barry Hart, "On the Problem of Utilizing Unilateral Action to Prevent Acts of Sea Piracy and Terrorism: A Proactive Approach to the Evolution of International Law", 32 Syracuse J. Int'l L. & Com. (2004), pp. 1 *et seq.*, at 26.

92 *Davidson*, Scott, "Dangerous Waters: Combating Maritime Piracy in Asia", 9 Asian Yb. Int'l L. (2004), pp. 3 *et seq.*, at 7.

93 "Conference Report of the 5th Tri-annual IMB Meeting on Piracy and Maritime Security", Maritime Studies (January/February 2005) at 22. In 2005, there were 23 vessels hijacked by pirates. *IMB*, "Piracy and Armed Robbery against Ships, Annual Report 2005" (31 January 2006), at 16.

Lumpur and escaped with several thousand dollars from the ship's safe. The ship, which was in the Straits north of Port Klang about 50 kilometers from the Malaysian capital, was apparently boarded by three armed men from a wooden ship around 3 a.m. The pirates forced the crew to hand over the cash from the safe and escaped.[94]

The second scenario took place when a ship carrying United Nations' food aid to Somali victims of the Indian Ocean tsunami was hijacked on her way from the Kenyan port of Mombasa to Bossaso in north-eastern Somalia. The pirates used this ship to hijack another vessel carrying cement, but released the two vessels when they were running out of fuel.[95]

The third scenario requires a greater deal of organizational skills. An attempt to board a vessel and then sell its cargo occurred on 14 June 2005 when Indonesian pirates hijacked an oil tanker off northern Malaysia in the Straits of Malacca. Police and naval forces laid siege to the ship and the pirates, armed with machetes, surrendered after 12 hours. Police also arrested two of the tanker's crew members and a Malaysian businessman believed to have masterminded the pirate attack. Police believed the pirates may have arranged international buyers for the 30,000 barrels of diesel worth about 5.3 million Singapore Dollars on the vessel, which was bound for Myanmar.[96] Only slightly more successful were the pirates who, in November 2002, seized the *Natris*, put the crew ashore, repainted the vessel and called at ports in India, Bangladesh and Myanmar before she was intercepted by Malaysian authorities in August 2005.[97]

The economic impact of piracy is considerable. While the damage to one particular vessel and her owner by an act of piracy might be very limited, one has to take account of the consequences for the economic development of whole regions and of the long-term reaction of shipping companies. Somalia's development, *e.g.*, will be hampered by the fact that shipping companies steer clear of its coastlines. Hence, they incur higher freight because ships will avoid the shortest routes through piracy-prone areas. Furthermore, the insurers might raise the premiums if a vessel regularly passes through these areas. The decision of the Lloyd's Insurance Market in London to charge higher premiums for vessels passing the Malacca Straits by classing them a "war risk" on 20 June 2005[98] was due to the risk of piracy, but also to information indicating that terrorists may be planning to use the Straits for an attack on maritime trade.[99]

There is great diversity of measures to combat piracy. To prevent the crime, ships may be equipped with so-called electrifying fences, acoustic and tracking

94 Kyodo News Service, 1 April 2005.

95 New York Times, 4 October 2005, p. A 10.

96 Singapore Shipping Times, 30 June 2005.

97 "Terror fears put squeeze on ships in Asian strait", International Herald Tribune, 25 August 2005, p. 1.

98 *Cf.* "'War-risk' tag angers Asean region's sipping industry", Financial Times, 16 August 2005, p. 2.

99 This decision has since then been heavily criticized due to a decreasing number of piratical attacks in the Straits of Malacca. *Cf.* "Aon rates Malacca Strait high risk in new piracy threat map", Lloyd's List, 27 April 2006, p. 1.

devices. An electrifying fence is a non-lethal device surrounding the vessel which uses a 9,000 volt pulse to deter boardings. If an intruder comes in contact with the fence, he receives a non-lethal shock and the alarm goes off.[100] However, for safety reasons, electrifying fences cannot be used on tankers and gas carriers.[101] The Long Range Acoustic Device (LRAD) sends sound waves to intruders causing pain and even hearing loss. The cruiseliner *Seabourn Spirit* was able to deter pirates off the Somalian coasts by using LRAD.[102]

Tracking systems allow shipping companies to monitor the exact location of their vessels. Tracking systems also often include the possibility for the crew to send an alarm message to the shipping company. Large ships are already required to carry such tracking devices under IMO Regulation SOLAS XI-2/6. Singapore also started to fit all small boats and yachts with them in order to prevent privacy near its coastlines.[103] Furthermore, the crew may also arm themselves. The arming of crew members or even private escorts for cargo vessels could, on the other hand, also lead to uncontrollable conflicts and increased violence endangering crew members.[104] Malaysia and Indonesia have therefore objected to the presence of private armed escort ships in the Malacca Straits.[105] In spite of these efforts, private escorts seem to have become a reality in the Straits of Malacca.[106] Other preventive measures would be to avoid anchoring or unnecessary berthing, shipping in coastal areas or particularly dangerous shipping lanes. The decision of the Lloyd's Insurance Market (*supra*) may have triggered a consideration of alternative shipping routes by the shipowners. Furthermore, this decision may itself have represented a successful measure since it might have contributed to increased security measures and thereby to a lower number of piracy incidents in the Malacca Straits. Eventually, the Joint War Committee of the Lloyd's Insurance Market was able to declassify the straits as a war risk zone.[107]

If an act of piracy has occurred, the coastal State may lay siege to the pirates, arrest them and finally sentence them. Due to the character of piracy as an international crime, every State (not only the coastal one) may seize the pirate ship and arrest the pirates if the crime occurred on the high seas or in the exclusive economic zone (Art. 105 LOSC).

However, there are several reasons why a seizure under Art. 105 LOSC is very rare. First, pirates usually attack in shallow, coastal areas inside the jurisdiction of

[100] For more information on the „Secure-Ship“ system, available at <www.secure-marine.com/ship/index.shtml>.

[101] *Mukundan*, Pottengal, "Piracy and Armed Robbery against Ships Today", 2 WMU J. of Maritime Affairs (2003), pp. 167 *et seq.*, at 179.

[102] "Wenn die Granate in die Bordwand donnert“, Frankfurter Allgemeine Zeitung, 2 December 2005, p. 18.

[103] Reuters, 2 July 2005.

[104] But see *Kovalev*, Aleksandr Antonovic, "Contemporary issues of the Law of the Sea" (Utrecht: eleven, 2004), at 148.

[105] Tehrantimes, 16 May 2005.

[106] "Private sector helps to ease piracy fears in Malacca Strait", Lloyd's List, 4 July 2006, p. 4.

[107] "Insurers drop Malacca Strait as war risk", Lloyd's List, 9 August 2006, p. 1.

a coastal State because their relatively small boats are not able to go out very far and because target vessels usually move particularly slowly in coastal areas or even anchor or berth there and thus constitute a feasible target. Secondly, the boats used by the pirates very often are not registered in any State. As such, they do not enjoy protection by any flag State and may be boarded at any time (Art. 110, para. 1, lit. d LOSC).

The statistics of the IMB and the IMO show that a significant number of attacks takes place in busy and confined waters and not on the high seas.[108] Two thirds of all acts of piracy and maritime robberies occur in the territorial waters of a coastal State.[109] In fact, within the last 20 years, only one prosecution of piracy under the provisions of the LOSC took place.[110] Exceptional in this regard is the situation in Somalia where pirates attacked ships as far as 400 nautical miles off the coast and apparently used "mother vessels" to launch these attacks.[111] On 21 January 2006, the U.S. navy captured a pirate ship inside the Somalian exclusive economic zone[112] which is probably currently the only area in the world where boarding and seizure of a pirate vessel under Arts. 110, para. 1 and 105 LOSC has significant relevance.

Due to the location of the crime and due to the fact that most States do not have the resources or are unwilling to respond effectively to a pirate attack, it is the coastal State which is the most appropriate entity to combat piracy.[113] In the territorial sea, other States than the coastal State do not have any jurisdiction for enforcement measures against piracy.[114] Recent international efforts have thus focussed on enhancing the security measures by coastal States, particularly in the Malacca Straits. One of the major problems in regions involving a multitude of coastal States is that pirates may escape patrol boats of one coastal State simply by entering the territorial sea of another coastal State which would then object to any

108 *Mukundan*, Pottengal, "Piracy and Armed Robbery against Ships Today", 2 WMU J. of Maritime Affairs (2003), pp. 167 *et seq.*, at 175.

109 *Jesus*, José Luis, "Protection of Foreign Ships against Piracy and Terrorism at Sea: Legal Aspects", 18 Int'l J. Mar. & Coast. L. (2005), pp. 363 *et seq.*, at 383.

110 *National Union of Marine, Aviation and Shipping Transport Officers*, "In the firing line" (2004), at 20. A Belgian court n this case ruled that the Greenpeace vessel *Sirius* had committed an act of piracy when it tried to prevent two Belgian vessels from dumping toxic waste in the North Sea; cf. Court of Appeals (Antwerp), 19 July 1985, European Transport Law (1985), pp. 536-543.

111 *IMB*, "Piracy and Armed Robbery against Ships, Annual Report 2005" (31 January 2006), at 16.

112 "US Navy seizes suspected pirate vessel off Somalia", Lloyd's List, 24 January 2006, p. 5.

113 *Cf. Diaz*, Leticia/*Dubner*, Barry Hart, "On the Problem of Utilizing Unilateral Action to Prevent Acts of Sea Piracy and Terrorism: A Proactive Approach to the Evolution of International Law", 32 Syracuse J. Int'l L. & Com. (2004), pp. 1 *et seq.*, at 7.

114 Even though the LOSC is not very explicit on the issue, all States are probably entitled to take actions against pirates in the EEZ's of other States. *Cf. Davidson*, Scott, "Dangerous Waters: Combating Maritime Piracy in Asia", 9 Asian Yb. Int'l L. (2004), pp. 3 *et seq.*, at 14-15.

enforcement measure by other States.[115] The general attitude of States bordering the Malacca Straits is that any financial help and the donation of patrol vessels is welcome, while they are very reluctant to let other States undertake patrols in their own coastal areas, particularly as far as it concerns the U.S. navy and coast guard.[116] A rare exception took place when Indonesia, Malaysia and Singapore asked India to help patrolling the Malacca Strait in June 2004.[117] Efforts by Malaysia, Indonesia and Singapore have been very mixed. Singapore, due to the small territorial sea and its well-equipped coast guard, has achieved the best results.[118] The coordinated patrols which started in July 2004 with 17 naval vessels of the three States have had varied degrees of success.[119] In June 2005, Malaysia has gone ahead to control its part of the straits with six patrol boats[120] and plans to build up a fleet of 72 boats with 4,000 personnel.[121] Indonesia received complaints about its lack of control by Japan[122] and then stepped up patrols one month later.[123] All three States have established coordinated patrols on the sea and in the air. In fact, the air patrols are joined by Thailand. Up to two maritime patrol aircraft from each nation are involved in the air surveillance scheme. Each aircraft must have one officer from each nation on board and is allowed to patrol above territorial waters of each State no less than three nautical miles from the shore.[124] Air surveillance can be especially effective in regions where boundary disputes lead to jurisdictional sensitivity and where therefore naval vessels are hesitant to enter.[125]

Furthermore, 16 Southeast Asian States have adopted the "Regional Cooperation Agreement on Prevention and Suppression of Piracy and Armed Robbery Against Ships in Asia" under which an anti-piracy center, financed by Japan, is set up in Singapore. There, States will gather information on piracy and share it with other States parties.[126] One needs to notice, though, that Malaysia and Indonesia

---

115 *Ibid.*, at 21-22.

116 "Rumsfeld seeks unity in fight against piracy", International Herald Tribune, 7 June 2005, p. 3.

117 The Peninsula, 9 May 2005.

118 *Eadie*, Edward N., "Relevance of International Criminal Law to Piracy in Asian Waters", Maritime Studies (May/June 2004), pp. 21 *et seq.*, at 25.

119 *Richardson*, Michael, "The Threats of Piracy and Maritime Terrorism in Southeast Asia", Maritime Studies (November/December 2004), pp. 18 *et seq.*, at 20.

120 Schiff & Hafen, Vol. 57, No. 6 (2005), at 6.

121 *IMB*, "Piracy and Armed Robbery against Ships, Annual Report 2005" (31 January 2006), at 30.

122 BBC Monitoring Asia & Pacific, 1 April 2005.

123 "Terror fears put squeeze on ships in Asian strait", International Herald Tribune, 25 August 2005, p. 1.

124 "Joint air patrol on Malacca Strait", Shipping Times, 8 September 2005.

125 *Eadie*, Edward N., "Relevance of International Criminal Law to Piracy in Asian Waters", Maritime Studies (May/June 2004), pp. 21 *et seq.*, at 31.

126 "Japan to fund Singapore anti-piracy center", Big News Network, 5 September 2005.

have not yet signed the agreement even though piracy represents a considerable problem in their waters.[127]

IMO has also signed a Memorandum of Understanding with the States bordering the Malacca Straits which suggests that all vessels travelling on the shipping lane install equipment that will allow them to inform authorities about pirate attacks or other security threats.[128]

When all other measures fail or are not available, the only solution is to settle an agreement with the pirates. In Somalia, no effective government exists and hence, no governmental patrol boats are controlling its coastal waters. Pirates were easily able to highjack a few ships in the summer of 2005 and demanded ransom for crew, cargo and vessel. The transitional government could only urge neighbouring States to send warships to patrol Somalian waters.[129] On a UN General Assembly meeting in 2001, the following general proactive approach was proposed: If a coastal state is unable or unwilling to prosecute pirates, then the flag State should have a role to play.[130] During its 24th session in 2005, the IMO Assembly authorized the IMO Secretary General to bring the matter of piracy off Somalian coasts to the UN Security Council.[131] Four months later, the Security Council reacted with a Presidential Statement encouraging "all member States whose naval vessels and military aircraft operate in international waters and airspace adjacent to the coast off Somalia to be vigilant to any incident of piracy therein and to take appropriate action to protect merchant shipping, in particular the transportation of humanitarian aid, against any such act, in line with relevant international law."[132]

In addition to its demand of patrolling by foreign navies, the transitional government of Somalia has meanwhile contracted with a U.S. security company to patrol Somalian waters.

A seizure in the territorial sea against the will of the coastal state would again raise the issue of conformity with public international law, but as of now, almost all interferences with pirate vessels (with the exception of some Somalian cases) do not fall under the scope of any provision of public international law. The compensation provisions in Arts. 106 and 110, para. 3 LOSC thus only play a marginal role.

As far as it regards those acts of armed robbery that do not constitute piracy because either only one vessel is involved or because the criminals do not act for private, but for public purposes, the Convention for the Suppression of Unlawful

---

127 "Asian anti-piracy pact to come into force", Lloyd's List, 21 April 2006, p. 3; "Asian alliance to fight pirates goes ahead despite dissenters", Lloyd's List, 22 June 2006, p. 1.

128 "Japan to fund Singapore anti-piracy center", Big News Network, 5 September 2005.

129 "Somalis seek help to stop pirates", BBC News, 13 October 2005.

130 *UN* Doc. A/56/58, "Oceans and the Law of the Sea: Report of the Secretary-General" (9 March 2001), at 39.

131 Lloyd's List, 25 November 2005; *IMO* Doc A.979(24) (23 November 2005).

132 *UN* Doc. S/PRST/2006/11, "Statement by the President of the Security Council" (15 March 2006) at 2-3; *cf.* also "UN approves IMO Somalia piracy plan", Lloyd's List, 20 March 2006, p. 1.

Acts against the Safety of Maritime Navigation (SUA Convention)[133] in 1988 tried to fill some loopholes by obliging States to criminalize these acts (see Arts. 3, para. 1, lit. a and 5 SUA Convention). In October 2005, this convention was complemented by a protocol which allowed boardings of foreign vessels involved in such crimes under certain circumstances. This SUA Convention and its 2005 Protocol mainly target acts of terrorism, but they are also applicable to armed robbers who do not use a pirate vessel, but who take over a vessel as fake crew members or passengers.

The scope of the SUA Convention shows that it is not easy to clearly distinguish between piracy and terrorism. Often, pirates may act both for private (*e.g.*, to steal money) and public (*e.g.*, to finance the fight against a central government and to undermine its security policy) purposes. Therefore, this analysis will now focus on terrorism as another potential ground for interferences with navigation.

II. Terrorism and weapons of mass destruction – the new dominant concern

Since 09/11, the international community has perceived an increased risk of a terrorist attack. Maritime trade has not been immune from this development. This part is therefore going to deal with the potential scenarios of a terrorist attack on maritime trade, their potential economic consequences and the proposed and implemented measures to prevent and react to these attacks. This overview shall serve the purpose of determining the relevance of interferences with navigation undertaken in order to prevent terrorism.

Maritime transport might be considered the "Achilles Heal" in the international transport chain because it enjoys a significant freedom from government control. This freedom which has allowed maritime transport to contribute to economic prosperity renders it uniquely vulnerable to exploitation by terrorist groups.[134]

Maritime transport involves a multitude of different cargos, thousands of intermediaries and great possibilities to hide one's own identity as shipowner or shipper using a complex web of international corporate registration practices.[135] The transportation of the so-called weapons of mass destruction does not necessarily have to be linked to terrorists since also States might have an interest in acquiring these weapons. However, the prevention of their transportation is usually discussed in the framework of measures against terrorism and, as will be seen, some measures do not distinguish between transportation by States and by private individuals suspected of supporting terrorism.

---

[133] *IMO* Doc. SUA/CONF/15/Rev.1, "Convention for the Suppression of Unlawful Acts against the Safety of Maritime Navigation", Rome, 10 March 1988; reprinted in Révue Générale de Droit International Public, Vol. 92, p. 477; 27 ILM (1988) p. 672.

[134] *OECD Maritime Transport Committee*, "Security in Maritime Transport: Risk Factors and Economic Impact" (2003), at 3.

[135] *Ibid.*, at 5.

Also, ships are an ideal base for a terrorist hostage-taking since they offer a self-contained unit with internal food, water and power supplies.[136] Finally, maritime trade (particularly oil tankers) and cruise ships present iconic symbols of the western economy and culture. They are as such ideal targets to spread a political message to the world.

1. Scenarios of terrorist attacks on maritime trade

As one possible scenario, terrorists could hijack a vessel and demand the satisfaction of certain postulations like the liberation of prisoners for the release of the vessel and its crew. Pirates in the Malacca Straits already use these means to gain their living and there is speculation that some terrorist groups might be involved in some of the hijackings in that area. The "Achille Lauro" hijacking by Palestinian terrorists in 1985 nevertheless remains the most famous among the cases of terrorist hijackings of a vessel.[137]

Terrorists could also destroy vessels and hereby cause extensive material and environmental damage and terror. Thus, *e.g.*, on 6 October 2002, terrorists rammed a small boat packed with explosives into the tanker *MT Limburg*. One crewmember died and approximately 90,000 barrels of oil poured into the Gulf of Aden near the Yemeni coastline.[138] In the same year, the FBI issued warnings that terrorists might be planning attacks by divers attaching explosives to the hulls of oil tankers.[139] A Syrian terrorist apparently planned to attack Israeli cruise ships docking on Turkey's Mediterranean coast, but was arrested before he could strike.[140] Naval vessels evidently constitute a very prestigious target for terrorists. On 19 August 2005, terrorists fired three rockets at two U.S. warships in the Red Sea Port of Aqaba. They missed their targets, but killed one Jordanian soldier and

---

136 *National Union of Marine, Aviation and Shipping Transport Officers*, "In the firing line" (2004) at 5.

137 *Cf.* also the case of the "Santa Maria" in which members of the Portuguese opposition hijacked a cruiseliner in the Caribbean in December 1961 in order to raise the attention of world press toward political events in Portugal under the Salazar regime. *Lagoni*, Rainer, "Piraterie und widerrechtliche Handlungen gegen die Seeschiffahrt", in *Ipsen*, Jörn *et al.* (eds.), "Recht-Staat-Gemeinwohl – Festschrift für Dietrich Rauschning" (Köln: Heymann, 2001), pp. 502 *et seq.*, at 519.

138 *Diaz*, Leticia/*Dubner*, Barry Hart, "On the Problem of Utilizing Unilateral Action to Prevent Acts of Sea Piracy and Terrorism: A Proactive Approach to the Evolution of International Law", 32 Syracuse J. Int'l L. & Com. (2004), pp. 1 *et seq.*, at 8-9.

139 *IMB*, "Piracy and Armed Robbery Against Ships, 2002 Annual Report" (2003), at 24.

140 "Turkey Charges Syrian in a Plot To Blow Up Israeli Cruise Ships", New York Times, 12 August 2005, p. A.10. The port of Antalya has since then established a sophisticated security regime. "Commercial focus restores confidence", Lloyd's List, 27 April 2006, p. 7.

hit the close-by Israeli resort of Eilat.[141] In 2002, the U.S. and allied nations disrupted a plot to attack ships transiting the Straits of Hormuz.[142]

Containers or even whole vessels could also be used as dirty bombs exploding in the middle of great cities or blocking important shipping routes. Of course, the steering of a large vessel requires great skills, but terrorists seem to have learned their first lessons. In March 2003, ten armed men seized the chemical tanker *Dewi Madrim* in the Malacca Straits off Indonesia's coast for the purpose of learning to steer it.[143] They spent an hour steering the vessel and then robbed it.[144] As far as it concerns containers, one must first take account that there are 15 million in circulation. In 2001, 232 million containers moved through container ports and only 2 percent of those arriving in the U.S. were physically examined.[145] Due to the stacking on vessels, it is not possible to check containers on the sea and inspections in ports are very expensive. Crews hardly ever know about the contents of containers. Therefore, it is rather easy for terrorists to transport a bomb into a port and let it explode in a prominent location. They may also use containers for their own transport. On 18 October 2001, port authorities in the southern Italian port of Gioia Tauro discovered an Egyptian-born Canadian stowaway in a container equipped with cellular phones, a computer and security passes for several U.S. airports. The final destination of the container was Canada.[146]

Finally, terrorists could act like shipowners or shippers, generating income by the operation of ships or transporting important material for the building of bombs in one of thousands of containers. Al-Qa'eda has been reported to own a fleet of up to 20 ships.[147] To carry out the bombings of the U.S. embassy in Kenya in 1998, Al-Qa'eda smuggled explosives into Mombassa on vessels.[148] The organization has probably taken the Tamil Tigers as an example. The latter operate 10-12 bulk freighters bearing Panamanian, Honduran and Liberian flags. These vessels generate income for the Tamil Tigers, but also carry some weapons (approximately 5 percent of the cargo).[149]

---

141 "Group with al-Qaeda links fires on US warships", Financial Times, 20 August 2005, p. 6.

142 Fact Sheet: Plots, Casings, and Infiltrations Referenced in President Bush's Remarks on the War on Terror, available at <www.whitehouse.gov/news/releases/2005/10/20051006-7.html>.

143 "Editorial, Piracy and Terrorism", New York Times, 10 April 2004, p. A14.

144 *USCINCAP Virtual Information Center*, Primer: Piracy in Asia (31 October 2003), at 24.

145 *National Union of Marine, Aviation and Shipping Transport Officers*, "In the firing line" (2004), at 7.

146 "Canada, Italy Work on Stowaway Case", Wall Street Journal, 29 October 2001, p. .19.

147 *National Union of Marine, Aviation and Shipping Transport Officers*, "In the firing line" (2004), at 9.

148 *Gunaratma*, Rohan, "Terrorist threat to shipping is 'imminent and growing'", Lloyd's List, 29 September 2004.

149 *OECD*, "Security in Maritime Transport: Risk Factors and Economic Impact" (2003), at 15.

Another possibility for terrorists to use maritime trade is to have some of their members enrol as seamen. There are 1.2 million seafarers, most of them employed by agencies in developing countries. It would be relatively easy for Al-Qa'eda to have their agents pose as seafarers and at some point take command of a ship or simply secretly immigrate into a target state. According to IMO, 6 percent of all seafarer certificates may be counterfeit and 9 percent of all seafarers are serving illegally.

As a preliminary result, it is submitted that the risk of a terrorist attack on maritime trade is real, but that thus far, much more people have been killed by pirates than by maritime terrorists and that the number of terrorist incidents has been very limited.

2. Potential economic impact of terrorist attacks on maritime trade

The economic impact of a terrorist attack on maritime trade could be enormous. If only one vessel is attacked, costs are limited to the reparation of the damage to the vessel, the cargo and the crew, an increase in insurance premiums for other vessels plying the same area and potentially environmental damage, some unemployment and other losses for the affected area itself. However, the impact would multiply if an attack disrupted traffic in a major port or in an important shipping route. The disruption of port traffic in all U.S. west coast ports for 11 days in October 2003 due to a strike provides for an interesting example. The strike entailed significant back-logs and warehousing costs increased extremely. There are estimates that the strike triggered costs of 466.9 million or even 19.4 billion U.S. dollars.[150] These are probably only the lower bounds because the estimates do not include any property and personal damage and losses in other countries. If one tries to estimate the costs of a potential terrorist attack, one has to take account of the fact that the costs will rise exponentially with the duration of the closure. It is thus submitted that the costs of a terrorist attack leading to the disruption of port traffic will more likely be in the billions than in the millions.

Of course, companies could anticipate these costs by establishing certain buffers in their inventories. In fact, due to 09/11, U.S. companies have already increased inventories from 1.36 months in 2001 to 1.43 months. This however, has also triggered costs of 50 to 80 billion U.S. dollars.[151] Furthermore, the indirect costs of a terrorist attack will most likely outnumber the direct impact by far. There is an estimate that these costs could be as high as 58 billion U.S. dollars for the United States alone.[152]

As far as it concerns the disruption of traffic in an important shipping lane, the costs depend on the amount of traffic regularly passing this lane and the burden of choosing alternative shipping routes. As for the Malacca Straits, approximately

---

150 *Ibid.*, at 19.

151 *Bemasek*, Anna "The friction economy: American business just got the bill for the terrorist attacks: $151 billion--a year", Fortune, 18 February 2002, p. 104.

152 *OECD Maritime Transport Committee*, "Security in Maritime Transport: Risk Factors and Economic Impact" (2003) at 55.

55,000 vessels are passing these Straits every year representing 80 percent of the total oil transport to China, Japan and South Korea and about 40 percent of global trade.[153] Any detour would consist of at least 600 nautical miles through the Indonesian archipelago which could make freight rates surge 500 percent or more. Due to the overwhelming importance of this region for maritime trade, any terrorist strike, even if it was not a major one, would send economic shockwaves around the world.[154]

3. Preventive and repressive measures to combat maritime terrorism

The responses of the international community to these threats are very diverse and have been taken on the domestic, the regional and the international level. One ought to distinguish between ship and port security measures and interdictions on the seas.

a) Ship and port security

The most prominent measure of the former is the International Ship and Port Facility Security Code (ISPS). A diplomatic conference under the auspices of the IMO adopted some amendments to the Safety of Life at Sea Convention (SOLAS) and the ISPS Code in December 2002. The amendments to SOLAS include an accelerated equipping of vessels with Automatic Identification Systems[155] and obligations to mark ships with a permanent identification number on the hull and inside the ship,[156] to keep records with safety information on the ship (Continuous Synopsis Records – CSR) including, *e.g.*, the name of the shipowner[157] and to install ship security alert systems by which a security alert can be sent from the ship to an authority on shore.[158] This authority will then be able to track the ship and initiate safety measures. The crew must be able to activate the system from the bridge and another place on the vessel and the system must not raise any alarm on board the ship. Starting in 2008, all ships of more than 300 gross tonnage also need to install long-range tracking equipment to transmit identity and location to authorized government agencies.[159]

The ISPS Code follows a risk management approach and obliges ships, shipping companies and ports to install their own risk management systems. Shipping companies have to designate a Company Security Officer (CSO) who is then responsible for the elaboration of Ship Security Plans (SSP), which, after approval by the flag State, are then placed on each ship. These plans enumerate the

153 "US Admiral seeks global information network", Lloyd's List, 2 February 2006, p. 3.

154 *Ibid.*

155 Modification of SOLAS, Chapter V. On the advantages and disadvantages of Automated Identification Systems see *Eason*, Craig, "Freedom and Security: The dilemma of vessel tracking", Lloyd's List, 21 April 2006, p. 7.

156 New SOLAS Chapter XI-1.Regulation XI-1/3.

157 New SOLAS Regulation XI-I/5.

158 New SOLAS Chapter XI-2.

159 "IMO agrees on tracking requirements", Lloyd's List, 23 May 2006, p. 1.

measures which need to be taken by the crew for each different security level set by ports. A Ship Security Officer (SSO) is responsible for the execution of the SSP. Flag States have to issue International Ship Security Certificates (ISSC) for ships complying with the new provisions. Without such an ISSC, a ship will not be allowed to proceed trading.

Ports have to designate Port Facility Security Officers who are responsible, after an assessment, to elaborate and execute Port Facility Security Plans indicating measures for three levels of security. Ports are also entitled to check compliance with SOLAS and ISPS provisions during ship inspections. If ships are non-compliant, available measures include delaying, detention and expulsion from the port.[160] A coastal State may also require a ship intending to enter its ports to notify in advance whether it complies with the requirements.[161] The SOLAS Amendments and the ISPS Code entered into force on 1 July 2004. In February 2005, almost 94 percent of the members to SOLAS have approved security plans for 97 percent of the declared port facilities (more than 9,600 ports worldwide).[162] Furthermore, far more than 90 percent of vessels falling under the scope of SOLAS and ISPS Code now have approved ISSC's.[163]

OECD estimates that measures concerning ships security would cost ship operating companies at least 1.279 billion U.S. dollars in the first year and 730 million U.S. dollars per year thereafter.[164] Concerning costs for port security measures, the OECD estimates that U.S. ports alone will incur costs of 963 million U.S. dollars in the first year and 509 million U.S. dollars in the years thereafter.[165] World-wide costs for port security measures will approximately be between 2 and 2.5 billion U.S. dollars per year.[166] Since ports apply different strategies in generating revenue to finance these security measures, there is a significant risk that competition between ports might in the end be increasingly distorted.[167]

The United States did not consider these measures sufficient to guarantee its own security. It has therefore adopted legislation going beyond the mentioned IMO measures. Vessels destined to a U.S. port now have to notify U.S. port authorities 96 hours prior to their arrival with information on cargo and crew. Car-

---

160 *Özcayir*, Oya, "The International Ship and Port Facility Security (ISPS) Code", 9 J. Int'l Maritime L. (2003), pp. 578 *et seq.*, at 581.

161 *UN* Doc. A/59/63, "Oceans and the Law of the Sea, Report of the Secretary General" (18 August 2004), at para. 81.

162 *IMO* Press Release, "Maritime Security on agenda as USCG Commandant visits IMO" (17 February 2005).

163 *IMO* Press Release, "Security compliance shows continued improvement" (6 August 2004). On the whole implementation process of the ISPS Code see *Asariotis*, Regina, "Implementation of the ISPS Code: an overview of recent developments", 11 J. Int'l Maritime L. (2005), pp. 266 *et seq.*, at 267-269.

164 *OECD Maritime Transport Committee*, "Security in Maritime Transport: Risk Factors and Economic Impact" (2003), at 39.

165 *Ibid.*, at 45.

166 *Asariotis*, Regina, "Implementation of the ISPS Code: an overview of recent developments", 11 J. Int'l Maritime L. (2005), pp. 266 *et seq.*, at 277.

167 "Brussels warns of port security 'distortions'", Lloyd's List, 4 August 2006, p. 3.

riers have to declare the cargo of a container 24 hours before the container is loaded on board a vessel bound for the U.S. no matter whether the cargo will be discharged in the U.S. The data of the bill of lading suffices, but there are plans to demand even more detailed data on the cargo.[168] The European Union has adopted a similar 24-hour-rule for external maritime trade.[169] For certain cargo, U.S. customs service will issue a "do not load" message. If the vessel nevertheless loads, it will not be allowed to discharge in a U.S. port. Hereby, container trade loses a considerable degree of its flexibility and thus also a part of its profitability since larger inventories will be needed and since just-in-time supply management will become harder.

Furthermore, the United States has announced the Container Security Initiative (CSI) under which it has concluded agreements with other port states to screen certain high-risk containers in foreign ports before loading. In return, cargoes from those ports are moved more quickly once they land in the United States. The agreements also allow U.S. customs inspectors to participate in the security measures in foreign ports. In May 2005, there were 36 non-U.S. ports participating in the CSI.[170]

In another U.S. program, the Customs-Trade Partnership against Terrorism (C-TPAT), companies are given preferential U.S. customs treatment if they adhere to security procedures. These include such steps as putting up fencing around manufacturing plants and watching over loaded containers as they move from the factory to the ship. Containers shipped by these companies are inspected only once every 306 times, instead of once every 47 times permitting faster movement of goods. In May 2005, there were 5,000 companies participating in C-TPAT.[171] The total costs of all these measures will most likely in the end be borne by the consumer. Industrial sources estimate that, due to the security measures, prices for goods traded by sea will increase by 1 to 3 percent.[172] The European Commission is planning similar legislation, allegedly avoiding excessive bureaucracy of C-TPAT.[173]

Security measures have also affected persons employed in the area of maritime trade. The personnel of U.S. ports is now obliged to carry transportation security cards. Foreign seafarers in U.S. ports have to apply for non-immigrant visas for any shore leave. Under the auspices of the International Labor Organization, there was adopted the Convention on Seafarer Identity Documents (C185) which was to guarantee at the same time secure identification of seafarers and non-bureaucratic shore leave opportunities for seafarers. This convention, though, has so far been

---

168 "New security rules for US-bound cargo in works: Bill of lading data will no longer be adequate, warns shipping body chief", Shipping Times, 19 September 2005.

169 "EU lines up container security expansion", Lloyd's List, 16 November 2005.

170 "Loopholes Seen in U.S. Efforts to Secure Ports", New York Times, 25 May 2005, p. A.6.

171 *Ibid.*

172 *OECD*, "Economic Outlook", No. 71 (June 2002), at 118.

173 "Brussels security code aims for fast-track shipping", Lloyd's List, 2 May 2006, p. 3.

ratified by only seven States[174] and has not been able to unify rules concerning shore leave in order to enable seafarers to leave their vessels while in port.[175] The United States has been extremely sceptical toward this convention, probably because it would require a certain degree of trust in foreign administrations.

Hence there is a great deal of measures against terrorism that do not include any interferences on the high seas and thus far, no major terrorist strike against maritime trade occurred. However, States are also increasingly using interferences with navigation outside their own territorial seas in order to combat terrorism.

b) Interception operations

After 09/11, western naval forces have been extensively involved in programmes of interception and inspection in areas such as the Middle East and the Mediterranean. These boardings have been undertaken for two main reasons. First, the United States and other States were concerned that after the invasion of Afghanistan, members of Al Qa'eda would attempt to escape western forces using maritime traffic. Secondly, these boardings shall prevent the transport of so-called "weapons of mass destruction" (WMD), particularly nuclear material which could be used for a terrorist attack. This risk is not mere theory. The International Atomic Energy Agency (IAEA) has already collected a database with hundreds of incidents involving illicit trafficking of nuclear and other radioactive material.[176] Scientists are no more linked to States or international alliances, information is readily available and WMD could be miniaturized by usage of information technology.[177] Interference with maritime transport could therefore be an efficient measure to prevent the dissemination of WMD.

Thus, within the UN-mandated "Operation Enduring Freedom", the naval "Task Force 150" consisting of 18 warships of different nations inspected almost 300 vessels near the Horn of Africa between 6 December 2004 and 31 March 2005.[178] Until late 2005, the German navy alone had inspected nearly 100 merchant vessels in this region.[179] Boardings in this area are however limited to the high seas and the exclusive economic zones. Only the United States and the United Kingdom have thus far gained approvals by coastal States to board vessels in their territorial seas.[180] In the Mediterranean Sea, NATO forces have been monitoring maritime traffic immediately after 09/11, particularly in the Eastern

[174] Azerbaijan, France, Hungary, Jordan, Nigeria, Moldova, Nigeria, available at <www.ilo.org/ilolex/cgi-lex/ratifce.pl?C185>.

[175] "Numast fights to ratify seafarers ID scheme", Lloyd's List, 8 August 2006, p. 1.

[176] *UN* Doc. A/59/63, "Oceans and the Law of the Sea, Report of the Secretary General" (18 August 2004), at para. 85.

[177] *Lehrman*, Thomas D., "Enhancing the Proliferation Security Initiative: The Case for a Decentralized Nonproliferation Architecture", 45 Va. J. Int'l L. (2004) 223, at 241.

[178] "Übergabe in drei Akten", available at <www.marine.de/01DB070000000001/CurrentBaseLink/W26CRAWX339INFODE>.

[179] „Was darf die Bundeswehr im Kampf gegen den Terror?“, Frankfurter Allgemeine Sonntagszeitung, 22 January 2005, p. 2.

[180] *Ibid.*

Mediterranean and the Straits of Gibraltar. On 29 April 2003, the "Task Force Endeavour" began boarding operations following a North Atlantic Council decision to enhance the effectiveness of the current naval operations against suspected terrorist activities in the Mediterranean. As of 8 January 2004, 37 vessels had been boarded by "Task Force Endeavour".[181] All boardings by Task Force 150 and Task Force Endeavour require the permission of the boarded vessel's captain.

In June 2003, a ship registered in the Comoros Islands and carrying 680 tons of explosives was intercepted by Greek forces about 240 kilometres from Athens. The vessel had been roaming the Mediterranean for six weeks and the papers on the ship listed as the recipient of the cargo a non-existing chemical company in Sudan.[182]

Again, the United States did not consider these multilateral efforts sufficient to prevent terrorist acts. The Law of the Sea seemed to lay insurmountable barriers rendering it very difficult to inspect and detain a vessel on the high seas. The United States failed to gain China's support for a UN Security Council resolution authorizing the interdiction of foreign vessels suspected of ferrying banned weapons on the high seas.[183] Furthermore, there are some uses of the oceans which comply with public international law and nevertheless pose a threat to international security. On 9 December 2002, two Spanish Navy vessels intercepted and boarded a North Korean cargo ship on the high seas, 600 miles off the coast of Yemen. Hidden beneath cargo, boarding crews discovered a stockpile of Scud missiles. After the initial interdiction and seizure, the vessel was permitted to continue to its final destination Yemen when it was discovered through consultations with the Yemeni president that his government had legally purchased the missiles.[184] The White House conceded at that time that there was no provision under international law that prohibited Yemen from purchasing conventional missiles from North Korea and that vessel and cargo therefore could not be confiscated.[185]

Faced with these problems, the United States on 31 May 2003 announced the "Proliferation Security Initiative" (PSI), a non-obligatory partnership with other nations committing themselves to conduct and to allow boardings in zones under their jurisdiction or on the high seas in order to combat terrorism.[186] More than 60

---

[181] "Operation Active Endeavour", available at <www.afsouth.nato.int/JFCN_Operations/ActiveEndeavour/Endeavour.htm>.

[182] "Greece impounds explosives-laden ship headed for Sudan", International Herald Tribune, 24 June 2003, p. 5.

[183] *Bergin*, Anthony, "The Proliferation Security Initiative – Implications for the Indian Ocean", 20 Int'l J. Mar. & Coast. L. (2005), pp. 85 *et seq.*, at 91 (2005).

[184] *de Almeida Nascimento*, Adelaida, "El Control de Buques Mercantes en Alta Mar por Parte de los Efectivos de la Armada Española que Participan en la Operación Libertad Duradera: El Episodio del So Sane", 55 REDI (2003) pp. 268 *et seq.*, at 272.

[185] *Cf.* "Reluctant U.S. Gives Assent For Missiles to Go to Yemen", New York Times, 12 December 2002, p. A.1.

[186] See *Department of State*, Proliferation Security Initiative: Statement of Interdiction Principles (4 September 2003), available at <http://usinfo.state.gov/products/pubs/proliferation/#statement>.

states have meanwhile become members of PSI.[187] PSI is an activity rather than a multilateral treaty and does not "provide a legal basis for interdicting vessels flagged to third States on the high seas."[188] Officials of the U.S. administration have asserted that PSI had scored some successes, but claimed that they were unable to reveal details for fear of disclosing and damaging sensitive operations and intelligence sources and methods. In May 2005, Secretary of State *Condoleezza Rice* noted that, in the previous nine months, the United States and PSI partners have cooperated on 11 successful interdiction efforts. However, she was very vague concerning the precise incidents, maybe because the cooperating states are concerned about retributions by terrorists.[189]

PSI cooperation stopped the transshipment of material and equipment bound for ballistic missile programs in countries of concern, including Iran. PSI partners also have worked with others to prevent Iran from procuring goods to support its nuclear program. And bilateral PSI cooperation prevented the ballistic missile program in another region from receiving equipment used to produce propellant for missiles.[190] In December 2003, the United States Navy intercepted and seized a small vessel near the Strait of Hormuz in the Persian Gulf. Found aboard were nearly two tons of illicit drugs, and more importantly to the ongoing campaign against terrorism, three Al-Qa'eda suspects. The seizure occurred in a strait used for international navigation, as that term is defined by the Law of the Sea Convention, where "all ships and aircraft enjoy the right of transit passage, which shall not be impeded."[191] In October 2003, the *BBC China*, a German-owned ship carrying centrifuge components for Libya's nuclear weapons program, was intercepted during a PSI exercise.[192] The ship was forced into port in Taranto, Italy. This might indirectly have resulted in *Moammar Qaddafi's* announcement of an end to his nation's covert nuclear weapons development program.

As part of the PSI, the United States has concluded ship boarding agreements with some important flag States like Panama and Liberia. These agreements establish procedures for the authorization of a flag State to board a vessel suspected of carrying illicit shipments of WMD. Most notably, some of these agreements stipulate that if the flag State does not respond to a request within a certain amount

---

187 "President's Statement on the Proliferation Security Initiative", available at <www.whitehouse.gov/news/releases/2005/05/20050531-1.html>.

188 *Klein*, Natalie, "Legal Implications of Australia's Maritime Identification System", 55 Int'l & Comparativle L. Quarterly (2006), pp. 337 *et seq.*, at 347.

189 "Rice to Discuss Antiproliferation Program", New York, 31 May 2005, p. A.3.

190 "Transforming our Counterproliferation Efforts in the Asia Region", available at <www.state.gov/t/us/rm/51129.htm>.

191 *Barry*, Ian Patrick, "The right of visit, search and seizure of foreign flagged vessels on the High Seas pursuant to customary international law: A defense of the proliferation security initiative", 33 Hofstra L. Rev. (2004/2005), pp. 299 *et seq.*, at 299.

192 "U.S. Seized Shipload of Nuclear Equipment Bound for Libya in October", New York Times, 1 January 2004, at A7.

of time,[193] then the requesting Party will be deemed to have been authorized to board the suspect vessel. The ship boarding agreements now cover more than 60 percent of the global commercial shipping fleet's dead weight tonnage.[194]

In spite of these aforementioned successes of PSI, it remains unknown how large the PSI impact on maritime trade really is. States members of PSI are concerned that they as interdicting states could be liable for any damages incurred by the target vessel, including to its cargo, and for any costs incurred by delays in passage of goods to the ship's final destination and that they therefore would prefer to have high confidence in information-sharing arrangements.[195] This alone raises the suspicion that the damage incurred on maritime trade by PSI is very significant. Furthermore, 95 percent of the ingredients for WMD are dual-use in nature, having both civilian and WMD applications.[196] Therefore, an efficient effort to find WMD shipments would require the boarding State to stop and search numerous ships which turn out to pose no threat at all.

Nobel Peace Prize Winner *Mohamed ElBaradei* has also expressed some scepticism about PSI because it is not rooted in the international non-proliferation regime and because it does not tackle the proliferation issue at its roots (*e.g.*, instability in the concerned regions).[197]

The latest measure to combat maritime terrorism is the new protocol[198] to the 1988 Convention for the Suppression of Unlawful Acts against the Safety of Maritime Navigation. This convention was originally meant to fight certain acts of maritime crime not falling under the piracy provisions of LOSC because of the two-vessel requirement and the private end criterion.[199] It introduced an obligation for States having some connection with the offence to establish jurisdiction and an obligation for all States to criminalize the offences covered by the convention and to either punish or extradite the offenders (*aut dedere aut judicare)*.[200] The new

---

193 Two hours in the Proliferation Security Initiative Ship Boarding Agreement with Liberia, "Proliferation Security Initiative Ship Boarding Agreement with Liberia" (11 February 2004), available at <www.state.gov/t/isn/c12387.htm>.

194 Media Note, The United States and Belize Proliferation Security Initiative Ship Boarding Agreement (4 August 2005), available at <www.state.gov/r/pa/prs/ps/2005/50787.htm>.

195 *Bergin*, Anthony, "The Proliferation Security Initiative – Implications for the Indian Ocean", 20 Int'l J. Mar. & Coast. L. (2005), pp. 85 *et seq.*, at 93.

196 *Beck*, Michael E., "The Promise and Limits of the PSI", The Monitor (Center for Int'l Trade and Security), Vol. 10, No. 1 (Spring 2004), at 16.

197 "Weapons of Mass Destruction and the Proliferation Dilemma: Interview with Dr. Mohamed ElBaradei: Director General of the International Atomic Energy Agency", 28 Fletcher F. World Aff. (2004) 29, at 39-40.

198 *IMO* Doc. LEG/CONF.15/21, "Protocol of 2005 to the Convention for the Suppression of Unlawful Acts against the Safety of Maritime Navigation" (1 November 2005).

199 *IMO* Doc. SUA/CONF/RD 13; *Joyner*, C.C., "The 1988 IMO Convention on the Safety of Maritime Navigation: Towards a Legal Remedy for Terrorism at Sea", 31 GYIL (1988), pp. 230 *et seq.*, at 242.

200 *Treves*, Tullio, "*The Rome Convention for the Suppression of Unlawful Acts Against the Safety of Maritime Navigation"*, in *Ronzitti*, Natalino (ed.), "Maritime Terrorism and International Law" (Dordrecht: Nijhoff, 1990), pp. 69 *et seq.*, at 71; *Lagoni*, Rainer,

protocol now contains a provision on boarding of vessels suspected of being involved in terrorist activities or carrying weapons of mass destruction. However, the protocol has not yet entered into force and the new provisions thus not yet found application.

This brief analysis has shown that the frequency of interferences on the high seas in order to fight terrorism or the transport of weapons of mass destruction has significantly increased. Legal grounds for these interferences could be (1) a United Nations mandate for a multilateral interdiction operation, (2) the consent by the flag State, (3) a ship boarding agreement, (4) the new protocol to the SUA Convention or (5) some interference right under customary international law such as self-defence. While the analysis may have given the impression that abusive interferences, particularly by the United States, have become common, one must admit that the United States has also implemented some safeguards for shipping interests. Large container vessels with the destination of a U.S. port are thus at least usually warned in advance that the U.S. Coast Guards intends to board them.[201]

This study will not analyze under what circumstances interferences with vessels suspected of supporting terrorism is lawful, but it will, in the following Chapters, set out the preconditions of liability of the boarding State under each of the mentioned grounds for interference.

III. Undocumented Migration

Undocumented Migration continues to be a major issue in international law and politics. Most migrants are destined to the United States, Southern Europe and Australia. Since land border controls have become more effective, migrants tend to choose the seas as a route of transport.

The common terminology distinguishes between "undocumented migrants" and "stowaways". The former are known by the carrier, but hide themselves from authorities of the State of their destination.[202] The latter do not pay for their voyage and therefore need to hide from the carrier and both the departure and the destination State.[203] An undocumented migrant usually travels on a rather small high speed boat and therefore can only travel a certain distance. Stowaways, on the other hand, hide themselves in the cargo holds of great vessels, often traveling great distances.

In numbers, the maritime trafficking of migrants today seems to be the much more significant issue as compared with the stowaway phenomenon. In the first

"Piraterie und widerrechtliche Handlungen gegen die Sicherheit der Seeschiffahrt", in *Ipsen*, Jörn *et al.* (eds.), "Recht – Staat – Gemeinwohl: Festschrift für Dietrich Rauschning" (Köln: Heymann, 2001), pp. 501 *et seq.*, at 525-529.

201 "Some Ships Get Coast Guard Tip Before Searches", New Times, 20 May 2006.

202 *Goy*, Raymond, "Le régime international des migrants illicites par voie de mer", 7 ADM (2002), pp. 249 *et seq.*, at 250.

203 *Goy*, Raymond, "Le régime international du passager clandestine", 6 ADM (2001), pp. 167 *et seq.*, at 170.

eleven months of 2005, the Spanish Coast Guard rescued 5,700 migrants off the Spanish coast.[204] The Spanish government counted a total of 567 boats carrying undocumented migrants from Africa to Spain.[205] Lately, the Canary Islands have become a new destination for undocumented migration receiving approximately 7,500 African migrants within the first 5 months of 2006.[206] Furthermore, Italy has seen a 50 percent increase in the number of African migrants crossing the Mediterranean Sea on the way to its shores in 2005.[207] Between 1999 and 30 July 2004, 597 incidents related to unsafe practices associated with the trafficking or transport of migrants involving 20,175 migrants were reported to IMO.[208] The real number of undocumented migrants is probably, as the name indicates, much higher.[209] Contrary to the European Union, the United States has been able to reduce the number of undocumented migrants traveling by sea. While in 1992, the U.S. Coast Guard interdicted 31,438 immigrants, this number went down to about 2,500 immigrants in 1997.[210] One of the reasons for this decrease has definitely been the political situation in the Caribbean with the end of the Haitian civil war in the mid-1990's. However, a significant part of the reduction of trafficking is also attributed to stepped-up Coast Guard interdictions after the United States concluded bilateral maritime agreements with many Caribbean States authorizing the U.S. Coast Guard to undertake interdictions in order to prevent migrant smuggling.[211]

As far as it concerns stowaways, the number of incidents reported to IMO from November 1998 to June 2004 was 2,342. Most of them were discovered in West Africa (33.6 per cent in 2002 and 47.8 per cent in 2003) and the Mediterranean, the Black Sea and the North Sea (combined 47.7 per cent in 2002 and 24.3 per cent in 2003).[212]

States have taken great efforts to reduce the numbers of undocumented migrants and of stowaways. However, these measures need to be different for the two distinct categories of migrants. Stowaways travel alone or in small groups. Furthermore, they hide in places which are difficult to inspect on the seas (*e.g.*,

---

204 "Navy deal to fight illegal migration", The Guardian, 3 December 2005, p. 19.

205 "Kurze Meldungen", Frankfurter Allgemeine Zeitung, 7 January 2006, p. 4.

206 "Keine deutsche Hilfe für Spanien", Frankfurter Allgemeine Zeitung, 27 May 2006, p. 1.

207 "650 Flüchtlinge auf den Kanaren", Frankfurter Allgemeine Zeitung, 15 May 2006.

208 *IMO* Doc. MSC.3/Circ.7.

209 *UN* Doc. A/60/63, "Oceans and the Law of the Sea, Report of the Secretary General" (4 March 2005), at para. 103.

210 *Kramek*, Joseph E., "Bilateral Maritime Counter-Drug and Immigrant Interdiction Agreements: Is this the world of the Future?", 31 U. Miami Inter-Am. L. Rev. (2000), pp. 121 *et seq.*, at 137-8.

211 *Ibid.* For the exchange of notes between the U.S. and Haiti see *Nash Leich*, Marian, "Contemporary Practice of the USA relating to international law", 76 AJIL (1982) pp. 374-377.

212 *UN* Doc. A/59/63, "Oceans and the Law of the Sea, Report of the Secretary General" (18 August 2004), at para. 94.

a container). Therefore, any government efforts have to concentrate on port State control.

A wider array of measures is available regarding undocumented migrants. Either the departure or the destination State may prevent the transport boat from leaving or entering its coastal zones. Furthermore, States are trying to intercept the boat on its voyage. Due to the rather short trips of these boats, such interdiction will usually occur in territorial waters or contiguous zones. The destination State has a considerable interest of receiving permission for interdictions in the territorial sea of the departure State, hereby rendering its interdictions more efficient. In order to get this authorization, potential destination States have adopted agreements with likely departure States (*see supra*). For example, the exchange of notes between Italy and Albania[213] authorizes Italian naval vessels (with Albanian officers on board) to stop vessels of all flags inside the Albanian territorial sea.[214]

Interdictions on the high seas thus far have played a rather minor role in the prevention of migrant smuggling. Furthermore, boats carrying undocumented migrants are often not registered in any State and can be legally interdicted on the high seas by any other State. An Italian court, *e.g.*, justified the intervention of the *Cemil Panuk* by Italian forces by treating the vessel as a ship without nationality.[215] Nevertheless, the international community deemed it necessary to draft a new ground for interferences on the high seas in cases of suspected migrant smuggling and adopted the 2000 Migrant Smuggling Protocol.[216] The associated compensation provision in this Protocol will therefore be subject to analysis together with the other compensation provisions.

Furthermore, the European Commissioner for Justice and Interior Affairs, Franco Frattini, has called for "setting up a permanent plan for European patrols in the Mediterranean to intercept illegal migrants."[217] Apparently, the new European agency Frontex is destined to control these European interdiction efforts.

Thus, the European plans raise many issues concerning the applicability of the Migrant Smuggling Protocol and concerning the liable entity if many member States cooperate within one International Organization. Finally, as the plans also propose interdiction measures near the African coasts,[218] they will definitely require coastal State consent. This study will deal with some of these issues and

---

213 Gazzeta Ufficiale dell Republica Italiana, suppl. n° 163 (15 July 1997).

214 *Goy*, Raymond, "Le régime international des migrants illicites par voie de mer", 7 ADM (2002), pp. 249 *et seq.*, at 286.

215 *Goy*, Raymond, "Le régime international des migrants illicites par voie de mer", 7 ADM (2002), pp. 249 *et seq.,* at 268-269; *Pamuk e altri*, Tribunale de Crotone (27 September 2001), 84 Rivista di diritto internazionale (2001), pp. 1155 *et seq.*; *cf.* also case note by *Andreone*, Gemma, "Pamuk and others", 11 Italian Yb. of Int'l L. (2001), pp. 273 *et seq.*

216 *UN* Doc. A/55/383, Annex III (2 Nov 2000); reprinted in 40 ILM (2001) 384.

217 "Spain urges Brussels to help with influx of migrants from Africa", The Independent, 24 May 2006, p. 19.

218 "EU faces complications in plan to halt migrants Member nations lack unified policies", International Herald Tribune, 25 May 2006, p. 8.

place special emphasis on the determination of the liable entity in multilateral boardings.

IV. Narcotic drugs and psychotropic substances

States have for centuries argued that the transport of certain cargoes was illicit and therefore constituted a ground for interference on the high seas. By declaring this transport illicit and claiming some degree of enforcement jurisdiction, States either aimed to protect the health or moral values of their population or simply enforced their own customs laws.[219] With the establishment of the territorial sea and the contiguous zone, States may now enforce their customs laws in a maritime zone extending up to 24 nautical miles from their shores[220] and an interference right on the high seas to enforce domestic legislation seems no more urgently necessary. Furthermore, smuggling has become less profitable because trade barriers were lifted in the liberalization of world trade.

However, apart from the transport of weapons of mass destruction (discussed *supra* in the framework of terrorism), there is one more cargo concerning which a great number of States demand the prohibition of transport and an interference right on the high seas: narcotic drugs and psychotropic substances.

It is estimated that there is a worldwide market of 200 million people or five percent of the world population for these drugs.[221] The value of the whole illicit drug market at the retail level is estimated to be USD 322 billion.[222] The greatest demand for narcotic drugs and psychotrophic substances exists in developed market economies in North America and Western Europe. However, since prohibition of production of these drugs is quite strictly enforced in these countries and since some drugs may be better cultivated in the climate of developing countries, the business of illicit drugs heavily depends on the transport over great distances. The United Nations estimates that criminal organizations gain USD 300 to USD 500 billion annually from narcotics trafficking.[223]

With approximately 161 millions consumers, cannabis is by far the most common street drug.[224] Its production is extremely dispersed and predominantly for

---

219 *Cf., e.g.*, the Convention between the United Kingdom and the United States respecting the Regulation of Liquor Traffic, concluded in Washington on 23 January 1924, LNTS, Vol. 27 (1924) 182; reprinted in 5 BYIL (1924) 187; see *Jessup*, Philip C., "The Law of Territorial Waters and Maritime Jurisdiction" (New York: Kraus reprint, 1927), at pp. 279-352.

220 *Cf.* Art. 33 LOSC.

221 *United Nations Office of Drugs and Crime*, "World Drug Report 2005", at 23.

222 *Ibid.*, at 127.

223 *UN* Doc. A/59/565, "High-level Panel on Threats, Challenges and Change, A more secure world: our shared responsibility" (2 December 2004), at para. 166.

224 *United Nations Office of Drugs and Crime*, "World Drug Report 2005", at 93.

the domestic market.[225] Morocco, though, seems to be the main producer of the cannabis resin (hashish), mainly transported to Western Europe.[226]

Amphetamine-type stimulants (ATS) come second, as far as it concerns consumption, with an estimated group of 26 million users.[227] Production concentrates in East and South-East Asia, North America and Europe.[228] Since production occurs close to the consumers, cross-border trafficking plays a minor role as compared to other drugs.

Opiates, with 16 million worldwide users, depend on the production of opium poppy which mainly takes place in Afghanistan, Myanmar and Laos.[229] The users, particularly those of heroin, are predominantly located in Asia, Europe and the United States.[230] Therefore, drug trafficking is a major issue in the business of opiates. Heroin probably represents the most dangerous major drug, responsible for 60 percent of treatment demand in Europe and Asia.[231]

Finally, Cocaine is another major drug with 14 million users worldwide where the business requires the transport over great distances.[232] Almost 50 percent of the users are living in North America and there are strong trends to higher consumption in Europe which is already now representing a quarter of worldwide usage.[233] Almost the entire coca cultivation and potential cocaine production, on the other hand, occurs in Columbia, Peru and Bolivia.[234] Central America and the Atlantic are therefore major trading routes for Cocaine.

The vast majority of illegal drugs crosses borders disguised as, or in, ordinary commercial or personal goods.[235] However, in recent decades, border controls on land have significantly increased, particularly on the U.S.-Mexican border and in Central/Eastern Europe. Furthermore, the transport of drugs on land often involves the crossing of a multitude of boundaries and involves a great number of potential cargo controls. Finally, the transport on land can also be quite expensive. Therefore, actors in the business of illicit drugs nowadays more and more frequently utilize maritime transport to move their goods to their customers.

As far as it concerns cocaine, the U.S. government estimates that virtually all of the cocaine produced in South America for consumption elsewhere travels by sea for some portion of its route between South America and its final destination (North America or Western Europe).[236] In 1997, an estimated 430 metric tons of

---

225 *Ibid.*, at 81-82.
226 *Ibid.*, at 83.
227 *Ibid.*, at 112.
228 *Ibid.*, at 99.
229 *Ibid.*, at 41.
230 *Ibid.*, at 57.
231 *Ibid.*, at 67.
232 *Ibid.*, at 76.
233 *Ibid.*, at 76.
234 *Ibid.*, at 62.
235 *Raustiala*, Kal, "Law, Liberalization & International Narcotics Trafficking", 32 J. Int'l L. & Politics (1999), pp. 89 *et seq.*, at 91.
236 *Williams*, Malcolm J., "Bilateral Maritime Agreements enhancing International Cooperation in the Suppression of Illicit Maritime Narcotics Trafficking", in *Nordquist*,

cocaine, 30 metric tons of heroin, and a large amount of marijuana were smuggled to the United States via the maritime, so-called "transit zone" (Gulf of Mexico, Caribbean, Eastern Pacific).[237]

There are different methods how to move illicit drugs by sea. One is to conceal the drugs within containers carried by large commercial vessels. In 1999, 64 per cent of the global seizure volume of cocaine reported to the World Customs Organization was intercepted in maritime containers.[238] Evidently, since containers are usually transported in stacks, it would be hard to inspect a container carrier on sea and the only reasonable measure to prevent transport of drugs would be controls in the port of the departure or the destination State.

Another method to transport is the combination of mother ships with small speed boats. Here, the mother ship will transport a large quantity of the illicit cargo over a great distance, stop outside the contiguous zone of the destination State and then distribute the cargo to a greater number of small speedboats which quickly carry the cargo to the shore, most often to unpopulated areas instead of ports. Any measure after the distribution to the small boats would most probably be too late and inefficient since they move too fast and only carry a comparably small quantity. Hence, reasonable prevention measures need to focus on interferences with the mother ships and on controls in the departure State.

A third method of maritime transport is to carry the drugs inside the territorial seas of third States and then use fast boats to bridge the final gap to the destination State. This method used to be very popular in the Caribbean and could also be useful for some smugglers in the Mediterranean.

It becomes evident that the destination State, which is most interested in the prevention of maritime transport of drugs, needs to rely on the cooperation of other States in its efforts against maritime drug smuggling. First, it could request the departure State to control the cargo leaving its ports. Secondly, it could ask flag States to authorize the inspection of its vessels either generally, or on a case-by-case basis. Finally, the destination State could demand intermediary States to either control their territorial sea with scrutiny or to allow the destination State to exercise this control on its own.

Under the auspices of the United Nations, delegations from a great number of States in 1988 adopted the United Nations Convention Against Illicit Traffic in Narcotic Drugs and Psychotropic Substances.[239] Its Art. 17 stipulates, *inter alia*, that parties "shall co-operate to the fullest extent possible to suppress illicit traffic by sea, in conformity with the international Law of the Sea" (para. 1), may board and search vessels of other States parties if these have granted authorization

---

Myron H. *et al.* (eds.), "Oceans Policy – New Institutions, Challenges, Opportunities" (The Hague: Nijhoff, 1999), pp. 179 *et seq.*, at 182.

237 *Hull*, James D./*Emerson*, Michael D. Emerson, "High 'Seize' Maritime Interdiction Works!", 125 U.S. Naval Institute Proceedings (Jan. 1999), pp. 64 *et seq.*, at 64-65.

238 *UN* Doc. A/60/63, "Oceans and the Law of the Sea, Report of the Secretary General" (4 March 2005), at para. 99.

239 *UN* Doc. E/CONF.82/15, United Nations Convention Against Illicit Traffic in Narcotic Drugs and Psychotropic Substances, opened for signature Dec. 20, 1988 (19 December 1988), reprinted in 28 ILM (1989) 493.

(paras. 3, 4) and "shall consider entering into bilateral or regional agreements or arrangements to carry out, or to enhance the effectiveness of, the provisions of this article" (para. 9). Even though this article did not modify the existing Law of the Sea as such, it initiated the conclusion of a considerable number of agreements between States concerned with drug trafficking and flag States. According to the United Nations Office on Drugs and Crime, at least 22 States have legislation in place permitting cooperation with other States in connection with countering illicit drug trafficking by sea and at least fourteen States have entered into bilateral or multilateral agreements on illicit trafficking by sea.[240] The most important multilateral agreement is probably the "Agreement on illicit traffic by sea, implementing Article 17 of the United Nations Convention against illicit traffic in narcotic drugs and psychotropic substances", adopted on 31 January 1995 under the auspices of the Council of Europe.[241]

Even more important in practice has been the policy followed by the United States. It has concluded a whole series of bilateral maritime agreements with twenty-nine Latin American and Caribbean States for the purpose of combating illicit drug and immigrant smuggling in the transit zone between South and North America.[242] These bilateral agreements streamline the process involved in obtaining permission from a foreign State not only to board one of their ships on the high seas, but also to enter their territorial sea and air space. Of the twenty-nine nations with which the United States has bilateral agreements, fourteen have allowed the United States to stop, board, and search foreign flagged vessels without the flag-State's case-by-case permission when those vessels are located on the high seas and are suspected of illicit traffic (ship-boarding)[243] and twelve have allowed the United States to enter their territorial seas to investigate vessels or aircraft

---

240 UN Doc. E/CN.7/2005/2/Add.3, "United Nations Economic and Social Council, Commission on Narcotic Drugs, The world drug problem – Third biennial report of the Executive Director Office on Drugs and Crime" (7 January 2005), at p. 11, paras. 48-49.

241 "Agreement on illicit traffic by sea, implementing Article 17 of the United Nations Convention against illicit traffic in narcotic drugs and psychotropic substances", European Treaty Series No. 156. This agreement has nevertheless only been ratified by only 11 States, available at <http://conventions.coe.int/Treaty/Commun/ChercheSig.asp?NT=156&CM=8&DF=10/7/2006&CL=ENG>.

242 *Kramek*, Joseph E., "Bilateral Maritime Counter-Drug and Immigrant Interdiction Agreements: Is this the world of the Future?", 31 U. Miami Inter-Am. L. Rev. (2000), pp. 121 *et seq.*, at 123. *Cf.* also, *Sorensen*, Christina E., "Drug Trafficking on the High Seas: A Move toward Universal Jurisdiction under International Law", 4 Emory Int'l L. Rev. (1990), pp. 207 *et seq.*, at 221-223.

243 Most noticeable is the Exchange of Notes between the United States and the United Kingdom, concluded on 13 November 1981, UK Treaty Series (1982), at 8; Cmnd. 8470. *Cf.* also *Siddle*, John, "Anglo-American Co-Operation in the Suppression of Drug Smuggling", 31 Int'l & Comp. L. Q. (1982), pp. 726 *et seq.*; *Gilmore*, William C., "Narcotics Interdiction at Sea: UK-US Cooperation", 13 Marine Policy (1989), pp. 218 *et seq.*, at 222-226.

located therein that are suspected of illegal activities.[244] Furthermore, sixteen States have concluded a "shiprider" agreement with the United States under which a law enforcement officer of one State is embarked onboard a law enforcement plane or ship of another State to permit certain measures of the ship.[245] Finally, twelve States have permitted the United States to conduct a hot pursuit extending to their territorial seas.[246] Very often, the United States also conducts boardings after the captain of the boarded vessel has declared his consent even in the absence of a bilateral agreement between his flag State and the United States.[247]

This practice has enabled the United States to reach a certain degree of success in its efforts against drug smuggling. In 2005, *e.g.*, the U.S. Coast Guard seized 303,187 pounds of cocaine and 10,026 pounds of marijuana.[248]

The drug business nevertheless seems to have adapted its operations and measures to combat drug trafficking need to become more and more sophisticated, involving secret services and law enforcement officials of many States. For example, in July 2005, Spanish police and customs agents seized a fishing vessel with a Brazilian flag carrying 2.5 tons of cocaine in international waters of the Atlantic Ocean. The operation was jointly conducted by members of the U.S. Drug Enforcement Agency, British authorities and the federal police forces of Brazil and Italy.[249] As a reaction to increased law enforcement by Spain, drug smugglers now more frequently use West African States as gateways to Western Europe. In 2004 and 2005, seizures of cocaine totalling 40 tons have been effected on the high seas on ships coming from Western Africa.[250]

This brief analysis has shown how relevant interferences on the high seas are in order to prevent drug trafficking by sea. However, it has also shown that the legal framework is properly described as a patchwork of multilateral conventions, bilateral agreements and *ad hoc* procedures to gain consent by the flag State. This study will analyze the preconditions for and the extent of responsibility of the boarding State under the 1988 United Nations Drugs Convention, the 1995 Council of Europe Agreement implementing this convention, bilateral agreements concluded by the United States and the requirements for a valid consent excluding the responsibility of the boarding State.

---

244 *Kramek*, Joseph E., "Bilateral Maritime Counter-Drug and Immigrant Interdiction Agreements: Is this the world of the Future?", 31 U. Miami Inter-Am. L. Rev. (2000), pp. 121 *et seq.*, at 133-134.

245 *Ibid.*, at 134.

246 *Ibid.*, at 135.

247 *Ibid.*, at 132; *Anderson*, Andrew W., "In the Wake of the DAUNTLESS: The Background and Development of Maritime Interdictions Operations", in *Clingan*, Jr., Thomas A. (ed.), "The Law of the Sea: What Lies Ahead, Proceedings of the 20th Annual Conference of the Law of the Sea Institute July 21-24" (Honolulu: University of Hawaii, 1988), pp. 15 *et seq.*, at 32.

248 *U.S. Coast Guard*, Drug Seizure Statistics, available at <www.uscg.mil/hq/g-o/g-opl/Drugs/Statswww.htm>.

249 China View, 21 July 2005.

250 "W Africa is cocaine hub says UN", Lloyd's List, 7 March 2005, p. 12.

V. Illegal fishing

The freedom of the high seas traditionally also includes the freedom of fishing on the high seas.[251] This aspect of the freedom of the high seas was based on the idea that the living resources of the high seas are inexploitable and that it was thus unnecessary to restrict this use of the high seas.[252] However, even *Grotius* recognized that it could be possible to prohibit fishing because "in a way it can be maintained that fish are exhaustible".[253]

The serious decline of fish stocks in the 20th century has shown that fish are indeed very much exhaustible.[254] This decline was due to a tremendous growth of the world fishing fleet, an increase of the harvesting and processing efficiency per vessel, an extension of the spatial reach of fishing vessels and governmental subsidies to the fishing business.[255]

Noting a continuous downward trend, the Food and Agricultural Organization estimates "that in 2003 about one-quarter of the stocks monitored were underexploited or moderately exploited (3 percent and 21 percent respectively) and could perhaps produce more. About half of the stocks (52 percent) were fully exploited and therefore producing catches that were close to their maximum sustainable limits, while approximately one-quarter were overexploited, depleted or recovering from depletion (16 percent, 7 percent and 1 percent respectively) and needed rebuilding."[256]

Public international law has somehow adapted to the depletion of fish stocks. First, *Hardin's* argument that common resources will always be overexploited because every user would only strive for short-term, maximum gains[257] led to the idea that some exclusive access may represent the most productive allocation.[258] Therefore, coastal States gained more jurisdiction by the establishment of an exclusive economic zone (EEZ) extending to 200 nautical miles from the shores,

---

251 *Cf.* Art. 87, para. 1, lit. e LOSC; Art. 2, para. 2 CHS.

252 *Orrego Vicuña*, Francisco, "The Changing International Law of High Seas Fisheries" (Cambridge: Cambridge University Press, 1999), at 4-5.

253 *Grotius*, Hugo, "The freedom of the seas: or the right which belongs to the Dutch to take part in the East Indian trade" (Translation, New York: Oxford University Press, 1913), at 43.

254 *Fauteux*, Paul, "L'initiative juridique canadienne sur la pêche en haute mer", 31 Can. Yb. Int'l L. (1993), pp. 33 *et seq.*, at 41-43.

255 *Stokke*, Olav Schram, *"Introduction"*, in *id.* (ed.), "Governing High Seas Fisheries – The Interplay of Global and Regional Regimes" (Oxford: Oxford University Press, 2001), pp. 3-5; *Orrego Vicuña*, Francisco, "The Changing International Law of High Seas Fisheries" (Cambridge: Cambridge University Press, 1999), at 55-60.

256 *Food and Agricultural Organization*, "The State of World Fisheries and Aquaculture 2004" (2004), at 32.

257 *Hardin*, Garrett, "The Tragedy of the Commons", Science (1938), pp. 1243-1248.

258 *McDougal*, Myres Smith/*Burke*, William T., "The Public Order of the Oceans" (New Haven: Yale University Press, 1962), at 749.

first accepted as customary international law[259] and then codified in the 1982 Law of the Sea Convention.[260] In this EEZ, the coastal State has sovereign rights and exclusive legislative and enforcement jurisdiction over all living resources.[261] Furthermore, the Law of the Sea Convention also obliged all States parties to exploit living resources of the high seas in a sustainable manner.[262] Regional fisheries organizations (RFO) for large parts of the high seas were established determining total allowable catches for the resources in their areas and quotas for flag States whose vessels want to fish in these areas.[263] The 1995 "Agreement for the Implementation of the Provisions of the United Nations Convention on the Law of the Sea of 10 December 1982 relating to the Conservation and Management of Straddling Fish Stocks and Highly Migratory Fish Stocks" (Fish Stocks Agreement)[264] obliges all parties to the Fish Stocks Agreement to follow decisions of the RFO's even if they may not be members of an RFO.[265] However, as the name indicates, the Fish Stocks Agreement is only applicable to certain species and does not cover a lot of species increasingly exposed to high seas fishing.

To enforce the restrictions on fishing on the high seas under the Fish Stocks Agreement, States may either undertake measures of port State control[266] or board and inspect fishing vessels of flag States parties to the Fish Stocks Agreement[267] under the preconditions codified in this agreement. However, few States have adopted boarding and inspection schemes because of lacking capacity.[268] Further-

---

259 The International Court of Justice recognized a twelve-mile Exclusive Fishing Zone in *Fisheries Jurisdiction Case (United Kingdom v. Iceland)*, Judgment of 25 July 1974, ICJ Reports 1974, pp. 4 *et seq.*, at 24, para. 52. Before the Third United Nations Conference ended, there was a large amount of State practice of claims to 200-mile-EEZ. *Churchill*, Robin R./*Lowe*, Alan Vaughan: "The Law of the Sea" (3rd ed., Manchester: Juris Publications, 1999), at 288.

260 Art. 57 LOSC.

261 Art. 56, para. 1, lit. a and Art. 73, para. 1 LOSC.

262 Arts. 117-119 LOSC.

263 For an excellent overview see *Rayfuse*, Rosemary Gail, "Non-Flag State Enforcement in High Seas Fisheries" (Leiden: Nijhoff, 2004), at 103-203. *Cf.* also *Churchill*, Robin R./*Lowe*, Alan Vaughan: "The Law of the Sea" (3rd ed., Manchester: Juris Publications, 1999), at 297-299.

264 *UN* Doc. A/CONF.164/37, "Agreement for the Implementation of the Provisions of the United Nations Convention on the Law of the Sea of 10 December 1982 relating to the Conservation and Management of Straddling Fish Stocks and Highly Migratory Fish Stocks", adopted on 4 August 1995, (8 September 1995); reprinted in 34 ILM (1995), at 1547.

265 Art. 8, para. 3 Fish Stocks Agreement; *Rayfuse*, Rosemary Gail, "Non-Flag State Enforcement in High Seas Fisheries" (Leiden: Nijhoff, 2004), at 44.

266 Art. 23 Fish Stocks Agreement; *Rayfuse*, Rosemary Gail, "Non-Flag State Enforcement in High Seas Fisheries" (Leiden: Nijhoff, 2004), at 76-78.

267 Arts. 20-22 Fish Stocks Agreement; *Rayfuse*, Rosemary Gail, "Non-Flag State Enforcement in High Seas Fisheries" (Leiden: Nijhoff, 2004), at 73-76.

268 *Lodge*, Michael W./*Nandan*, Satya N., "Some Suggestions Towards Better Implementation of the United Nations Agreement on Straddling Fish Stocks and Highly

more, a considerable enforcement gap still exists for vessels with the nationality of a State that is not member to any RFO or the Fish Stocks Agreement.

Contrary to interferences with navigation on the high seas, interferences with the activities of fishing vessels mainly occur for an economic purpose rather than a security purpose. In the long term, such control is advantageous for the whole fishing business because it is meant to support rather than restrict this important industry. In 2000, total world trade of fish and fishery products was estimated to have an export value of USD 55.2 billion.[269] It is only through a larger degree of control of high seas fisheries that a sustainable management of fishery resources could be achieved and one of the means to gain such control are interferences on the high seas. Therefore, the freedom of fishing on the high seas plays a minor role in the contemporary international policy and law. Some even go as far to argue that the right to fish on the high seas is limited by the rights and duties and interests of the coastal states.[270]

Boardings of vessels on the grounds of illegal fishing are much more common than for other grounds of interference. However, most of these seizures take place inside the exclusive economic zones of coastal States and national laws concerning the responsibility of the coastal States apply. Even if a vessel is suspected of illegal fishing inside the exclusive economic zone of a coastal State, this State will often not be able to reach that fishing vessel while it is still inside that zone. The Law of the Sea then allows the coastal State under quite strict requirements to pursue the fishing vessel onto the high seas (Art. 111, para. 1 LOSC). Such "hot pursuit" may become a complex procedure. In the case of the *Viarsa 1*, for example, the Australian customs service sighted the Uruguyan-flagged *Viarsa 1* inside the Australian exclusive economic zone, unsuccessfully ordered it to stop and then pursued it over a distance of 3,900 nautical miles with the help of South African and British naval vessels before the *Viarsa 1* was finally apprehended 2,000 nautical miles south-west of Cape Town.[271] An Australian jury nevertheless found that the evidence was not sufficiently convincing to rule that the *Viarsa 1* had illegally fished inside the Australian exclusive economic zone. The Australian fisheries minister's reaction was to state that he had "no regrets over the incident that involved Australia in a 21-day chase across three oceans" and that he "would repeat the exercise tomorrow if a foreign fishing vessel is sighted by an Australian patrol vessel inside the Australian Fishing Zone without a permit".[272] If fishing vessels may thus be subject to boardings and pursuit without committing any unlawful action, one necessarily needs to question whether the shipowner needs to bear the

---

Migratory Fish Stocks of 1995", 20 Int'l J. Mar. & Coast. L. (2005), pp. 345 *et seq.*, at 364, n. 69.

[269] *UN* Doc. A/60/63, "Ocean and the Law of the Sea, Report of the Secretary General" (4 March 2005), at 50, para. 182.

[270] *FAO* Doc. FI/HSF/TC/92/7, "Legal Issues Concerning High Seas Fishing" (May 1992).

[271] *Molenaar*, Erik Jaap, "Multilateral Hot Pursuit and Illegal Fishing in the Southern Ocean: The Pursuits of the Viarsa 1 and the South Tomi", 19 Int'l J. Mar. & Coast. L. (2004), pp. 19 *et seq.*, at 19-20.

[272] *Senator Ian MacDonald*, "Viarsa 1 verdict, Media Release DAFF05/218M" (5 November 2005), available at <www.mffc.gov.au>.

costs of such measures. The shipowner of the *Viarsa 1* has already demanded the release of his vessel and claimed compensation of 8 million Australian dollars.[273] The Australian court ruling on the compensation issue may well apply Art. 111, para. 8 LOSC, the compensation provision dealing with matters of hot pursuit. This study will elaborate the preconditions for and the consequences of a claim under Art. 111, para. 8 LOSC, an article not only important for fishing vessels, but for any kind of hot pursuit on the high seas.

Furthermore, it will also deal with interferences with the navigation of fishing vessels under the 1995 Fish Stocks Agreement and the requirements for responsibility of the interfering State under that agreement.

VI. Pollution

One of the rationales of the freedom of navigation was that it does not collide with other uses of the ocean and should therefore not be restricted. However, the previous passage has shown that fishing constitutes another usually free use. According to Art. 87, para. 2 LOSC, the freedom of navigation "shall be exercised by all States with due regard for the interests of other States in their exercise of the freedom of the high seas." A vessel enjoying freedom of navigation, which pollutes the sea and thereby harms fish stocks, significantly impedes the enjoyment by fishing vessels of the freedom of fishing.

Fisheries, however, are by far not the only asset of the ocean which deserves protection from pollution. Within the last fifty years, the international community has realized that a healthy marine environment covering more than 70 percent of the earth's surface bears an immeasurable value of which fish for consumption only constitutes a one aspect. The Law of the Sea Convention has therefore codified rules for the marine environment in a separate part (Part XII), independent of the rules on fisheries (*e.g.*, Part VII, Section 2). In the fundamental provision of Art. 192 LOSC, the convention obliges all States to "protect and preserve the marine environment". While this provision, though not without controversy, has been described as a norm of *ius cogens*,[274] the need to avoid pollution of the marine environment from all kinds of sources has found great acceptance.

However, despite these obligations, pollution by ships continues to be a major problem of maritime transport. Ships frequently endanger the marine environment by polluting accidents, operational discharges, air pollution, dumping, incineration, physical damage to marine habitats, use of toxic anti-fouling paints on ships' hulls, ballast water discharge and intense underwater anthropogenic noise.[275] Ini-

---

273 "Australian Jury Acquitts Viarsa I of Poaching Charge" (7 November 2005), available at <www.sartma.com/art.php?artid=2141&skip=1>.

274 *Lagoni*, Rainer, "Die Abwehr von Gefahren für die marine Umwelt", 32 Berichte der Deutschen Gesellschaft für Völkerrecht (1992), pp. 87 *et seq.*, at 123, 146-149. *Cf.* also the critical remarks by *Rauschning* (*ibid.*, at 160) and *Platzöder* (*ibid.*, at 167).

275 *UN* Doc. A/60/63, "Oceans and the Law of the Sea, Report of the Secretary General" (4 March 2005), at para. 112.

tially, great oil spills such as the *Torrey Canyon* in 1967, the *Amoco Cadiz* in 1978 and the *Exxon Valdez* in 1989 have increased the awareness that certain standards were necessary for shipping in order to avoid pollution.[276] In recent years, the other forms of ship-based pollution have also enjoyed growing attention.

Art. 211, para. 1 LOSC obliges all States to adopt international standards for shipping to prevent pollution. The International Maritime Organization (IMO) has been extremely successful in elaborating these standards for shipping in a great number of usually widely ratified international conventions. Furthermore, regional conventions complemented existing conventions and the United States and the European Union have adopted extensive legislation against marine pollution. The measures in these pieces of legislation include the prohibition of certain ships and the prescription of certain equipment on ships,[277] the imposition of civil liability on shipowners and other actors for certain kinds of pollution[278] and, probably the newest trend, the criminalization of certain conduct which causes marine pollution.[279]

However, the enforcement of standards for ships is predominantly left to flag States and to port States exercising port State control.[280] Only one convention allows the interference with navigation of a foreign vessel on the high seas in order to avoid pollution. The 1969 "International Convention Relating to Inter-

---

276 *Churchill*, Robin R./*Lowe*, Alan Vaughan: "The Law of the Sea" (3rd ed., Manchester: Juris Publications, 1999), at 297-299.

277 Most important is probably the "International Convention for the Prevention of Pollution from Ships" (MARPOL), adopted on 2 November 1973, 12 ILM (1973), at 1319. MARPOL had a multitude of amendments. See *International Maritime Organization*, "MARPOL 73/78: articles, protocols, annexes, unified interpretations of the international convention for the prevention of pollution from ships, 1973, as modified by the protocol of 1978 relating thereto" (2002). See also "Convention on the Prevention of Marine Pollution by Dumping of Wastes and Other Matter", adopted on 29 December 1972, 11 ILM (1972), at 1294; *IMO* Doc. AFS/CONF/26, "International Convention on the Control of Harmful Anti-Fouling Systems", adopted on 5 October 2001.

278 See, *e.g.*, "International Convention on Civil Liability for Oil Pollution Damage", adopted on 29 November 1969, 13 ILM (1969), at 1048 and its amendments; "International Convention on Liability and Compensation for Damage in connection with the Carriage of Hazardous and Noxious Substances by Sea", adopted on 3 May 1996, 35 ILM (1996), at 1406; *IMO* Doc. LEG/CONF 12/19, "International Convention on Civil Liability for Bunker Oil Pollution Damage", adopted on 23 March 2001 (27 March 2001).

279 See, *e.g.*, "Federal Water Pollution Act", 33 U.S.C. § 1319(c)(1); "Oil Pollution Act", 33 U.S.C. § 1321(b)(5); *European Commission*, COM(2003) 92 final, "Proposal for a Directive on ship-source pollution and on the introduction of sanctions, including criminal sanctions, for pollution offences" (5 March 2003). The United States has prosecuted 30 criminal cases between 1995 and 2005 involving intentional discharge of oil, 21 of which have come since 2002. A total of $133m in criminal fines has been levied since 1998. "US signals zero tolerance for polluters", Lloyd's List, 9 February 2006, p. 1.

280 *Cf.* Arts. 218-220 LOSC.

vention on the High Seas in Cases of Oil Pollution Casualties" (Intervention Convention)[281] stipulates in its Article I, para. 1 that "[p]arties to the present Convention may take such measures on the high seas as may be necessary to prevent, mitigate or eliminate grave and imminent danger to their coastline or related interests from pollution or threat of pollution of the sea by oil, following upon a maritime casualty or acts related to such a casualty, which may reasonably be expected to result in major harmful consequences." As Art. 221 LOSC indicates, this interference power remained unchanged after the entry into force of the 1982 Law of the Sea Convention.

No incident is known to the author where a coastal State actually relied on Art. I, para. 1 of the Intervention Convention. A European Commission-sponsored research project nevertheless suggests to broaden the limits to intervention powers in the convention in order to better prevent pollution of European waters by an amendment of the Intervention Convention.[282]

Interferences with navigation in order to prevent pollution therefore currently play a minimal role in the Law of the Sea, but might soonly increase in numbers. This study will dedicate some emphasis on an analysis of the interfering State's responsibility under the Intervention Convention.

VII. Fading away and back-up grounds for interferences

Art. 110, para. 1 LOSC provides for some more grounds for interferences with navigation on the high seas. Under this provision, States may also board vessels suspected of being engaged in illegal broadcasting or slave-trading or of having no nationality.

The two former grounds for interferences are of no practical concern any more and reliance upon them has practically died out. The unauthorized broadcasting from vessels in international waters constituted a problem for coastal States, particularly in the Baltic, the Irish and the North Sea, because since their inhabitants could receive the broadcasts from the seas, States were unable to enforce their broadcasting monopolies, their prohibition of commercial advertising and copyright and tax law. Furthermore, pirate broadcasting often collided with wavelengths which had already been allocated.[283] Meanwhile, coastal States have liberalized their regulation of commercial advertising and their broadcasting monopolies, rendering it less profitable to broadcast from the high seas. Furthermore, all European States have criminalized any support to pirate broadcasting, hereby undermining all financial, personal and logistic support for the pirate sta-

---

281 "International Convention Relating to Intervention on the High Seas in Cases of Oil Pollution Casualties", adopted on 29 November 1969, reprinted in 9 ILM (1969), at 25.

282 "EU to push for coastal rights overhaul", Lloyd's List, 26 May 2006, p. 3; "EU seeks to extend territorial powers", Lloyd's List, 19 July 2006, p. 1.

283 *Cf. Hunnings*, N. March, "Pirate Broadcasting in European Waters", 14 Int'l & Comp. L. Q. (1965), pp. 410 *et seq.*, at 410-413; *Haucke*, Michael, "Piratensender auf See" (München: Beck, 1969), at 2-8.

tions.[284] Therefore, pirate broadcasting does not have any great relevance any more and States do not need to rely on Art. 110, para. 1, lit. c LOSC in order to combat pirate broadcasting.

Slavery and slave trade, on the other hand, have been outlawed decades before[285] and the International Court of Justice even considers it to be an obligation for all State to fight slavery wherever it occurs.[286] Slavery has persisted though, particularly in some regions of the world. However, the transport of slaves in large numbers on vessels, as it was known from Africa to North and Central America until the 19th century, and which was the rationale behind a claimed interference right with the navigation of vessels on the high seas, today does not exist any more in any considerable degree.[287] The interference right laid down in Art. 110, para. 1, lit. b LOSC therefore does not play a major role in practice.

Contrary to these dying-out grounds for interference, States much more frequently rely on another ground codified in Art. 110, para. 1 LOSC: the boarding of vessels suspected of being stateless. If a vessel does not have any nationality at all, it enjoys no protection of any State.[288] Since many criminals or persons whose activity's legality at least is controversial use small, fast, but unregistered boats for their business, interfering States often argue that the interference is justified because the vessel was suspected of being stateless.

Probably the most famous example of such interference is the *So San*. In that case, the Spanish navy on 9 December 2002 boarded this North Korean vessel which was carrying Scud missiles to Yemen. After this transport turned out to be lawful, the Spanish navy argued that the interference was justified since the vessel was not flying a flag and the national markings were obscured by paint and therefore raised the suspicion that the vessel was stateless.[289] Lacking enforcement

---

[284] *Woodcliffe*, J.C., "The demise of unauthorized broadcasting from ships in international waters", 1 Int'l J. Estuarine & Coast. L. (1986), pp. 402 *et seq.*, at 403. "European Agreement for the Prevention of Broadcasts Transmitted from Stations Outside National Territories", adopted on 22 January 1965, UNTS, Vo. 634, at 239, reprinted in 4 ILM (1965), at 115.

[285] "General Act of the Brussels Conference relating to the African Slave Trade", adopted on 2 July 1890, Consolidated Treaty Series, Vol. 173, at 292; "Slavery Convention", adopted on 25 September 1926, LNTS, Vol. 60, at 253; "Supplementary Convention on the Abolition of Slavery, the Slave Trade and Institutions and Practices similar to Slavery", adopted on 7 September 1956, UNTS, Vol. 266, at 3.

[286] *Barcelona Traction, Light and Power Company, Limited (Belgium v. Spain),* Judgment of 5 February 1970, ICJ Reports 1970, pp. 4 *et seq.*, at 33, para. 34.

[287] *Lucchini*, Laurent/*Voelckel*, Michel, "Droit de la mer", Vol. 2, Part. 2 (Paris: Pedone, 1996), at 147.

[288] *Naim Molvan v. Attorney-General (The Asya)*, 81 Lloyd's Law Reports (1948), at 277. It may also be argued that at least the individuals on board the ship enjoy the protection of the State of nationality. *Cf. Churchill*, Robin R./*Lowe*, Alan Vaughan: "The Law of the Sea" (3rd ed., Manchester: Juris Publications, 1999), at 214; *United States v. Marquez* 759 F.2d 864, 867 (11th Cir. 1985).

[289] *Barry*, Ian Patrick, "The right of visit, search and seizure of foreign flagged vessels on the High Seas pursuant to customary international law: A defense of the proliferation security initiative", 33 Hofstra L. Rev. (2004/2005), pp. 299 *et seq.*, at 299-300; *Byers*,

jurisdiction, coastal States often put pressure on flag States to denationalize some of their vessels because of their unlawful conduct, so that they may then board and seize these vessels.[290]

However, not every unregistered vessel is at the same time stateless because a State may not require the registration of ships below a certain size, but may nonetheless regard such ships as having its nationality if they are owned by its nationals.[291] Furthermore, one must seriously question whether this interference right justifies the search of a vessel, as Spain claimed in the *So San* incident, after the crew has shown satisfactory registration documentation.

Hence, even though exact numbers are not available, one can estimate that many interferences on the high seas take place on the ground of the vessel being suspicious of having no nationality. One can also assume that many States abuse this interference right as a "back-up" if other grounds are not sufficient and if the navigation of the boarded vessel constitutes, in one way or the other (*e.g.*, illegal fishing, transport of weapons), an economic or security concern for the interfering State. Finally, States often use the interference right to inspect the transported cargo even though the right was meant to justify verification of the nationality only. These interferences therefore play a major role in practice and are a considerable threat to the freedom of navigation. Art. 110, para. 3 LOSC will hence play a central role in this study.

C. Legal limits for interferences and the role of State responsibility

The above considerations have shown the persistent conflict between the freedom of navigation being of overwhelming economic importance and a great number of security concerns of which some may be more or less satisfied by interferences with the navigation of foreign vessels on the high seas. The challenge for public international law lies in finding a reasonable balance between these two important values. Such reasonable balance should prevent abuse by interfering States.

One of the measures to achieve this is, of course, the test of reasonableness itself. This test assesses the lawfulness of an interference by taking account factors such as "the significance of the interest sought to be protected by the state claiming [an interference right], the relationship between the authority claimed and the interest at stake, the types of activities affected, the intensity of their occurrence, the significance of such activities for the general community, the modality and degree of interference with affected uses and the duration of the interference."[292]

Michael, "Policing the High Seas: The Proliferation Security Initiative", 98 AJIL (2004), pp. 526 *et seq.*, at 526.

290 *McDorman*, Ted L., "Stateless Fishing Vessels, International Law and the U.N. High Seas Fisheries Conference", 25 J. Mar. L. & Com. (1994), pp. 531 *et seq.*, at 532.

291 *Ibid.*, at 533.

292 *McDougal*, Myres Smith/*Burke*, William T., The Public Order of the Oceans" (New Haven: Yale University Press, 1962), at 765.

Depending on the maritime zone involved, the test nevertheless involves a certain presumption in favour of free navigation which is stronger on the high seas than it is inside the exclusive economic zone.[293] Furthermore, any claimed interference right needs to be one that is universally claimed because otherwise "the legal regime of the sea would quickly deteriorate into either complete chaos or unilateral dominion."[294]

However, the mere decision that an interference has been unreasonable and therefore unlawful would be of little help for the flag State, the ship owner and for cargo interests. Furthermore, some interfering States would probably accept the decision, but nevertheless continue their abusive conduct. Therefore, it is submitted that the law of State responsibility is particularly necessary in the case of interferences on the high seas.

There are quite a few dogmatic approaches justifying the existence of a law of State responsibility. Thus, the principle of State responsibility has been founded on the idea that public international law constitutes a legal order in which only States dispose of original legal personality and hence are subjects of rights and obligations. As in every legal order, the violation of the right of another subject entails the obligation to repair the consequences of such a violation.[295]

Anzilotti described the legal consequences deriving from an internationally wrongful act exclusively in terms of a binding bilateral relationship thereby established between the wrongdoing State and the injured State, in which the obligation of the former State to make reparation is set against the "subjective" right of the latter State to require reparation.[296]

Another view, associated with *Kelsen*, started from the idea that the legal order is a coercive order and saw the authorization accorded to the injured State to apply a coercive sanction against the responsible State as the primary legal consequence flowing directly from the wrongful act.[297] According to this view, general international law empowered the injured State to react to a wrong; the obligation to make reparation was treated as subsidiary, a way by which the responsible State could avoid the application of coercion.

A third view, which came to prevail, held that the consequences of an internationally wrongful act cannot be limited either to reparation or to a "sanction".[298] In international law, as in any system of law, the wrongful act may give rise to vari-

---

293 *Ibid.*

294 *Ibid.*, at 794.

295 *Cf. Anzilotti*, Dionisio, "Teoria generale della responsabilitá dello stato nel diritto internazionale", Vol. 1 (1902) at 25, 62; *Schoen*, Paul, "Die völkerrechtliche Haftung der Staaten aus unerlaubten Handlungen", (Breslau: Kern, 1917), at 18; *Strupp*, Karl, "Das völkerrechtliche Delikt" (Stuttgart: Kohlhammer, 1920), at 4.

296 *Anzilotti*, Dionisio, "Teoria generale della responsabilitá dello stato nel diritto internazionale", Vol. 1 (1902), at 62.

297 See *Kelsen*, Hans, "Principles of International Law" (2nd ed., New York: Holt, Rinehart, Winston, 1967), at 22.

298 See, *e.g., Ago*, Roberto, "Le délit international", 68 RdC (1939-II), pp. 417 *et seq.*, at 430-440; *Lauterpacht*, Hersch, "Oppenheim's International Law", Vol. 1 (8th ed., London: Longmans, Green, 1955), at 352-354.

ous types of legal relations, depending on the circumstances. Thus, arbitrator *Huber* held that "... responsibility is the necessary corollary of a right. All rights of an international character involve international responsibility."[299]

The importance of the law of State responsibility for public international law as a legal order has in strong terms been advocated by *Basdevant*: "les règles de la responsabilité sont en quelque sorte les règles-clefs de tout ordre juridique... on peut affirmer que la valeur pratique d'un ordre juridique déterminé dépend de l'efficacité et de l'étendue des règles sur la responsabilité."[300]

Brownlie, by the way, considers the basis for responsibility to be "in religious thought and in the secular morality of which law is the outwork."[301]

Public international law provides for an egalitarian order of all States. Basically, there is no authority above States to guarantee the enforcement of the rules of public international law. The law of State responsibility therefore constitutes a necessary regulatory mechanism.[302] Thus, one might state that "[du fait contraire au droit, la responsabilité] fait, au lieu d'une négation du droit, une simple irrégularité, c'est-à-dire un objet du droit – un fait juridique – dont le droit définit minutieusement les conséquences."[303] Particularly within the last decades, the law of State responsibility has become a major instrument to control legality.[304]

It has the important function to deter States from using their rights abusively. As far as it concerns interferences with navigation, "States are likely to use their powers with caution as they may risk having to compensate the vessel for loss or damage sustained by unjustifiable enforcement action."[305] One example of such an abuse might have occurred in May 2006 when the Japanese coast guard boarded and detained a North Korean vessel which had been involved in drug smuggling in 2002 (!), presumably in order "to force North Korea to give more details about the fate of Japanese citizens kidnapped by North Korean agents in the 1970s and

---

299 *Spanish Zone of Morocco*, RIAA, Vol. II, pp. 615 *et seq.*, at 641. *Cf.* also *Corfu Channel (United Kingdom v. Albania)*, Judgment of 9 April 1949, ICJ Reports 1949, pp. 4 *et seq.*, at 23.

300 *Basdevant*, Jules, "Actes de la Conférence SDN", vol. 7 (1930), cited by *Quéneudec*, Jean-Pierre, "La responsabilité internationale de l'Etat pour les fautes personelles de ses agents" (Paris: Pichon et Durand-Auzias, 1966), at 5.

301 *Brownlie*, Ian, "State Responsiblity" (Oxford: Clarendon Press, 1983), at 1.

302 *Cf. Daillier*, Patrick/*Pellet*, Alain, "Droit international public" (7th ed., Paris: L.G.D.J., 2002), at 762; *De Visscher*, Charles, "Les responsabilités des États", Bibl. Viss. 2 (1924), pp. 87 *et seq.*, at 90; *Eagleton*, Clyde, "The responsibility of states in international law" (New York City: New York University Press, 1924), at 5-6; *Delbez*, Louis, "Les principes généraux du Droit international public" (3rd ed., Paris: Pichon et Durand-Auzias, 1964), at 357.

303 *de la Pradelle*, Géraud, "Les conflits de loi en matière de nullités" (Paris: Dalloz, 1967), at 7.

304 *Dupuy*, Pierre-Marie, "Responsabilité et légalité", in *Société française pour le droit international* (ed.), "La responsabilité dans le système international" (Paris: Pedone, 1990), pp. 263 *et seq.*, at 264.

305 *Molenaar*, Erik Jaap, "Multilateral Hot Pursuit and Illegal Fishing in the Southern Ocean: The Pursuits of the Viarsa 1 and the South Tomi", 19 Int'l J. Mar. & Coast. L. (2004), pp. 19 *et seq.*, at 36.

1980s."[306] Apparently, Japan was not concerned with any compensation claims by the shipowner or the flag State North Korea, which is not a party to any of the conventions discussed in this study. Furthermore, the law of State responsibility may also have some punishing aspects substituting an illusory criminal authority for States.[307] Of course, this function requires the subjects of international law to utilize the available remedies, which they have only reluctantly done in the past.[308]

Another important function of the law of State responsibility is to prevent international conflicts. Before a State may lawfully resort to force as a reaction to the violation of international law by another State, it must at least demand reparation.[309] State responsibility thus represents an instrument to restore and maintain peace and friendship. Furthermore, if States do not have the possibility of claiming compensation, they might recur to other countermeasures like economic sanctions which can also intensify a conflict. One example took place when the Solomon Islands and Papua New Guinea seized U.S. vessels fishing in zones of coastal jurisdiction and the U.S. reacted by imposing retaliatory embargoes.[310] Any such reprisals are likely to harm both parties, in particular the weaker state,[311] while the law of State responsibility would only restitute the situation which existed before the occurrence of the first claimed violation of international law in a conflict.

All of these considerations have focused on the law of State responsibility as a system regulating the relations between States only. And this is indeed the traditional approach to the law of State responsibility even if a State claims the damage to one of its nationals.

However, the status of the individual in international law has significantly grown and it has been widely accepted that an individual may in certain cases possess legal personality in public international law.[312] From a policy point of view, one could therefore also argue that a law of State responsibility shall protect individuals as well. If a State may be responsible in respect of damages to indi-

---

306 "Japan Coast Guard boards North Korea 'drug running' ship", Lloyd's List, 15 May 2006, p. 3.

307 *Cottereau*, Gilles, "Système juridique et notion de responsabilité", in *Société française pour le droit international* (ed.), "La responsabilité dans le système international" (Paris: Pedone, 1991), pp. 1 *et seq.*, at 6.

308 *Zemanek*, Karl, "Does the Prospect of Incurring Responsibility Improve the Observance of International Law?", in *Ragazzi*, Maurizio (ed.), "International Responsibility Today – Essays in Memory of Oscar Schachter" (Leiden: Nijhoff, 2005), pp. 125 *et seq.*, at 126.

309 *Cf. van Bynkershoek*, Cornelius, "Quaestionum Iuris Publici Libri Duo", Vol. I, ch. I, para. 2; ch. II, para. 6 (1737).

310 *Saunders*, Phillip/*Williamson*, Hugh, "Small Islands and Archipelagic States", in *Crickard*, Fred W. *et al.* (eds.), "Multinational Naval Cooperation and Foreign Policy into the 21st century" (Aldershot: Ashgate, 1998), pp. 170 *et seq.*, at 177.

311 *Cf. Roelofsen*, Cornelis G., "The Claim of Some Citizens of Stettin against the Dutch Republic and its Adjudication", in *Gill*, Terry D. *et al.* (eds.), "Reflections on Principles and Practice in International Law" (The Hague: Nijhoff, 2000), pp. 175 *et seq.*, at 176-7.

312 *Partsch*, Karl Joseph, "Individuals in International Law", in *Bernhardt*, Rudolf (ed.), "Encyclopedia of Public International Law", Vol. 2 (Amsterdam: North-Holland, 1995), pp. 957 *et seq.*, at 958.

viduals, then the existence of an obligation to repair the damage will deter States from inflicting damage to individuals and the awarded compensation will palliate the suffering of the individual.

From the perspective of the individual, the certainty of being compensated in cases of certain interferences would render the risks of maritime transport more calculable, which is of extreme importance in the business of maritime transport where investments (and potential damages) are enormous and a multitude of factors needs to be considered.

Finally, State responsibility also shifts the risk of damage from the shipowner and the cargo interests to the interfering State. According to the economic analysis of law, whoever is conducting a dangerous activity which eventually leads to damage suffered by somebody else shall also bear the responsibility for the damage if the activity was undertaken for his own benefit because for him, it would usually cost the least to prevent the damage.[313] Basically, who profits from an operation shall be liable for it.[314] Admittedly, these principles have been developed for tort law, but it seems reasonable to apply them to the law of State responsibility.

In cases of interventions with navigation on the high seas, one ought to distinguish between the different grounds for interferences. Some interferences are undertaken for the benefit of the population of the interfering State (*e.g.*, terrorism, pollution, drug trafficking, migrant smuggling), but some also aim to protect maritime transport as such and the interests of beneficial owners and crew members (piracy, terrorism). One might even argue that values of the mankind as a whole might benefit from interferences if one considers human rights (migrant smuggling) or the marine environment (pollution, high seas fishing) such values. It seems quite illusory though that a State would really spend considerable efforts to interfere with navigation for the sake of humanity.

Hence, the interfering State in the majority of interferences acts for its own or at least its own population's benefit. From an economic point of view, damage caused by these interferences should therefore generally be borne by the interfering State. One must add that this should not be the case if the boarded vessel herself bears the responsibility for the interference, because she provoked the interference either by infringing international law or by at least reprehensibly causing suspicion for such an infringement.[315]

Such a system of State responsibility would definitely be desirable *de lege ferenda*. Whether it also corresponds to the *lex lata* as laid down in international conventions and customary international law, the following chapters will attempt to determine.

---

313 *Cf. Cooter*, Robert/*Ulen*, Thomas, "Law and Economics" (4th ed., Boston: Pearson Addison-Wesley, 2004), at 310; *Brown*, John Prather, "Toward an Economic Theory of Liability", 2 The Journal of Legal Studies (1973), at 323.

314 *Cf.* also *Wagner*, Gerhard, "Vor § 823", in *Rebmann*, Kurt *et al.* (eds.), "Münchener Kommentar zum Bürgerlichen Gesetzbuch" (4th ed., München: Beck, 2004), pp. 1487-1488, at para. 43.

315 *Cf. Posner*, Richard A., "Economic Analysis of Law" (6th ed., New York: Aspen Publications, 2003), at 178. The law of State responsibility recognizes this exemption with the concept of contributory negligence. See Art. 39 ASR.

Chapter II: Principles drawn from the treaty provisions on State responsibility for interferences with navigation on the high seas

The Law of the Sea with the Law of the Sea Convention and a great number of IMO conventions represents one area of public international law which is very densely codified. Even though the Law of the Sea Convention alone with its 320 articles and 11 annexes has rightly been called the "Constitution of the Oceans", it represents only a small part of the codified Law of the Sea. This is particularly true for the matter of interferences with navigation on the high seas because over decades, States became aware of new security concerns and adopted separate conventions for these particular concerns. Each convention which permitted an interference on the high seas accompanied this authorization with a provision on compensation. This definitely shows how important the States parties to all these conventions deemed the issue of State responsibility.

However, these compensation provisions do not quite follow one line of wording and this study will try to elaborate common principles of (or differences between) these provisions. These are the provisions to be studied:

- Art. 106 LOSC
- Art. 110, para. 3 LOSC
- Art. 111, para. 8 LOSC
- Art. VI of the 1969 Intervention Convention
- Art. 21, para. 18 Fish Stocks Agreement
- Art. 9, para. 2 Migrant Smuggling Protocol
- Art. 8bis, para. 10, lit. b of the 2005 Protocol to the SUA Convention

Other compensation provisions such as Art. 7 of the International Convention for the Prevention of Marine Pollution from Ships (MARPOL) and Rule 19, lit. f in Chapter I of the International Convention for the Safety of Life at Sea (SOLAS) will not be analyzed in detail because they were drafted in order to modify interference powers in ports (Port State Control). They do however, as will be shown, play a certain role in the interpretation of some of the mentioned compensation provisions because they were relied upon in the drafting procedure.

The rules on treaty interpretation will be of critical importance in this analysis and therefore deserve a brief presentation (A.). Instead of interpreting each compensation provision one after the other, this study will focus on some main issues which come up by purely reading these provisions and which may render the law laid down in these provisions different from the general law on State responsibility. Most important here is the question whether the flag State, the ship or her owner is the entitled entity to claim compensation (B.). Furthermore, some of the provisions might render a State liable for conduct not prohibited by public international law (C.). The question whether a State also bears responsibility for attempted interferences constitutes another special issue, particularly for cases of hot pursuit (D.). Since many interferences involve a multitude of States, rules concerning the liable entity need to be determined (E.). Also, the conduct of the claimant and persons whose conduct is attributable to him seems to have different effects depending on which compensation provision one applies (F.). The preconditions and effects of consent to an interference with navigation deserve further attention (G.). Finally, the extent of State responsibility, in particularly the damages which may be claimed, will be analyzed (H.), before this chapter will conclude with some elaborations on procedural issues like the burden of proof, competing claims of protection and a potential obligation of the protecting State to forward the compensation to the individual victim (J.).

A. Treaty interpretation

Since a great deal of the existing public international law concerning the responsibility for interferences with navigation is laid down in international conventions, the interpretation of the relevant provisions within these conventions is of critical importance.

The determination of rules on treaty interpretation used to be a considerable problem for an international lawyer. As late as 1974, *Elias* stated that "customary international law has not established a set of precise rules or canons of treaty interpretation. What we have instead are certain maxims or norms of interpretation put forward by some publicists…"[1] Some authors even went as far as denying the existence of any rules on treaty interpretation and describing their application in any particular case as an "*ex post facto* rationalisation of a conclusion reached on other ground or a cover for judicial creativeness."[2]

Since then, however, the law on treaty interpretation has developed into a very sophisticated area of public international law. In fact, it has been one of the more successful projects undertaken by the International Law Commission which has elaborated the Vienna Convention on the Law of Treaties (VCLT) with its Articles 31-33 on treaty interpretation.[3] With ratifications by 107 States parties, the VCLT

---

1 *Elias*, Taslim Olawale, "The Modern Law of Treaties" (Dobbs Ferry: Oceana Publications, 1974), at 71.

2 *Stone*, Julius, "Fictional elements in treaty interpretation – A Study in the International Judicial Process", 1 Sydney L. Rev. (1953-1955), pp. 344 *et seq.*, at 360, 364.

3 "Vienna Convention on the Law of Treaties", adopted on 23 May 1969, UNTS, Vol. 1155, at 331.

has had considerable success.[4] However, some important States such as France have not ratified the VCLT. The application of Arts. 31-33 VCLT to widely-ratified multilateral conventions thus poses problems. Furthermore, according to Art. 4 VCLT, the convention only applies to treaties concluded after the entry into force of the VCLT. The VCLT entered into force on 27 January 1980.[5] Most conventions relevant for this study such as the Law of the Sea Convention, the SUA Convention or the Migrant Smuggling Protocol have indeed been concluded after the entry into force of the VCLT. Others, such as the 1969 Intervention Convention, have not and thus do not directly fall into the scope of the VCLT.

These difficulties can nevertheless be overcome because, contrary to the more controversial provisions such as Art. 53 VCLT, the VCLT provisions relevant to this study have been accepted as customary international law.[6] Therefore, any interpretation of the conventions containing compensation provisions for interferences with navigation need to be based on the principles codified in Art. 31 and 32 VCLT.

Before this study will turn to the application of these principles, they deserve a brief general presentation.

Art. 31 VCLT describes three different methods of treaty interpretation, namely the interpretation of the text, its context and its object and purpose. The goal of each method is to derive the intentions of the parties to the treaty. Art. 31 VCLT is entitled "General rule of interpretation"/"Règle générale d'interprétation", the singular noun thus indicates that Article 31 VCLT contains only one rule and that one must consider each of the three methods in the interpretation of a treaty provision.[7] Furthermore, all of the three methods and the interpretation resulting from their application need to be checked for "good faith" drawing inspiration from the *bona fides* of the parties to the treaty.[8]

---

4 <http://untreaty.un.org>.

5 *Ibid.*

6 For Art. 31 VCLT: *Territorial Dispute (Libya/Chad)*, Judgment of 13 February 1994, ICJ Reports 1994, pp. 6 *et seq.*, at para. 41; *Maritime Delimitation and Territorial Questions (Qatar v. Bahrain)*, Judgment of 15 February 1995 on Jurisdiction and Admissibility, ICJ Reports 1995, pp. 6 *et seq.*, at para. 33; *Oil Platforms (Iran/USA)*, Judgment of 12 December 1996 on Preliminary Objections, ICJ Reports 1996/II, pp. 812 *et seq.*, at para. 23; *Kasikili/Sedudu Island (Botswana/Namibia)*, Judgment of 13 December 1999, ICJ Reports 1999/II, pp. 1045 *et seq.*, at para. 18. For Art. 32 VCLT: *Territorial Dispute (Libya/Chad)*, Judgment of 13 February 1994, ICJ Reports 1994, pp. 6 *et seq.*, at paras. 41, 55; *Maritime Delimitation and Territorial Questions (Qatar v. Bahrain)*, Judgment of 15 February 1995 on Jurisdiction and Admissibility, ICJ Reports 1995, pp. 6 *et seq.*, at para. 40; *Kasikili/Sedudu Island (Botswana/Namibia)*, Judgment of 13 December 1999, ICJ Reports 1999/II, pp. 1045 *et seq.*, at paras. 20, 46; *Arbitral Award of 31 July 1989 (Guinea Bissau v. Senegal)*, Judgment of 12 November 1991, ICJ Reports 1991, pp. 52 *et seq.*, at para. 48.

7 *Aust*, Anthony, "Modern Treaty Law and Practice" (Cambridge: Cambridge University Press, 2000), at 186-7.

8 *Yasseen*, M.K., "L'interprétation des traités d'après la Convention de Vienne sur le Droit des Traités", 151 RdC (1976-III), pp. 20 *et seq.*, at 22.

I. Interpretation of the wording

The textual interpretation analyzes the ordinary meaning of the terms in the provision since this ordinary meaning is most likely to reflect what the parties intended.[9] The starting point is usually the grammatical meaning of the terms. The terms must be interpreted according to the meaning which they possessed, or which would have been attributed to them, and in the light of current linguistic usage, at the time when the treaty was originally concluded.[10]

Different from the ordinary meaning, terms of a treaty may also have a special meaning (Art. 31, para. 4 VCLT), but the burden of proof of the special meaning will rest on the party invoking this meaning.[11]

Generally, the wording of all authentic texts of a treaty has the same relevance. An international lawyer should therefore consult all authentic texts and interpret their meaning. Even though in practice, international courts such as the ICJ often only consult the English and French texts,[12] such approach inadequately recognizes the value attributed by all States parties to an authentic text in another language.

According to Art. 33, para. 3 VCLT, the terms of a treaty are presumed to have the same meaning in each authentic text. This is so because all authentic versions constitute a single treaty.[13] In spite of this presumption, reliance on all authentic texts will often result in differences of meaning between the different texts. The international lawyer then has to adopt the meaning which best reconciles the texts (Art. 33, para. 4 VCLT). When the meaning is ambiguous or obscure in one text it may be clearer in another and there may nevertheless be no need to attempt to reconcile them.[14]

Also, the International Law Commission broke with the pre-existing conservative doctrine that an international tribunal would be bound to adopt the more limited (less intruding into the sovereignty of States parties) interpretation which

---

9 *Aust*, Anthony, "Modern Treaty Law and Practice" (Cambridge: Cambridge University Press, 2000), at 186-7.

10 *Fitzmaurice*, Gerald, "The Law and Procedure of the International Court of Justice 1951-4: Treaty Interpretation and Other Treaty Points", 33 BYIL (1957), pp. 203 *et seq.*, at 212; *cf.* also *Rights of Nationals of the United States of America in Morocco (France v. United States)*, Judgment of 27 August 1952, ICJ Reports 1952, at 189; *Lord McNair*, Arnold Duncan, "The Law of Treaties" (Oxford: Clarendon Press, 1961), at 365.

11 Yearbook of the International Law Commission (1966-II), at 222; *Legal Status of Eastern Greenland*, Judgment of 5 April 1933, (1933) PCIJ, ser. A/B, No. 53, pp. 22 *et seq.*, at 49.

12 *Hardy*, Jean, "The Interpretation of Plurilingual Treaties by International Courts and Tribunals", 37 BYIL (1961), pp. 72 *et seq.*, at 143.

13 Yearbook of the International Law Commission (1966-II), at 225.

14 *Aust*, Anthony, "Modern Treaty Law and Practice" (Cambridge: Cambridge University Press, 2000), at 205; but see *Young Loan Arbitration*, 59 Int'l L. Reports, at 529-30.

can be made to harmonize the two versions.[15] Rather than a principle of restrictive interpretation leading to the adoption of the lowest common denominator, the intentions of the parties need to be determined on a case-by-case method.[16]

Finally, in practice, international lawyers often place more reliance on an authentic text in the language in which the treaty was negotiated and drafted, particularly if it is unambiguous.[17] This approach, though frequent in practice, is nevertheless dogmatically problematic if one, on the one hand, considers the *travaux préparatoires* to be subsidiary (*infra*) and, on the other hand, places emphasis on the drafting and negotiating language. Hence, the priority of this language should only prevail under the conditions of Art. 32 VCLT.

II. Interpretation of the context

The contextual interpretation takes notice of the treaty as a whole, including the preamble and its annexes. For a document to become part of the context of a treaty, it must be concerned with the substance of the treaty, clarify certain concepts in the treaty or limit its field of application.[18] It must also be drawn up on the occasion of the conclusion of the treaty.[19] Finally, this relationship must have been accepted by all the parties (Art. 31, para. 2 VCLT).

The context, in a wider sense, also includes subsequent agreements relating to the interpretation of the treaty, subsequent practice in the application of the treaty and the applicable general international law (Art. 31, para. 3 VCLT). The rationale for the inclusion of subsequent agreements is that because State parties are empowered to modify or terminate a treaty, they are also entitled to interpret it.[20] However, such an international treaty cannot realistically be regarded as such a subsequent agreement on interpretation, unless it has the consensus support of all the parties, or there is no objection.[21]

---

15 *Mavrommatis Palestine Concession (Greece/United Kingdom)*, Judgment of 30 August 1924, (1924) PCIJ Ser. A No. 2, pp. 5 *et seq.*, at 19.

16 *Sinclair*, Ian, "The Vienna Convention on the Law of Treaties" (Manchester: University Press, 1984), at 149-151; Yearbook of the International Law Commission (1966-II), at 225.

17 *Sinclair*, Ian, "The Vienna Convention on the Law of Treaties" (Manchester: University Press, 1984), at 147-152; *Aust*, Anthony, "Modern Treaty Law and Practice" (Cambridge: Cambridge University Press, 2000), at 205-206.

18 *Yasseen*, M.K., "L'interprétation des traités d'après la Convention de Vienne sur le Droit des Traités", 151 RdC (1976-III), pp. 20 *et seq.*, at 37.

19 *Sinclair*, Ian, "The Vienna Convention on the Law of Treaties" (Manchester: University Press, 1984), at 129.

20 *Sinclair*, Ian, "The Vienna Convention on the Law of Treaties" (Manchester: University Press, 1984), at 136; *Delimitation of the Polish-Czecholovakian frontier (question of Jaworzina)*, Advisory Opinion of 6 December 1923, [1923] PCIJ Ser. B No. 8, pp. 5 *et seq.*, at 37.

21 *Pauwelyn*, Joost, "The Role of Public International Law in the WTO: How Far Can We Go?", 95 AJIL (2001), pp. 535 *et seq.*, at 575-6; *McLachlan*, C., "The Principle of

The same is basically true for the subsequent practice of States parties. The reasoning for the relevance of subsequent State practice is that the way in which a treaty is actually applied by the parties is a good indication of what they understand it to mean, provided the practice is consistent, and is common to, or accepted by, all the parties.[22] In order to prove such subsequent practice, it is not required to demonstrate customary international law because it is not necessary to show that each party has engaged in a practice, only that all have accepted it, albeit tacitly.[23] One isolated fact usually does not constitute subsequent practice, because it rather means a sequence of facts or acts.[24] Any conduct not falling under the scope of "subsequent practice" may be considered as supplementary means of interpretation.[25]

The "relevant rules of international law applicable in the relations between the parties" (Art. 31, para. 3, lit. c) VCLT) represent not only the international law at the time the treaty was concluded, but also contemporary international law.[26] The latter, nonetheless, can only be applied if the States parties to the treaty so intended.[27] The issue therefore depends on whether the parties initially considered the relevant term to be evolutionary (which, for example, one could allege concerning "public policy", "protection of morals" or "domestic jurisdiction") or to be static.[28]

An evolutionary interpretation allows the international lawyer to consider changing values and social context when applying international law. This point is particularly well observed in international human rights law, but might be less relevant to a treaty such as the Law of the Sea Convention.[29] The evolutionary interpretation furthermore does not permit a tribunal to engage in a process of

---

Systemic Integration and Article 31(3)(c) of the Vienna Convention", 54 ICLQ (2005), pp. 279 *et seq.*, at para. 16.

22 See *US-France Air Services Arbitration 1963*, 54 ILR 303; *US-UK Heathrow User Charges Arbitration*, 102 ILR 261, 353.

23 *Aust*, Anthony, "Modern Treaty Law and Practice" (Cambridge: Cambridge University Press, 2000), at 186-7.; *Elias*, Taslim Olawale, "The Modern Law of Treaties" (Dobbs Ferry: Oceana Publications, 1974), at 76.

24 *Sinclair*, Ian, "The Vienna Convention on the Law of Treaties" (Manchester: University Press, 1984), at 137.

25 *Ibid.*, at 138.

26 *Thirlway*, Hugh, "The Law and Procedure of the International Court of Justice 1960-1989", 62 BYIL (1991), pp. 16 *et seq.*, at 16-17; *Higgins*, Rosalyn, "Some Observations on the Inter-Temporal Rule in International Law", in *Makarczyk*, Jerzy (ed.), "Theory of International Law at the Threshold of the 21st Century" (The Hague: Kluwer Law International, 1996), pp. 173 *et seq.*, at 173; *id.*, "Time and the Law: International Perspectives on an Old Problem", 46 ICLQ (1997), pp. 501 *et seq.*, at 515-519.

27 *de Arechaga*, Jimenez, Yearbook of the International Law Commission (1964-I), at 34, para. 10.

28 *Cf. Legal Consequences for States of the continued presence of South Africa in Namibia*, Advisory Opinion of 21 June 1971, ICJ Reports 1971, at 31.

29 *Boyle*, Alan, "Further Development of the Law of the Sea Convention: Mechanisms for Change", 54 ICLQ (2005), pp. 563 *et seq.*, at 567.

constant revision or updating of a treaty such as the Law of the Sea Convention every time a newer treaty is concluded that relates to similar matters.[30] Such judicial holdings would probably represent a "révision détournée".[31] Thus, for example, Ireland did not succeed in its argument in the *Mox Plant Case* when it attempted to rewrite the Law of the Sea Convention by relying on provisions in other treaties.[32]

Generally, if one deals with provisions from other conventions while interpreting a certain article of a multilateral convention such as the Law of the Sea Convention, regional treaties are of no great relevance. A global multilateral treaty, particularly one in implementation of the Law of the Sea Convention (for example, the 1995 UN Fish Stocks Agreement), has greater potential for influencing interpretation of the convention than a solitary regional agreement.[33]

III. Object and purpose

Finally, the third method of treaty interpretation mentioned in Art. 31 VCLT is the interpretation of object and purpose of a provision. The determination of the object and purpose, however, tends to be difficult without resorting to the *travaux préparatoires* of the provision. Since the latter may only be resorted to as a means of supplementary interpretation (*cf.* Art. 32, para. 1 VCLT), interpretation of object and purpose, in spite of its prominent place in Art. 31, para. 1 VCLT, often plays a minor role in the interpretation of treaties.[34] The attempt to derive from the "object and purpose" the common intentions of the parties[35] often ends up to become the search of the pot of gold at the end of the rainbow.[36] Application of this method must never entail attributing to treaty provisions a meaning which would be contrary to their letter and spirit.[37]

30 *Ibid.*, at 568.

31 *Gabcíkovo-Nagymaros (Hungary/Slovakia)*, Separate Opinion Judge Bedjaoui, ICJ Reports 1997, at para. 12.

32 *Mox Plant Arbitration (Ireland v. United Kingdom)*, Order Nr. 3, 24 June 2003, Permanent Court of Arbitration, at para. 18.

33 *Boyle*, Alan, "Further Development of the Law of the Sea Convention: Mechanisms for Change", 54 ICLQ (2005), pp. 563 *et seq.*, at 569.

34 *Aust*, Anthony, "Modern Treaty Law and Practice" (Cambridge: Cambridge University Press, 2000), at 188; *Sinclair*, Ian, "The Vienna Convention on the Law of Treaties" (Manchester: University Press, 1984), at 118.

35 *Degan*, Vladimir Duro, "L'interprétation des accords en droit international" (The Hague: Nijhoff, 1963), at 134.

36 *Sinclair*, Ian, "The Vienna Convention on the Law of Treaties" (Manchester: University Press, 1984), at 130.

37 *Interpretation of Peace Treaties with Bulgaria, Hungary and Romania*, Advisory Opinion of 18 July 1950, ICJ Reports 1950, pp. 221 *et seq.*, 229.

However, the method can be elusive[38] and it seems reasonable to apply the principle *ut res magis valeat quam pereat* within the scope of the interpretation of object and purpose.[39] According to this principle, if a treaty is capable of being given two interpretations one of which would give real effect to the treaty whilst the other would not, that interpretation should be adopted which gives the treaty the proper effect. One might presume that it is always the intention of parties acting in good faith (*cf. supra*) to adopt provisions which give full effect to a treaty.

The International Court of Justice, finally, seems to gather object and purpose of a treaty primarily from the text of the treaty and particularly from the preamble.[40] Since both other methods under Art. 31 VCLT already consider these, the approach by the ICJ shows all the more how inter-related the different methods of Art. 31 VCLT really are.

IV. A hierarchy of methods under Art. 31 VCLT

If one acknowledges, as the ICJ did, "the primary necessity of interpreting an instrument in accordance with the intentions of the parties at the time of its conclusion,"[41] a major issue will be which of the three methods is closest to these intentions and may thus have a certain superiority over the other methods.

For a long time, authors have alleged that the textual interpretation is in a certain way superior over the other methods. *O'Connell*, for example, writes that "[t]he problem of treaty interpretation … is one of ascertaining the logic inherent in the treaty, and pretending that this is what the parties desired. In so far as this logic can be discovered by reference to the terms of the treaty itself, it is impermissible to depart from those terms."[42] He also sees a certain precedence of the textual approach in the wording of Art. 31, para. 1 VCLT.[43] *Reuter* even states that

---

38 *Cf. Aust*, Anthony, "Modern Treaty Law and Practice" (Cambridge: Cambridge University Press, 2000), at 110.

39 *Elias*, Taslim Olawale, "The Modern Law of Treaties" (Dobbs Ferry: Oceana Publications, 1974), at 74.

40 *Jacobs*, Francis G., "Varieties of approach to treaty interpretation: with special reference to the draft Convention on the Law of Treaties before the Vienna diplomatic conference", 18 ICLQ (1969), pp. 318 *et seq.*, at 337. See, *e.g.*, *Rights of Nationals of the United States of America in Morocco (France v. United States)*, Judgment of 27 August 1952, ICJ Reports 1952, at 196; *Golder v. United Kingdom*, European Court of Human Rights, Judgment of 21 February 1975, 57 ILR at 217; *Beagle Channel Arbitration*, 17 ILM (1978), at 634, para. 19.

41 *Legal Consequences for States of the Continued Presence of South Africa in Namibia (South West Africa) notwithstanding Security Council Resolution 276 (1970)*, Advisory Opinion of 21 June 1971, ICJ Reports 1971, pp. 16 *et seq.*, at 31; *Aegean Sea Continental Shelf (Greece v. Turkey)*, Judgment of 19 December 1978, ICJ Reports 1978, pp. 3 *et seq.*, at 32-3.

42 *O'Connell*, Daniel Patrick, "International Law", Vol. 1 (2nd ed., London: Stevens, 1970), at 253.

43 *Ibid.*, at 255.

"the primacy of the text, especially in international law, is the cardinal rule for any interpretation."[44] A conservative view based upon the sovereignty of States would also argue that the textual approach limits the sovereignty of States the least because, in international law, the legislative and judicial processes are by the free consent of the parties, and that the textual approach should therefore prevail.[45] Furthermore, there are some indications in the jurisprudence of the ICJ for a primacy of the text.[46]

However, the International Law Commission, when drafting the Vienna Convention on the Law of Treaties, resolutely rejected the view that in interpreting a treaty, one must give greater weight to one particular factor, such as the text.[47] Also, one may quote Judge *Anzilotti* who wrote that "I do not see how it is possible to say that an article of a convention is clear until the subject and aim of the convention have been ascertained for the article only assumes its true import in this convention and in relation thereto."[48] Reliance on one method to the detriment of the others would probably be contrary to the jurisprudence of the International Court of Justice.[49] Even though the ICJ has held that "[i]nterpretation must be based above all upon the text of the treaty,"[50] it has never ruled that it is superior to, *e.g.*, the contextual interpretation.

It is therefore submitted that no formal hierarchy between the methods of treaty interpretation under Art. 31 VCLT exists, but that the starting point for every treaty interpretation needs to be the textual interpretation.

V. Supplementary means of interpretation

As already mentioned above, recourse to the *travaux préparatoires* only constitutes a supplementary means of interpretation. According to Art. 32, para. 1 VCLT, such recourse may only take place if the results of the interpretation

44 *Reuter*, Paul, "Introduction to the Law of Treaties" (2nd ed., London: Kegan Paul International, 1995) at 96, para. 142.

45 *Ibid.*

46 *Territorial Dispute (Libya/Chad)*, Judgment of 14 February 1994, ICJ Reports 1994, pp. 4 *et seq.*, at 19-20, para. 41; *Elias*, Taslim Olawale, "The Modern Law of Treaties" (Dobbs Ferry: Oceana Publications, 1974), at 72. *Cf.* also *Competence of the General Assembly for the Admission of a State to the United Nations*, Advisory Opinion of 3 March 1950, ICJ Reports 1950, pp. 8 *et seq.*; *Access to, and anchorage in the Port of Danzig, of Polish war vessels*, Advisory Opinion of 11 Dezember 1931, (1931) PCIJ, Ser. A/B, No. 43, pp. 128 *et seq.*, at 144.

47 *Aust*, Anthony, "Modern Treaty Law and Practice" (Cambridge: Cambridge University Press, 2000), at 185.

48 *Interpretation of the Convention of 1919 concerning Employment of Women during the Night*, (1932) PCIJ Series A/B, No. 50, Dissenting Opinion Anzilotti, pp. 365 *et seq.*, at 383.

49 *Cf. Thirlway*, Hugh, "The Law and Procedure of the International Court of Justice 1960-1989", 62 BYIL(1991), pp. 16 *et seq.*, at 16-17.

50 *Territorial Dispute (Libya/Chad)*, Judgment of 14 February 1994, ICJ Reports 1994, pp. 4 *et seq.*, at 19-20, para. 41.

according to Art. 31 VCLT leave the meaning of the provision ambiguous or obscure or if the results are manifestly absurd or unreasonable.[51]

The reasoning behind this subsidiarity is diverse. First, one might argue that interpretation involves an elucidation of the meaning of the text, not a fresh investigation as to the supposed intentions of the parties.[52] Secondly, the fact that acceding parties have not been involved in the negotiations decreases the value of the *travaux préparatoires*. The intentions recorded in the preparatory work are not final.[53] Thirdly, preparatory work is uncertain ground since its content is not precisely defined nor rigorously certified, and it reveals the shortcomings or possible blunders of the negotiators as well as their reluctance to confront the true difficulties.[54] Fourthly, the obscurity of a text will often find its origin in the *travaux préparatoires* themselves.[55] And finally, the *travaux préparatoires* do not reveal what has been agreed during private corridor discussions.[56]

Nevertheless, there is a certain need to invoke *travaux préparatoires* even in disputes to which States are parties which did not take part in the negotiation of a multilateral treaty.[57] Any other rule would be extremely inconvenient given the number of new states which have emerged since the Second World War, and the quantity of multilateral treaties made during that period to which new states have subsequently become parties.[58] To hold otherwise would disrupt the unity of a multilateral treaty, since it would imply that two different methods of interpretation should be employed.[59] There should only be an exception concerning *travaux préparatoires* kept secret by the negotiating parties[60] and the value of *travaux préparatoires* generally depends on authenticity, completeness and availability.

In practice, recourse to *travaux préparatoires* is quite frequent because disputes usually only arise if treaty provisions are obscure and ambiguous and because

51 *Conditions of Admission of a State to Membership in the United Nations (Article 4 of the Charter)*, Advisory Opinion of 28 May 1948, ICJ Reports 1948, at 63.

52 *Aust*, Anthony, "Modern Treaty Law and Practice" (Cambridge: Cambridge University Press, 2000), at 187.

53 *Reuter*, Paul, "Introduction to the Law of Treaties" (2nd ed., London: Kegan Paul International, 1995), at 97, para. 146.

54 *Ibid.*, at 97-8, para. 146.

55 *Sinclair*, Ian, "The Vienna Convention on the Law of Treaties" (Manchester: University Press, 1984), at 142.

56 *Yasseen*, M.K., "L'interprétation des traités d'après la Convention de Vienne sur le Droit des Traités", 151 RdC (1976-III), pp. 20 *et seq.*, at 85.

57 *Cf. Briggs*, Herbert W., "The travaux préparatoires of the Vienna Convention on the Law of Treaties", 65 AJIL (1971), pp. 705 *et seq.*, at 709.

58 *Sinclair*, Ian, "The Vienna Convention on the Law of Treaties" (Manchester: University Press, 1984), at 142-144. But see *Territorial Jurisdiction of the International Commission of the River Oder*, Judgment of 10 September 1929, (1929) PCIJ Ser. A, No. 23, pp. 4 *et seq.*, at 30.

59 *Sinclair*, Ian, "The Vienna Convention on the Law of Treaties" (Manchester: University Press, 1984), at 144.

60 *Yasseen*, M.K., "L'interprétation des traités d'après la Convention de Vienne sur le Droit des Traités", 151 RdC (1976-III), pp. 20 *et seq.*, at 90.

parties very often argue by referring to the *travaux préparatoires*.[61] It seems likely that judges in international tribunals will even have recourse to *travaux préparatoires* if the ordinary meaning appears to be clear and it is evident from the *travaux préparatoires* that the ordinary meaning does not represent the intention of the parties.[62] However, on the other hand, the ICJ has expressly held that Art. 32 VCLT constitutes customary international law.[63] Despite some differences between the views of some practitioners and the existing customary law, the latter will be taken as basis for this study.

Finally, one may add that another supplementary means to interpret a treaty under Art. 32 VCLT are the "circumstances of the conclusion of the treaty". Such circumstances are, *e.g.*, the historic events which led the parties to the conclusion[64] or the individual attitudes of the States parties such as being members of a certain grouping of States.[65]

Since the ILC wanted to leave the existing customary international law unaffected, the list of interpretation methods in Arts. 31-33 VCLT is probably not exhaustive.[66] However, the adoption and growing importance of the VCLT has more or less streamlined the law of treaty interpretation and the frequent reliance by the ICJ on Arts. 31 and 32 VCLT has slowly degraded other principles of treaty interpretation.

B. An individual right to claim compensation?

Having thus laid down the basic principles of treaty interpretation, this study will now continue with the analysis of some problematic issues of the mentioned compensation provisions in different Law of the Sea conventions dealing with the

---

61 *Sinclair*, Ian, "The Vienna Convention on the Law of Treaties" (Manchester: University Press, 1984), at 142

62 *Schwebel*, Stephen M., "May Preparatory Work be Used to Correct Rather than Confirm the „Clear" Meaning of a Treaty Provision?", in *Makarczyk*, Jerzy (ed.), "Theory of International Law at the Threshold of the 21st Century" (The Hague: Kluwer Law International, 1996), pp. 541 *et seq.*; *Aust*, Anthony, "Modern Treaty Law and Practice" (Cambridge: Cambridge University Press, 2000), at 197.

63 *Territorial Dispute (Libya/Chad)*, Judgment of 13 February 1994, ICJ Reports 1994, pp. 6 *et seq.*, at paras. 41, 55; *Maritime Delimitation and Territorial Questions (Qatar v. Bahrain)*, Judgment of 15 February 1995 on Jurisdiction and Admissibility, ICJ Reports 1995, pp. 6 *et seq.*, at para. 40; *Kasikili/Sedudu Island (Botswana/Namibia)*, Judgment of 13 December 1999, ICJ Reports 1999/II, pp. 1045 *et seq.*, at paras. 20, 46; *Arbitral Award of 31 July 1989 (Guinea Bissau v. Senegal)*, Judgment of 12 November 1991, ICJ Reports 1991, pp. 52 *et seq.*, at para. 48.

64 *Yasseen*, M.K., "L'interprétation des traités d'après la Convention de Vienne sur le Droit des Traités", 151 RdC (1976-III), pp. 20 *et seq.*, at 90.

65 *Sinclair*, Ian, "The Vienna Convention on the Law of Treaties" (Manchester: University Press, 1984), at 141.

66 *Sinclair*, Ian, "The Vienna Convention on the Law of Treaties" (Manchester: University Press, 1984), at 153; *Cf.* last sentence of the VCLT preamble.

responsibility for interferences with navigation on the high seas. These provisions have experienced surprisingly little attention by court decisions and authors even though they raise some very interesting questions.

In practice, most important is the question whether the compensation provisions grant a right to a private entity such as the ship owner. This question is of great relevance because if a private entity had the right to claim compensation under public international law, States might be obliged to provide for remedies in their domestic legal system and the private entity would no more be dependent upon the willingness of its State of nationality or flag State to exercise diplomatic or flag State protection. Of course, an entitlement to claim compensation does not by itself lead to the ability of the individual to appear as a party before an international tribunal, but the mere obligation to provide for domestic remedies would definitely significantly increase the protection of individuals engaged in maritime transport.

In order to determine the entity entitled to claim compensation, an interpretation of all relevant compensation provisions will focus on analyzing whether they entitle the flag State or a private entity affected by the interference with navigation. The identification of the private entity is contained in the interpretation of the context ("The meaning of the ship", 2. h)), since all other interpretation methods are not very revealing concerning the issue which of the private entities interested in the navigation of a vessel represents the entitled entity under the respective provision.

I. The ordinary meaning of the relevant provisions

The basis of all relevant compensation provisions seems to be Art. 110, para. 3 LOSC. It has a very broad scope since it deals with the responsibility for the boarding of foreign vessels on the high seas for various grounds (Art. 110, para. 1 LOSC). Furthermore, Art. 22, para. 3 CHS embodied the same provision which thus might have served as an example for conventions adopted after 1958.

The wording of Art. 110, para. 3 LOSC quite unequivocally indicates that "the ship" is the entity entitled to claim compensation: "If the suspicions prove to be unfounded, and provided that the ship boarded has not committed any act justifying them, it shall be compensated for any loss or damage that may have been sustained." The provision says that "it shall be compensated" and "it" can only mean the ship because the only noun used in the previous terms of the provision that "it" could reasonably refer to is the ship. The same indication holds true for the French ("le navire est indemnisé"), the Spanish ("dicho buque será indemnizado") and the Russian text ("судно … ему должны быть возмещены"). One could only counter-argue that the texts do not explicitly mention by whom the ship shall be compensated and that therefore the flag State could still act as intermediary claiming compensation from the responsible State on behalf of the vessel and then forwarding the compensation to the vessel. However, an entitlement of "the ship" seems much closer to the text and it would at first sight seem odd if the drafters had wanted an entitlement of the flag State without explicitly naming it.

The actual meaning of the term "the ship" is however quite obscure. Does it grant the ship herself a personality? Does it refer to a particular private entity interested in the business of the ship such as the shipowner, cargo interests or even the flag State? Or is it simply a catch-all term covering all of these interests at the same time? The mere interpretation of the wording indicates the first. However, these are only indications reached on the preliminary basis of textual interpretation. No conclusion can be reached before having recourse to the other methods of treaty interpretation.

The wording of provisions concerning the hot pursuit of vessels on the high seas (Art. 111, para. 8 LOSC) and concerning the boarding of vessels suspected of migrant smuggling (Art. 9, para. 2 Migrant Smuggling Protocol) are very similar to Art. 110, para. 3 LOSC. Thus, the same considerations as to Art. 110, para. 3 LOSC apply to them. Without having recourse to other methods of interpretation, other authors have on several occasions considered Art. 111, para. 8 LOSC to grant a right to the ship.[67]

Another type of provision does not directly suggest any party entitled to claim compensation. Instead, these provisions merely provide for the responsibility of the boarding State. Such provisions are Art. VI of the Intervention Convention, Art. 21, para. 18 of the Straddling Fish Stocks Agreement and Art. 8bis, para. 10, lit. b of the 2005 Protocol to the SUA Convention. However, this latter provision contains a final sentence according to which "States Parties shall provide effective recourse in respect of such damage, harm or loss." Since inter-State relations are usually dealt with on the international level, the provision indicates that some private entity shall be entitled to claim compensation before a domestic court. The 2005 Protocol to the SUA Convention thus not only (implicitly) deals with the entitled entity, but also the means to enforce the claim. Furthermore, doubts remain concerning the ordinary meaning of Art. VI Intervention Convention if one considers the (authentic, *cf.* Art. XVII Intervention Convention) French text of the provision: "Toute Partie à la Convention qui a pris des mesures en contravention avec les dispositions de la présente Convention, causant à autrui un préjudice, est tenue de *le* dédommager pour autant que les mesures dépassent ce qui est raisonnablement nécessaire pour parvenir aux fins mentionnées à l'article premier" (emphasis added). This text indicates that whoever suffered damage by a disproportionate interference shall be entitled to claim compensation. Since the French text in this respect turns out to be more precise than the English text, it is more valuable for the interpretation of the provision's ordinary meaning.

Finally, a third type quite clearly seems to entitle the flag State of the affected vessel to claim compensation from the interfering State.[68] The sole example of

---

67 *Molenaar*, Erik Jaap, "Multilateral Hot Pursuit and Illegal Fishing in the Southern Ocean: The Pursuits of the Viarsa 1 and the South Tomi", 19 Int'l J. Mar. & Coast. L. (2004), pp. 19 *et seq.*, at 37; *Wollenberg*, Simon Friedrich Wilhelm, "Die Nacheile zur See – eine dogmatische Betrachtung", 42 AVR (2004), pp. 217 *et seq.*, at 231-232; *The M/V Saiga (No. 2) (St. Vincent and the Grenadines v. Guinea)*, Separate Opinion Rao, ITLOS Reports 1999, pp. 126 *et seq.*, at 130, para. 14.

68 *Cf. ibid.*

such a provision is Art. 106 LOSC: "Where the seizure of a ship or aircraft on suspicion of piracy has been effected without adequate grounds, the State making the seizure shall be liable to the State the nationality of which is possessed by the ship or aircraft for any loss or damage caused by the seizure." This article nevertheless only applies to seizures undertaken on grounds of piracy.

Thus, while a textual interpretation provides for some preliminary results concerning the first and third type of compensation provision, it does not quite solve the issue concerning the second type of provisions.

II. Context

The contextual interpretation of a provision as the second primary method of treaty interpretation first needs to consider the whole treaty, particularly the provisions with some relationship to the analyzed provision and the preamble.

1. The structure of the Law of the Sea Convention

In this regard, the relationship between Arts. 106, 110, para. 3 and 111, para. 8 LOSC seems of great importance. Drafters and States parties must have been aware of the different terminology used for Art. 106 LOSC, on the one hand, and the other two provisions, on the other hand, particularly because all the provisions are situated in the same part of the Law of the Sea Convention. The use of different terms thus generally leads to the presumption of a difference in substantial meaning as well.

Furthermore, other provisions of the Law of the Sea Convention such as Arts. 17, 21, para. 4, 58, para. 1, 58, para. 3, 62, para. 4 and 116 LOSC also explicitly mention a right of the "ship". Therefore, an entitlement of the "ship" does not seem to be foreign to the Law of the Sea Convention and the drafting of Arts. 110, para. 3 and 111, para. 8 LOSC cannot be merely erroneous.

Also, if one considers the different scope of application of the provisions, the drafters might have had sound reason to deal with them differently. Since Art. 110, para. 3 LOSC also covers responsibility for boardings of suspected pirate vessels (*cf.* Art. 110, para. 1, lit. a LOSC), there is no major difference as to the criminal conduct of the vessel which is interfered with. However, three differences might have some relevance.

First, a seizure constitutes a major intrusion into the property of the shipowner, the bareboat charterer and potential cargo interests. Contrary to a seizure, the mere boarding and inspection usually cause less damage. This could speak in favour of an interpretation granting the "ship" at least the same rights in the case of a seizure as in the case of a boarding.

Secondly, however, the boardings covered by Arts. 110, para. 3 and 111, para. 8 LOSC start and usually also end on the high seas at great distance to the shores. A seizure, on the other hand, will often be accompanied by court proceedings, such as the prosecution of the alleged pirates. Boardings and inspections on the high seas receive little publicity, especially if they do not lead to the discovery of criminal activity. Hence, there is a certain concern that States might abuse their naval powers on the high seas. This second consideration might justify the different regulation of seizures and boardings under the Law of the Sea Convention being more favourable to private interests.

Thirdly, the relatively small damage coupled with the higher frequency of boardings as opposed to seizures would probably overstrain the means of dispute resolution between States. Therefore, the drafters might have deemed it more adequate to focus on domestic remedies. Again, this does not render inter-State dispute resolution obsolete, but the claim of the "ship" before domestic tribunals of the boarding State offers an efficient alternative.

Hence, there are indeed sound reasons for entitling a private entity the right to claim compensation in cases of boardings on the high seas and cases of hot pursuit, while a claim of the flag State may constitute a sufficient remedy in the case of the seizure of a pirate ship.

Finally, one ought to consider that the Law of the Sea criminalizes certain conduct of private entities for which their flag State usually does not bear any responsibility. If a private entity thus becomes (criminally) responsible under public international law, it seems logical to grant in return some rights to such entities if they are related to the individual criminal responsibility.[69] The right to compensation could constitute such a right.

2. The conventions succeeding the Law of the Sea Convention

Most of the other conventions authorizing interferences on the high seas were adopted after the conclusion of the Third United Nations Conference on the Law of the Sea in 1982. Their drafting therefore has been very much influenced by the terms used in the Law of the Sea Convention. Art. 9, para. 2 of the Migrant Smuggling Protocol basically copies Art. 110, para. 3 LOSC. Furthermore, the Migrant Smuggling Protocol is not meant to modify the existing Law of the Sea[70] and therefore its Art. 9, para. 2 also probably wants to rely on Art. 110, para. 3 LOSC.

21, para. 18 of the Straddlings Fish Stocks Agreement and Art. 8bis, para. 10, lit. b of the 2005 Protocol to the SUA Convention, on the other hand, seem to be derived from Art. 232 LOSC. Therefore, one might follow that the drafters preferred a substantial meaning different from Art. 110, para. 3 LOSC.

The 1988 United Nations Convention Against Illicit Traffic in Narcotic Drugs and Psychotropic Substances does not contain any explicit provision on liability. According to Art. 17, para. 9 of this convention, "[t]he Parties shall consider entering into bilateral or regional agreements or arrangements to carry out, or to

---

69 *Cf. Zemanek*, Karl, "Does the Prospect of Incurring Responsibility Improve the Observance of International Law?", in *Ragazzi*, Maurizio (ed.), "International Responsibility Today – Essays in Memory of Oscar Schachter" (Leiden: Nijhoff, 2005), pp. 125 *et seq.*, at 133.

70 Art. 9(3) Migrant Smuggling Protocol. *Cf. Hinrichs*, Ximena, "Measures against smuggling of migrants at sea: A Law of the Sea Perspective", 36 Révue Belge de Droit International (2003), pp. 413 *et seq.*, at 430-1.

enhance the effectiveness of, the provisions of this article." Art. 26, para. 2 of the European Agreement on Illicit Traffic by Sea, implementing Article 17 of the United Nations Convention against Illicit Traffic in Narcotic Drugs and Psychotrophic Substances (Implementation Agreement) does not explicitly mention any party entitled to claim the responsibility of the interfering State. Concerning the interpretation of this provision, the explanatory report of the Council of Europe has great authority. It was adopted at the same time as the agreement and published with it. Therefore, it should be seen as part of the context of the agreement and not as *travaux préparatoires*.[71] According to this report, the committee of governmental experts under the authority of the European Committee on Crime Problems "decided not to limit any provisions on damage to inter-state relations but sought to go further".[72] Also, the committee considered Art. 110, para. 3 LOSC to constitute customary international law and explicitly wanted Art. 26 of the Implementation Agreement to be interpreted in the light of Art. 110, para. 3 LOSC.[73] The assumption that a private entity other than the flag State would claim the responsibility of the interfering State underlies the whole commentary on Art. 26 of the Implementation Agreement. Thus, the Implementation Agreement constitutes important State practice in favour of an entitlement of a private entity both under the Implementation Agreement and under Art. 110, para. 3 LOSC.

Art. VI of the Intervention Convention, finally, compared to the other compensation provisions, does not seem to have any direct predecessor or successor. Therefore, the drafters either wanted to come up with something new or were unaware of the close relationship to Art. 22, para. 3 CHS.

3. Subsequent practice

Since the Convention on the High Seas has been adopted in 1958, only three cases are known to the author where one of the provisions has been applied in practice. The International Tribunal for the Law of the Sea (ITLOS) in 1999 had to rule on the lawfulness of a hot pursuit by Guinean authorities. The flag State, St. Vincent and the Grenadines, claimed compensation on behalf of the vessel and her crew members. In the oral argument, both parties agreed that Art. 111, para. 8 LOSC obliges a State to compensate the ship.[74]

---

[71] *Sinclair*, Ian, "The Vienna Convention on the Law of Treaties" (Manchester: University Press, 1984), at 129-130; *Aust*, Anthony, "Modern Treaty Law and Practice" (Cambridge: Cambridge University Press, 2000), at 191.

[72] "Agreement on Illicit Traffic by Sea implementing Article 17 of the United Nations Convention against Illicit Traffic in Narcotic Drugs and Psychotropic Substances" (ETS No. 156), Explanatory Report, at para. 90.

[73] *Ibid.*, at para. 94.

[74] *The M/V "Saiga" (No. 2) Case (St. Vincent and the Grenadines v. Guinea)*, Oral Argument of St. Vincent and the Grenadines, 19 March 1999, ITLOS Pleadings 1999, pp. 1208 *et seq.*, at 1225; *ibid.*, Oral Argument of Guinea, 20 March 1999, ITLOS Pleadings 1999, pp. 1233 *et seq.*, at 1265-1266.

ITLOS, in its judgment, briefly noted that the claim of the flag State was based on both Art. 111, para. 8 LOSC and general international law,[75] but then recapitulated principles of general international law and applied them to the case at hand.[76] Not in any regard did the Tribunal deal with the particularities of Art. 111, para. 8 LOSC. Presumably, the Tribunal was quite uncomfortable being faced with Art. 111, para. 8 LOSC and evaded its application by relying on general international law. Furthermore, it was not necessary for ITLOS to rule on the issue because the applicant State could have exercised flag State protection on behalf of the private interests related to the ship and thereby claim the violation of a right of these interests such as Art. 111, para. 8 LOSC.

In the United States, two cases argued before the Court of Appeals for the Fifth Circuit give certain, though not uniform indications concerning individual rights under the Convention on the High Seas. Since Art. 22, para. 3 CHS is almost identical with Art. 110, para. 3 LOSC and served as starting point for its drafting, the elaborations by the Court of Appeals for the Fifth Circuit could be relevant for the interpretation of Art. 110, para. 3 LOSC.

In the case of *United States v. Cadena*, the Fifth Circuit Court of Appeals followed a very cautious approach. It had to rule on a case in which the United States Coast Guard had boarded and seized a vessel of either Canadian or Colombian nationality 200 nautical miles off the United States coast. The captain of the vessel claimed that the search violated Art. 22, para. 1 CHS. The United States has been a party to this convention since 1961, but Canada and Colombia had only signed it without successive ratification.

The Court held that the CHS was therefore not applicable to the case at hand, but nevertheless elaborated on the application of the Convention to citizens and vessels of non-member States: "Art. 22 of the Convention, for example, specifies the right to compensation for damages suffered as a consequences of its violation; *if only this remedy is available to citizens or vessels of member nations*, citizens of non-member nations ought not enjoy the benefits of greater prophylaxis ... by virtue of their nation's failure to ratify"[77] (emphasis added). Even though the Court did not apply the Convention on the High Seas to the case at hand, the language of the judgments indicates that Art. 22, para. 3 CHS may constitute a remedy for "citizens or vessels of member nations".

The second case, *United States v. Postal*, dealt with two boardings on 15 September 1976 of a sailing vessel registered in the Grand Cayman Islands. The first boarding took place 8.75 nautical miles off the United States coastline. The Court apparently was uncertain whether the boarding occurred within or outside the United States territorial sea. It nevertheless applied Art. 22 CHS to the case at

75 In its final formal submission, St. Vincent and the Grenadines based its claim solely on Art. 111, para. 8 LOSC. *The M/V "Saiga" (No. 2) Case (St. Vincent and the Grenadines v. Guinea)*, Oral Argument of St. Vincent and the Grenadines, 19 March 1999, ITLOS Pleadings 1999, pp. 1208 *et seq.*, at 1231.

76 *The M/V "Saiga" (No. 2) Case (St. Vincent and the Grenadines v. Guinea)*, Judgment of 1 July 1999, ITLOS Reports 1999, pp. 10 *et seq.*, at 64-67, paras. 167-177.

77 *United States v. Cadena*, 585 F.2d 1252, 1261 (5th Cir. 1978).

hand. The Court of Appeals held that the boarding was justified under Art. 22, para. 1 CHS. The vessel was suspicious to have United States nationality because she was flying no flag and exhibiting neither name nor home port on her stern, because the crew pretended to be Australian, but spoke no accent and because the manoeuvres of the vessels apparently tried to evade any boarding.[78] However, even though the boarding officers found out that the vessel was indeed registered in the Grand Cayman Islands and the suspicions thus "proved to be unfounded", Art. 22, para. 3 CHS was not applied to the first boarding. Presumably, the claimants had not based any compensation claim upon Art. 22, para. 3 CHS because the first boarding had not led to great damage.

The Coast Guard abstained from inspecting the hold during the first boarding and temporarily left the vessel. It nevertheless remained suspicious and pursued the vessel for two and a half to three hours. Then, the Coast Guard Operations Center in Miami ordered to search the holds of the vessel. The search eventually took place 16.3 nautical miles off the United States coastline. The Coast Guard seized eight thousand pounds of Marihuana worth 2.5 million U.S. dollars. The Court held that the boarding was unjustified because one requirement for a legal hot pursuit had not been met[79] and because Art. 22 CHS was only applicable to merchant ships.[80]

Thus, the Court ruled that Art. 6 CHS (exclusivity of flag State jurisdiction) had been violated by the United States Coast Guard. However, after an extensive interpretation of the provision particularly referring to the U.S. government[81] and U.S. authors,[82] the Court came to the conclusion that Art. 6 CHS was not self-executing and therefore would bar the jurisdiction of the Court. Quite evidently, this also meant that the boarded vessel remained forfeited and that the owner could not claim any compensation.

The interpretative value of this decision is dubious. First, one could argue that the Court of Appeals for the Fifth Circuit has implicitly held that Art. 22, para. 3 CHS does not represent a self-executing provision. However, on the other hand, the decision focused on a provision that is much more widely considered to constitute a right of the flag State, namely Art. 6 CHS. Furthermore, Art. 22 CHS, contrary to Art. 110 LOSC, is limited to "foreign merchant ships". Finally, one also ought to distinguish between the ability to enforce before domestic court a

---

78 *United States v. Postal*, 589 F.2d 862, 871 (5th Cir. 1979).

79 Art. 23, para. 3, cl. 2 CHS (identical to Art. 111, para. 4, cl. 2 LOSC): "The pursuit may only be commences after a visual or auditory signal to stop has been given at a distance which enables it to be seen or heard by the foreign ship." In the case at hand, such signs were only given immediately before the second boarding, thus outside the territorial sea.

80 In *United States v. Postal*, the claimants claimed their vessel to be a pleasure craft. *United States v. Postal*, 589 F.2d 862, 873 (5th Cir. 1979).

81 *United States v. Postal*, 589 F.2d 862, 881-882 (5th Cir. 1979).

82 *Cf. Ficken*, Ivan W., "The 1935 Anti-Smuggling Act Applied to Hovering Narcotics Smugglers beyond the Contiguous Zone: An Assessment under International Law", 29 U. Miami L. Rev. (1974-1975), pp. 700 *et seq.*, at 724 (stating that it is doubtful whether the Convention on the High Seas has changed any exiting internal legislation).

right granted under public international law and the existence of the right as such. The first issue is governed by constitutional law applied by the domestic court and may depend on the application of principles like "self-executory" treaties. The second issue is exclusively a matter of public international law and needs to be confined to treaty interpretation. The Court of Appeals for the Fifth Circuit focused on constitutional issues, but nevertheless pretended to apply principles of treaty interpretation.

Considering both United States court decisions, the State practice of the United States is far from conclusive and contains indications into both directions. Unfortunately, the court decisions thus gain little relevance for this study, but only show how controversial the issue may be.

Suffice it to add one more example of the extremely scarce State practice: In the case of the Algerian emergency, France visited a great number of vessels within a distance of approximately 50 kilometers off the Algerian coast in order to prevent the transport of arms and munitions to Algerian forces. In at least the case of one vessel, the *Helga Böge*, France paid compensation directly to the shipowner, after the detention proved to be unfounded.[83] *Wolff Heintschel von Heinegg* regards this to have been the regular French practice during the Algerian emergency.[84] This could indicate that France considers Art. 110, para. 3 LOSC to constitute an individual right of private entities, but one could as well question whether France considered itself legally obliged to pay this compensation or whether the payment represented an act of benevolence (*ex gratia* payment).

4. Rules of general international law

The contextual interpretation needs to take account of the "relevant rules of international law applicable in the relations between the parties" (Art. 31, para. 3, lit. c) VCLT). As far as compensation provisions are concerned, the general law of State responsibility is most relevant. This part of general international law traditionally does not know of any entitlement of an individual to claim the responsibility of another State. Instead, the general law of State responsibility is traditionally construed to be limited to inter-State relations and thus only States may claim the responsibility of another State.[85] If a State violates an international obligation and hereby inflicts damage on an individual of another State, this latter State may claim the responsibility of the first State by exercising diplomatic protection. This traditional concept definitely constitutes a consequence of the conservative per-

---

83 *Heintschel von Heinegg*, Wolff, "Visit, Search, Diversion, and Capture in Naval Warfare: Part II, Developments since 1945", 30 Can. Yb. Int'l L. (1992), pp. 89 *et seq.*, at 101.

84 *Ibid.* But see *Vollmar*, Sabine, "Das Durchsuchungsrecht im Frieden aus Gründen des Selbstschutzes" (Bonn, 1966), at 12-3.

85 *Cf.* Art. 33, para. 1 Articles on State Reponsibility.

ception of public international law according to which only States are subjects of public international law.[86]

The German Federal Constitutional Court (Bundesverfassungsgericht) recently held that Art. 3 of the Convention respecting the Laws and Customs of War on Land (also known as "Hague IV"), according to which "[a] belligerent party which violates the provisions of the said Regulations shall, if the case demands, be liable to pay compensation", does not create an individual right.[87] However, one ought to add that the Bundesverfassungsgericht in its decision needed to apply international humanitarian law to a situation which occurred in the Second World War at a time when human rights and a strengthened status of the individual were still unknown in public international law.[88] Furthermore, the wording of the provision is different from some of the analyzed provisions since it does not indicate any individual entitlement and since it conditions the liability by the terms "if the case demands".[89] The decision of the Bundesverfassungsgericht is thus of little value to the interpretation of the relevant compensation provisions. In fact, the Bundesverfassungsgericht held in a different decision that the obligation of a State to provide for restitution in kind, if it has committed an internationally wrongful act, represents customary international law and is directly applicable in the German legal system.[90] This obligation can thus generally be invoked against the federal government by private entities before German courts.

The Articles on State Responsibility by the International Law Commission have exempted all issues concerning the ability of private entities to claim the responsibility of a State and, for this reason, have been heavily criticized as not reflecting the contemporary public international law in respect of the protection of individuals.[91]

In modern public international law, particularly since the end of World War II, private entities have increasingly gained individual rights. Most often, these material rights have not been linked with means to enforce them, but this does not deny

---

86 *Dahm*, Georg/*Delbrück*, Jost/*Wolfrum*, Rüdiger, "Völkerrecht", Vol. 1, Part 2 (2nd ed., Berlin: de Gruyter, 2002), at 259-260; *Brown Weiss*, Edith, "Invoking State Responsibility in the Twenty-First Century", 96 AJIL (2002), 798 *et seq.*, at 798.

87 BVerfG, 2 BvR 1476/03 (15 February 2006), at para. 20.

88 *Ibid.*, at para. 22.

89 *Ibid.*

90 BVerfG, 46 ZaöRV (1986), pp. 289 *et seq.*

91 *Brown Weiss*, Edith, "Invoking State Responsibility in the Twenty-First Century", 96 AJIL (2002), 798 *et seq.*, at 799; *Pisillo Mazzeschi*, Riccardo, "The Marginal Role of the Individual in the ILC'Articles on State Responsibility", 14 Italian Yb. of Int'l L. (2004), pp. 39 *et seq.*, at 42-43; *Zemanek*, Karl, "Does the Prospect of Incurring Responsibility Improve the Observance of International Law?", in *Ragazzi*, Maurizio (ed.), "International Responsibility Today – Essays in Memory of Oscar Schachter" (Leiden: Nijhoff, 2005), pp. 125 *et seq.*, at 134. *Cf.* also *Roucounas*, Emmanuel, "Facteurs privés et droit international public", 299 RdC (2002- VI), pp. 9 *et seq.*, at 323.

their existence as such.[92] The International Court of Justice has also recognized the status of the individual as subject of public international law in certain cases.[93]

After the Permanent Court of International Justice decided in 1928 that individual rights can be derived from international treaties if the parties so intended and that States may be obliged to enforce these individual rights in their domestic legal systems,[94] national courts have been more and more willing to apply such rights.[95]

Some treaties have even enabled private entities to invoke the responsibility of another State or even their State of nationality for the violation of such an individual right and sometimes even to claim damages.[96] This is true, for example, under those human rights treaties, which provide a right of petition to a court or some other body for affected individuals. Under the First Optional Protocol to the International Covenant on Civil and Political Rights (ICCPR), individuals have the right to make written representations to the United Nations Human Rights Committee to claim the violation of the ICCPR by a State which has accepted the protocol.[97] Based on the model of this protocol, States parties to the Convention on the Elimination of Discrimination Against Women adopted an Optional Protocol which gives individuals similar rights.[98] Furthermore, the Convention against Torture and other Forms of Cruel, Inhuman and Degrading Treatment or Punishment[99] and the International Convention on the Elimination of All Form of Racial

---

[92] *Lauterpacht*, Hersch, "International Law and Human Rights" (London: Stevens, 1950), at 27, 48, 61, 159-160; *Schaumann*, Wilfried, "Die Gleichheit der Staaten" (Wien: Springer, 1957), at 94-95, 97.

[93] *LaGrand Case (Germany v. United States of America),* Judgment of 27 June 2001, ICJ Reports 2001, pp. 466 *et seq.*, para. 77; *Case Concerning Avena and Other Mexican Nationals (Mexico v. United States of America)*, Judgment of 31 March 2004, reprinted in 43 ILM (2004), pp. 581 *et seq.*, para. 40. *Cf.* also Inter-American Court of Human Rights, *The Right to Information on Consular Assistance in the Framework of the Guarantees of Due Process of Law*, Advisory Opinion of 1 October 1999, reprinted in Human Rights Law Journal (2000), pp. 24 *et seq.*

[94] *Jurisdiction of the Courts of Danzig*, Advisory Opinion of 3 March 1928, (1928) PCIJ Series B, No. 15, pp. 4 *et seq.*

[95] Supreme Court of Danzig, 4 ZaöRV (1934), pp. 947 *et seq.*; RGZ 117, 284; BGHZ 17, 309, 313.

[96] For a detailed enumeration of such treaties see *Dahm*, Georg/*Delbrück*, Jost/*Wolfrum*, Rüdiger, "Völkerrecht", Vol. 1, Part 2 (2nd ed., Berlin: de Gruyter, 2002), at 263-264 and *Jennings*, Robert/*Watts*, Arthur, "Oppenheim's International Law", Vol. 2 (9th ed., Harlow: Longman, 1992), at 847-848.

[97] "International Covenant on Civil and Political Rights", adopted on 16 December 1966, UNTS, Vol. 999, pp. 171 *et seq.*; "First Optional Protocol", UNTS, Vol. 999, pp. 302 *et seq.*

[98] "Convention on the Elimination of Discrimination Against Women", adopted on 1 March 1980, UNTS, Vol. 1249, pp. 13 *et seq.*; "Optional Protocol", General Assembly Resolution 54/4, annex (6 October 1999).

[99] "Convention against Torture and other Forms of Cruel, Inhuman and Degrading Treatment or Punishment", adopted on 10 December 1984, UNTS, Vol. 1465, pp. 85 *et seq.*

Discrimination[100] establish individual complaint procedures, which States can opt into.

On the regional level, individuals may claim the violation of the European Convention for the Protection of Human Rights and Fundamental Freedoms and even claim damages before the European Court of Human Rights.[101] Under the American Convention on Human Rights, individuals may file complaints with the Inter-American Commission on Human Rights.[102]

The Commission on Human Rights even states that in general international law, the individual victim at least in cases of gross violations of human rights has a right to reparation including compensation against the responsible State.[103]

Invocation of State responsibility is not strictly limited to human rights. Under the North American Agreement on Environmental Cooperation, private entities may lodge complaints that a State party "is failing to effectively enforce its environmental law."[104] Also, under the Optional Rules for Arbitration of Disputes Relating to Natural Resources and/or the Environment of the Permanent Court of Arbitration (PCA), private entities may now file complaints against States for the violation of environmental and natural resources law.[105]

In the area of investments disputes, many bilateral or regional investment protection agreements concluded between States and private corporations provide for the possibility that corporations file claims in arbitration or conciliation proceedings.[106] The most prominent forum is the International Centre for the Settlement of Investment Disputes (ICSID).[107] These agreements might have been a consequence of the difficulties private entities previously had to file claims under

[100] "International Convention on the Elimination of All Form of Racial Discrimination", adopted on 21 December 1965, UNTS, Vol. 660, pp. 195 *et seq.*

[101] *Cf., e.g.,* Arts. 34, 41 European Convention for the Protection of Human Rights and Fundamental Freedoms, UNTS, Vol. 213 (1955), pp. 221 *et seq.*

[102] Art. 44 of the American Convention on Human Rights, adopted on 22 November 1969, UNTS, Vol. 1144, pp. 123 *et seq.*

[103] *Commission on Human Rights*, "Study Concerning the Right to Restitution, Compensation and Rehabilitation for Victims of Gross Violations of Human Rights and Fundamental Freedoms", *UN* Doc. E/CN.4/Sub.2/1993.8 (2 July 1993), at 53, para. 133.

[104] Art. 14 of the North American Agreement on Environmental Cooperation, adopted on 14 September 1993, 32 ILM (1993), pp. 1480 *et seq.*

[105] "Permanent Court of Arbitration Optional Rules for Arbitration of Disputes Relating to Natural Resources and/or the Environment", adopted on 19 June 2001, available at <www.pca-cpa.org/ENGLISH/EDR/ENRrules.htm>.

[106] Commentary on Art. 33 ASR, para. 4, reprinted in *Crawford*, James, "The International Law Commission's Articles on State Responsibility" (Cambridge: Cambridge University Press, 2002), at 210; *Brown Weiss*, Edith, "Invoking State Responsibility in the Twenty-First Century", 96 AJIL (2002), 798 *et seq.*

[107] *Cf.* "Convention for the Settlement of Investment Disputes between States of Nationals of Other States", adopted on 18 March 1965, UNTS, Vol. 575, pp. 159 *et seq.*

public international law according to the jurisprudence of the International Court of Justice.[108]

Even the law on diplomatic protection increasingly recognizes that a State, in exercising diplomatic protection on behalf of its nationals, no more exclusively claims own rights,[109] but also protects substantial rights of its nationals under public international law.[110] The special rapporteur of the International Law Commission, *Mohamed Bennouna*, submitted a report which was quite critical about the traditional doctrine and favoured individual rights under public international law.[111] Within the International Law Association, there seems to be great support for a new approach to the law of diplomatic protection according to which the State of nationality is claiming the rights of its nationals.[112]

Presently, the International Law Commission apparently upholds the *Mavrommatis* doctrine, but realizes that it is merely a fiction in order to establish remedies for States acting on behalf of their nationals.[113] Thus, the ILC implicitly recognizes material rights of individuals without granting them the procedural remedies to enforce them.

Therefore, general international law favours certain individual rights and there are even some procedures available to claim these rights before international institutions.[114] It is submitted that only because remedies for private entities before international tribunals are rare, existing materials individual rights to claim compensation have thus far found little attention in public international law.

5. Invocation of State responsibility by private entities in maritime matters

Furthermore, invocation of State responsibility by a private entity is not unknown to the Law of the Sea. As early as 1841, the so-called Quintuple Treaty provided that domestic courts shall grant compensation to the captain, the shipowner and

---

108 *Sornarajah*, Muthucumaraswamy, "State Responsibility and Bilateral Investment Treaties", 20 Journal of World Trade Law (1986), pp. 79 *et seq.*, at 87.

109 Such was the traditional approach. *Cf. Mavrommatis Palestine Concession Case (Greece v. United Kingdom)*, Judgment of 30 August 1924, (1924) PCIJ Series A, No. 2, pp. 4 *et seq.*, at 12.

110 *Orrego Vicuña*, Francisco, "The Protection of Shareholders under International Law: Making State Responsibility More Accessible", in *Ragazzi*, Maurizio (ed.), "International Responsibility Today – Essays in Memory of Oscar Schachter" (Leiden: Nijhoff, 2005), pp. 161 *et seq.*, at 165.

111 *UN* Doc. A/CN.4/484 (4 February 1998), *Bennouna*, Mohamed, "Preliminary Report on Diplomatic Protection", at para. 32.

112 *ILA*, "Report of the Sixty-Ninth Conference, Committee on Diplomatic Protection of Persons and Property" (2000), pp. 604 *et seq.*, at 633-634. *Cf.* also *García Amador*, F. V., "State Responsibility – Some New Problems", 94 RdC (1958-II), pp. 421 *et seq.*, at 472.

113 *UN* Doc. A/CN.4/506 (7 March 2000), *Dugard*, John R., "First Report on Diplomatic Protection", at 7, para. 20.

114 *Cf.* also *Seegers*, Martin, "Das Individualrecht auf Wiedergutmachung" (Münster: LIT, 2006), at 85-162.

cargo owners if a vessel of a contracting State was stopped on grounds of slave trade without reasonable suspicion.[115] Interestingly, the liable entity under the treaty was the commander of the interfering vessel and not the interfering State, probably an outflow of the influence of the Prussian municipal law on State liability. Apparently, the States parties at the time did not yet adhere to the view that public international law would only create rights and obligations to States. In the following decades, quite a few conventions dealing with matters of the Law of the Sea provided for detailed proceedings in which the shipowners and other private entities could claim compensation for wrongful interferences.[116] These proceedings either took place on the sea with the naval officer granting compensation[117] or before a domestic court.[118]

In the law of naval warfare, most States have established prize courts where private entities may appear as parties to claim compensation for the damage caused by a violation of the rules of naval warfare.[119] Even though the establishment of these prize courts was based on domestic law, the custom in the two world wars has amounted to an obligation to provide for proceedings where private entities of other States may appear ("toute prise doit être jugée").[120] The reason for

---

[115] Article XIII, Traité entre l'Autriche, la France, la Grande-Bretagne et la Russie, sur la repression de la traite d'esclaves d'Afrique, adopted on 20 December 1841, Martens Nouveau Receuil Général de Traités, Vol. 2 (1841), pp. 392 *et seq.*, at 401.

[116] Article 33, Convention internationale pour règler la police de la pêche dans la mer du Nord en dehors des eaux territoriales, adopted on 6 May 1882, Martens Nouveau Recueil Général de Traités, Deuxième Série, Vol. 9 (1884), pp. 556 *et seq.*, at 562; Article. LIII of the Acte général de la Conférence anti-esclavagiste, adopted on 2 July 1890, Martens Nouveau Recueil Général de Traités, Deuxième Série, Vol. 16 (1891), pp. 3 *et seq.*, at 19; Art. 21 of the Convention for the Control of the Trade in arms and ammunition, adopted on 10 September 1919, LNTS(1922), pp. 331 *et seq.*, at 352; Annex II, para. 8 e) of the Convention on Supervision of International Trade in Arms and Ammunition and in Implements of War, adopted on 17 June 1925, reprinted in Carnegie Endowment (ed.), "International legislation: a collection of the texts of multipartite international instruments of general interest", Vol. 3 (1931), pp. 1634 *et seq.*

[117] Article 33 of the Convention internationale pour règler la police de la pêche dans la mer du Nord en dehors des eaux territoriales; Art. 33 of the Convention for regulating the fisheries outside territorial waters in the ocean surrounding the Faroë Islands and Iceland (Denmark/United Kingdom), adopted on 24 June 1901, reprinted in *United Nations*, "Laws and Regulations on the Regimes of the High Seas", Vol. 1 (1951), at 232, 237.

[118] Article. LIII of the Acte général de la Conférence anti-esclavagiste; Art. 21 of the Convention for the Control of the Trade in arms and ammunition; Annex II, para. 8 e) of the Convention on Supervision of International Trade in Arms and Ammunition and in Implements of War.

[119] *Verzijl*, Jan Hendrik Willem, "Le droit des prises de la Grande Guerre" (Leyde: Sijthoff, 1924), at 6-17.

[120] *Rousseau*, Charles, "Le droit des conflits armés" (Paris: Pedone, 1983), at 322-323.

this obligation was that a vessel may only be condemned by a prize court in the State of the captor.[121]

The right of private entities to claim compensation in a prize court was codified in Art. 64 of the 1909 London Declaration[122] which stipulates that "the parties interested have the right to compensation, unless there were good reasons for capturing the vessel or goods". Contrary to some other issues of this provision, the fact that a private entity might enjoy a right under the provision was never controversial during its negotiations. In this respect, Art. 64 of the 1909 London Declaration therefore acquired the status of customary international law.[123]

In the years after 1949 in the conflict between the Communists and the National Chinese government, the latter seized many merchant vessels in the Street of Formosa. Even though not applying the London Declaration or referring to the law of naval warfare (the conflict was, strictly speaking, not a war between two sovereign States), it offered to directly give "satisfaction" to those vessels which had been engaged in "legitimate neutral shipping".[124] This statement might represent evidence of *opinio juris* concerning an obligation to compensate innocent vessels whose navigation had been interfered with.

Moreover, the entitlement of the "ship" to claim compensation seems to be well accepted in the law concerning port State control. In its provisions on port State control, the Law of the Sea Convention does not directly deal with the issue of the entitled entity.[125] For port State control on grounds of pollution, the International Convention for the Prevention of Pollution from Ships (MARPOL)[126] is most relevant. According to its Art. 7, para. 2, "[w]hen a ship is unduly detained or delayed under Article 4, 5 or 6 of the present Convention, *it* shall be entitled to compensation for any loss or damage suffered" (emphasis added). Also, the part of the International Convention for the Safety of Life at Sea (SOLAS) which deals with enforcement by port State control stipulates in Chapter XI-2 Reg. 3.1 no. 1 2nd sentence that "[w]hen Contracting Governments exercise control ..., all possible efforts shall be made to avoid a ship being unduly detained or delayed. If a ship is thereby unduly detained, or delayed, *it* shall be entitled to compensation for any loss or damage suffered" (emphasis added).

To strengthen the enforcement of the MARPOL and SOLAS provisions, regional memorandums of understanding (MOU) were adopted. The three major

---

[121] *Colombos*, Constantin John, "The International Law of the Sea" (6th ed., London: Longman, 1967), at 797, para. 926.

[122] "Declaration concerning the Laws of Naval War", adopted on 16 February 1909, reprinted in 3 AJIL, Supplement (1909), pp. 179 *et seq.*

[123] *Cf.* also *Colombos*, Constantin John, "A Treatise on the Law of Prize" (2nd ed., London: The Grotius Society, 1940), at 25-26.

[124] *Cf. UN* Doc. A/AC/SR-51-55, para. 14; cited by *Vollmar*, Sabine, "Das Durchsuchungsrecht im Frieden aus Gründen des Selbstschutzes" (Bonn, 1966), at 7.

[125] *Cf.* Art. 232 LOSC: "States shall be liable for damage or loss attributable to them arising from measures taken pursuant to section 6 when such measures are unlawful or exceed those reasonably required in the light of available information. States shall provide for recourse in their courts for actions in respect of such damage or loss."

[126] Adopted on 2 November 1973, reprinted in 12 ILM (1973), pp. 1319 *et seq.*

MOU's contain provisions stipulating that "[n]othing in the memorandum affects rights created by provisions of relevant instruments relating to compensation for undue detention or delay."[127] Hence, the parties to these MOU's adhered, *inter alia*, to Art. 7, para. 2 MARPOL. Inspite of the unambiguous text of the Paris MOU,[128] it has been questioned whether the relevant MOU's constitute legally binding instruments since they may only reflect the understanding as to matters of fact or the conduct of the States parties.[129] Notwithstanding this controversial issue, the Paris MOU, in the first years of its existence, has hardly been used by any shipowner to receive compensation for wrongful port State control measures.[130]

The Council Directive 95/21/EC on port State control,[131] on the other hand, provides in Art. 9, para. 7 that "[i]f a ship is unduly detained or delayed, the owner or operator shall be entitled to compensation for any loss or damage suffered. In any instance of alleged undue detention or delay the burden of proof shall lie with the owner or operator of the ship."[132] It is not uncommon for a directive to create direct rights of individuals. Even though according to Art. 249 of the Treaty establishing the European Community,[133] a directive "shall be binding as to the result to be achieved, upon each Member State to which it is addressed, but shall leave to the national authorities the choice of form and methods," a provision of a directive can have direct effect.[134] It only needs to be sufficiently clear and exact to be capable of being applied directly by a national court and the time limit for

127 Rule 3.18 of the 1982 Paris MOU, reprinted in *Özcayir*, Z. Oya, "Port State Control" (2nd ed., London: LLP, 2004), at 543; Rule 3.13 of the 1993 Tokyo MOU, available at <www.tokyo-mou.org/memorand.pdf>; Rule 3.11 of the 1992 Acuerdo de Vina del Mar Agreement on Port State control of 1992, available at <http://200.45.69.62/PDF/Cuerpo%20principal%20Acuerdo_i.PDF>; Rule 3.11 of the MOU on Port State Control in the Caribbean Region, reprinted in ILM (1997), pp. 237 *et seq.*; Rule 3.10 of the MOU on Port State Control for the Indian Ocean Region, reprinted in "Indian Ocean MOU on Port State Control Annual Report 2002", at 41.

128 *Cf.* the title of section 1 of the MOU: "Commitments".

129 *Kasoulides*, George C., "Port State Control and Jurisdiction" (Dordrecht: Nijhoff, 1992), at 143.

130 *Ibid.*, 158.

131 *EC* Council Directive 05/21/EC of 19 June 1995, 1995 O.J. (L 157), pp. 1 *et seq.*

132 This provision has not been modified by the following amendments to Council Directive 95/21/EC: *EC* Council Directive 98/25/EC of 27 April 1998, 1998 O.J. (L 133), pp. 19 *et seq.*; *EC* Commission Directive 98/42/EC of 19 June 1998, 1998 O.J. (L 184), pp. 40 *et seq.*; *EC* Commission Directive 1999/97/EC of 13 December 1999, 1999 O.J. (L 331), pp. 67 *et seq.*; *EC* Directive 2001/106/EC of the European Parliament and of the Council of 19 December 2001, 2002 O.J. (L 19), pp. 17 *et seq.*; *EC* Directive 2002/84/EC of the European Parliament and of the Council of 5 November 2002, 2002 O.J. (L 324), pp. 53 *et seq.*

133 "Treaty establishing the European Community", Consolidated Version of 24 December 2002, 2003 O.J. C/325, pp. 1 *et seq.*

134 *Craig*, Paul & *de Búrca*, Graínne, "EU Law: Text Cases and Materials" (3rd ed., Oxford, Oxford University Press, 2003), at 202.

the implementation of the directive into national law must have run out.[135] The fact that the directive explicitly mentions the "owner or operator" and hence an individual favours the argument that such a direct right has been created. Thus, the shipowner does not need to rely on the protection by the flag State to claim compensation under the directive.

Moreover, the directive shows that member States of the European Communities provide great respect for Art. 7, para. 2 MARPOL since they simply copied it into the directive. Since it is unlikely that the EU Member States aimed to change the existing Law of the Sea in this respect, they probably considered Art. 7, para. 2 MARPOL to create a right under public international law to some private entity related to the ship.

Finally, as far as it concerns available remedies before international tribunals, the International Tribunal for the Law of the Sea, contrary to the International Court of Justice, is potentially open to private entities. Art. 20 of the ITLOS Statute provides that "[t]he Tribunal shall be open to entities other than States Parties in any case expressly provided for in Part XI or in any case submitted pursuant to any other agreement conferring jurisdiction on the Tribunal which is accepted by all the parties to that case". While the first alternative refers to sea-bed mining in the area of the sea-bed beyond national jurisdiction, the second alternative could be of relevance to interferences on the high seas. For example, shipping companies could conclude agreements with States interested in the fight against terrorism. These agreements could oblige the shipping companies to screen their cargoes, but also refer to the limited possibilities of interferences on the high seas by the State party to the agreement whether or not such conduct would be in conformity with flag State jurisdiction. If the agreement conferred jurisdiction on ITLOS, then the shipping company might directly rely on Art. 110, para. 3 LOSC or a similar compensation provision and claim compensation.[136] This alternative has "not been fully explored",[137] but it nevertheless constitutes a considerable remedy for private entities in the future.

Art. 292, para. 2 LOSC also allows private entities to claim the release of a vessel "on behalf of the flag State". While the provision does not allow a direct access of an individual to the International Tribunal for the Law of the Sea, it at least permits "the flag State … to authorize an individual or association, such as the ship owner, a shipping association or a labor union, to make an application for release."[138] In most cases of prompt release before the Tribunal, the application

---

[135] *Streinz*, Rudolf, Europarecht (5th ed., Heidelberg: Müller, 2001), at para. 402; European Court of Justice, Case 8/81, *Becker ./. Finanzamt Münster*, 1982 E.C.R., pp. 53 *et seq.*; Case 41/74, *Van Duyn v. Home Office*, 1974 ECR, pp. 1337 *et seq.*, at para. 12.

[136] It is a controversial and unresolved issue whether the agreement needs to be "related to the purposes of the [Law of the Sea] Convention" (Art. 288, para. 2 LOSC) or whether "any agreement" may confer jurisdiction on ITLOS (Art. 21 ITLOS Statute), *cf. Wolfrum*, Rüdiger, "Statement to the Informal Meeting of Legal Advisers of Ministries of Foreign Affairs" (24 October 2005), at 10-11, available at <www.itlos.org>.

[137] *Ibid.*, at 10.

[138] *Oxman*, Bernard H., "Human Rights and the United Nations Convention on the Law of the Sea", 36 Colum. J. Transnat'l L. (1997), pp. 399 *et seq.*, at 423.

was made by private individuals "on behalf of the flag State."[139] Thus, while formally upholding the status of the flag State as a party, private entities may in fact act as agents of the State protecting their own interests, a scenario which has become particularly important in cases involving open registers.

The above considerations have shown that an interpretation of the compensation provisions leading to an entitlement of private entities would not at the same time result in an anomaly in public international law. In fact, modern international law is slowly developing to recognize the status of private entities as bearers of rights and obligations. Suffice it to add that all compensation provisions shall be interpreted in the light of the contemporary public international law.[140] Hence, a progressive interpretation of Art. 110, para. 3 LOSC and the other provisions open to such an interpretation based on the development of public international law might well lead to an entitlement of the "ship".

6. The primary right affected by the interference

Under general international law, State responsibility usually only exists toward the entity whose right has been violated by the conduct of the responsible State.[141] Therefore, any private entity also needs to show a violation of its own rights when it claims the responsibility of a State. The issue of whether the "ship" or the flag State may be entitled to claim compensation under the diverse compensation provisions might thus depend on whether the claim is based on a violation of rights of the flag State or of the "ship".

Such a right could either be derived from the Law of the Sea or from the International Law on Human Rights.

a) Freedom of navigation: a right of the flag State or of the "ship"?

The first and foremost candidate for such a primary right is the freedom of navigation. All of the analyzed provisions stipulate that in certain cases of interferences with navigation, compensation shall be paid. The compensation provisions are therefore directly linked to the freedom of navigation in order to prevent abusive infringements. In particular, Arts. 106, 110, para. 3 and 111, para. 8

---

139 See, *e.g.*, ITLOS, *The "Grand Prince" Case (Belize v. France)*, Prompt Release, Judgment of 20 April 2001, ITLOS Reports 2001, pp. 17 *et seq.*, at 20, paras. 1-2; *The "Chaisiri Reefer 2" Case (Panama v. Yemen)*, Prompt Release, Order 2001/3 of 6 July 2001, ITLOS Reports 2001, pp. 76 *et seq.*, at 76, para. 1;.*The "Juno Trader" Case (St. Vincent and the Grenadines v. Guinea-Bissau)*, Prompt Release, Judgment of 18 December 2004, ITLOS Reports 2004, pp. 17 *et seq.*, at 21, para. 1.

140 *Thirlway*, Hugh, "The Law and Procedure of the International Court of Justice 1960-1989", 62 BYIL(1991), pp. 16 *et seq.*, at 16-17; *Higgins*, Rosalyn, "Some Observations on the Inter-Temporal Rule in International Law", in *Makarczyk*, Jerzy (ed.), "Theory of International Law at the Threshold of the 21st Century" (The Hague: Kluwer Law International, 1996), pp. 173 *et seq.*; *id.*, "Time and the Law: International Perspectives on an Old Problem", 46 ICLQ (1997, pp. 501 *et seq.*, at 515-519.

141 *Cf.* Art. 42, lit. a of the Articles on State Responsibility.

LOSC are all situated in Part VII of the Law of the Sea Convention for which the freedom of the high seas (Art. 87 LOSC) represents the central provision. Thus, it becomes important for this study whether this freedom represents a right of the flag State and/or of private entities.

After enumerating the different freedoms of the high seas, Art. 87, para. 2 stipulates that "[t]hese freedoms shall be exercised by all States" / "[c]haque Etat exerce ces libertés" / "[e]stas libertades serán ejercidas por todos los Estados" / "Все государства осуществляют эти свободы". These terms quite unequivocally indicate that the freedom of navigation, together with the other freedoms of the high seas, represents a right of the flag State. This is indeed the most common understanding of the freedom of navigation.[142]

However, the strength of this textual argument could be weakened by a comparison with Art. 17 LOSC. According to this provision "ships of all States … enjoy the right of innocent passage through the territorial sea."[143] Evidently, the coastal State enjoys much more sovereignty in the territorial sea than it does on the high seas. It would seem odd therefore if the ship had more rights in the territorial sea than she has on the high seas. In spite of the wording of the provision, the right to innocent passage is nevertheless commonly understood to constitute an exclusive right of the flag State.[144] Thus, the wording of Art. 17 LOSC is not sufficient to cast doubts on the common understanding of the freedom of navigation.

Furthermore, the wording of Art. 87, para. 2 LOSC and the common understanding of the freedom of navigation could be due to an overcome concept of public international law according to which only States, and not private entities, may enjoy rights. There have been some indications in favour of an individual right. *Pufendorf*, *e.g.*, wrote that the ocean needs to be free by the law of "humanity", not the law of nations.[145] At the end of World War I, the Italian draft for a League of Nations Constitution included a provision which stipulated: "Les

---

142 *Cf. Colombos*, Constantin John, "The International Law of the Sea" (6th ed., London: Longman, 1967), at 66; *O'Connell*, Daniel Patrick, "The International Law of the Sea", Vol. 2 (Oxford: Clarendon Press, 1984), at 796-798.

143 Judge Alvarez confirms that the right of passage belongs to „the ship". *Corfu Channel Case (United Kingdom v. Albania)*, Separate Opinion Alvarez, ICJ Reports 1949, pp. 39 *et seq.*, at 49.

144 *Cf., e.g., Lauterpacht*, Hersch, "Oppenheim's International Law", Vol. 1 (7th ed., London: Longman, 1948), at para. 188 (arguing that in customary international law, each State has the right to have vessels under its flag allowed to navigate innocently in the territorial sea of another State); *Corfu Channel (United Kingdom v. Albania)*, Judgment of 9 April 1949, ICJ Reports 1949, pp. 4 *et seq.*, at 22 (referring to the "obligation not to allow knowingly [the] territory to be used for acts contrary to the *rights of other States*" [emphasis added] in connection to the right of innocent passage in the Albanian territorial sea). The International Law Commission based its draft of the predecessor of Art. 17 LOSC on this judgment by the ICJ, see ILC Yearbook 1953/II, at 71.

145 *Pufendorff*, Samuel, Acht Bücher vom Natur- und Völcker-Rechte, Vol. 4, Kapitel V (1711), Cited by *Gidel*, Gilbert, "Le droit international de la mer", Vol. 1 (Paris-Châteauroux: Mellottée, 1932), at 198.

navires marchands de tout pavillon ont le droit de naviguer librement sur les mers."[146] The 1927 draft treaty on piracy was commented in the following terms: "If, after inspection of the suspected vessel, the suspicion proves to have been unfounded, the captain of the suspected vessel is entitled to reparation or compensation, according to circumstances."[147] However, there is no indication that these drafts were actually meant to create individual rights, particularly if one considers the period when they were written, a time when public international law was dominated by the notion of sovereignty without recognizing the personality of private entities.

In the course of centuries, the freedom of navigation may have developed from an instrument to combat maritime dominion to an important aspect of globalization and trade liberalization (*supra*). Maritime transport is now almost exclusively undertaken by private entities and the role of flag States has gradually decreased. The main direct beneficiaries of the freedom of navigation therefore today may represent private entities involved in maritime transport.[148] The freedom of navigation is thus "for the benefit of shipping in general."[149] Only indirectly, their States of origin and the States importing or exporting goods carried by maritime transport benefit from the freedom of navigation. Hence, an extremely progressive interpretation of the freedom of navigation might argue for the existence of an individual right of freedom of navigation, coexisting with a complementary right of flag States. An isolated, exclusive right of the ship owner, on the other hand, cannot be acceptable since that would mean that vessels without nationality would benefit from the freedom of navigation, a contradiction to the enforcement powers in Art. 110, para. 1, lit. d LOSC.

However, the previous considerations are definitely of minor importance as compared to (1) the unequivocal wording of Art. 87, para. 2 LOSC and (2) the widely recognized practice of States. While the practical influence of some flag States on shipowners under their flag may have decreased, the Law of the Sea still places great weight in the role of flag States with their rights and obligations under public international law. The mentioned considerations only underline that individual interests may be taken into account without giving private entities an individual right to navigate on the high seas.

Judge *Wolfrum*, in his separate opinion in the *M/V Saiga (No. 2) Case*, on the other hand, draws some arguments from the Law of the Sea Convention in favour of the freedom of navigation representing a right both of the flag State and of

---

[146] *Cf. Gidel*, Gilbert, "Le droit international de la mer", Vol. 1 (Paris-Châteauroux: Mellottée, 1932), at 199; *Krüger*, Herbert, "Schiffahrtsfreiheit", in *Schlochauer*, Hans-Jürgen (ed.), "Wörterbuch des Völkerrechts" (2nd ed., Berlin: de Gruyter, 1962), at 206.

[147] *League of Nations* Doc. C.196.M.70.1927.V., "Report of the Sub-Committee of the League of Nations Committee of Experts for the Progressive Codification of International Law", Draft Provisions for the Suppression of Piracy, Art. 6, at 119.

[148] *Cf. The M/V "Saiga" (No. 2) (St. Vincent and the Grenadines v. Guinea)*, Separate Opinion Laing, ITLOS Reports 1999, pp. 154 *et seq.*, at 169-171, paras. 23-26.

[149] *Cf. Corfu Channel Case (United Kingdom v. Albania)*, Judgment of 9 April 1949, ICJ Reports 1949, pp. 4 *et seq.*, at 22.

private entities: First, "according to article 292, paragraph 2, of the Convention the application for the prompt release of a vessel may be made by the flag State or on its behalf. The second alternative of that provision opens the possibility for the flag State to entrust the entity whose interests are directly at stake to initiate the respective proceedings. This … recognizes that disputes concerning the exercise of freedom of navigation, in general, involve rights of natural or juridical persons which may prevail over the rights of States."[150]

Secondly, "Article 295 of the Convention provides that local remedies are to be exhausted, where required under international law, before a dispute between States Parties may be submitted to a dispute settlement procedure provided for under the Convention. If … disputes concerning the interpretation or application are only disputes between States Parties arising from alleged violations of States' rights, article 295 of the Convention would be meaningless. This, however, would violate one of the most basic rules concerning the interpretation of international treaties, namely that interpretation should not render a provision inoperative."[151]

Judge *Wolfrum* concludes that "the concept of freedom of navigation has as its addressees States as well as individual or private entities" and that "[e]very other interpretation would run counter the objective of the Convention on the Law of the Sea."[152] He submits that a wording similar to Art. 116 LOSC ("All States have the right *for their nationals* to engage in fishing on the high seas." (emphasis added)) would have more precisely qualified the freedom of navigation.[153]

This conclusion by Judge *Wolfrum* probably overestimates the importance of Articles 292 and 295 LOSC as compared to the fundamental freedom of navigation which has found its meaning in the State practice over centuries. The Law of the Sea Convention introduced the new remedy of prompt release proceedings, but its Art. 292 LOSC nevertheless recognizes that the freedom of navigation represents a right of the flag State only. Otherwise, a private entity would not be required to file a claim "on behalf of the flag State", but could claim the violation of an own right. Furthermore, Art. 295 LOSC simply refers to the current state of public international law without indicating where in the Law of the Sea Convention individual rights are affected. Such reference to public international law does not suffice to attribute a new meaning to the freedom of navigation. It is therefore not surprising that Judge *Wolfrum* has never repeated his arguments in his later treatises on the high seas.[154] Such piece of literature might have been the more appropriate place to come forward with a new view on the freedom of navigation than one of 11 separate or dissenting opinions to the first decision of a newly established tribunal.

---

150 *The M/V "Saiga" (No. 2) (St. Vincent and the Grenadines v. Guinea)*, Separate Opinion Wolfrum, ITLOS Reports 1999, pp. 92 *et seq.*, at 109-110, para. 51.

151 *Ibid.*

152 *Ibid. Cf.* also *ibid.,* Dissenting Opinion Warioba, ITLOS Reports 1999, pp. 195 *et seq.*, at 217.

153 *The M/V "Saiga" (No. 2) (St. Vincent and the Grenadines v. Guinea)*, Separate Opinion Wolfrum, ITLOS Reports 1999, pp. 92 *et seq.*, at 110, para. 53.

154 *Cf., e.g., Wolfrum*, Rüdiger, "Hohe See und Tiefseeboden", in *Graf Vitzthum*, Wolfgang (ed.), "Handbuch des Seerechts" (München: Beck, 2006), pp. 293 *et seq.*

Evidently, ITLOS did not follow Judge *Wolfrum's* reasoning and, without providing explicit arguments, held that the right of freedom of navigation exclusively belongs to the flag State and that therefore the requirement of exhaustion of local remedies does not apply if the applicant State claims a violation of this right.[155] The decision by the Tribunal may have been criticized for its lack of explanation,[156] but it nevertheless has shown that all attempts to include the protection of individual rights in the freedom of navigation have thus far been in vain.

Similarly, one cannot extract an individual right from the exclusive jurisdiction of the flag State as laid down in Art. 92 LOSC. This provision prohibits the exercise of jurisdiction to other States than the flag States, but such a regulation of jurisdictional competences does not amount to any entitlement of a private entity.

Therefore, the Law of the Sea Convention does not contain a right of private entities to be safe from interferences on the high seas by States other than the flag State. Does this contradict the potential existence of an individual right to compensation in cases of some interferences? The previous considerations have shown that the interests of private entities definitely play a role for the interpretation and application of the freedom of navigation and of the exclusive jurisdiction of the flag State. The interplay between these two cornerstones of the Law of the Sea provides an important umbrella protecting the interests of private entities. However, the flag State remains an essential actor because it represents the only entity being able to claim the violation of the freedom of navigation.

Thus, even though the Law of the Sea Convention does not attribute a right to a private entity to be exempt from interferences on the high seas by other States than the flag State, it provides sound reason why a private entity might nevertheless be entitled to claim compensation in the case of certain interferences.

b) The relevance of the right to property

The primary right of a private entitiy might also lie in the human right to freely enjoy own property. Human rights have traditionally been considered to represent treaty obligations between States parties. One State is "committed vis-à-vis other States to respect and to ensure respect" of human rights whose beneficiaries in reality are private entities.[157] Therefore, a wrong to a national of another State was traditionally perceived to constitute a wrong to that other State.[158] However, if one State violates one of these human rights, secondary rules apply and a new relation-

---

155 *The M/V "Saiga" (No. 2) (St. Vincent and the Grenadines v. Guinea)*, Judgment of 1 July 1999, ITLOS Reports 1999, pp. 10 *et seq.*, at 45, para. 97.

156 *Cf. Bellayer-Roille*, Alexandra, "L'arrêt du Tribunal international du droit de la mer du 1er juillet 1999 – Affaire du navire "Saiga" N° 2", 19 ADMO (2001), pp. 111 *et seq.*, at 138-140.

157 *Roucounas*, Emmanuel, "*Non-State Actors: Areas of International Responsibility in Need of Further Exploration*", in *Ragazzi*, Maurizio (ed.), "International Responsibility Today – Essays in Memory of Oscar Schachter" (Leiden: Nijhoff, 2005), pp. 391 *et seq.*, at 399.

158 *Cf. Mavrommatis Palestine Concession Case (Greece v. United Kingdom)*, Judgment of 30 August 1924, (1924) PCIJ Series A, No. 2, at 12.

ship emerges. In this relationship, the responsible State bears an obligation to compensate the victim who, particularly in situations of human rights abuses, may be a private entity.[159] This alone shows that an entitlement to compensation could also exist if the primary right which has been violated does not belong to the private entity, but its State of nationality.

Even more progressive is the increasingly accepted approach that human rights constitute individual rights of private entities and that these entities have thereby become subjects of public international law.[160]

If one may thus find a human right which would be infringed by an interference with the navigation of a foreign vessel on the high seas, then the right to compensation under the controversial compensation provisions may reasonably belong to private entities and not to the flag State.

The most likely right which could be infringed might be the right to property. This right allows individuals to own property, not to be arbitrarily deprived of it, but also simply to freely enjoy one's own possessions.[161] If an interfering State boards a vessel on the high seas, the passage of the vessel is hindered and one might argue that such temporary blockade prejudices the right to property of the shipowner and potentially also of cargo-related interests. The fact that the Law of the Sea Convention and other conventions impose liability on a State for certain interferences has "clear, albeit indirect, implications for ... property rights."[162]

The status of the right to property has for a long time been rather controversial since not all human rights texts included such a right. While the Universal Declaration on Human Rights[163] provides in Art. 17, para. 1 that "[e]veryone has the right to own property", the declaration has largely remained a non-binding instrument.[164] The right does not appear in any of the International Covenants of 1966.[165] Even the European Convention on Human Rights does not contain the right to property, but all the members of the Council of Europe except Switzerland, Monaco and Andorra have meanwhile ratified the First Protocol to the Con-

---

159 *Roucounas*, Emmanuel, "Facteurs privés et droit international public", 299 RdC (2002), pp. 9 *et seq.*, at 347-348.

160 *Kälin*, Walter/*Künzli*, Jörg, "Universeller Menschenrechtsschutz" (Basel: Helbing & Lichtenhahn, 2005), at 17.

161 *Clayton*, Richard/*Tomlinson*, Hugh, "The Law of Human Rights", Vol. 1 (Oxford: Oxford University Press, 2000), at 1292.

162 *Oxman*, Bernard H., "Human Rights and the United Nations Convention on the Law of the Sea", 36 Colum. J. Transnat'l L. (1997), pp. 399 *et seq.*, at 420.

163 *United Nations*, General Assembly Resolution 217 A(III) (10 December 1948).

164 *Kälin*, Walter/*Künzli*, Jörg, "Universeller Menschenrechtsschutz" (Basel: Helbing & Lichtenhahn, 2005), at 77. But see *Humphrey*, John P., "The International Bill of Rights: Scope and Implementation", 17 Wm. & Mary L. Rev. (1975-76), pp. 527 et *seq.*, at 529; *Sohn*, Louis B., "The Human Rights Law of the Charter", 12 Tex. Int'l L. J. (1977), pp. 129 *et seq.*, at 133.

165 "International Covenant on Civil and Political Rights", adopted on 16 December 1966, UNTS, Vol. 999, pp. 171 *et seq.*; "International Covenant on Economic Social and Cultural Rights", adopted on 16 December 1966, UNTS, Vol. 993, pp. 3 *et seq.*

vention expressly recognizing such a right.[166] The Restatement of the Foreign Relations Law of the United States, a private codification of customary international law by international lawyers, does not mention the right to property as a customary human right.[167] Finally, many constitutions in the world do not explicitly protect the right to property.[168] The mere fact that some States still adhere to communist ideology renders it unlikely that the right to property has acquired the status of customary international law.

However, the States members of the League of Nations recognized as early as 1929 that a State may not unreasonably deprive foreign nationals of their property.[169] This obligation differs from the human right to property because the obliged entity is not the State of nationality of the claimant, but the State of his residence.[170] The obligation to protect the property of foreign nationals within the own jurisdiction has become a rule of customary international law.[171] Thus, for example, a State may not expropriate foreign property without providing for prompt, adequate and effective compensation.[172]

Such situations are in a certain respect similar to interferences on the high seas. In the latter case, the interfering State prevents the free use by the shipowner of his property. Even though the interference occurs on the high seas, the conduct by navy, coast guard or other government vessel occurs under the jurisdiction of the interfering State. Also, the activity of merchant vessels navigating in order to undertake international trade is very much comparable to the situation of an international company investing in a certain country. Furthermore, one might argue that if foreign property is protected within the territory of another State, then all States must *a fortiori* respect foreign property on the high seas where their degree of jurisdiction is much more limited.

The only concern one might raise is that according to many authors, States still enjoy a certain degree of discretion when dealing with foreign property on their

---

166 *Cf.* "Dates of ratification of the European Convention on Human Rights and Additional Protocols", available at <www.echr.coe.int>.

167 *American Law Institute*, "Third Restatement of the Foreign Relations Law of the United States" (St. Paul, 1987), at 161.

168 *Clayton*, Richard/*Tomlinson*, Hugh, "The Law of Human Rights", Vol. 1 (Oxford: Oxford University Press, 2000), at 1293 (citing *In re Certification of the Constitution of RSA 1996*, South African Constitutional Court, 10 Butterworths Constitutional Law Reports (1996), pp. 1253 *et seq.*, paras. 72-73).

169 *Cf. League of Nations* Document C.75.M.69.1929.V, "Conference for the Codification of International Law, Volume 3, Responsibility of States for Damage caused in their Territory to the Person or Property of Foreigners (1929), at 253.

170 *Jennings*, Robert/*Watts*, Arthur, "Oppenheim's International Law", Vol. 2 (9th ed., Harlow: Longman, 1992), at 910-911.

171 *Seidl-Hohenveldern*, Ignaz, "Aliens, Property", in *Bernhardt*, Rudolf (ed.), "Encyclopedia of Public International Law", Vol. 1 (Amsterdam: North-Holland, 1992), at 116.

172 *Cf. Domke*, Martin, "Foreign Nationalizations – Some Aspects of Contemporary International Law", 55 AJIL (1961), pp. 585 *et seq.*, at 603-610; *Sohn*, Louis B./*Baxter*, R.R., "Responsibility of States for Injuries to the Economic Interests of Aliens", *ibid.*, pp. 545 *et seq.*, at 553, 557.

territory and that the only serious limitations of this discretion affect expropriations and fair trials.[173] Compared to an expropriation, the mere boarding of a foreign vessel infringes upon the right to property to a considerably lower degree.

However, it is submitted that the Law of the Sea with its freedom of navigation significantly limits the exercise of jurisdiction on the high seas (*cf.* Art. 92 LOSC) and that the comparison to the protection of aliens on foreign territory suffices to weigh in favour of an individual right of private entities interested in the navigation of a vessel to claim compensation in cases of interferences with navigation.

Nonetheless, international human rights law has not yet established a customary right to property against the State of nationality. In analogy, one might argue that private entities do not enjoy a right to claim compensation against their own flag State if this State interferes with the navigation of their vessels. This underlines the preliminary result reached above that the flag State, the sole entity entitled to freedom of navigation, remains an important actor in the relationship between private entities, their flag State and the interfering State.

7. Conclusion

The context of the analyzed provisions shows that, if the wording of a compensation provision mentions the term "ship" or "vessel", a private entity might be entitled to claim compensation first because private entities have increasingly acquired rights in public international law and even invoked the violation of these rights before international institutions and secondly because both the Law of the Sea and the Law on the Protection of Foreign Investment show that even without the violation of a primary right of its own, private entities may nevertheless enjoy a certain protection, particulary by the possibility to claim compensation from the interfering State.

However, since the freedom of navigation constitutes an exclusive right of the flag State and since this right is so closely linked to any right to compensation in cases of interferences on the high seas, this analysis has also shown that no private entity may claim compensation against its own flag State in the case of such interference. Evidently, this only applies to the compensation provisions relevant for this study and do not affect other available remedies, *e.g.*, under domestic law.

8. Meaning of "the ship"

The above considerations have nevertheless not been able to clarify the meaning of the term "the ship". A contextual interpretation might also help clarifying the meaning of this term. There are some definitions of "the ship" in international law,[174] but these do not help to determine an entity entitled to claim compensation

---

[173] *Cf. Brownlie*, Ian, "Principles of Public International Law" (6th ed., Oxford: Oxford University Press, 2003), at 508-509; *Jennings*, Robert/*Watts*, Arthur, "Oppenheim's International Law", Vol. 2 (9th ed., Harlow: Longman, 1992), at 911-912.

[174] *Cf. Hasselmann*, Cord-Georg, "Die Freiheit der Handelsschiffahrt" (Kehl am Rhein: Engel, 1986), at 55-61; *Gidel*, Gilbert, "Le droit international de la mer", Vol. 1 (Paris-Châteauroux: Mellottée, 1932), at 70.

because they distinguish the ship from other structures on the sea rather than identify a legal personality. The German law implementing MARPOL stipulates in Art. 1 c that the term "ship" in Art. 7, para. 2 MARPOL includes the owner and the operator of the ship.[175] Even though this interpretation indicates that an international maritime convention, in particular MARPOL, may entitle the shipowner as a private entity, the interpretation is limited to one party and to one convention only and therefore only has indicative value concerning the compensation provisions most relevant for this study.

Possible meanings of these provisions are a) that the ship herself is granted a legal personality, b) that the shipowner and/or some other private entities interested in her operation may claim compensation or c) that the provision catches all of them depending on the legal system where compensation is claimed.

None of the conventions containing the relevant compensation provisions explicitly provides for the possibility that either the ship or another private entity may settle its dispute with the interfering State before an international forum. The possibility of ITLOS jurisdiction (*supra*) has thus far remained hypothetical. Hence, the claimant will either have to rely on diplomatic protection by his State of nationality (most probably the flag State) or will have to pursue his claim before a domestic court. Such domestic court would in principle apply domestic law. Since a definition in public international law of the term "the ship" is missing, the interpretation of the term may therefore as well consider domestic legal systems.

If one takes into account the maritime laws of different States, it becomes apparent that only in some States, such as the United States[176] or the United Kingdom,[177] the ship has a legal personality. While the typical *in rem* action in the United States and the United Kingdom only knows the ship as defendant, the ship may even pursue claims in the French legal system.[178] The German legal system, on the other hand, does not grant any legal personality to the ship.

The national maritime laws thus significantly differ. According to most laws, the ship has no legal personality and thus could not claim compensation from another party.[179] The drafters of Art. 110, para. 3 LOSC and of similar compensation provisions probably were not willing to introduce new legal personalities into domestic remedies. Instead, it seems most likely that the drafters aimed to leave it to each domestic law to determine who will be entitled to claim compensation from the interfering State. The only precondition derived from Art. 110, para. 3

[175] Gesetz zu dem Internationalen Übereinkommen von 1973 zur Verhütung der Meeresverschmutzung durch Schiffe und zu dem Protokoll von 1978 zu diesem Übereinkommen, Art. 1 lit. c, 18 September 1998, BGBl. II, at 2546.

[176] *Schoenbaum*, Thomas J., "Admiralty and Maritime Law", Vol. 2 (4th ed., St. Paul: Thomson West, 2004), at 401.

[177] *Hill*, Christopher, "Maritime Law" (6th ed., London: LLP, 2003), at 88.

[178] *Rodière*, René/*du Pontavice*, Emmanuel, "Droit maritime" (12th ed., Paris: Dalloz, 1997), at 39; *Werner*, Auguste-Raynald, "Traité de droit maritime général" (Genève: Droz, 1964), at 190-194.

[179] *Cf. Lagoni*, Rainer, "Der Hamburger Hafen, die internationale Handelsschiffahrt und das Völkerrecht", 26 AVR (1988), pp. 261 *et seq.*, at 295.

LOSC could be that the person claiming compensation must have suffered damage or loss caused by the interference with the navigation of the vessel. Thus, one might agree with Judge *Rao* that "the expression 'ship' here is a symbolic reference to everything on the ship and every person involved or interested in the operations of the ship. In short, all interests directly affected by the wrongful arrest of a ship are entitled to be compensated for any loss or damage that may have been sustained by such arrest."[180]

However, one must also take into consideration that cargo interests may recur to contractual remedies against the shipowner or bare boat charterer in the case of damage caused by a governmental interference with navigation on the high seas. Furthermore, for the sake of legal certainty, it seems reasonable that the interfering State is only faced with a limited number of claimants. Finally, the term "ship" itself makes it hard to include anybody owning a piece of property on the ship. Therefore, it is submitted that if the domestic legal system does not recognize the legal personality of the ship herself, then only the shipowner or the bareboat charterer may rely on one of the relevant compensation provisions as private individuals.

III. Object and purpose

As the third method under Art. 31 VCLT, the object and purpose of the relevant compensation provisions will be considered in their interpretation. Without having recourse to the *travaux préparatoires* though, one may only make a few presumptions about these provisions.

First, one ought to presume that drafters and States parties had more in mind than merely duplicating the pre-existing principles on State responsibility. Otherwise, the Law of the Sea Convention would not stipulate in Art. 304 LOSC that "[t]he provisions of this Convention regarding responsibility and liability for damage are without prejudice to the application of existing rules and the development of further rules regarding responsibility and liability under international law."

Secondly, the compensation provisions are all related to the establishment of new permissions to interfere with navigation on the high seas. As such, they are emblematic of the great concern for the freedom of navigation that arises any time a new permission for interferences is discussed. One purpose of the compensation provisions therefore is to deter potential boarding States from undertaking any abusive interferences and thereby from undermining the freedom of navigation. Such deterrence would probably be more efficient if an interfering State were not only concerned by potential claims of the other flag State, but would also face claims by private entities who suffered damage resulting from the interference.

Thirdly, another purpose of the provisions could be to strengthen the protection of maritime transport. The preamble of the Law of the Sea Convention implicitly

[180] *The M/V "Saiga" (No. 2) (St. Vincent and the Grenadines v. Guinea)*, Separate Opinion Rao, ITLOS Reports 1999, pp. 126 *et seq.*, at 130, para 15.

recognizes this importance since it aims to "facilitate international communication." Concerning this protection, it would definitely be useful for private entities involved in maritime transport if they had the opportunity to claim compensation from States interfering with their navigation without having to rely on their flag States.

Hence, the interpretation of object and purpose, weak as it may be, strengthens the preliminary results achieved by having recourse to the other methods under Art. 31 VCLT.

IV. Preparatory work

According to an interpretation under Art. 31 VCLT, there are thus strong arguments derived from all three methods in favour of a direct right of vessels at least under Arts. 110, para. 3, 111, para. 8 LOSC and similar provisions. This result may be confirmed by recourse to "supplementary means of interpretation, including the preparatory work of the treaty and the circumstances of its conclusion" (Art. 32 VCLT). This analysis will start with a study of the *travaux préparatoires* of the Law of the Sea Convention, before it will then deal with the other, more special conventions.

1. The Law of the Sea Convention

Arts. 106, 110, para. 3 and Art. 111, para. 8 LOSC were verbatim taken over from the 1958 Convention on the High Seas (CHS).[181] During the Third Conference on the Law of the Sea, it was the common understanding that most of the CHS provisions "must remain in force ... and should be incorporated in any new comprehensive convention."[182] Thus, these provisions were never questioned during the conference. In fact, their exact wording was already used for the text presented by the chairman of the Second Committee[183] and in the Single Negotiating Text presented by the President of the Conference.[184] Thus, the *travaux préparatoires* of the LOSC are not very useful in the interpretation of Arts. 106, 110, para. 3 and 111, para. 8 LOSC.

For that reason, one must go back to the drafting of the CHS. This convention was elaborated by the International Law Commission. As far as it concerns the predecessors of Arts. 110, para. 3 and Art. 111, para. 8 LOSC, the provisions of

---

[181] "Convention on the High Seas", adopted on 29 April 1958, UNTS, Vol. 450, pp. 11 *et seq.*; 62 states parties, <http://untreaty.un.org>.

[182] *UN* Doc. A/CONF.62/C.2/L.54, "Working Paper on the High Seas by Belgium, Denmark, France, Germany (Federal Republic of), Ireland, Italy, Luxembourg, Netherlands and United Kingdom of Great Britain and Northern Ireland" (12 August 1974), reprinted in Third United Nations Conference on the Law of the Sea, Official Records, Vol. 3 (1975), p. 229.

[183] *UN* Doc. A/CONF.62/WP.8/REV.1/PART II, Arts. 94, 98(3) and 99(8).

[184] *UN* Doc. A/CONF.62/WP.10, Arts. 106, 110(3) and 111(8).

the CHS are original drafts by the International Law Commission and the First United Nations Conference on the Law of the Sea. The 1930 Draft Convention on the Legal Status of the Territorial Sea, which was negotiated by the Conference for the Codification of International Law of the League of Nations, contained an article on hot pursuit, but no provision on the responsibility of the interfering state.[185]

Concerning the predecessor of Art. 106 LOSC, the special rapporteur of the ILC, *J.P.A. François*, in preparing the articles on piracy, had heavily relied on the Draft Convention on Piracy prepared by the Harvard Research in International Law and the Comment to the Draft by Professor *Brigham*.[186] In this draft convention,[187] both Art. 10 (dealing with liability for the seizure of pirate ships) and Art. 11, para. 2 (dealing with liability for visit and search of pirate ships) expressly stipulate that "the state making the [interference/seizure] shall be liable to the state to which the ship belongs". The comment to these articles underlines the impression that the concerns of States were dominant in the drafting of the provisions. The comment takes account of a then-existing view in the doctrine that "a war ship may stop and search and even seize a foreign ship on the high sea on suspicion of piracy without liability".[188] However, the comment denies this view because "the great majority of states would refuse to concede an unconditional right of visit or seizure" since "the dangers of loss and annoyance to commerce and of international friction from officious inspection of ships on the high sea by foreign cruisers or police boats greatly outweigh the chances of a pirate here and there escaping capture of the deterring influence of liability under this Article."[189] Even though the comment thus cautiously recognizes the importance of free navigation for "commerce", it clearly argues by exclusively referring to the concerns of governments. This also reflects the then-existing predominance of the sovereignty of States in public international law with little concern for the interests of individuals. It also confirms the already quite unequivocal wording of the provisions in the draft conventions. Since *J.P.A. François* considered both the draft convention and its commentary, their reasoning underlies the whole drafting history of Art. 106 LOSC.

As far as it concerns the predecessor to Art. 110, para. 3 LOSC, the special rapporteur chose a totally different wording and proposed a draft article in his provisional articles which was very similar to the contemporary Art. 110, para. 3 LOSC

185 *Cf. Berg*, Andreas, "Die Kodifikationsbemühungen des Völkerbundes auf dem Gebiet des Seerechts" (Hamburg, 1999), at 160; *Lagoni*, Rainer, "Zum Recht der Nacheile (Art. 111 SRÜ)", in *Epping*, Volker *et al.* (eds.), "Brücken bauen und begehen – Festschrift für Knut Ipsen" (München: Beck, 2000), pp. 213 *et seq.*, at 216.

186 *UN* Doc. A/CN.4/SER.A/1955, "Summary Records of the Seventh Session", reprinted in Yearbook of the International Law Commission (1955-I), at 19, 25; *UN* Doc. A/3159 (1956), "Report of the International Law Commission", reprinted in Yearbook of the International Law Commission (1956-II), at 253, 282.

187 "Draft Convention on Piracy", reprinted in 26 AJIL Supplement (1932), at 742.

188 Comment on Arts. 10, 11 Draft Convention on Piracy, reprinted in 26 AJIL Supplement (1932), at 838, 839.

189 *Ibid.*

and which indicated a right of the ship.[190] Even though both the Netherlands[191] and Norway[192] complained that Art. 19 of the provisional articles (the predecessor of Art. 106 LOSC) and Art. 21, para. 3 of the provisional articles (the predecessor of Art. 110, para. 3 LOSC) used different terms and even though the ILC agreed that Art. 21, para. 3 of the provisional articles should be amended accordingly,[193] Art. 46, para. 3 of the final ILC draft retained the same terminology.[194] Later, in its commentary to this article, the ILC even wrote that "[t]he State to which the warship belongs must compensate the merchant ship..."[195]

The matter was then submitted to the First United Nations Conference on the Law of the Sea. During this conference, Norway repeated its complaint about the difference between the provisions concerning the seizure of pirate ships and the right to visit.[196] Again, no changes occurred.[197] Furthermore, the predecessor of Art. 111, para. 8 LOSC was added on the demand of the United Kingdom[198] because compensation in cases of wrongful hot pursuit was "just as necessary ... as in Art. 46 [right of visit]".[199] The final article on hot pursuit as adopted by the Conference (Art. 23, para. 8 CHS) was similar to the provision on compensation for wrongful boarding in that it stipulated that the ship "shall be compensated".

What results can be drawn from these *travaux préparatoires*? Obviously, little attention has been paid to compensation issues by the drafters of the predecessors of Art. 110, para. 3 LOSC and Art. 111, para. 8 LOSC. The First Conference on the Law of the Sea was furthermore marked by a lack of time. The statement by *J.P.A. François* and the reaction by the ILC are also very telling. The members of the ILC agreed that the provision concerning the right of visit should be amended.

---

190 "1955 Report of the International Law Commission to the General Assembly", Art. 21(3), reprinted in Yearbook of the International Law Commission (1955-II), at 26.

191 *UN* Doc. A/CN.4/99/Add.1 (16 March 1956), "Comments by the Netherlands on the provisional articles concerning the regime of the High Seas", reprinted in: Yearbook of the International Law Commission (1956-II), at 62, 65.

192 *UN* Doc. A/CN.4/99/Add. 1, "Letter dated 27 March from the Permanent Mission of Norway to the United Nations", reprinted in Yearbook of the International Law Commission (1956-II), at 67.

193 *UN* Doc. A/CN.4/SER.A/1956, "Summary Records of the 343rd meeting", Yearbook of the International Law Commission 1956-I, at para. 66.

194 *UN* Doc. A/3159, "1956 Report of the International Law Commission to the General Assembly", reprinted in Yearbook of the International Law Commission (1956-II), pp. 253 *et seq.*, at 261.

195 *Ibid.*, at 284.

196 "Statement by Mr. Seyersted (United Kingdom), Twenty-eighth meeting" 9 April 1958), United Nations Conference on the Law of the Sea, Official Records, Vol. 4 (1958), at 79, para. 28.

197 The Norwegian proposal was rejected 19 votes to 13, with 20 abstentions. "Twenty-ninth meeting" (10 April 1958), United Nations Conference on the Law of the Sea, Official Records, Vol. 4 (1958), at 84.

198 *UN* Doc. A/CONF.13/C.2/L.96/Rev.1.

199 "Statement by Mr. Grant (United Kingdom), Twenty-eighth meeting" (9 April 1958), United Nations Conference on the Law of the Sea, Official Records, Vol. 4 (1958), at 79, para. 4. Israel had a similar proposal, *ibid.*, at 82, para. 34.

However, an explanation why the drafters omitted to redraft the predecessor of Art. 110, para. 3 LOSC is hard to find. One could even presume that there were indeed some cautious proponents of a right of the ship because the commentary quite clearly underlines the terminology of the provision ("the State must compensate … the ship").

While the *travaux préparatoires* concerning Art. 106 LOSC rather clearly confirm that no right of a private entity to claim compensation is granted by the provision, the interpretation of the *travaux préparatoires* of both Art. 110, para. 3 and Art. 111, para. 8 LOSC is quite inconclusive. Neither does it confirm the result achieved by the interpretation under Art. 31 VCLT, nor is it able to seriously question it.

2. The Intervention Convention

The considerable doubts as to the substantial meaning of Art. VI Intervention Convention (*supra*) could be lifted by having recourse to the *travaux préparatoires* of the convention. The Intervention Convention, together with its private law counterpart, the International Convention on Civil Liability for Oil Pollution Damage, represents a reaction to the 1967 *Torrey Canyon* incident. On 8 May 1967, the Council of the Inter-Governmental Maritime Consultative Organization (the predecessor of the International Maritime Organization) decided to study as a matter of urgency and to report on, *inter alia*, the following: "The extent to which a State directly threatened or affected by a casualty which takes place outside its territorial sea can, or should be enabled to, take measures to protect its coastline, harbours, territorial sea or amenities, even when such measures may affect the interests of shipowners, salvage companies and insurers and even of a flag government."[200]

An Ad Hoc Legal Committee, which later became the regular Legal Committee of the IMO, was created and decided, on its first session on 21 June 1967 that "member governments should summarize their national legislation and regulatory practice"[201] The United Kingdom and Germany expressed their intention to offer guidance papers on the issue.[202] The United States submitted a working paper which clearly outlined that no authority exists to take action on the high seas.[203]

The Legal Committee then split up into two informal working groups, one of them dealing with public law matters under the chairmanship of Professor *W. Riphagen* (Netherlands). During the First Session of this Working Group, the United Kingdom submitted a guidance paper proposing conditions justifying a coastal State to take action on the high seas in order to forestall pollution. As safe-

200 *IMCO* Doc. C/ES.III/5 (8 May 1967), "Conclusions of the Council on the Action to be taken on the problems brought to light by the los of the 'Torrey Canyon'", item 15.

201 *IMCO* Doc. LEG I/5 (23 June 1967), "Ad Hoc Legal Committee, First Session, Report to the Council", at 2.

202 *Ibid.*, at 3.

203 *IMCO* Doc. LEG I/WP.1 (21 June 1967), "Existing Authority and Limitations for United States Actions in 'Torrey Canyon Type'".

guards to maritime transport, the guidance paper proposed the principle of proportionality and an obligation of the coastal State to compensate the shipowner and other interested parties for action in violation of the principle of proportionality.[204] The working group endorsed these draft provisions and submitted that a multilateral convention covering these matters should be envisaged.[205] The Legal Committee adhered to these proposals and called for an diplomatic conference.[206]

While these first proposals do not indicate the entity entitled to claim compensation, some comments by delegates tend to favour the entitlement of private entities. Thus, the Liberian delegation wondered whether the right to compensation was not illusory because it seemed unlikely that a State would agree to arbitration in a dispute with a private party of another State's nationality.[207] Australian authorities stated that "[i]f a State has undisputed authority to deal with any pollution in a manner which it deems best in its national interest, it would appear to be a natural corollary that *a shipowner should be protected against any economic loss* that the action of the affected State might occasion, provided that the disaster was not due to the negligence of himself or his servants…" (emphasis added).[208]

The first draft article VI then stipulated that "[a] State which takes measures or purports to take measures falling within the scope of this Convention, which are not justified by its provisions, shall pay compensation for any financial loss suffered thereby."[209] During the Third Session of the Working Group, the United Kingdom noted that no indication was given as to whom compensation should be paid and suggested that the words "to any State or any person physical or corporate" be included.[210] Belgium seemed to favour the entitlement of a private entity

---

204 *IMCO* Doc. LEG/WG(I).I/WP.1 (15 August 1967), "Right of the Coastal State to take Action to forestall pollution or other damage, United Kingdom Guidance Paper", at 3. *Cf.* also the following comment by Greece: "In the event of a casualty due to force majeure or fortuitous circumstances, the shipowner should be entitled to compensation from the threatened State for any undue damage to his ship caused by action of this State. In the same way, in the event of a casualty due to negligence of the ship's master, the shipowner should also be entitled to compensation for any undue damage to his ship caused by action of the threatened State subsequently considered as unnecessary, or for costs incurred in excess of what was actually required for forestalling pollution." *IMCO* Doc. LEG/WG(I).I/WP.8 (11 September 1967), "Comments of Kingdom of Greece on United Kingdom guidance paper", at 4.

205 *IMCO* Doc. LEG/WG(I).I/2 (18 September 1967), "Legal Committee Working Group I, First Session, Report to the Legal Committee", at 4, 6.

206 *IMCO* Doc. LEG II/4 (11 December 1967), "Legal Committee, Second Session, Conclusions reached and Future Work Programme Proposed", at 2, 3.

207 *IMCO* Doc. LEG II/SR.2 (29 December 1967), "Legal Committee, Second Session, Summary Record of the Second Meeting", at 12.

208 *IMCO* Doc. LEG II/WP.1 (20 October 1967), "Comments of Australian and Nigerian authorities on United Kingdom guidance paper", at 3.

209 *IMCO* Doc. LEG/WG(I).III/3 (31 May 1968), "Legal Committee Working Group I, Report to the Legal Committee by Working Group I on the work of its second and third sessions", Annex I, at 4.

210 *IMCO* Doc. LEG III/SR.7 (1 August 1968), "Legal Committee, Third Session, Summary Record of the Seventh Meeting", at 18.

as well since it noted that the "only legally valid course open would be for the victim to sue the coastal State through the courts [of the coastal State], and, if that failed, to rely on its own State to take its case to the international courts by exercising diplomatic protection."[211]

Spain, however, did not share these thoughts. On the contrary, its delegates stated that "the article was unnecessary since it merely repeated the principle of international liability of States under international law… If the issue at stake involved granting rights to private parties to claim compensation against a State, the Committee was entering a new field of international law which would entail considerable discussion… There was no real case for including any provision of that nature and the whole of Article VI should be deleted."[212]

As a matter the clarification, *Riphagen*, the chairman of the Working Group, assured that "[t]he question of who should be paid compensation had been left open purposely by the Working Group after consideration of an alternative text." As regards deletion of the whole, he said that he personally felt there was no need to have a separate article, since some oblique reference to the settlement of disputes was made anyway in Article VIII. On the other hand, he had no concrete objection to the article and believed that the difficulties it gave rise to were overrated.[213]

The United Kingdom then gave in and argued that there merely were presentational rather than legal reasons for the article, which made ratification more acceptable for States with large mercantile fleets. In cases of insuperable difficulties, the United Kingdom would reluctantly agree to the deletion of the Article, if it was provided elsewhere that compensation would be payable to the parties injured as a result of unjustified action.[214] Thus, the United Kingdom seems to have accepted that private parties should no more be directly entitled by the compensation provision. Only the International Chamber of Shipping (for obvious reasons) thereafter still spoke of "rights of the shipowners."[215]

Summarizing the discussion, *Riphagen* favoured keeping the provision for political reasons: "Those who wanted the article deleted did so by reason of possible drafting difficulties which were not opposed to its principle. Other delegations had reasons of substance (though no legal substance) for wanting Article VI retained and such views, he believed, should therefore take precedence."[216] Thus, Article VI of the Intervention Convention was not meant to modify the existing international law on State responsibility, but rather served the (political) purpose of deterring abusive interferences.

The Legal Committee then agreed upon the following draft article: "Any State which, within the scope of the present Convention, has taken measures in contravention of its provisions, causing damage to others, shall be obliged to pay com-

[211] *Ibid.*, at 19.
[212] *Ibid.*, at 21-22.
[213] *Ibid.*
[214] *Ibid.*, at 23.
[215] *Ibid.*, at 24.
[216] *Ibid.*, at 24.

pensation."[217] The Legal Committee also found the draft articles to be "sufficiently developed to serve as the basis of work for a diplomatic conference convened for the purpose of adopting a Convention on the subject."[218]

On 28 November 1968, the Assembly of the Inter-Governmental Maritime Consultative Organization decided to convene an international conference to consider the adoption of a convention or conventions on questions relating to marine pollution damage.[219]

Before the Conference started on 10 November 1969 in the Palais des Congrès in Brussels, States were able to send their observations on the draft articles.

Among these, the Liberian comment is most interesting. The Government of Liberia strongly urged "that there be an opportunity for direct action by private parties affected by steps taken by a coastal State and that its proposal in that respect be adopted. After all, it is the private interest which will be suffering the loss in the event of improper or disproportionate action taken by a coastal State, and such private party should not have its rights determined only by the slow and uncertain procedures of international arbitration between Governments."[220] However, this submission together with a Canadian proposal to introduce a direct action of the shipowner and cargo interests clearly failed.[221] The Canadian delegation apparently aimed at introducing a new remedy and had changed its view since in its observation of September 1969 it had still stated that "any rights implied by the freedom of navigation are proper to States and not private parties; in consequence, the flag State shall have a right to claim compensation in cases where a coastal State takes action on the high seas against a ship threatening pollution damage where such action goes beyond what is reasonably necessary to deal with the threat."[222]

During the Conference, the Committee of the Whole on the Public Law Convention negotiated the draft articles. Some statements of delegates clearly underline that Article VI Intervention Convention only grants a right to States, and not to private entities. Thus, when Canada proposed to link both the public and the private law Convention in the compensation issue, the United States argued that

[217] *IMCO* Doc. LEG III/2 (18 June 1968), "Legal Committee, Third Session, Report to the Council", Annex, at 4.

[218] *IMCO* Doc. LEG IV/6 (15 November 1968), "Legal Committee, Fourth Session, Report to the Council on the work of its third and fourth Sessions", at 2, para. 5.

[219] *IMCO* Doc. A/ES.IV/Res.171 (28 November 1968), "Convening of a Conference on 'Torrey Canyon' Matters".

[220] *IMCO* Doc. LEG/CONF/3/Add.1 (15 October 1969), "Observations and Proposals of Governments concerning Draft Articles on the Right of a Coastal State to intervene when a Casualty which causes, or might cause, pollution of the sea [by oil] occurs on the High Seas", at 7.

[221] *IMCO* Doc. LEG/CONF/C.1/SR.18 (7 May 1971), Committee of the Whole I, Summary Record of the Eighteenth Meeting, at 12-13.

[222] *IMCO* Doc. LEG/CONF/3 (September 1969), "International Conference on Marine Pollution Damage, Observations submitted by Governments on draft articles on the right of a coastal State to intervene when a casualty which causes or might cause pollution of the sea [by oil] occurs on the High Seas", at 2.

"[t]hose suggestions would mean that the *injured State* would not receive full compensation, and would give protection to the coastal State"[223] (emphasis added).

A similar proposal led Greece to the following statement: "It would confer on the coastal State the right to evade its obligation under the Convention to pay compensation to the *flag State* in respect of excessive damage..." (emphasis added).[224] Even Liberia seemed to have recognized the exclusive inter-State relationship established by Art. VI Intervention Convention: "If the shipper had entirely different national links from the vessel involved in an incident, he would not even be involved in the claims as *between the flag State and the coastal State*, and there could then be no justification for withholding the compensation due pending the settlement of the *claims by the two States*."[225]

The Committee of the Whole on the Public Law Convention made some minor amendments to the draft article and Article VI was then finally adopted by the Plenary Meeting of the Conference on 29 November 1969. The *travaux préparatoires* thus clearly indicate that Art. VI Intervention Convention was not meant to create a right of a private entity to claim compensation.

3. The Straddling Fish Stocks Agreement

On 22 December 1992, the United Nations General Assembly established the United Nations Conference on Straddling Fish Stocks and Highly Migratory Fish Stocks to negotiate, draft and adopt the Agreement for the Implementation of the Provisions of the United Nations Convention on the Law of the Sea of 10 December 1982 relating to the Conservation and Management of Straddling Fish Stocks and Highly Migratory Fish Stocks (Fish Stocks Agreement).[226] The mandate of the conference was, *inter alia*, to achieve results "fully consistent with the provisions of the United Nations Convention on the Law of the Sea."[227] The conference held six sessions (5 to 17 days each) in the period from 19 April 1993 to 4 August 1995. After the determination of issues to be covered by the Fish Stocks Agreement, the Chairman of the Conference drafted a first Negotiating Text which dealt with enforcement by flag States and regional fisheries organizations, but which did not contain any provision on compensation.[228] The succeeding negotiations focused on issues such as the precautionary approach. The next text, the Draft Agreement of 23 August 1994 again did not cover any compensation issues.[229] The provision on enforcement in the Second Draft Agreement of 11 April 1995,

[223] *IMCO* Doc. LEG/CONF/C.1/SR.17 (7 May 1971), "Committee of the Whole I, Summary Record of the Seventeenth Meeting", at 8.

[224] *IMCO* Doc. LEG/CONF/C.1/SR.18 (7 May 1971), "Committee of the Whole I, Summary Record of the Eighteenth Meeting", at 4.

[225] *Ibid.*

[226] *UN* Doc. A/RES/47/192 (29 January 1993), "United Nations Conference on Straddling Fish Stock and Highly Migratory Fish Stocks".

[227] *Ibid.*

[228] *UN* Doc. A/Conf.164/13 (23 November 1993), "First Negotiating Text".

[229] *UN* Doc. A/Conf.164/22 (23 August 1994), "Draft Agreement".

due to its contentious and innovative nature,[230] became much more detailed and was coupled with many safeguards, but again, a compensation provision was missing.[231] Finally, the Chairman of the Conference elaborated a Third Draft Agreement with the same compensation provision as was later adopted by the Conference.[232] The provision probably emanates from a conference room paper not available to the public, also drafted by the Chairman of the Conference.

It is very hard to find any reference to the compensation provision in the *travaux préparatoires*. Apparently, the delegations devoted very little attention to the issue. Only the Russian Federation, at the very start of the conference, proposed that "[m]aterial and other liability for unjustified seizure of a vessel beyond the outer limits of the exclusive economic zone should be borne by the State effecting the seizure."[233]

However, the fact that the delegations first dealt with port State enforcement and then slowly started to draft the boarding provisions including the provision on compensation leads to the presumption that they mainly took into consideration Part XII, Section 6 of the Law of the Sea Convention. This largely explains why the wording of Art. 232 LOSC seems to have been taken as an example for the compensation provision. The meaning of Art. 232 LOSC hence is of substantial value for the interpretation of Art. 21, para. 18 Fish Stocks Agreement.

Art. 232 LOSC, specifically its second sentence, clearly indicates that private entities instead of the flag State should be able to claim the responsibility of the interfering State. The provision thus "requires a State to provide for recourse in its courts against itself or its responsible agency or instrumentality."[234] Such recourse would only make sense if a private entity were the entitled claimant.

Furthermore, the *travaux préparatoires* of Art. 232 LOSC indicate an entitlement of a private entity. In the beginning of the Third United Nations Conference on the Law of the Sea, both Greece and the Federal Republic of Germany submitted proposals according to which the ship should be entitled to compensation.[235]

---

230 *Lodge*, Michael W./*Nandan*, Satya N., "Some Suggestions Towards Better Implementation of the United Nations Agreement on Straddling Fish Stocks and Highly Migratory Fish Stocks of 1995", 20 Int'l J. Mar. & Coast. L. (2005), pp. 345 *et seq.*, at 363, n. 69.

231 *UN* Doc. A/Conf.164/22/Rev.1 (11 April 1995), "Second Draft Agreement", at 19-21.

232 *UN* Doc. A/Conf.164/33 (3 August 1995), "Third Draft Agreement", at 22.

233 *UN* Doc. A/CONF.164/L.26 (26 July 1993), "Some Considerations regarding the question of securing compliance with conservation measures for straddling fish stocks and highly migratory fish stocks (Submitted by the delegation of the Russian Federation)", at 2.

234 *Oxman*, Bernard H., "Human Rights and the United Nations Convention on the Law of the Sea", 36 Colum. J. Transnat'l L. (1997), pp. 399 *et seq.*, at 420.

235 *UN* Doc. A/CONF.62/C.3/L.4 (23 July 1974), "Greece: Draft articles on the enforcement of the provisions on the protection of the marine environment", Art. 9, para. 2, reprinted in "Third United Nations Conference on the Law of the Sea, Official Records", Vol. 3, at 247, 248; *UN* Doc. A/CONF.62/C.3/L.7 (1 August 1974), "Federal Republic of Germany: draft articles on enforcement of regulations concerning the protection of the marine environment against vessel-source pollution", Art. 5, para. 4,

These proposals then led to a provision submitted by nine governments (including the Federal Republic of Germany and Greece) which was already quite similar to the later Art. 232 LOSC.[236] An attempt by the Union of Soviet Socialist Republics to adopt a provision similar to Art. VI Intervention Convention was not successful.[237] The Informal Single Negotiating Text explicitly stipulated that "[t]he coastal State must provide for recourse in its courts in respect of loss or damage from … measures … where they exceed those which were reasonably necessary in view of the existing information."[238] This wording already indicates that private entities should be able to claim damages from the coastal State in domestic courts. All later versions of the provision then contain this obligation to provide for a remedy under domestic law and implicitly insinuate a right of private entities under the provision.[239] Thus, in this regard, the Greek and German proposal prevailed and Art. 232 LOSC embodied, in a modified way, a proposal entitling private entities to claim compensation before domestic courts.

Contrary to Art. 232 LOSC though, Art. 21, para. 18 Fish Stocks Agreement does not explicitly oblige States parties to provide for effective recourse in their courts for actions in respect of damage resulting from unjustified enforcement measures. Thus, the considerations concerning the *travaux préparatoires* of Art. 232 LOSC only apply to a limited extent. One could even argue that the drafters of Art. 21, para. 18 Fish Stocks Agreement intentionally avoided the second sentence of Art. 232 LOSC in order to exclude the entitlement of a private entity. Altogether, the *travaux préparatoires* of Art. 21, para. 18 Fish Stocks Agreement therefore remain quite unclear concerning the entitlement of private entities to claim compensation.

---

reprinted in "Third United Nations Conference on the Law of the Sea, Official Records", Vol. 3, at 250, 251.

236 *UN* Doc. A/CONF.62/C.3/L.24 (21 March 1975), "Belgium, Bulgaria, Denmark, German Democratic Republic, Federal Republic of Germany, Greece, Netherlands, Poland and United Kingdom of Great Britain and Northern Ireland: draft articles on the prevention, reduction and control of marine pollution", Art. 6, para. 3, reprinted in "Third United Nations Conference on the Law of the Sea, Official Records", Vol. 4, at 210, 212.

237 *UN* Doc. A/CONF.62/C.3/L.25 (25 March 1975), "Union of Soviet Socialist Republics. Additional draft articles on prevention of pollution of the marine environment", Art. 4, para. 2, reprinted in "Third United Nations Conference on the Law of the Sea, Official Records", Vol. 4, at 212, 213.

238 *UN* Doc. A/CONF.62/WP.8/PART III (7 May 1975), "Informal single negotiating text", Art. 37, reprinted in "Third United Nations Conference on the Law of the Sea, Official Records", Vol. 4, pp. 137 *et seq.*, at 176.

239 *Cf. UN* Doc. A/CONF.62/WP.8/Rev.1/PART III (6 May 1976), "Revised single negotiating text", Art. 41, reprinted in "Third United Nations Conference on the Law of the Sea, Official Records", Vol. 5, at 173, 180; *UN* Doc. A/CONF.62/WP.10 (15 July 1977), "Informal Composite Negotiating Text", Art. 233, reprinted in "Third United Nations Conference on the Law of the Sea, Official Records", Vol. 8, pp. 1 *et seq.*, at 40.

4. The Migrant Smuggling Protocol

On 15 November 2000, the United Nations General Assembly adopted the Protocol against the Smuggling of Migrants by Land, Sea and Air, supplementing the United Nations Convention against Transnational Organized Crime (Migrant Smuggling Protocol)[240]. The Migrant Smuggling Protocol entered into force on 28 January 2004 and has, as of 7 October 2006, 100 States Parties.[241] Its Art. 9, para. 2 deals with the liability of States interfering with the navigation of vessels under foreign flags.

The *travaux préparatoires* provide for a great deal of insight into the rationale behind Art. 9, para. 2 of the Migrant Smuggling Protocol. The UN General Assembly, on 9 December 1998, established an Ad Hoc Committee to elaborate a comprehensive convention dealing with, *inter alia*, smuggling of migrants by sea.[242] For the first session of the Ad Hoc Committee, Italy and Austria submitted proposals containing a right to stop and divert foreign vessels in order to prevent the flow of individuals to the boarding State's territory.[243] Reflecting all comments and proposals during the First Session from 19 to 29 January 1999, a Draft Protocol was then elaborated with a provision very similar to the later adopted Art. 8 Migrant Smuggling Protocol, but without any compensation provision.[244] For the drafting of the predecessor of Art. 8 Migrant Smuggling Protocol, the parties derived language from Art. 17 of the United Nations Convention against Illicit Traffic in Narcotic Drugs and Psychotrophic Substances of 1988.[245] This convention, however, does not contain any compensation provision and simply leaves the international Law of the Sea unchanged, as its Art. 17, para. 11 indicates. In the Revised Draft Migrant Smuggling Protocol of 22 November 1999, no modifications relevant to the subject at hand occurred.[246]

However, during the Sixth Session of the Ad Hoc Committee, China, as one of the biggest flag States apparently concerned about abusive interferences with navigation, proposed to include the following compensation provision: "If a suspicion proves to be unfounded and the vessel being suspected has not committed any act to justify further suspicion, a State Party that has taken action in accor-

---

240 *UN* Doc. A/RES/55/25, "Annex III to the United Nations Convention against Transnational Organized Crime".

241 <www.unodc.org/unodc/en/crime_cicp_signatures_migrants.html>.

242 *UN* Doc. A/RES/53/111 (20 January 1999), "Resolution 53/111".

243 *UN* Doc. A/AC.254/4/Add.1 (15 December 1998), "Draft elements for an international legal instrument against illegal trafficking and transport of migrants, Proposal submitted by Austria and Italy".

244 *UN* Doc. A/AC.254/4/Add.1/Rev.1 (13 May 1999), Draft Protocol against the Smuggling of Migrants by Land, Air and Sea, Supplementing the United Nations Convention against Transnational Organized Crime.

245 *UN* Doc. A/AC.254/4/Add.1/Rev.1 (13 May 1999), "Draft Protocol against the Smuggling of Migrants by Land, Air and Sea, Supplementing the United Nations Convention against Transnational Organized Crime", at 7-9, notes 27-43.

246 *UN* Doc. A/AC.254/4/Add.1/Rev.3 (22 November 1999), "Revised draft Protocol against the Smuggling of Migrants by Land, Air and Sea,2 Supplementing the United Nations Convention against Transnational Organized Crime".

dance with this article shall make compensation for any loss or damage that may have been sustained to that vessel."[247] This proposal copied parts of Art. 110, para. 3 LOSC, but avoided the language indicating a potential legal personality and an entitlement of the vessel. Thus, the Chinese delegation seems to have favoured the traditional approach to State responsibility as a relationship between States only. Furthermore, the proposal replaced the term "ship" by the term "vessel" in order to maintain consistency in the terminology of the Protocol.[248] This latter modification therefore has no substantial meaning.

The Ad Hoc Committee did not entirely accept the Chinese submission. Instead, the new draft of 27 December 1999 stipulated: "Where measures taken pursuant to this Protocol prove to be unfounded, the vessel shall be compensated for any loss or damage that may have been sustained, provided that the vessel has not committed any act justifying the measures taken."[249] This draft clearly rejects the Chinese approach concerning the entitlement of the vessel and confirms the wording of Art. 110, para. 3 LOSC in this regard. Apparently, the wide majority of delegations in the committee favoured an entitlement of the vessel or of private entities related to her.

During the ninth session of the Ad Hoc Committee, some delegations expressed concerns with respect to who might be able to claim compensation, from whom and in what forum; furthermore, some delegations were unsure whether the term "the vessel" meant the shipowner or another party.[250] However, there was consent that the compensation provision should be in line with the existing Law of the Sea as stipulated in Art. 110, para. 3 LOSC and the draft remained unchanged.[251] Apparently, all delegations presumed that the right to compensation does not belong to the flag State, but to either the shipowner or another party.

On the eleventh and last session of the Ad Hoc Committee, the provision was subject to some last minor amendments before the draft Protocol was approved on 24 October 2000.[252]

The *travaux préparatoires* thus clearly confirm the results of the interpretation according to Art. 31 VCLT. Under certain circumstances, the Migrant Smuggling Protocol grants a right to claim compensation to private entities who directly suffered damages resulting from an interference with the navigation of a vessel. At the same time, the *travaux préparatoires* of the Migrant Smuggling Protocol also

---

247 *UN* Doc. A/AC.254/5/Add.15 (24 November 1999), "Proposals and contributions received from Governments, Addendum", at 2.

248 *UN* Doc. A/AC.254/4/Add.1/Rev.4 (27 December 1999) "Revised draft Protocol against the Smuggling of Migrants by Land, Air and Sea,2 Supplementing the United Nations Convention against Transnational Organized Crime", at 13, note 102.

249 *Ibid.*

250 *UN* Doc. A/AC.254/4/Add.1/Rev.6 (19 July 2000), "Revised draft Protocol against the Smuggling of Migrants by Land, Air and Sea, Supplementing the United Nations Convention against Transnational Organized Crime".

251 *Ibid.*

252 *UN* Doc. A/55/383 (2 November 2000), "Crime Prevention and criminal justice, Report of the Ad Hoc Committee on the Elaboration of a Convention against Transnational Organized Crime on the work of its first to eleventh sessions", at 21, para. 118.

strengthen the interpretation of Art. 110, para. 3 LOSC because they constitute "subsequent practice" of States parties to the Law of the Sea Convention, interpreting Art. 110, para. 3 LOSC in the mentioned manner.

Suffice it to add that El Salvador deemed it necessary to post a reservation in regard to Art. 9, para. 2 Migrant Smuggling Protocol. It declared "that only in the event of the revision of criminal judgements shall the State, in keeping with its domestic legislation, by law compensate the victims of judicial errors that have been duly proved."[253] Doubtful as this approach may be since it seems to limit responsibility to cases of wrongful court decisions (excluding all kinds of abusive law enforcement), the reservation shows that El Salvador considers a potential liability to exist vis-à-vis the private entity who becomes a "victim" of a criminal judgment and not the flag State of the affected vessel.

5. The 2005 Protocol to the SUA Convention

The 2005 Protocol to the SUA Convention was adopted by a diplomatic conference held under the auspices of the International Maritime Organization in October 2005. During that conference, the compensation provision was neither changed nor commented. The major drafting and discussions took place in the IMO Legal Committee, a Correspondence Group and a Working Group set up by the Legal Committee.

Since negotiations took place in English, this study only considers the English versions of the relevant documents. The new SUA protocol finds its origin in Resolution A.924(22) of the IMO General Assembly which "request[ed] ... the Legal Committee ... to undertake on a high priority basis a review to ascertain whether there is a need to update the [SUA Convention]."[254] In April 2002, the Legal Committee then started to consider amendments, established a correspondence group under the leadership of the United States and invited all interested International Organizations to participate.[255] Within the correspondence group, a provision concerning the boarding of foreign vessels was quickly proposed. Many delegates demanded safeguards, but at first, a provision on compensation was not discussed.[256] Reacting to the concerns by other States, the United States proposed the following provision, basically copying Art. 110, para. 3 LOSC and Art. 22, para. 3 CHS: "Where the grounds for measures taken pursuant to this Article prove to be unfounded, the ship shall be compensated for any loss or damage that

253 <www.unodc.org/unodc/en/crime_cicp_signatures_migrants.html#declaration>.

254 *IMO* Doc. A 22/Res.924 (22 January 2002), "Review of Measures and Procedures to prevent Acts of Terrorism which threaten the Security of Passenger and Crews and the Safety of Ships", at 2.

255 *IMO* Doc. LEG/84/14 (7 May 2002), "Report of the Legal Committee on the work of its Eighty-Fourth Session", at paras. 65-76.

256 *IMO* Doc. LEG/85/11 (5 November 2002), "Report of the Legal Committee on the work of its Eighty-Fifth Session", at para. 101.

may have been sustained, provided that the ship has not committed any act justifying the measures taken."[257]

The other delegates reacted quite positively, but, probably due to the lack of jurisprudence concerning Art. 110, para. 3 LOSC, demanded further clarifications.[258] Eventually, the negotiations concerning the compensation provision turned out to become rather controversial.[259] Apparently confused by the wording, one delegation suggested that not only the ship, but individuals such as the shipowner and persons on board the ship who suffer loss or injury as a result of the boarding should be entitled to compensation in such cases; furthermore, it was noted that the current wording left it unclear as to which State, the flag State or the requesting/boarding State, should pay the compensation;[260] another delegate proposed Article 232 LOSC as a model for a provision on compensation; finally, the view was expressed that the compensation provisions might also depend on the scope of offences which might have an impact on the frequency of boardings.[261]

Bearing these suggestions in mind, the United States then modified its draft and, based on Art. 232 LOSC, proposed the following provision: "Where the grounds for measures taken pursuant to this Article prove to be unfounded, States Parties shall be liable for damage or loss attributable to them, consistent with their national laws, arising from action taken pursuant to this Article when such action is unlawful or exceeds that reasonably required in light of available information to implement the provisions of this Article, provided that the vessel has not committed any act justifying the measures taken."[262] It is interesting that this provision would have limited the responsibility in at least one respect. A State would be liable only if its national law so provides. Hence, several delegations demanded that the phrase "consistent with their national laws" should be deleted since the determination of compensation should not be limited by the law of the State which is liable for the damage or loss.[263] It was also noted that the terms might create a loophole for public vessels.[264] Since international tribunals usually do not apply national law and since public vessels do not enjoy immunity before international tribunals, these comments indicate that the delegates presumed that domestic

---

257 *IMO* Doc. LEG 86/5 (26 February 2003), "Draft amendments to the SUA Convention and Protocol Submitted by the United States", at 11.

258 *IMO* Doc. LEG/86/15 (2 May 2003), "Report of the Legal Committee on the work of its Eighty-Sixth Session", at para. 74.

259 *Wolfrum*, Rüdiger, "Hohe See und Tiefseeboden", in *Graf Vitzthum*, Wolfgang (ed.), "Handbuch des Seerechts" (München: Beck, 2006), pp. 293 *et seq.*, at 311.

260 Under the 2005 Protocol, the boarding State has to ask for permission by the flag State before it may board a vessel suspected of being involved in a criminal activity covered by the SUA Convention and its 2005 Protocol.

261 *IMO* Doc. LEG/86/15 (2 May 2003), "Report of the Legal Committee on the work of its Eighty-Sixth Session", at para. 75.

262 *IMO* Doc. LEG 87/5/1 (8 August 2003), "Draft amendments to the SUA Convention and SUA Protocol Submitted by the United States", Annex 2, at 10.

263 *IMO* Doc. LEG 87/17 (23 October 2003), "Report of the Legal Committee on the work of its Eighty-Seventh Session", at para. 127.

264 *Ibid.*, Annex 3, p. 12, note 39.

courts of the interfering State would have jurisdiction to decide on the compensation issue and that private entities should have the right to claim compensation directly from the interfering State.

New suggestions at the 87th session of the Legal Committee included that seafarers should also be entitled to compensation for any infringement of this provision and for any damage to their property.[265] Furthermore, many participants suggested that the text be shortened and clarified and reliance on Articles 232, 106, and 110, para 3 LOSC were offered as potential sources for a rewrite, as well as the explicit text of the Fish Stocks Agreement.[266]

The United States showed some reluctance to change its draft and only modified it slightly. This draft was again heavily criticized because of its continued reference to national law and because, allegedly like imprecise provisions in other conventions, it inadequately protected the shipowner against delays and damage to the ship.[267] Mexico proposed the creation of a direct action against liable States and the obligation to provide for speedy arrangements for dealing with claims in national legal systems.[268] However, these proposed changes were meant to introduce an own remedy with its own arbitral procedure which need to be distinguished from the material right to claim compensation. The Legal Committee sent the provisions to an inter-sessional working group.

During the first meeting of this working group, Mexico proposed a draft establishing joint and several liability of boarding and authorizing State and a direct action for all interested claimants.[269] This proposal, which would have provided for the liability of the flag State vis-à-vis ships under its own flag, was rejected by many other delegates.[270]

Apparently frustrated with the debates, Brazil[271] and Germany[272] submitted proposals based on Art. 110, para. 3 LOSC. However, other delegations found the issue to be more complex and proposed to include provisions on dispute settlement with access to arbitration or an international tribunal, clarification of the

---

265 *IMO* Doc. LEG 87/5/2 (11 September 2003), "Submission by the International Confederation of Free Trade Unions (ICFTU)", at para. 14.

266 IMO Doc. LEG 87/17 (23 October 2003), "Report of the Legal Committee on the work of its Eighty-Seventh Session", Annex 3, at 12, note 41.

267 *IMO* Doc. LEG 88/13 (18 May 2004), "Report of the Legal Committee on the work of its Eighty-Eighth Session", at paras. 74-76.

268 *IMO* Doc. LEG 88/3/1 (19 March 2004), "Comments and proposals submitted by Mexico", at para. 8.

269 *IMO* Doc. LEG/SUA/WG.1/2/8, "Suggested amendment to article 8bis 8b (Safeguards) submitted by Mexico", at para. 5.

270 *IMO* Doc. LEG/SUA/WG.1/3 (26 July 2004), "Report of the Working Group", at para. 96.

271 *IMO* Doc. LEG/SUA/WG.1/2/4 (9 July 2004), "Draft amendments to the SUA Convention and SUA Protocol, Comments on US delegation's proposed revisions to the proposed Protocol to the SUA Convention (Annex 1) Submitted by Brazil", at para. 14.

272 *IMO* Doc. LEG/SUA/WG.1/WP.8 (15 July 2004), "Proposal regarding Article 8bis paragraph (c) submitted by Germany".

applicable national law and jurisdictions available to the claimant and a means of ensuring the execution or enforcement of court judgements.[273] The working group could not agree on a new draft.

During the 89th session of the Legal Committee in October 2004, Mexico proposed another rather detailed article on compensation including a right of direct action and a private arbitration system.[274] This proposal found no support because some States were constitutionally prohibited to implement such an arbitration scheme and because it contradicted provisions of the draft protocol according to which the authorizing flag State may subject its authorization to conditions, also relating to liability.[275] Furthermore, the direct action is a particularity of marine insurance, and as such alien to public international law. However, the comments show that delegates considered a direct right of the ship against any interfering State to be existent.

Germany suggested that the following phrase from Art. 232 LOSC should be added: "State Parties shall provide for recourse for actions in respect of such damage or loss."[276] This suggestion received some in principle support.[277] The United States considered these opinions and proposed the following draft article: "[States Parties] shall be liable for any damage or loss attributable to them arising from measures taken pursuant to this Article when: (i) the grounds for such measures prove to be unfounded, provided that the ship has not committed any act justifying the measures taken; or (ii) such measures are unlawful or exceed that reasonably required in light of available information to implement the provisions of this Article. States Parties shall provide for effective recourse in respect of such damage." The additional sentence introduces the obligation for States parties to introduce a legal remedy in their domestic systems.[278] This again strongly suggests a right for private entities to claim damages because an intermediary flag State exercising diplomatic protection is no more necessary in such a procedure.

When the Intersessional Working Group met for its second session in early 2005, one of the few remaining issues was whether it was necessary to clarify the liable entity. Some delegations were concerned that the flag State could be liable for its mere authorization; other delegations alleged that the flag State could only be liable if, for example, it was acting as the boarding State, or the damage or loss

---

[273] *IMO* Doc. LEG/SUA/WG.1/3 (26 July 2004), « Report of the Working Group", at para. 97.

[274] *IMO* Doc. LEG 89/4/2 (17 September 2004), "Draft article 8bis, paragraph 8(b) (Security measures and compensation) submitted by Mexico", at para. 11.

[275] *IMO* Doc. LEG 89/16 (4 November 2004), "Report of the Legal Committee on the work of its Eighty-Ninth Session", at para. 74.

[276] *IMO* Doc. LEG 89/WP.4 (25 October 2004), "Submission by Germany", at para. 1.

[277] *IMO* Doc. LEG 89/16 (4 November 2004), "Report of the Legal Committee on the work of its Eighty-Ninth Session", at para. 77.

[278] *Cf. Kieserman*, Brad J., "Preventing and Defeating Terrorism at Sea: Practical Considerations for Implementation of the Draft Protocol to the Convention for the Suppression of Unlawful Acts Against the Safety of Maritime Navigation (SUA)", in *Nordquist*, Myron H. *et al.* (eds.), "Recent Developments in the Law of the Sea and China" (Leiden: Nijhoff, 2006), pp. 425 *et seq.*, 448.

was attributable to a condition it imposed on the boarding authorization, or if it granted authorization on grounds that proved to be unfounded.[279] To protect the flag State from liability merely for authorizing a boarding in accordance with the protocol, some delegations proposed the addition of the following terms: "The authorization to boarding by a flag State shall not per se amount to its liability."[280] This shows that the delegates were of the opinion that the freedom of navigation belongs to the flag State and that only the violation of other rights might lead to its liability.

Greece then proposed to stipulate that courts in both the flag State and the boarding State would have jurisdiction to award damages.[281] This proposal did not succeed and one can therefore presume that the courts of the interfering State would remain competent to decide on the compensation issue.

The provision resulting from the Second Meeting was almost identical to the final outcome of the Diplomatic Conference adopting the new SUA Protocol. The only drafting change after the Second Meeting was to add the words "harm or loss" at the end of the second sentence as a technical correction in order to achieve consistency.[282]

Any later discussions in the Legal Committee did not change the terms of the provision, but may nevertheless be interesting concerning its interpretation. Thus, the Chinese delegation insisted that in some jurisdictions, it is very difficult to recover pure economic loss incurred as a result of delays; in view of the traditional construction of the words "loss or damage" in relevant provisions of the transport conventions, it would be necessary to insert the word "delay" after "loss or damage".[283] Even though some delegations had pointed out that "loss or damage" should be interpreted to cover the concept of delay, it would have been helpful, according to China, to have "delay" explicitly stated in order to minimize any undesirable misinterpretation."[284] The lack of support shows that the Chinese concerns have not been convincing.[285] It also underlines that it will be for domestic courts to decide on compensation issues.

On 14 October 2005, the diplomatic conference adopted the protocol revising the SUA Convention without much discussion about the compensation provision even though the conference was more "politically charged" than any other IMO Conference.[286] The protocol will be open to signature from 14 February 2006 (four

---

[279] *IMO* Doc. LEG/SUA/WG.2/4 (9 February 2005), "Report of the Working Group", at para. 62.

[280] *Ibid.*, at para. 64.

[281] *IMO* Doc. LEG/SUA/WG.2/WP.5 (1 February 2005), "Submission by Greece".

[282] *IMO* Doc. LEG/90/15 (9 May 2005), "Report of the Legal Committee on the work of its Ninetieth Session", at para. 96.

[283] *IMO* Doc. LEG/90/4/6 (18 March 2005), "Comments and proposals submitted by China", at para. 5.

[284] *Ibid.*

[285] *Cf. IMO* Doc. LEG/90/15 (9 May 2005), "Report of the Legal Committee on the work of its Ninetieth Session", at para. 95.

[286] *IMO* Doc. LEG/CONF.15/INF.5 (21 October 2005), "Closing State of E.E. Mitropoulos, IMO Secretary-General".

months after conclusion of the diplomatic conference!) to 13 February 2007 (Art. 17(1) of the Protocol) and the amendments will enter into force ninety days following the date on which twelve States have either signed it without reservation as to ratification, acceptance or approval, or have deposited an instrument of ratification (Art. 18(1) of the Protocol). It will thus take a considerable amount of time for the new provisions to become effective.

V. Conclusion

As a result of this interpretation, shipowners and bareboat charterers who have directly suffered damages as a consequence of an interference with the navigation of a vessel are entitled to claim compensation under Arts. 110, para. 3 and 111, para. 8 LOSC, Art. 9, para. 2 Migrant Smuggling Protocol and Art. 8bis, para. 10, lit. b SUA Protocol. Of course, this does not mean that a private entity may sue another State before an international tribunal because generally, no jurisdiction for such a dispute exists. One must clearly distinguish between the individual right to compensation and the availability of remedies under public international or domestic law.[287] But it means at least that the interfering State has to compensate the private entities which suffered losses and has to incorporate this remedy into its domestic legal system.

Therefore, the Law of the Sea, just like other areas of public international law, recognizes the personality of private entities to a limited and precisely circumscribed extent. Unlike other areas of public international law, this special status of private entities in the Law of the Sea has remained largely undiscovered by most authors.[288]

The entitlement of a private entity does not at the same time lead to a loss of the functions of the flag State. Instead, this State may still exercise the well-accepted flag State protection and claim damages on behalf of the private entities protected by the flag. Hence, there may be a "double series of holders of the corresponding right to receive reparation", a phenomenon well known to human rights law as well.[289]

---

[287] *Mann*, Frederick Alexander, "The Consequences of an International Wrong in International and National Law", 48 BYIL(1977), pp. 1 *et seq.*, at 5.

[288] See, *e.g.*, *König*, Doris, "Questionnaire International Law of the Sea", in *Zimmermann*, Andreas *et al.* (eds.), "Unity and Diversity in International Law" (Berlin: Duncker & Humblot, 2006), pp. 27 *et seq.*, at 32; *Geiß*, Robin, "Non-State Actors: Their Role and Impact on the Fragmentation of International Law", *ibid.*, pp. 303 *et seq.*, at 325-326. See also *Wolfrum*, Rüdiger, "Hohe See und Tiefseeboden", in *Graf Vitzthum*, Wolfgang (ed.), "Handbuch des Seerechts" (München: Beck, 2006), pp. 293 *et seq.*, at 309, note 112 (wrongfully applying Art. 106 LOSC to situations covered by Art. 110 LOSC).

[289] *Pisillo Mazzeschi*, Riccardo, "International Oligations to Provide for Reparation Claims?", in *Randelzhofer*, Albrecht *et al.* (eds.), "State Responsibility and the Individual: Reparation in Instances of Grave Violations of Human Rights" (The Hague: Nijhoff, 1999), pp. 149 *et seq.*, at 152 *et seq.*

Generally, as the interpretation of the context shows, no private entity may base a claim for compensation against the flag State on any of the relevant compensation provisions. The flag State continues to be the exclusive bearer of the freedom of navigation and thus a claim for compensation in a case related to the freedom of navigation may not be directed against this flag State.

As far as it concerns Art. 106 LOSC and Art. VI Intervention Convention, they clearly only entitle the flag State to claim compensation for seizures of suspected pirate ships and for interferences in order to prevent major pollution by oil tankers. Hence, they adhere to the traditional law on State responsibility.

The substantial meaning of Art. 21, para. 18 Fish Stocks Agreement in this regard, finally, remains unclear and will hopefully be clarified by State practice or the jurisprudence of an international tribunal in the near future.

C. The act entailing responsibility: requirement of wrongfulness?

In the general law on State responsibility, the basic principle is that a breach of international law by a State entails its international responsibility.[290] Only in certain limited cases may a State bear responsibility for lawful conduct.[291] In these cases, the responsible State usually has control over a dangerous activity which causes almost unavoidable damage.[292] Interferences on the high seas do not necessarily fall under this category. However, many authors have described some of the analyzed compensation provisions as establishing State liability for the injurious consequences of lawful conduct.[293] This study will therefore attempt to determine

290 *Phosphates in Morocco*, Preliminary Objections, Judgment of 14 June 1938, PCIJ Series A/B, No. 72, pp. 10 *et seq.*, at 28; *The S.S. Wimbledon*, Judgment of 17 August 1923, PCIJ Series A, No. 1, pp. 15 *et seq.*, at 30; *Factory at Chorzów*, Merits, Judgment of 13 September 1928, PCIJ Series A, No. 17, pp. 4 *et seq.*, at 29; *Corfu Channel (United Kingdom v. Albania)*, Judgment of 9 April 1949, ICJ Reports 1949, pp. 4 *et seq.*, at 23.

291 *Cf., e.g.,* Art. VII of the 1967Outer Space Treaty, UNTS, Vol. 610, at 205; Art. II of the 1972 Convention on International Liability for Damage Caused by Space Objects, UNTS, Vol. 961, at 187.

292 *Harndt*, Raimundt, "Völkerrechtliche Haftung für die schädlichen Folgen nicht verbotenen Verhaltens" (Berlin: Duncker & Humblot, 1993), at 590; *Dupuy*, Pierre-Marie, "La responsibilité internationale des États pour les dommages d'originie technologique et industrielle" (Paris: Pedone, 1976), at 222.

293 *Sorensen*, Max, "Principes de droit international public", 101 RdC (1960-III), pp. 2 *et seq.*, at 221; *Akehurst*, Michael B., "International Liability for injurious consequences arising out of acts not prohibited by international law", 16 Netherlands Ybk. Int'l L. (1985), pp. 3 *et seq.*, at 10; *Brownlie*, Ian, "Principles of Public International Law" (6th ed., Oxford: Oxford University Press, 2003), at 234; *Treves*, Tullio, "La Navigation", in *Dupuy*, René-Jean/*Vignes*, Daniel (eds.), "Traité du nouveau droit de la mer" (Paris: Economica, 1985), pp. 687 *et seq.*, at 700; *Ipsen*, Knut, "Völkerrechtliche Verantwortlichkeit und Völkerstrafrecht", in *id.*, "Völkerrecht" (5th ed., München: Beck, 2004),

those of the compensation provisions which do indeed provide for such liability and distinguish them from the other compensation provisions which follow a more traditional approach.

I. Art. 110, para. 3 LOSC, the prototype of liability for lawful conduct in the Law of the Sea

Again, Art. 110, para. 3 LOSC, due to its overwhelming importance and due to its pioneering role for other compensation provisions, shall be the starting point for this study.

A successful claim for compensation under Art. 110, para. 3 LOSC requires that "the suspicions prove to be unfounded and ... that the ship boarded has not committed any act justifying them". Thus, while a boarding might have been justified under Art. 110, para. 1 LOSC because a "reasonable ground" for suspicions existed, the interfering state might still have to pay compensation under certain conditions. The provision in Art. 110, para. 3 LOSC therefore represents one of the few examples where a State has to pay compensation for the consequences of a lawful activity causing damage.[294] Since an internationally wrongful act is not required, one cannot, in a case of Art. 110, para. 3 LOSC, demand any fault on the part of the interfering state: its liability is strict.[295] The drafting of Art. 110, para. 3 LOSC was probably influenced by the United States Supreme Court decision on *The Marianna Flora*, which held that "the party seizes at his peril, and is liable to costs and damages if he fails to establish the forfeiture".[296]

Object and purpose of Art. 110, para. 3 LOSC is to prevent abusive interferences and to increase the degree of diligence exercised by the naval officers considering a boarding.[297] The imposition of liability for lawful conduct would definitely help achieving these purposes.

Therefore, wording, context and object and purpose of Art. 110, para. 3 LOSC quite evidently reveal that the responsibility under the provision is for lawful conduct. This interpretation is furthermore confirmed by the *travaux préparatoires*. In its comment to the draft articles by the International Law Commission, Yugoslavia demanded that "the search of merchant ships by warships should not be dis-

pp. 615 *et seq.*, at 633; *Harndt*, Raimundt, "Völkerrechtliche Haftung für die schädlichen Folgen nicht verbotenen Verhaltens" (Berlin: Duncker & Humblot, 1993), at 805; *Schröder*, Meinhard, "Verantwortlichkeit, Völkerstrafrecht, Streitbeilegung und Sanktionen", in *Graf Vitzthum*, Wolfgang, "Völkerrecht" (2nd ed., Berlin: de Gruyter, 2001), pp. 545 *et seq.*, at 559.

294 *Schröder*, Meinhard, "Verantwortlichkeit, Völkerstrafrecht, Streitbeilegung und Sanktionen", in *Graf Vitzthum*, Wolfgang, "Völkerrecht" (2nd ed., Berlin: de Gruyter, 2001), pp. 545 *et seq.*, at 559.

295 *Brownlie*, Ian, "Principles of Public International Law" (6th ed., Oxford: Oxford University Press, 2003), at 234.

296 *The Marianna Flora*, 1 Wheaton 1 (1826).

297 *Randelzhofer*, Albrecht, "Probleme der völkerrechtlichen Gefährdungshaftung", 24 Berichte der Deutschen Gesellschaft für Völkerrecht (1984), pp. 35 *et seq.*, at 49.

couraged by too strict sanctions" and wanted to insert a fault requirement.[298] The ILC rejected this demand because "this severe penalty seems justified in order to prevent the right of visit being abused."[299] Furthermore, South Africa commented that "anything less than absolute liability for damages if a vessel is boarded without justification, would be a derogation from the principle of the freedom of the high seas."[300]

Finally, the special rapporteur first proposed two different compensation provisions for boardings in cases of suspected piracy and suspected slave-trading. The later provision explicitly required an illegal measure.[301] In his sixth report, however, the special rapporteur favoured the first alternative not requiring any illegal conduct by the boarding party in respect of both grounds of interference.[302] During the discussions within the International Law Commision, the special rapporteur explained that he had chosen this text because a judge then would not have to judge the motives for the boarding.[303] The two provisions were thus merged into the predecessor of Art. 110, para. 3 LOSC. Apparently, the drafters rejected the idea that only an illegal boarding should lead to the liability of the interfering State.

Therefore, the *travaux préparatoires* clearly support the previous results of the interpretation of Art. 110, para. 3 LOSC. This provision does not require an unlawful interference by the interfering State. According to *Albrecht Randelzhofer*, Art. 22, para. 3 CHS even represents the first provision in an international convention imposing liability for lawful conduct.[304] Its importance for the interpretation of the other provisions thus is not to be underestimated. The provision furthermore represents a certain anomaly in the law on State responsibility according to which liability for lawful conduct is usually provided in cases of ultra-hazardous activities, a category mere boardings on the high seas would hardly belong to.[305]

---

298 *UN* Doc. A/CN.4/99/Add.1, "Letter dated 20 March 1956 from the Permanent Mission of Yugoslavia to the United Nations", reprinted in Yearbook of the International Law Commission (1956-II), pp. 94 *et seq.*, at 97.

299 Comment on Art. 46 of the ILC Draft, para. 3, reprinted in Yearbook of the International Law Commission (1956-II), at 284.

300 *UN* Doc. A/CN.4/99/Add.1, p. 3, 7, reprinted in Yearbook of the International Law Commission (1956-II), pp. 78 *et seq.*, at 79.

301 *UN* Doc. A/CN.4/42, p. 20, 22, reprinted in Yearbook of the International Law Commission (1951-II), at 85.

302 *UN* Doc. A/CN.4/79, "Draft Article 21, Sixième rapport de J.P.A. François", reprinted in Yearbook of the International Law Commission (1954-II), pp. 7 *et seq.*, at 14, 15.

303 *UN* Doc. A/CN.4/SR.288 (10 May 1955), "Summary records of the seventh session of the International Law Commission, 288th meeting", reprinted in Yearbook of the International Law Commission (1955-I), at 26, para. 13.

304 *Randelzhofer*, Albrecht, "Probleme der völkerrechtlichen Gefährdungshaftung", 24 Berichte der Deutschen Gesellschaft für Völkerrecht (1984), pp. 35 *et seq.*, at 49.

305 *Ibid.*, at 56.

II. Hot pursuit under Art. 111, para. 8 LOSC

The provisions in Art. 111, para. 8 LOSC and in Art. 106 LOSC might nevertheless have a different meaning. Art. 111, para. 8 LOSC requires that "the circumstances do not justify the exercise of the right of hot pursuit"/"dans des circonstances ne justifiant pas l'exercice du droit de poursuite"/"en circunstancias que no justifiquen el ejercicio del derecho de persecución"/ "в условиях, которые не оправдывают осуществления права преследования по горячим следам". Hence, according to the wording, when a measure of hot pursuit is not justified and leads to damage, the interfering State has to pay compensation. An unjustified hot pursuit *prima facie* constitutes an internationally wrongful act and thus Art. 111, para. 8 LOSC seems to be in line with the general law of State responsibility in this respect.

Concerning the object and purpose of Art. 111, para. 8 LOSC, one could take into account that hot pursuit is regarded as an extension of coastal jurisdiction and therefore probably also as a lesser intrusion into the freedom of the high seas as compared with Art. 110 LOSC. The contextual interpretation of Art. 111, para. 8 LOSC has to compare it to the wording of Art. 110, para. 3 LOSC. The fact that the terms of Art. 111, para. 8 LOSC, contrary to the terms of Art. 110, para. 3 LOSC, indicate the requirement of an unlawful measure significantly strengthens this indication.

However, the contextual interpretation also has to take account of "any relevant rules of international law applicable in the relations between the parties" (Art. 31, para. 3, lit. c VCLT). Before the adoption of the CHS, it was well established in international law that a vessel undertaking measures of hot pursuit seizes at her own peril.[306] May this rebut the presumption reached by the unequivocal wording of Art. 111, para. 8 LOSC?

A supplementary interpretation of the *travaux préparatoires* might shed some light on this issue. The provision was inserted at the First United Nations Conference on the Law of the Sea after the ILC had already submitted its draft. The United Kingdom had proposed the paragraph because "a clause providing for the payment of compensation for loss or damage sustained in the circumstances which did not justify the exercise of the right of hot pursuit was just as necessary in art. 47 [hot pursuit] as in article 46 [right of visit]."[307] However, the comment on the Israeli proposal for a similar provision shows that the delegates in the Second Committee might have been unaware of the special character of the predecessor of

[306] *The Marianna Flora*, 1 Wheaton 1 (1826); *Colombos*, Constantin John, "The International Law of the Sea" (6th ed., London: Longman, 1967), at 168; *Williams*, Glanville L., "The Juridical Basis of Hot Pursuit", 20 British. Yb. of Int'l. L. (1939), pp. 82 *et seq.*, at 96.

[307] "Statement of Mr. Grant (United Kingdom), Twenty-Eighth Meeting" (9 April 1958), para. 4, "United Nations Conference on the Law of the Sea, Official Records", Vol. 4 (1958), at 79.

Art. 110, para. 3 LOSC not requiring an internationally wrongful act.[308] Another example of this misunderstanding is the Soviet proposal during the Third United Nations Conference on the Law of the Sea for a part concerning "General Safeguards" which was to delete duplications,[309] but in fact would have eliminated the special character of Art. 110, para. 3 LOSC. The *travaux préparatoires* therefore have a very ambiguous character and do not provide for any substantial result as to the nature of Art. 111, para. 8 LOSC.

Thus, it is submitted that the interpretation of the unambiguous wording of Art. 111, para. 8 LOSC cannot be rebutted[310] by an arguable context interpretation and an unfruitful historic interpretation. Compensation under Art. 111, para. 8 LOSC need not be made if the circumstances are sufficiently suspicious to justify hot pursuit, even if the suspicions later prove to be unfounded. Only an illegal hot pursuit leads to an obligation to pay compensation under Art. 111, para. 8 LOSC.[311]

III. The seizure of pirate ships under Art. 106 LOSC

Art. 106 LOSC obliges to compensate when a pirate ship has been seized "without adequate grounds"/"sans motif suffisant"/"sin motives suficientes"/"без достаточных оснований". The exception to the freedom of the high seas concerning the seizure of pirate ships is contained in Art. 105 LOSC and (unlike Art. 110, para. 1 and 111, para. 1 LOSC) does not refer to any "adequate grounds". The wordings of Articles 105 and 106 LOSC nevertheless indicate that a seizure of a non-pirate ship without adequate grounds constitutes an internationally wrongful act which is a requirement for the obligation to compensate under Art. 106 LOSC.

However, Art. 106 LOSC stipulates that the legal consequence will be "liability". This term is nowadays often understood to be distinct from the notion of

308 "Paragraph 3 of article 46 provides for the payment of compensation in respect of loss or damage to a ship when boarded or delayed without good reason." *UN* Doc. A/CONF.13/C.2/L.116, "Proposal by Israel" (9 April 1958), reprinted in "United Nations Conference on the Law of the Sea, Official Records", Vol. 4 (1958), pp. 148 *et seq.*, at 149.

309 *UN* Doc. A/CONF.62/RCNG/2, "Informal Proposal reported by the Chairman of the Third Committee", reprinted in "Third United Nations Conference on the Law of the Sea, Official Records", Vol. 10 (1978), pp. 126 *et seq.*, at 173, 187.

310 *Cf.* the adherence of the ICJ to the textual interpretation being the most important. *Territorial Dispute (Libya /Chad),* Judgment of 13 February 1994, ICJ Reports 1994, pp. 6 *et seq.*, at para. 41; *Fitzmaurice*, Malgosia, "The practical working of the Law of Treaties", in *Evans*, Malcolm D. (ed.), "International Law" (2003), pp. 173 *et seq.*, at 186-7.

311 The same result reach Reuland and Wollenberg, though without any reference to treaty interpretation. *Reuland*, Robert C., "The Customary Right of Hot Pursuit onto the High Seas: Annotations to Article 111 of the Law of the Sea Convention", 33 Va. J. Int'l L. (1992-1993), pp. 557 *et seq.*, at 587; *Wollenberg*, Simon Friedrich Wilhelm, "Die Nacheile zur See – eine dogmatische Betrachtung", 42 AVR (2004), pp. 217 *et seq.*, at 231.

"state responsibility" in that it does not require an internationally wrongful act.[312] This is nevertheless not the ordinary meaning of the term since liability is defined as "1. The quality or state of being legally obligated or accountable; legal responsibility to another or to society, enforceable by civil remedy or criminal punishment. 2. A financial or pecuniary obligation."[313] As opposed to "strict liability", the simple term "liability" usually requires a wrongful act. Furthermore, the distinction undertaken by the International Law Commission is probably due to the fact that it preferred to leave the topic of responsibility for lawful activities for later considerations.[314] When Art. 20 CHS (the predecessor of Art. 106 LOSC) was drafted, the delegates were unaware of such a distinction. Thus, the interpretation of the term "liability" does not modify the preliminary result.

This outcome might however be contrary to object and purpose and the context of Art. 106 LOSC. An interfering state would, according to the interpretation of the wording, less likely incur liability when seizing a suspected pirate ship than when boarding a suspicious vessel. If one takes into consideration the character of the seizure of a vessel which infringes the freedom of navigation far more than a simple boarding, and if one furthermore considers that piracy is one of the suspicions named in Art. 110, para. 1 LOSC, this different regulation seems contradictory and cannot be explained by the special character of piracy as a universal crime. Furthermore, "the right of seizure [should usually] depend upon the result of the exercise of the right to search."[315] However, three other considerations equally apply. First, a seizure usually involves court proceedings in the legal system of the interfering State. This could have been seen as an adequate safeguard for free navigation not requiring any stricter liability for the interfering State in cases of seizures. Secondly, the special character of Art. 110, para. 3 LOSC may be explained by the nature of boardings which occur on the high seas and where, due to lack of judicial control, additional safeguards to prevent abuse by interfering States were deemed necessary. Thirdly, it should be important to render dispute resolution as easy as possible if the conduct the claimant is complaining of occurs on the high seas where evidence is hard to establish. Liability for lawful conduct is much easier to prove and therefore probably more adequate in cases of Art. 110 LOSC. In cases of seizures, on the other hand, the amount of damage seems to justify more complicated court proceedings.

In addition, one should consider that an inspection during a boarding is ordinarily satisfactory to determine whether the suspicions "prove to be unfounded." Any seizure nevertheless undertaken afterwards needs to be considered an internationally wrongful act. Therefore, the different meanings of Art. 106 LOSC and

---

312 *Cf. UN* Doc. A/56/10, "Report of the International Law Commission, 53rd Session" (2001), at 382.

313 Black's Law Dictionary (8th ed., St. Paul: West Group, 2004), at 932.

314 *Cf. Boyle*, Alan E., "State Responsibility and International Liability for injurious consequences of acts not prohibited by international law: A necessary distinction?", in *Provost*, René (ed.), "State Responsibility in International Law" (Aldershot: Ashgate, 2002), pp. 141 *et seq.*, at 142.

315 *Cf. The Nancy*, 37 Ct.Cl. 401 (1902).

Art. 110, para. 3 LOSC are justified by the different character of seizures and simple boardings.

An interpretation of the *travaux préparatoires* leads to the same result as concerning the question of a direct right or a personality of ships. The ILC had promised to bring the two articles concerning liability for seizure of pirate ships and for boardings of suspicious vessels into line, but omitted to do so. This might provide an argument for the two articles having the same meaning, but the supplementary interpretation of the *travaux préparatoires* cannot overrule the result of an interpretation according to Art. 31 VCLT.

Therefore, the meanings of Art. 106 and Art. 110, para. 3 LOSC significantly differ.[316] The seizure of a suspected pirate ship only leads to an obligation to compensate if no "adequate grounds" for the suspicion were present. Art. 106 LOSC thus requires an internationally wrongful act.

IV. Interferences under the Intervention Convention

Art. VI of the Intervention Convention quite explicitly requires wrongful conduct of the responsible State. According to its wording, only the State which "has taken measures in contravention of the provisions of the present Convention" is obliged to pay compensation. Thus, only an act in breach of the provisions of the Intervention Convention entails the responsibility of the interfering State.

This interpretation is confirmed by the *travaux préparatoires*. The United Kingdom in its guidance paper had proposed an obligation of the coastal State to compensate for action in violation of the principle of proportionality only.[317] Both the Working Group[318] and the Legal Committee[319] endorsed this proposal. On the third session of the Working Group, however, the following provision was drafted: "A State which takes measures or purports to take measures falling within the scope of this Convention, which are not justified by its provisions, shall pay compensation for any financial loss suffered thereby."[320] Following a proposal of Belgium, Spain and the United Kingdom, [321] the Legal Committee slightly modified the provision in the following terms: "Any State which, within the scope of the present Convention, has taken measures in contravention of its provisions,

316 No distinction in *Gureev*, S.A., "Jurisdiktion des Flaggenstaats auf Hoher See", in Akademie der Wissenschaften der UdSSR (ed.), "Modernes Seevölkerrecht" (translated by Elmar Rauch, Baden-Baden: Nomos, 1978), pp. 171 *et seq.*, at 199.

317 *IMCO* Doc. LEG/WG(I).I/2, (18 September 1967), "Legal Committee Working Group I, First Session, Report to the Legal Committee", at 4, 6.

318 *Ibid.*

319 *IMCO* Doc. LEG II/4, (11 December 1967), "Legal Committee, Second Session, Conclusions reached and Future Work Programme Proposed", at 2, 3.

320 *IMCO* Doc. LEG/WG(I).III/3 (31 May 1968), "Legal Committee Working Group I, Report to the Legal Committee by Working Group I on the work of its second and third sessions", Annex I, at 4.

321 *IMCO* Doc. LEG/WG(I).III/3 (13 June 1968), "Proposal of the Delegations of Belgium, Spain and the United Kingdom for Article VI".

causing damage to others, shall be obliged to pay compensation."[322] Thus, not only a breach of the principle of proportionality, but all violations of provisions of the Intervention Convention generally entail the responsibility of the interfering State.

Some delegates put forward the idea that compensation should not only be payable only for damage caused by measures which contravene the provisions of the proposed Convention, but that compensation should also be payable for damage caused by measures which are taken in contravention of other rules of (general and conventional) international law, if any.[323] Canada, on the contrary proposed a provision according to which "[a]ny State which has taken measures *which are inconsistent with Article V*, and which causes damage to the ship or cargo interests, shall be liable for such damage ..." (emphasis added).[324] Both proposals failed, because the majority of delegations present did neither want to extend nor restrict the scope of the compensation provision.

Finally, Norway proposed to clarify the draft article in respect of the terms "within the scope of the present Convention" because the wording may lead to the misunderstanding that a coastal State which has taken unjustified action against oil pollution may exonerate itself from liability by invoking that its action went beyond what has been provided for in Article I and V and was therefore not included in the "scope of the Convention".[325] The proposal to replace "within the scope of the present Convention, has taken measures in contravention of its provisions" with the terms "has taken measures in contravention of the provisions of the present Convention" was successful and the final wording of the provision accomplished.[326]

Hence, Art. VI of the Intervention Convention adheres to the general law on State responsibility in so far as it requires an internationally wrongful act. However, instead of merely referring to the general law on State responsibility (such as Art. 304 LOSC), Art. VI Intervention Convention limits its scope to violations of the convention as such.

---

322 *IMCO* Doc. LEG III/2 (18 June 1968), "Legal Committee, Third Session, Report to the Council", Annex, at 4.

323 *IMCO* Doc. LEG IV/6, p. 3 (15 November 1968), "Legal Committee, Fourth Session, Report to the Council on the work of its third and fourth Sessions", at 3, para. 9(b).

324 This part was to ensure that a coastal State was liable only for that part of its actions that was in excess of the action permitted under the Convention. *Cf. IMCO* Doc. LEG/CONF/C.1/SR. 11 (7 May 1971), "Committee of the Whole I, Summary Record of the Eleventh Meeting", at 13.

325 *IMCO* Doc. LEG/CONF/3 (September 1969), "International Conference on Marine Pollution Damage, Observations submitted by Governments on draft articles on the right of a coastal State to intervene when a casualty which causes or might cause pollution of the sea [by oil] occurs on the High Seas", at 35-37.

326 *IMCO* Doc. LEG/CONF/C.1/SR. 11 (7 May 1971), "Committee of the Whole I, Summary Record of the Eleventh Meeting", at 13-14.

V. Liability for interfering with the navigation of fishing vessels under the Fish Stocks Agreement

Art. 21, para. 18 Fish Stocks Agreement contains two alternatives. First, an interfering State is liable for "action taken pursuant to this article when such action is unlawful". This alternative thus clearly requires an internationally wrongful act. Under the second alternative, the action needs to have "exceed[ed] that reasonably required in the light of available information to implement the provisions of this article." Thus, the second alternative provides for liability for disproportionate measures. Does this alternative at the same time establish a liability for lawful conduct? This would mean that the principle of proportionality has not acquired the status of either a general principle of international law or of customary international law. However, the principle of proportionality has indeed, according to some authors, become a general principle of international law.[327] Since this status has nevertheless been questioned by other authors,[328] the inclusion of the principle in the compensation provision might have had clarifying effect at least.

Art. 21, para. 18 Fish Stocks Agreement basically copies Art. 232 LOSC. The negotiations in the drafting of the latter provision were very much influenced by the Intervention Convention[329] where the whole issue of proportionality played a major role. Most probably, the status of the principle of proportionality was quite uncertain at the time Art. 232 LOSC was drafted. This confirms the clarifying effect of the second alternative of Art. 232 LOSC

Therefore, it is submitted that Art. 21, para. 18 Fish Stocks Agreement codifies the principle of proportionality in its second alternative and that it considers the breach of this principle to be illicit at least under the agreement. The compensation provision thus only imposes responsibility for unlawful conduct of States parties.

VI. Interferences in order to combat Migrant Smuggling

Art. 9, para. 2 Migrant Smuggling Protocol at first sight seems to follow the character of Art. 110, para. 3 LOSC. The only difference in the wording is that

---

327 *Cf. Delbrück*, Jost, "Proportionality", in *Bernhardt*, Rudolf (ed.), "Encyclopedia of Public International Law", Vol. 3 (Amsterdam: North-Holland, 1997), pp. 1140 *et seq.*, at 1144; *Gardam*, Judith Gail, "Proportionality and Force in International Law", 87 AJIL (1993), pp. 391 *et seq.*, 393; *Krugmann*, Michael, "Der Grundsatz der Verhältnismäßigkeit im Völkerrecht" (Berlin: Duncker & Humblot, 2004), at 11.

328 *Stein*, Torsten, "Proportionality revisited – Überlegungen zum Grundsatz der Verhältnismäßigkeit im internationalen Recht", in *Dicke*, Klaus *et al.* (ed.), "Weltinnenrecht – Liber amicorum Jost Delbrück" (Berlin: Duncker & Humblot), pp. 727 *et seq.*, at 737; *Higgins*, Rosalyn, "Problems and Process – International Law and How We Use It" (Oxford: Clarendon Press, 1995), at 218, 236.

329 *Cf*, *UN* Doc. A/CONF.62/C.3/L.25 (25 March 1975), "Union of Soviet Socialist Republics, Additional draft articles on prevention of pollution of the marine environment", Art. 4, para. 2, reprinted in "Third United Nations Conference on the Law of the Sea, Official Records", Vol. 4, pp. 212 *et seq.*, at 213.

Art. 9, para. 2 Migrant Smuggling Protocol refers to the "grounds for measures taken pursuant to article 8" while Art. 110, para. 3 LOSC merely refers to "suspicions".

The reason for this difference lies in the context of both provisions. Under the Migrant Smuggling Protocol, the boarding of a foreign vessel always requires (1) the authorization or the request by the flag State to board one of its vessels and (2) "reasonable grounds to suspect that a vessel … is engaged in the smuggling of migrants by sea". If an authorization or request by the flag State is missing, the interference remains unlawful. If however, the flag State has authorized the boarding, then, according to the traditional approach to freedom of navigation, any interference with navigation becomes lawful. If the suspicions later prove to be wrong and the vessel was not engaged in the smuggling of migrants, then the interfering State nevertheless bears responsibility under Art. 9, para. 2 Migrant Smuggling Protocol. Therefore, according to the context of the provision, the nature of Art. 9, para 2 Migrant Smuggling Protocol is comparable to Art. 110, para. 3 LOSC in that a possibility exists that the interfering State may bear responsibility for lawful conduct.

This interpretation finds confirmation in the *travaux préparatoires* of the provision. The People's Republic of China first submitted the following compensation provision which copied major parts of Art. 110, para. 3 LOSC: "If a suspicion proves to be unfounded and the vessel being suspected has not committed any act to justify further suspicion, a State Party that has taken action in accordance with this article shall make compensation for any loss or damage that may have been sustained to that vessel."[330] The proposal insinuated the nature of the liability for lawful conduct of the boarding State since the State was responsible even for action taken "in accordance with this article".

The Ad Hoc Committee did not entirely accept the Chinese submission. Instead, the new draft of 27 December 1999 stipulated: "Where measures taken pursuant to this Protocol prove to be unfounded, the vessel shall be compensated for any loss or damage that may have been sustained, provided that the vessel has not committed any act justifying the measures taken."[331] Under this provision, liability required unfounded "measures" instead of unfounded "suspicions". Such a wording would rather indicate responsibility for unlawful conduct. According to the *travaux préparatoires*, the modification was due to the fact that there was "no prior reference to suspicion in this article".[332] However, this ignores that Art. 7bis, para. 1 of this draft beyond doubt referred to "reasonable grounds to suspect that a vessel … is engaged in the smuggling of migrants".

During the ninth session of the Ad Hoc Committee, there was consent that the compensation provisions should be in line with the existing Law of the Sea as

[330] *UN* Doc. A/AC.254/5/Add.15 (24 November 1999), "Proposals and contributions received from Governments", Addendum, at 2.

[331] *UN* Doc. A/AC.254/4/Add.1/Rev.4 (27 December 1999), "Revised draft Protocol against the Smuggling of Migrants by Land, Air and Sea, Supplementing the United Nations Convention against Transnational Organized Crime".

[332] *Ibid.*, at 13, note 102.

stipulated in Art. 110, para. 3 LOSC and the draft remained unchanged.[333] Apparently, all delegations aimed to modify the wording of Art. 110, para 3 LOSC in order to apply it to the slightly different boarding procedures under the Migrant Smuggling Protocol, but wanted to leave the basic character of the provision unchanged.

During the last session of the Ad Hoc Committee, the provision was subject to some last amendments before the draft Protocol was approved on 24 October 2000.[334] The terms "measures taken pursuant to this Protocol" were replaced by the terms "grounds for measures taken pursuant to article 8". This amendment more clearly specifies the measures falling under the provision and it also again at least tends toward a liability for lawful conduct since one ground under Art. 8, para. 2 MSP is reasonable suspicion. Thus, the *travaux préparatoires*, particularly the adherence to Art. 110, para. 3 LOSC, provide strong argument why Art. 9, para 2 Migrant Smuggling Protocol does at least partially oblige to compensate even for lawful conduct of States parties.

VII. Terrorism interdiction operations under the 2005 SUA Protocol

Art. 8bis, para. 10, lit. b SUA Protocol, finally, seems to combine the terms of the other compensation provisions. The first alternative (i) basically copies Art. 110, para. 3 LOSC and the second alternative (ii) duplicates Art. 21, para. 18 Fish Stocks Agreement.

The extensive wording is due to a compromise reached in the drafting. There, delegates proposed to use Arts. 106, 110, para. 3 and 232 LOSC and Art. 21, para. 18 Fish Stocks Agreement as potential sources for the compensation provision.[335] The United States first submitted a draft based on Art. 110, para. 3 LOSC.[336] After some criticism, their second draft resembled Art. 232 LOSC and Art. 21, para. 18 Fish Stocks Agreement.[337] One delegation then heavily criticized that the second draft would limit responsibility to unlawful measures.[338] The United States amended their draft in this respect and came up with the final, extremely detailed provision.

---

333 *Ibid.*

334 *UN* Doc. A/55/383 (2 November 2000), "Crime Prevention and criminal justice, Report of the Ad Hoc Committee on the Elaboration of a Convention against Transnational Organized Crime on the work of its first to eleventh sessions", at 21, para. 118.

335 *IMO* Doc. LEG 87/17 (23 October 2003), "Report of the Legal Committee on the work of its Eighty-Seventh Session", Annex 3, at 12, note 41.

336 *IMO* Doc. LEG 86/5 (26 February 2003), "Draft amendments to the SUA Convention and Protocol Submitted by the United States", at 11.

337 *IMO* Doc. LEG 87/5/1 (8 August 2003), "Draft amendments to the SUA Convention and SUA Protocol Submitted by the United States", Annex 2, at 10.

338 *IMO* Doc. LEG 87/17 (23 October 2003), "Report of the Legal Committee on the work of its Eighty-Seventh Session", at para. 128.

Therefore, at least under the first alternative in Art. 8bis, para. 10, lit. b SUA Protocol, States engaged in maritime interdiction operation may bear responsibility for lawful conduct.

VIII. The effect of the special nature of the compensation provisions

The previous analysis has shown that most compensation provisions relevant to this study impose liability for lawful conduct on States interfering with navigation on the high seas and thus significantly differ from the general law on State responsibility. In how far does this special nature of the compensation provisions have any effect in practice?

First of all, the deterrent effect of a compensation provision is likely to increase if a State, though well aware that it may be justified in certain interferences on the high seas, always needs to be concerned that it may face compensation claims.

Secondly, the content of liability for lawful conduct might differ significantly from the consequences of responsibility for internationally wrongful acts. According to the general law on State responsibility, a State that has committed an internationally wrongful act must generally establish the situation that would exist if the internationally wrongful act had not been committed.[339] Basically, it must restitute in kind or, if that is not possible, pay compensation, including lost profits (indirect damages, *lucrum cessans*).[340] Reparation may also, if restitution and compensation do not suffice, include satisfaction (Art. 37 ASR).

Concerning liability for lawful conduct, the burden on the liable State may not be quite as extensive. The Permanent Court of International Justice ruled in 1928 that only in cases of unlawful takings of property, the State must compensate for "indirect damages", while in a case where an expropriation was lawful, the expropriating State must only compensate "the value of the undertaking at the time of dispossession, plus interest to the day of payment."[341]

From this decision, a common understanding developed in the doctrine concerning the expropriation of foreign property that liability for lawful conduct is limited to monetary compensation of the *damnum emergens*, while the *lucrum cessans* is not covered by such liability.[342] *Prima facie*, it would seem reasonable

[339] *Factory at Chorzów (Germany/Poland)*, Merits, Judgment of 13 September 1928, (1928) PCIJ Series A, No. 17, at 47; *Dupuy*, Pierre-Marie, "Le fait générateur de la responsabilité internationale des États", 188 RdC (1984-V), pp. 9 *et seq.*, at 94.

[340] Commentary on Art. 36, paras. 28-31, in *Crawford*, James, "The International Law Commission's Articles on State Responsibility" (Cambridge: Cambridge University Press, 2002), at 229-230.

[341] *Factory at Chorzów (Germany/Poland)*, Merits, Judgment of 13 September 1928, (1928) PCIJ Series A, No. 17, at 47.

[342] *Bindschedler*, Rudolf L., "La protection de la propriété en droit international public", 90 RdC (1956-II), pp. 173 *et seq.*, at 245-246; *Bin Cheng*, "The Rationale of Compensation for Expropriation", 44 Transactions of the Grotius Society (1958/1959), pp. 267 *et seq.*, 290; *Böckstiegel*, Karl-Heinz, "Die allgemeinen Grundsätze des Völkerrechts über Eigentumsentziehung" (Berlin: De Gruyter, 1963), at 94-95; *Ammann*,

to apply the same principles to cases of interferences with navigation. Such interferences also infringe the right of the shipowner to enjoy free use of his property. They are thus comparable to constraints on economic activities such as expropriations of foreign property.

The rationale for the denial of *lucrum cessans* in cases of lawful expropriations is that the owners of a company can never be certain that circumstances in the State where they undertake economic activities will not change in the future and that future profits therefore cannot be awarded when the expropriation is lawful.[343] It seems questionable whether this consideration applies to the same degree to shipowners because they do indeed have great trust in the freedom of navigation and the exclusive jurisdiction of their flag State. In their business calculations, they heavily rely on free, unhindered navigation since any interference could cause delay and damages and might significantly diminish their margin of profits.

Furthermore, another distinction between expropriations, on the one hand, and interferences with navigation, on the other, seems appropriate. The expropriation of foreign property only becomes lawful when a prompt and adequate compensation has been granted to the owners. Therefore, strictly speaking, the obligation to compensate is not the consequence of a lawful act, but instead compensation represents a requirement for the act (the expropriation) to become lawful.[344]

In cases of interferences with navigation, other requirements such as reasonable suspicion exist for the interference to become lawful. The interfering State, even though its conduct was justified, remains liable in certain cases such as when the "suspicions prove to be unfounded" (Art. 110, para. 3 LOSC).

Therefore, it seems premature to conclude from cases and doctrine exclusively dealing with expropriations that liability for lawful conduct only covers *damnum emergens* and not *lucrum cessans*. This issue will be analyzed in a separate part of this study dealing with the extent of responsibility under the different compensation provisions.

However, as opposed to State responsibility for internationally wrongful acts, liability for lawful conduct generally only entails an obligation to compensate and

---

Ulrich, "Der Schutz ausländischer Privatinvestitionen in Entwicklungsländern" (Zürich: Polygraphischer Verlag, 1967), at 66; *Fatouros*, Arghyris A., "Legal Security for International Investment", in *Friedmann*, Wolfgang G. *et al.* (eds.), "Legal Aspects of Foreign Investment" (Boston: Little Brown, 1959), pp. 699 *et seq.*, at 728; *UN* Doc. A/CN.4/119 (26 February 1959), *Garcia Amador*, F.V. "Responsibility of the State for injuries caused in its territory to the person or property of aliens, Fourth Report on International Responsibility", para. 64, reprinted in Yearbook of the International Law Commission (1959-II), pp. 1 *et seq.*, at 17 (1959-II); *Sorensen*, Max, "Principes de droit international public", 101 RdC (1960-III), pp. 2 *et seq.*, at 178-179.

343 *Fatouros*, Arghyris A., "Legal Security for International Investment", in *Friedmann*, Wolfgang G. *et al.* (eds.), "Legal Aspects of Foreign Investment" (Boston: Little Brown, 1959), pp. 699 *et seq.*, at 728-729. *Cf.* also *The Oscar Chinn Case (United Kingdom/Belgium)*, Judgment of 12 December 1934, (1934) PCIJ Series A/B No. 63, at 88.

344 *Cf. Bindschedler*, Rudolf L., "La protection de la propriété en droit international public", 90 RdC (1956-II), pp. 173 *et seq.*, at 246.

probably also, if possible, to restitute in kind (*restitutio in integrum*).[345] As will be seen *infra* (H.II.), the compensation provisions relevant to this study are even limited to compensation excluding *restitutio in integrum* without affecting the availability of a claim by the flag State for restitution in kind under the general law on state responsibility. Because liability for lawful acts is not meant to punish the liable State in any way or to prevent the repetition of certain conduct, but rather to allocate a loss,[346] satisfaction as a form of reparation is not available if the claimant only demonstrates that the responsible State has committed an internationally lawful act.

Finally, another, quite obvious difference lies in the effects of a possible justification of the reprehensible conduct. Such justification only exempts from the responsibility for unlawful conduct, but generally does not have any consequences for the liability for lawful conduct.[347]

IX. Conclusion

Concluding, the nature of some of the analyzed compensation provisions is quite atypical to public international law. These compensation provisions (namely Art. 110, para. 3 LOSC, Art. 9, para. 2 Migrant Smuggling Protocol and Art. 8bis, para. 10, lit. b of the 2005 SUA Protocol) provide for liability for lawful conduct of the interfering States, but the consequences of this liability may not be similar to the quite well-established consequences of "liability" for lawful expropriations of foreign property. Neither are the cases covered by the compensation provisions comparable to the situations within the scope of the ongoing work of the International Law Commission on the issue of "International liability for injurious consequences arising out of acts not prohibited by international law". The draft principles emanating from the ILC project only cover cases of loss from transboundary harm arising from hazardous activities and thereby more precisely target matters comparable to the *Trail Smelter Arbitration Case*.[348]

Thus, the relevant compensation provisions generally oblige the liable State to compensate for damage caused by lawful interferences with navigation on the high seas and to provide for *restitutio in integrum*. Satisfaction may only be claimed if the interference has been unlawful. Contrary to the law on expropriations of foreign property, loss of profits might be available under the analyzed

---

345 *UN* Doc. A/CN.4/413 (6 April 1988), *Barboza*, Julio "Fourth report on international liability for injurious consequences arising out of acts not prohibited by international law", para. 49, reprinted in Yearbook of the INternational Law Commission (1988-II-1), pp. 251 *et seq.*, at 259.

346 *UN* Doc. A/CN.4/423 (25 April 1989), *Barboza*, Julio, "Fifth report on international liability for injurious consequences arising out of acts not prohibited by international law", paras. 69-70, reprinted in Yearbook of the INternational Law Commission (1989-II-1), pp. 131 *et seq.*, at 141.

347 *Cf. Randelzhofer*, Albrecht, "Probleme der völkerrechtlichen Gefährdungshaftung", 24 Berichte der Deutschen Gesellschaft für Völkerrecht (1984), pp. 35 *et seq.*, at 64.

348 *Trail Smelter Arbitration (United States/Canada)*, 3 RIAA (1941), at 1965.

compensation provisions even when the conduct of the respondent State has been lawful. This issue (the extent of responsibility) will be the subject of a different part of this study (*infra*).

D. Responsibility for attempted interferences

All of the compensation provisions explicitly deal with situations where a vessel has been stopped on the high seas and where thus the freedom of navigation has been significantly impaired. The measures mentioned in the compensation provisions usually include the boarding, the detention, diversion and seizure of vessels. However, not every attempt to board a suspicious vessel is deemed by success. The suspicious vessel may try to escape to waters under the jurisdiction of a coastal State, forcing the interfering State to stop its pursuit or the suspicious vessel may simply manage to get away due to higher speed or due to problems encountered by the pursuing warship. Does such an attempted interference also fall under the relevant compensation provisions?

Quite naturally, this issue has mainly been discussed in cases of hot pursuit, which may extend over thousands of nautical miles and where the issue therefore is most relevant. Art. 111, para. 8 LOSC, like the other compensation provisions, does not explicitly stipulate the legal consequences of a pursuit from which the pursued vessel has escaped. Such a pursuit may nonetheless have caused considerable damage on the part of the pursued vessel because her journey was delayed, additional fuel had to be utilized, hull and machinery were damaged or because cargo had to be jettisoned in order to maintain a certain speed.

In the literature, *Myres S. McDougal* and *Willam T. Burke* were probably the first to raise (but not necessarily answer) the issue.[349] *Nicholas M. Poulantzas*, in his major treatise on hot pursuit, proposed to solve the question by applying the "functional method of interpretation of treaties, which takes into consideration the general function of the treaty at the time when the case for interpretation appears and in view of the social needs."[350]He came to the conclusion that Art. 111, para. 8 LOSC contains an obligation to compensate in the case of an unsuccessful hot pursuit.

Rindfleisch denies such a right because the unsuccessful pursuit itself cannot be a violation of public international law and because State responsibility for lawful conduct is exceptional in public international law.[351] This latter interpretation implies that any State may lawfully harass merchant ships of other States on the high seas without committing a violation of public international law. It also implies that the freedom of navigation only protects against boardings, inspections

---

[349] *McDougal*, Myres Smith/*Burke*, William T., "The Public Order of the Oceans" (New Haven: Yale University Press, 1962), at 919. *Cf.* also *Sobarzo*, Alejandro, "Régimen jurídico del alta mar" (México: Ed. Porrúa, 1970), at 155.

[350] *Poulantzas*, Nicholas M., "The Right of Hot Pursuit in International Law" (2nd ed., The Hague: Nijhoff, 2002), at 257.

[351] *Rindfleisch*, Stefan, "Das Recht der Nacheile zur See" (Hamburg: LIT, 2001), at 175.

and seizures, but not against harassments such as a shot over the bow and other encounters. This would open the high seas for abuse by powerful navies and coast guards and significantly impair the free enjoyment of the oceans and thus run counter the very essence of object and purpose of the freedom of navigation.

While the reasoning of Rindfleisch's argument is thus not to be followed, his result is in line with an interpretation of Art. 111, para. 8 LOSC under the Vienna Convention on the Law of Treaties. If one considers first the unequivocal wording of Art. 111, para. 8 LOSC ("where a ship has been *stopped* or *arrested*" (emphasis added)), secondly the special character of the provision with an entitlement of private entities, and thirdly the fact that neither the drafters nor the delegations present at the First and the Third United Nations Conference on the Law of the Sea paid attention to situations where the pursued vessel manages to escape a hot pursuit, then it seems hard to follow *Poulantzas's* interpretation of the provision and it seems much more likely that unsuccessful attempts to interfere with the navigation of a foreign vessel underlie the general regime of State responsibility requiring a claim by a flag State and an internationally wrongful act by the respondent State.

Contrary to *Poulantzas*, it is submitted that such result also copes with the "function" of the provision. A merchant vessel which tries to escape a boarding increases the costs of a pursuit both for the interfering State and for the shipowner. The latter, however, has an important safeguard at its disposal once the boarding takes place because if his cargo is innocent, he will be able to claim compensation under Art. 111, para. 8 LOSC. If he or his employees nevertheless decide to attempt an escape, such conduct would run counter his obligation to limit the damage suffered (see *infra*). It is definitely not the "function" of Art. 111, para. 8 LOSC to reward such recalcitrant shipowners with a right to claim compensation.

Therefore, Art. 111, para. 8 LOSC does not entitle shipowners who managed to escape a hot pursuit to claim compensation from the unsuccessful pursuer. This result evidently does not effect extistent remedies under the general law on State responsibility (*cf.* Art. 304 LOSC).

E. The liable entity – particularly in situations of multilateral boardings

As all maritime operations, interferences with the navigation of a vessel on the high seas often involve a great number of different States. The issue therefore arises which State might be responsible for such interferences. Basically, one ought to distinguish two different situations. First, a boarding might involve only two different potentially responsible States, such as the flag State of the boarded party and the State to which the boarding vessel belongs. Such a situation occurs, *e.g.*, if the boarding State requests the authorization of the flag State for the boarding or if the flag State asks another State to board and inspect one of its vessels. This study will attempt to determine the potential liable States in the case of such bilateral boardings (1.).

Secondly, an international or regional organization might establish a whole system of interferences concerning vessels navigating in a certain region or concerning vessels of a certain type or of a certain flag State. Since no international or regional organization thus far has its own ship register, States parties to these organizations need to undertake the interdictions as such. The issue then becomes whether the organization, the boarding member State or both are responsible for the actual operation (2.).

I. Bilateral boardings

Apart from wide-ranging interdiction operations within the framework of International Organizations, most interferences on the high seas involve only two States: the flag State and the boarding State. However, other States may be involved in the boarding by, *e.g.*, providing information to the boarding State. Responsibility at first sight seems to rest with the interfering State.[352] The issue therefore becomes whether some room is left for a potential liability of other States such as the flag State or whether the interfering State remains exclusively liable.

1. The few indications in the analyzed provisions

Art. 110, para. 3 LOSC, Art. 111, para. 8 LOSC and Art. 9, para. 2 Migrant Smuggling Protocol all do not explicitly name the liable entity. Instead, they are written from the perspective of the ship ("it shall be compensated"). Since Art. 304 LOSC explicitly refers to the general law on State responsibility, and since Art. 9, para. 2 Migrant Smuggling Protocol adheres to the principles laid down in Art. 110, para. 3 LOSC, the general law on State responsibility seems applicable to these three provisions. The commentary by the International Law Commission on Art. 22, para. 3 CHS (the predecessor of Art. 110, para. 3 LOSC) nevertheless quite unambiguously states that "[t]he State to which the warship belongs must compensate the merchant ship [...]."[353]

According to Art. VI Intervention Convention, only the party "which has taken measures in contravention of the provisions of the present Convention" shall be liable to pay compensation. Thus, only the State which breaches the Intervention Convention is liable under the provision. Likewise, Art. 106 LOSC states that "the State making the seizure shall be liable". This seems to indicate that only the interfering State as such could be liable under these provisions. However, interpretation of the context according to Art. 31, para. 2 VCLT at least obliges to consider the general law on State responsibility.

---

352 *Cf. Talmon*, Stefan, "Responsibility of International Organizations: Does the European Community require Special Treatment", in *Ragazzi*, Maurizio (ed.), "International Responsibility Today – Essays in Memory of Oscar Schachter" (Leiden: Nijhoff, 2005), pp. 405 *et seq.*, at 411.

353 *UN* Doc. A/3159, at 30, reprinted in Yearbook of the International Law Commission (1956-II), at 284.

Art. 21, para. 18 Fish Stocks Agreement stipulates that "States shall be liable for damage or loss *attributable to them*" (emphasis added). This language probably alludes to the principles of attribution as included in the general law on State responsibility. It also implies that not only the State to whom the vessels doing the boarding may be liable, but that such a boarding may be attributable to another State as well.

Under Art. 8bis, para. 10, lit. b SUA Protocol, finally, "States shall be liable", but "authorization to board by a flag State shall not per se give rise to its liability". This provision most explicitly recognizes the issue that more than one State may be liable for a boarding. On the one hand, a mere authorization is not sufficient to entail the responsibility of the flag State, but on the other hand, the provision, by using the terms *per se*, leaves room for situations where the flag State authorizes a boarding and remains involved in the operation to such a degree that it bears responsibility for the boarding.

The more detailed regulation in the SUA Protocol probably represents a result of the unfruitful negotiations concerning the Migrant Smuggling Protocol. Under both agreements, a lawful boarding always requires the authorization of the flag State. When the Migrant Smuggling Protocol was drafted, some delegations expressed concerns with respect to who might be able to claim compensation, from whom and in what forum.[354] Since there was consent that the compensation should be in line with the existing Law of the Sea as stipulated in Art. 110, para. 3 LOSC, the draft nevertheless remained unchanged.[355]

The same concerns reappeared when the SUA Protocol was drafted.[356] Reacting to these concerns, the United States, apparently relying upon Art. 21, para. 18 Fish Stocks Agreement, submitted a draft according to which "States Parties shall be liable for damage or loss attributable to them".[357] When China proposed that only the requesting State shall be responsible under the new provision,[358] it found no support.

When the Intersessional Working Group met for its second session in early 2005, one of the few remaining issues was whether it was necessary to clarify the liable entity. Some delegations were concerned that the flag State could be liable for its mere authorization; other delegations alleged that "the flag State could only be liable if, for example, it was acting as the boarding State, or the damage or loss was attributable to a condition it imposed on the boarding authorization, or if it

354 *UN* Doc. A/AC.254/4/Add.1/Rev.6 (19 July 2000), "Revised draft Protocol against the Smuggling of Migrants by Land, Air and Sea,2 Supplementing the United Nations Convention against Transnational Organized Crime".

355 *Ibid.*

356 *Ibid.*, para. 75.

357 *IMO* Doc. LEG 87/5/1 (8 August 2003), "Draft amendments to the SUA Convention and SUA Protocol Submitted by the United States", Annex 2, at 10; *cf.* also *Ronzitti*, Natalino, "Coastal State Jurisdiction over Refugees and Migrants at Sea", in *Ando*, Nisuke *et al.* (eds.), "Liber amicorum Judge Shigeru Oda", Vol. 2 (The Hague, Kluwer Law International, 2002), pp. 1271 *et seq.*, at 1284.

358 *IMO* Doc. LEG 89/4/3 (22 September 2004), "Comments and proposals submitted by China", at para. 12.

granted authorization on grounds that proved to be unfounded."[359] To protect the flag State from liability merely for authorizing a boarding in accordance with the protocol, some delegations proposed the addition of the following terms, which then found entry into the provision: "The authorization to boarding by a flag State shall not per se amount to its liability."[360]

These *travaux préparatoires* are very revealing concerning the liable entity under Art. 8bis, para. 10, lit. b SUA Protocol, but also concerning the relevance of the general law on State responsibility for the issue both under the SUA Protocol and under other compensation provisions in the Law of the Sea. The rejection of China's proposal shows that not only the requesting, but also the boarding State may bear responsibility for a boarding requested by another State. Furthermore, the authorization of the flag State as such is not sufficient to entail responsibility, but other factors must come along. There seems to have been consensus during the negotiations that this issue depended on the question of attribution and that the general law on State responsibility remains applicable in this respect, with the only confinement that an authorization does not suffice for attribution of a boarding to a flag State. Since the freedom of navigation is an exclusive right of the flag State, one must require that any claim for compensation directed against the flag State needs to be linked with the violation of other, individual rights, such as a human right.

With this exception, all compensation provisions thus rely on the principles on attribution and participation in the general law of State responsibility which will therefore now be discussed.

2. The principles in the general law on State responsibility

A State could either be liable for a boarding if this interference is attributable to it (1) or if the State participated in the boarding by another State in a certain way (2).

a) Attribution

As far as it concerns the first situation, the basic rule is that a State is liable for the conduct of its organs and officials (Art. 4 Articles on State Responsibility (ASR)). The International Court of Justice in the *Cumaraswamy Case* held that Art. 4 ASR constitutes customary international law.[361] Besides, the whole set of Articles on State Responsibility has been drafted like a treaty and plays an important role in the determination of the content of public international law.[362] Moreover, the first

---

359 *IMO* Doc. LEG/SUA/WG.2/4 (9 February 2005), "Report of the Working Group", at para. 62.

360 *Ibid.*, para. 64.

361 *Difference Relating to Immunity from Legal Process of a Special Rapporteur of the Commission on Human Rights*, Advisory Opinion of 29 April 1999, ICJ Reports 1999, pp. 62 *et seq.*, at 87, para. 62.

362 *Treves*, Tullio, "The International Law Commission's Articles on State Responsibility and the Settlement of Disputes", in *Ragazzi*, Maurizio (ed.), "International Responsibility Today – Essays in Memory of Oscar Schachter" (Leiden: Nijhoff, 2005),

part of the Articles on State Responsibility (Articles 1 to 27 ASR) equally applies to the responsibility of a State vis-à-vis entities "other than States" [363] and thus also to situations where private entities claim the responsibility of a State under public international law.

According to Art. 4 ASR, the scope of State responsibility for official acts is broad and the definition of "organ" for this purpose comprehensive and inclusive. There is no distinction based on the level of seniority of the relevant officials in the State hierarchy. As long as these officials are acting in their official capacity, State responsibility is engaged.[364] Even *ultra vires* acts are attributable to a State if an organ acted within its official capacity.[365] It is sufficient if the organs have "acted at least to all appearances as competent officials or organs, or they must have used powers or methods appropriate to their official capacity."[366] If interferences on the high seas are undertaken by naval or coast guard officials acting in their official capacity, then these acts are usually attributable to the State which employs them, thus most likely the flag State of the naval or coast guard vessel.

All provisions in the Law of the Sea authorize interferences with navigation only to warships and other governmental vessels such as the coast guard, including auxiliary aircraft and helicopters. Boardings by private vessels therefore do not play any role in the Law of the Sea and their attribution to a State will not be discussed here.

Under what conditions, however, may the boarding by a warship be attributable to a third State other than the flag State? The first possibility to attribute such a boarding would be to consider the warship to be placed at the disposal of another State. The boarding will then be considered an act of the latter State if the warship or coast guard vessel "is acting in the exercise of elements of the governmental authority of the State at whose disposal it is placed" (Art. 6 ASR).[367] This means that the vessel acts with the consent, under the authority of and for the purposes of

pp. 223 *et seq.*, at 225; *Caron*, David D., "The ILC Articles on State Responsibility, the Paradoxical Relationship between Form and Authority", 96 AJIL (2002), pp. 857 *et seq.*, at 858.

363 Commentary on Art. 28 ASR, para. 3, in *Crawford*, James, "The International Law Commission's Articles on State Responsibility" (Cambridge: Cambridge University Press, 2002), at 192.

364 *LaGrand (Germany v. United States of America)*, Provisional Measures, Order of 3 March 1999, ICJ Reports 1999, pp. 9 *et seq.*, at para. 28; *Crawford*, James/*Olleson*, Simon, "The Nature and Forms of International Responsibility", in *Evans*, Malcolm D. (ed.), "International Law" (2003), pp. 455 *et seq.*

365 *Union Bridge Company Claim (United States v. United Kingdom)*, 6 RIAA (1924). pp. 138 *et seq.*

366 *Caire Case*, 5 RIAA (1929), pp. 516 *et seq.*, at 530; *cf.* also *Youmans Case*, 4 RIAA (1926), pp. 110 *et seq.*

367 As to the status of this principle as customary international law see *Dahm*, Georg/*Delbrück*, Jost/*Wolfrum*, Rüdiger, "Völkerrecht", Vol. 1, Part 3 (2nd ed., Berlin: de Gruyter, 2002), at 917.

the State to whom the operation is attributed.[368] The mere authorization by the boarded vessel's flag State is therefore not sufficient under the general law on State responsibility to attribute a naval law enforcement operation to the authorizing State.[369] Quite to the contrary, it would require that the flag State of the warship leaves control and command over the vessel exclusively to the other State. Examples of such interferences are not known to the author.[370]

The second possibility to attribute an interference to a State other than the flag State of the interfering vessel is that this other State adopts the interference *ex post* as its own and thus translates it into an own act of state.[371] Again, this possibility, which was mainly construed for the attribution of acts by private persons, only exists in extremely limited circumstances. The State to which the conduct is to be attributed needs to have assumed the responsibility, a mere verbal approval or endorsement is generally not sufficient.[372] Therefore, an *ex post* authorization of an interference by another State does not necessarily entail the responsibility of the authorizing State. Instead, it would seem necessary that the authorizing State shows gratitude to the interfering State because the authorizing State has in fact benefited from the interference. Furthermore, one ought to require that the authorizing State takes over the position of the interfering State in a potential dispute with private entities who had suffered damage by the interference.

Such situations have not yet arisen. The quite strict preconditions show that it is very unlikely that an interference will be attributed to a State other than the flag State of the interfering warship. The mere authorization thus does not seem to impose a great risk for the flag State as far as it concerns a potential liability.

b) Participation

In the general law on State responsibility, the principle of independent responsibility applies.[373] An authorizing or otherwise involved State may nevertheless bear responsibility for the boarding by another State if it has participated in the inter-

---

368 Commentary on Art. 6, para. 2, in: *Crawford*, James, "The International Law Commission's Articles on State Responsibility" (Cambridge: Cambridge University Press, 2002), at 103.

369 *Xhavara & others v. Italy & Albania* (Application No. 39473-98), European Court of Human Rights, Decision of 11 January 2001 (holding that Albania is not responsible for the interference by an Italian vessel based on the authorization in a convention between Italy and Albania).

370 One has to distinguish the case where a State donates warships to another State so that the latter is able to efficiently control parts of the ocean. In such a case, the warship acquires the nationality of the latter State and loses all links to the former.

371 Art. 11 ASR; *United States Diplomatic and Consular Staff in Tehran (United States v. Iran),* Judgment of 24 May 1980, ICJ Reports 1980, pp. 3 *et seq.*, paras. 73-4.

372 Commentary on Art. 11 ASR, para. 6, in *Crawford*, James, "The International Law Commission's Articles on State Responsibility" (Cambridge: Cambridge University Press, 2002), at 123.

373 Commentary on Chapter IV, para. 1, in *Crawford*, James, "The International Law Commission's Articles on State Responsibility" (Cambridge: Cambridge University Press, 2002), at 145.

ference. In such a case, the interference remains attributable to the interfering State, but the participation of the authorizing State could amount to own internationally wrongful conduct for which the authorizing State is responsible.

The Articles on State Responsibility provide for two possibilities under which the participating State may bear responsibility for the conduct of another State.

(1) Aid and assistance

First, the participating State may be responsible for its "aid or assistance" (Art. 16 ASR). Could the authorization of a boarding amount to such aid or assistance? While an authorization definitely contributes to the boarding of a foreign vessel (in the cases covered by the Migrant Smuggling Protocol and the SUA Convention, it even constitutes one precondition for a lawful boarding), Art. 16 ASR imposes two further requirements for the responsibility of the participating State. This State must have had "knowledge of the internationally wrongful act" and the act must have been "internationally wrongful if committed by that State". Thus, the responsibility of an authorizing State depends on the question whether the freedom of navigation constitutes a right of the flag State or also a right of private entities (*supra*). As has been shown, the freedom of navigation solely belongs to the flag State. Therefore, the authorization of the flag State renders the boarding as such lawful and no "internationally wrongful act" occurs. Furthermore, any boarding by the flag State cannot be internationally wrongful and therefore the authorization by the flag State to another State does not entail the responsibility of the flag State.

Cases where the flag State authorizes a boarding by another State need to be distinguished from cases where a third State aids the interfering State by, *e.g.*, providing information such as the position of the vessel to be boarded or her presumed illicit cargo. Here, the responsibility of the participating State depends on whether it had knowledge of the circumstances of the boarding.

(2) Direction and control

Secondly, the participating State may also be responsible for a boarding if it had directed and controlled the interfering State (Art. 17 ASR).[374] Again, according to this principle, the participating State must have had "knowledge of the internationally wrongful act" and the act must have been "internationally wrongful if committed by that State". "Control" requires the "domination over the commission of wrongful conduct and not simply oversight", and "direction" constitutes "more than incitement or suggestion but rather connotes actual direction of an operative kind."[375] In what kind of situations of interferences on the high seas may

---

[374] *Cf.* also *Crawford*, James/*Olleson*, Simon, "The Nature and Forms of International Responsibility", in *Evans*, Malcolm D. (ed.), "International Law" (2003), pp. 455 *et seq.*, at 457.

[375] Commentary on Art. 17 ASR, para. 7, in *Crawford*, James, "The International Law Commission's Articles on State Responsibility" (Cambridge: Cambridge University Press, 2002), at 154.

such conditions exist? It may, for example, be the case if a maritime power determines a vessel it wants to board and inspect, but is missing naval vessels in the region to undertake the interference. When this maritime power then strongly urges another State to stop the vessel until own naval vessels reach it and take over the suspect vessel, one could presume that the conduct of the "other" State was under the direction and control of the first State.

However, the case law underlying Art. 17 ASR primarily deals with situations where one State was heavily dependent upon another such as in protectorates, federations or territorial occupation.[376] Thus, one ought to be careful to apply the principle to situations where the degree of control has not attained the level present in occupation, but where one State follows directions of another State merely to maintain friendly relations to the latter. The only case known to the author where the responsibility of a dominant State for the conduct of an entirely independent State was alleged dates from 1911 and the case was resolved through an indemnification by the acting (not the dominant) State.[377] Therefore, it seems more than questionable whether Art. 17 ASR would apply to independent States cooperating in interferences with navigation on the high seas. Instead, it seems more reasonable to require the attribution of such interferences to the dominant State.[378]

(3) Vicarious liability for internationally lawful conduct?

All of these cases, in which the participating State may be responsible, require an "internationally wrongful act". However, some of the analyzed compensation provisions in the Law of the Sea also provide for liability if the interference was lawful (*supra*). Such responsibility is atypical to the law of State responsibility and applies only in limited, most often codified circumstances. The Draft Articles on the Prevention of Transboundary Harm from Hazardous Activities[379] do not mention the liability of any participating State other than the State from whose territory or jurisdiction the harm has been caused.

The rationale for the existence of liability for lawful conduct is to shift the risk of suffering a loss from the injured entity to the (liable) causer of the injury or the entity which has profited from the activity which caused the damage. It may well occur that a participating State has profited from the lawful boarding by another State for which the "ship" may then claim compensation or that a participating State has caused the boarding by delivering information or requesting the interference. Hence, it seems adequate to analogously apply the principles of partici-

---

376 *Cf.* commentary on Art. 28 Draft ASR, in UN Doc. A/34/10, p. 95, "Report of the International Law Commission on the work of its thirty-first session", at para. 10.

377 *Bouvé*, Clement L., "Russia's liability in tort for Persia's breach of contract", 6 AJIL (1912), pp. 389 *et seq.*, at 391-393.

378 *Cf. Verdross-Drossberg*, Alfred, "Theorie der mittelbaren Staatenhaftung", 1 Österreichische Zeitschrift für Öffentliches Recht (Neue Folge) (1948), pp. 388 *et seq.*, at 418-421.

379 *UN* Doc. A/56/10 (2004), "International Law Commission, Report of the fifty-sixth session", pp. 153 *et seq.*.

pation to these cases without requiring the existence of an internationally wrongful act.

Therefore, one might presume that in cases where the interfering State is responsible for a lawful interference, a participating State may, according to the principles laid down in the Articles on State Responsibility and under certain circumstances justifying an analogous application, bear responsibility for its participation in the interference.

3. Joint and several liability?

The application of the above-mentioned principles could lead to the responsibility of more than one State. While the principles on attribution attribute the conduct of organs of one State to another State and therefore trigger the responsibility of the latter only, Articles 16 and 17 ASR derive the responsibility of a participating State from the conduct of another State for which this latter State remains entirely responsible.

Two issues thus come up: First, does the participating State also bear the whole responsibility for the interference with navigation? Secondly, what is the relationship between the responsibilities of the two States? These two issues are linked in the interesting question whether the law of State responsibility adheres to the general principle of joint and several liability according to which the claimant may demand compensation of the whole damage from any responsible party and the responsible parties then need to deal with their different degrees of contribution in a separate proceeding without the original claimant.[380]

The principle of joint and several liability may either have acquired the status of a general principle of international law or have become a rule of customary international law. Since, due to different traditions in civil and common law, it is difficult to derive any general principle from domestic legal systems as to the nature of the relationship,[381] and since there is hardly any State practice or decisions by international tribunals,[382] it seems doubtful whether one may describe this relationship as "joint and several liability".[383]

The different domestic legal systems dealing with liability between private parties[384] describe the relationship in different terms, but essentially most domestic

---

380 "Black's Law Dictionary" (7th ed., St. Paul: West Group, 1999), at 926.

381 *Cf. Weir*, Tony, "Complex Liabilities", in *Tunc*, André (ed.), "International Encyclopedia of Comparative Law", Vol. 11, Part. 2 (Tübingen: Mohr, 1986), Chapter 12, pp. 12/01 *et seq.*, at 12/80-12/81, paras. 79-81; but see *Brownlie*, Ian, "State Responsiblity" (Oxford: Clarendon Press, 1983), at 189.

382 *Noyes*, John E./*Smith*, Brian D., "State Responsibility and the Principle of Joint and Several Liability", 13 Yale J. Int'l L. (1988), pp. 225 *et seq.*, at 226.

383 Such the proposal in *Ronzitti*, Natalino, "Coastal State Jurisdiction over Refugees and Migrants at Sea", in *Ando*, Nisuke *et al.* (eds.), "Liber amicorum Judge Shigeru Oda", Vol. 2 (The Hague, Kluwer Law International, 2002), pp. 1271 *et seq.*, at 1284.

384 This relationship is most relevant for the elaboration of general principles of international law because in public international law, States and other subjects of international law act on a level of equality like private entities in private law. *Cf.*

regimes of private law entitle the victim of a tort to claim the whole damage suffered from any single tortfeasor even if there have been more than one persons causing the damage.[385] As far as it concerns maritime law, which might be more relevant to situations of high seas interferences, many domestic maritime laws do not provide for several and joint liability and instead apply the principle of comparative fault.[386] However, both English and U.S. maritime law apply joint and several liability to claims by innocent third parties for damage to cargoes[387] and vessels.[388] Furthermore, the principles on contribution (the relationship between two responsible parties) diverge to a considerable degree in the different domestic legal systems.[389] Reference to domestic laws is thus not quite conclusive and definitely not sufficient to meet the high requirements of a general principle of international law.

The principle of joint and several liability may nevertheless have acquired the status of a rule of customary international law. The fact that two international conventions provide for a sophisticated system of concurrent liability[390] is not sufficient to prove the existence of a custom and may even favour its denial because the negotiators meant to create something new.[391]

In the case of *Anglo Chinese Shipping Co. v. United States*, the claimant complained of the retention of one of its vessels by the Allied forces occupying Japan. The vessel had been seized by Japan during World War II. The United States Court of Claims, in an *obiter dictum*, noted that "the occupation of Japan was a joint venture, participated in by the United States of America, the United Kingdom, China, and Russia; and whatever benefit the occupying powers derived from the use of the plaintiff's vessel ... was derived by all of them in common and not by any one more than another."[392] Furthermore, the Court found no need to decide "whether [the rule of joint and several liability] should be applied to sovereign

---

Lauterpacht, Hersch, "Private Law Sources and Analogies of International Law" (London, 1927), at 81.

385 *Noyes*, John E./*Smith*, Brian D., "State Responsibility and the Principle of Joint and Several Liability", 13 Yale J. Int'l L. (1988), pp. 225 *et seq.*, at 251-258.

386 *Cf. The Milan*, 167 Eng. Rep. 167 (1861); *United States v. Reliable Transfer Co.*, 421 U.S. 397 (1975); Article 4 of the Brussels Collision Liability Convention, adopted on 23 September 1910, reprinted in Martens Nouveau Recueil, Ser. 3, Vol. 7, pp. 711 *et seq.*, at 719.

387 *Aktieselskabet Cuzco v. The Sucarseco*, 294 U.S. 394 (1935); *The Chattahoochee*, 173 U.S. 540, 540, 549-552 (1899); *The Atlas*, 93 U.S. 302.

388 *The Alabama & The Game-cock*, 92 U.S. 695 (1875); *The Cairnbahn*, [1914] P. 25 (C.A.).

389 *Noyes*, John E./*Smith*, Brian D., "State Responsibility and the Principle of Joint and Several Liability", 13 Yale J. Int'l L. (1988), pp. 225 *et seq.*, at 256.

390 Article VI of the Treaty on Principles Governing the Activities of States in the Exploration and Use of Outer Space, Including the Moon and Other Celestial Bodies, adopted on 27 January 1967, UNTS, Vol. 610, pp. 205 *et seq.*; Art. XXII, para. 3 of the Convention on International Liability for Damage Caused by Space Objects, adopted on 29 March 1972, UNTS, Vol. 961, pp. 187 *et seq.*

391 *Cf.* 66 Annuaire de l'Institut de Droit International (1995-I), at 328.

392 *Anglo Chinese Shipping Co. v. United States*, 127 F.Supp. 553, 554 (Court of Claims).

nations engaged in a joint enterprise."[393] Apparently, the Court suggests that the claimant should have brought his claims against all four allied powers and not only the United States. The rule of joint and several liability, on the other hand, would allow exactly such separate claim against one respondent and a court could award the whole damage to the claimant. Thus, the Court of Claims tended against the application of the principle of joint and several liability in public international law.

In another case, however, the United States demanded full compensation from both Hungary and the Union of Socialist Soviet Republics (USSR) for the alleged cooperation in the interception and detention of a U.S. military aircraft and its crew.[394] While the International Court of Justice did not have the chance to rule on the issue in that case, one might interpret the *Corfu Channel Case* in favour of a principle of joint and several liability. The ICJ there held that Albania was entirely responsible for the damage suffered by the British navy even though presumably Yugoslavia had laid the mines which caused the damage.[395] *Ian Brownlie* has argued that the United Kingdom had been able to claim the whole damage from one of two tortfeasors and that the ICJ thus seems to have applied the principle of joint and several liability.[396] In a more recent case, the ICJ held that the possibility of the responsibility of other States than the respondent Australia did not render Nauru's claim for compensation inadmissible.[397] In the eventual settlement of the case, the United Kingdom and New Zealand nevertheless contributed to the compensation by Australia on an *ex gratia* basis.[398]

The International Law Commission proposes to distinguish two situations. "Where the assistance is a necessary element in the wrongful act in absence of which it could not have occurred, the injury suffered can be concurrently [borne by] the assisting and the acting State. In other cases, however, the difference may be very material: the assistance may have been only an incidental factor in the commission of the primary act, and may have contributed only to a minor degree, if at all, to the injury suffered. By assisting another State to commit an internationally wrongful act, a State should not necessarily be held to indemnify the victim for all the consequences of the act, but only for those which flow from its own

---

393 *Ibid.*, at 557.

394 *Treatment in Hungary of Aircraft and Crew of United States of America (United States v. Hungary)*, ICJ Pleadings 1954 (16 February 1954), at 8-10, 38-39; *Treatment in Hungary of Aircraft and Crew of United States of America (United States v. U.S.S.R.)*, ICJ Pleadings 1954 (16 February 1954), at 42, 43-44, 58-59.

395 *Corfu Channel Case (United Kingdom v. Albania)*, Judgment of 9 April 1949, ICJ Reports 1949, pp. 4 *et seq.*, at 36.

396 *Brownlie*, Ian, "Principles of Public International Law" (3rd ed., Oxford: Clarendon, 1979), at 456 (this comment is not part of the most recent 6th edition).

397 *Case Concerning Certain Phospate Lands in Naura (Nauru v. Australia)*, Judgment of 26 June 1949 on Preliminary Objections, ICJ Reports 1992, pp. 240 *et seq.*, at 258-259, para. 48.

398 *Brownlie*, Ian, "Principles of Public International Law" (6th ed., Oxford: Oxford University Press, 2003), at 440.

conduct."[399] It is thus possible that the participating State may, in addition to the State undertaking the interference, be responsible for the whole damage caused by an interference. Unfortunately, no rigid principle can be elaborated concerning this issue. Instead, a solution needs to be found on a case-by-case basis considering the degree of participation and cooperation, particularly the importance of the participation for the interference with navigation. In addition, one might apportion the responsibility according to the degree of information available to each responsible party (how reasonable was the suspicion to board the vessel for each party?) and the available possibilities to mitigate the damage suffered by the victim. Finally, one could also take into account in whose interest the interference was essentially undertaken.

Joint and several liability may even be more acceptable in situations where the responsible States have acted in conformity with public international law, but nevertheless are obliged to pay compensation. In such situations, the responsible States do not need to admit any wrongful conduct and the mere compensation will often not constitute a major burden on their budgets.[400] Thus, in situations covered by some of the analyzed compensation provisions, States may in the future accept a regime of joint and several liability.

As far as it concerns the second issue (the relationship between the two liabilities), the International Law Commission proposes that the two responsible States incur independent responsibilities which may be invoked by the claimants in different proceedings (Art. 47 para. 1 ASR). It is thus suggested that in contemporary public international law, the claimant may demand reparation and claim compensation from each of the responsible States. This does nonetheless not mean that the claimant always needs to claim the whole damage suffered from any one of the responsible States.

Furthermore, the claimant is barred from receiving an indemnification higher than the amount of the damage suffered (Art. 47, para. 2 ASR).[401] Whether the reasoning behind this provision is the prohibition of unjust enrichment,[402] the

---

399 Commentary on Art. 16 ASR, para. 11, in *Crawford*, James, "The International Law Commission's Articles on State Responsibility" (Cambridge: Cambridge University Press, 2002), at 151.

400 *Noyes*, John E./*Smith*, Brian D., "State Responsibility and the Principle of Joint and Several Liability", 13 Yale J. Int'l L. (1988), pp. 225 *et seq.*, at 264.

401 *Cf.* also *Case concerning the Factory at Chorzów (Germany/Poland)*, Merits, Judgment of 13 September 1928, (1928) PCIJ Series A, No. 17, at 49; *Reparation for Injuries suffered in the Service of the United Nations*, Advisory Opinion of 11 April 1949, ICJ Reports 1949, pp. 174 *et seq.*, at 176.

402 *Cf. Schreuer*, Christoph, "Unjust Enrichment", in *Bernhardt*, Rudolf (ed.), "Encyclopedia of Public International Law", Vol. 4 (Amsterdam: North-Holland, 2000), pp. 1243 *et seq.*, at 1243; *Cook Case (United States v. Mexico)*, 4 RIAA (1927), pp. 213 *et seq.*, at 218 (1927); *Fabiani Case (France v. Venezuela)* (1896), quoted in *Whiteman*, Marjorie M., "Damages in International Law", Vol. 2 (Washington, U.S. Government Printing Office, 1937), at 1786; *Case concerning the Factory at Chorzów (Germany/ Poland), Merits*, Judgment of 13 September 1928, (1928) PCIJ Series A, No. 17, at 31.

principle of equity[403] or the prohibition of an abuse of rights is immaterial. Therefore, it is possible under these conditions that a court will hold a State responsible, but as far as it concerns compensation will refer to an award against another State before another forum. The claimant is thus only barred from receiving additional compensation, but not from getting the court decision that more than one State was in fact responsible for the damages suffered.

Even though no case is known where one responsible State had recourse against another in order to receive contribution, such possibility is not precluded by the Articles on State Responsibility. Therefore, the relationship between the two responsibilities is very much similar to joint and several liability (common law) or solidary liability (civil law).

From a practical point of view, these rules provide for an effective protection of the victim which does not need to bring all potential responsible States before a domestic or international tribunal. Due to the difficulties of consensual jurisdiction before international tribunals[404] and principles of State immunity before foreign courts, such requirement would unnecessarily burden the claimant.

On the other hand, the mentioned rules also take into account the concerns of potential responsible States since not every act of participation necessarily entails the responsibility for the whole damage suffered by the victim. Furthermore, the award of compensation, *prima facie*, does not have any effect on the eventual recourse by the respondent against other responsible States since any court decision "has no binding force except between the parties and in respect of that particular case."[405]

II. Interdictions within the framework of International Organizations

A great number of interferences on the high seas have been undertaken within the framework of International Organizations, particularly in the enforcement of sanction simposed by the United Nations Security Council. This part will first determine what role such interdictions play in contemporary maritime transport (a)). Then, this study will attempt to analyze issues of attribution of interdictions to either the International Organization or its member States (b)) before finally dealing with the issue whether member States of these International Organizations may also bear responsibility if the interdiction is attributable to the organization (c)).

---

403 *Cf. Janis*, M.W., "Equity in International Law", in: *Bernhardt*, Rudolf (ed.), "Encyclopedia of Public International Law", Vol. 2 (Amsterdam: North-Holland, 1995), pp. 109 *et seq.*, at 109.

404 *Noyes*, John E./*Smith*, Brian D., "State Responsibility and the Principle of Joint and Several Liability", 13 Yale J. Int'l L. (1988), pp. 225 *et seq.*

405 *Cf.* Art. 59 of the Statute of the International Court of Justice; Art. 33, para. 2 of the Statute of the International Tribunal for the Law of the Sea.

1. The scope of interferences involving International Organizations

Law and practice of International Organizations has significantly developed after World War II. The international community first established such organizations mainly in order to provide for international security. A certain number of international conflicts and civil wars show that the authorization of maritime interdictions and the undertaking of them have become important means of International Organizations to enforce international law.

After Southern Rhodesia had declared its independence of the United Kingdom on 11 November 1965, the United Nations Security Council imposed an embargo on Southern Rhodesia[406] and authorized the United Kingdom to prevent the arrival of vessels reasonably believed to be carrying oil destined for Southern Rhodesia through the port of Beiria, Mozambique, if necessary by the use of force.[407] Between November 1965 and December 1966, the British navy identified 1,600 vessels, among which were 500 tankers; about twelve vessels were stopped and inspected.[408] In total, 24 British naval units were involved in the enforcement of the embargo.[409] Container ships had to limit their cargo on deck to no more than three containers stacked on top of each other, but inspection on sea was nevertheless impossible and thus the forces routinely diverted vessels into ports.[410] Over a period of two years, 17,800 vessels were intercepted, 7,400 boarded and 410 diverted.[411]

More than three decades later, in the Gulf War, the United Nations Security Council prohibited all imports and exports to and from Iraq[412] and shortly thereafter authorized all measures to halt inward and outward maritime shipping with the purpose of inspecting and verifying the cargo and in order to enforce the previous prohibition.[413] Authorized entities were those member states of the United Nations which were cooperating with the Government of Kuwait and which were deploying maritime forces in the area.[414] A coalition of 19 States then used a total

---

406 Security Council Resolution 217 (1965).

407 Security Council Resolution 221 (1966).

408 *Rousseau*, Charles, Rev. Gén. Dr. Int'l Publ. (1967), at 471. *Cf.* also *Soons*, Alfred H.A., "Enforcing the economic embargo at sea", in *Gowlland-Debbas*, Vera (ed.), "United Nations Sanctions and International Law" (The Hague: Kluwer Law International, 2001), pp. 307 *et seq.*, at 311-2.

409 *Rousseau*, Charles, "Chronique des faits internationaux", Rev. Gén. Dr. Int'l Publ. (1967), at 472.

410 *Astley*, J./*Schmitt*, M.N., "The Law of the Sea and Naval Operations", 42 A.F. L. Rev. (1997), pp. 119 *et seq.*, at 144.

411 *Ibid.*, at 146 n. 110. Voelckel, as of 15 April 1991, counted the following numbers: 1,203 boardings, 66 diversion, 14 warning shots. *Cf. Voelckel*, Michel, "Le Navire et les Situations Internationales de Crise", in *Société Française de Droit International* (ed.), "Le Navire en Droit international" (Paris: Pedone, 1992), pp. 183 *et seq.*, at 202 n. 66.

412 Security Council Resolution 661 (1990).

413 Security Council Resolution 665 (1990).

414 United States, United Kingdom, France, Spain, Netherlands, Italy, Belgium, Denmark, Greece, Norway, Canada, Australia and Argentina. See *Pagani*, Fabrizio, "Le misure di

of 95 naval vessels to control maritime transport in the Persian Gulf.[415] By February 1992, these forces had intercepted a total of 12,937 merchant vessels, boarded 3,504 of them and diverted 222 of them to different ports.[416]

In the civil war in the former Yugoslavia, the Security Council imposed different embargos which became more comprehensive over the years.[417] Since the Security Council had not explicitly authorized the boarding of foreign vessels, the Western European Union (WEU) and the North Atlantic Treaty Organization (NATO) only started surveillance measures to implement the embargos.[418] U.S., French and Spanish naval vessels identified all cargo vessels and interrogated the captains via radio in the South and Middle Adriatic Sea. If a vessel was suspicious, the naval vessels informed the flag State, but did not board the vessel. Until November 1992, 3,600 vessels were identified, 71 were suspected of violating the embargo.[419]

In a second phase of the conflict, the Security Council then authorized "[S]tates acting nationally or through regional agencies or arrangements" to take proportionate measures to stop vessels for the sake of enforcement of the embargoes[420] and finally even authorized enforcement measures even in the territorial sea of Serbia and Montenegro.[421] In the period from 22 November 1992 to 18 June 1996, 74,192 vessels challenged, 5,951 boarded and inspected, 1,480 diverted and inspected in port.[422] However, even though authorized to do so, the naval vessels implementing the embargo did not use force in their operations.[423]

When the democratically elected President of Haiti, *Jean-Bertrand Aristide*, was overthrown in 1993 by a military coup, the Security Council reacted with an

---

interdizione navale in relazione alle sanzioni adottate dall'ONU", 76 Rivista di diritto internazionale (1993), pp. 720 *et seq.*, at 725.

415 *Scholz*, Oliver, "Die Durchsetzung von Zwangsmaßnahmen nach Art. 41 der Satzung der Vereinten Nationen, insbesondere mit militärischen Mitteln" (Frankfurt am Main: Lang, 1998), at 41.

416 *Moore*, John F., "The U.S. Navy in 1991", 118 Naval Institute Proceedings (May 1992), pp. 133 *et seq.*, at 136.

417 Security Council Resolution 713 (25 September 1991) (no arms or military equipment transported to the whole territory of the former Yugoslavia); Security Council Resolution 757 (30 May 1992) (almost complete embargo against Serbia and Montenegro); Security Council Resolution 820 (1993) (prohibition of all commercial maritime traffic to ports of Serbia and Montenegro).

418 Agence Europe, 11 July 1992, at 3-4.

419 *UN* Doc. S/24847 (25 November 1992).

420 Security Council Resolution 787 (15 November 1992).

421 Security Council Resolution 820 (17 April 1993).

422 *Sokolsky*, Joel J., "Colbert's Heirs: The United States, NATO and Multilateral Naval Cooperation in the Post Cold War Era", in *Crickard*, Fred W. *et al.* (eds.), "Multinational Naval Cooperation and Foreign Policy into the 21st century" (Aldershot: Ashgate, 1998), pp. 69 *et seq.*, at 88.

423 *UN* Doc. S/1996/946 (15 November 1996), "Final Report of the Security Council Committee established pursuant to resolution 724 (1991) concerning Yugoslavia", at 32, para. 79 (b).

embargo[424] and called upon all member States to use "measures commensurate with the specific circumstances" to enforce the embargo.[425] Particularly the United States followed this call and, by February 1994, U.S. Coast Guard vessels alone had boarded 62 vessels on their way to Haiti.[426] However, the embargo remained quite inefficient because the Haitian government was able to import large quantities by land transport from the Dominican Republic.[427]

In 1997, the Security Council authorized the Economic Community of West African States (ECOWAS) to enforce the embargo imposed upon Sierra Leone.[428] The implementation of this embargo, however, did not have much success and, instead of preventing the transport of petroleum and arms, led to increased suffering of the civilian population.[429]

In September 2001, the United States initiated the "Operation Enduring Freedom" in their fight against. Part of its agenda is to control the waters surrounding the Horn of Africa and to prevent the transportation of terrorists and their cargoes. The legal grounds for these measures are Art. 51 UN Charter, Art. 5 of the North Atlantic Treaty[430] and the Security Council Resolutions 1368 (2001) and 1373 (2001). Unfortunately, most States involved in these operations have kept most statistics about boardings and inspections confidential.

Reacting to a significant increase of piratical incidents near Somalia and to an urgent call of the International Maritime Organization,[431] the President of the Security Council recently delivered a Presidential Statement[432] encouraging "Member States whose naval vessels and military aircraft operate in international waters and airspace adjacent to the coast of Somalia to be vigilant to any incident of piracy therein and to take appropriate action to protect merchant shipping, in particular the transportation of humanitarian aid, against any such act, in line with relevant international law." Quite immediately after this call, the United States navy fired upon a presumed pirate ship.[433] The legal nature of Presidential Statements of the Security Council remains quite controversial, but there is substantial

---

424 Security Council Resolution 841 (16 June 1993) and Security Council Resolution 873 (13 October 1993).

425 Security Council Resolution 875 (16 October 1993).

426 *Truver*, Scott C., "The U.S. Navy in Review", Naval Institute Proceedings (May 1994), pp. 114 *et seq.*, at 116.

427 *Scholz*, Oliver, "Die Durchsetzung von Zwangsmaßnahmen nach Art. 41 der Satzung der Vereinten Nationen, insbesondere mit militärischen Mitteln" (Frankfurt am Main: Lang, 1998), at 50.

428 Security Council Resolution 1132 (8 October 1997).

429 *Berger*, Lee F., "State practice evidence of the humanitarian intervention doctrine: The ECOWAS Intervention in Sierra Leone", 11 Ind. Int'l & Comp. L. Rev. (2001), pp. 605 *et seq.*, at 621.

430 North Atlantic Treaty, adopted on 4 April 1949, UNTS, Vol. 34, pp. 243 *et seq.*

431 *IMO* Doc. A.979(24) (6 February 2006), "Piracy and Armed Robbery against ships in waters off the coast of Somalia", IMO General Assembly Resolution of 23 November 2005.

432 *UN* Doc. S/PRST/2006/11 (15 March 2006), "Statement by the President of the Security Council".

433 "One dead in US Navy clash with 'pirates'", Lloyd's List, 21 March 2006.

argument that such statements may, under certain circumstances, have the status of binding decisions in the sense of Art. 25 UN Charter.[434] In the case at hand, however, the Presidential Statement merely reproduced the existing customary international law authorizing the search and visit of suspected pirate ships. Therefore, the situation is not comparable to an interdiction within the framework of an International Organization. Instead, interfering States use their powers under customary international law and bear the whole responsibility for these interferences.

2. Responsibility of the international or regional organization?

The issue in all of these operations becomes whether the United Nations, the regional organization or the individual State whose naval vessel undertakes the boarding bears responsibility for potential damage caused by it.

It seems to be well established in public international law that International Organizations may acquire an international legal personality and may thus become the bearer of rights and obligations in public international law.[435] As a consequence, they may also be responsible for certain conduct.[436] Even though the International Law Commission has stated in Art. 57 ASR that "[t]hese articles are without prejudice to any question of the responsibility under international law of an International Organization", it is largely accepted that the general law on State responsibility applies equally to International Organizations, with some necessary modifications.[437]

Therefore, if one applies the general principles on attribution, the responsibility of International Organizations for interdiction operations depends on their degree of control over a particular interference giving rise to a compensation claim. When this degree has acquired the status of "effective control", particularly when the acting organs have been placed at the disposal of the organization,[438] one might attribute the interference to the International Organization. The International Law

---

[434] *Talmon*, Stefan, "The Statements by the President of the Security Council", 2 Chinese J. of Int'l L. (2003), pp. 419 *et seq.*, at 447-449.

[435] *Cf. Reparation for injuries suffered in the service of the United Nations*, Advisory Opinion of 11 April 1949, ICJ Reports 1949, pp. 174 *et seq.*, at 179.

[436] *Herdegen*, Mathias, "Bemerkungen zur Zwangsliquidation und zum Haftungsdurchgriff bei internationalen Organisationen", 47 ZaöRV (1987), pp. 537 *et seq.*, at 549, 554; *Seidl-Hohenveldern*, Ignaz, "Piercing the Corporate Veil of International Organizations: The International Tin Council Case in the English Court of Appeals", 32 GYIL (1989), pp. 43 *et seq.*, at 47; *Hartwig*, Matthias, "Die Haftung der Mitgliedstaaten für Internationale Organisationen" (Berlin: Springer, 1993), at 294.

[437] *Cf. UN* Doc. A/51/389 (20 September 1996), "Report on the administrative and budgetary aspects of the financing of the United Nations peacekeeping operations", at para. 6; *Sands*, Philippe/*Klein*, Pierre, "Bowett's Law of International Institutions" (London: Sweet & Maxwell, 2001), at 519-520.

[438] *Schmalenbach*, Kirsten, "Die Haftung Internationaler Organisationen" (Frankfurt am Main: Lang, 2004), at 105.

Commission has recognized this principle,[439] but avoided to explicitly codify that once the International Organization has effective control over an organ, the latter's conduct may no more be attributable to the State.[440] Probably due to criticism by the doctrine,[441] the International Law Commission at least denied such dual attribution in its commentary to the draft articles.[442]

Most maritime interception operations have been multilateral in name, but national in practice. The key aspects of these operations, such as command and control, rules of engagement and communications were mostly left to individual (leading) nations.[443] Thus, one could argue that if a loss is imputable to the command as such, the individual nation having such command would be responsible for it. On the other hand, if rules of command are violated by the forces of another nation and if this conduct leads to damage, then this other nation would also bear responsibility for it.

a) The United Nations

The ICJ has held that the United Nations have been granted legal personality by their member States.[444] Furthermore, the Law of the Sea Convention implicitly recognizes this legal personality of the United Nations in Art. 93 LOSC. The Security Council is one the "principal organs" of the United Nations (Art. 7 Charter of the United Nations). Therefore, the United Nations would bear responsibility for interferences if these were attributable to the Security Council as one of its organs even if the Security Council acted *ultra vires*.[445] According to some of the Security Council Resolutions imposing naval embargoes, the authorized measures remain "under the authority of the Security Council."[446] Does this mean the Security Council enjoyed sufficient command over the enforcement of these embargoes to bear responsibility for interferences with navigation in the framework of such enforcement?

---

439 Draft Article 5 of the ILC's Draft Articles on the Responsibility of International Organizations, reprinted in *UN* Doc. A/59/10 (2004), "Report of the International Law Commission on the Work of its Fifty-Seventh Session", at 109.

440 *Cf.* Art. 5 ASR.

441 *Talmon*, Stefan, "Responsibility of International Organizations: Does the European Community require Special Treatment", in *Ragazzi*, Maurizio (ed.), "International Responsibility Today – Essays in Memory of Oscar Schachter" (Leiden: Nijhoff, 2005), pp. 405 *et seq.*, at 413-414.

442 Commentary on Draft Article 5 of the ILC's Draft Articles on the Responsibility of International Organizations, para 1, reprinted in *UN* Doc. A/59/10, p. 110 (2004), "Report of the International Law Commission on the Work of its Fifty-Seventh Session", at 110.

443 *Zeigler*, Richard, "Ubi Sumus? Quo vadimus?: Charting the Course of Maritime Interception Operations", 43 Naval L. Rev. (1996), pp. 1 *et seq.*, at 2.

444 *Reparation for injuries suffered in the service of the United Nations*, Advisory Opinion of 11 April 1949, ICJ Reports 1949, pp. 174 *et seq.*, at 179.

445 *Cf. UN* Doc. A/CN.4/541 (2 April 2004), *Gaja*, Giorgio, "Second Report on the Responsibility of International Organizations", at 23-27, paras. 51-59.

446 Security Council Resolution 665 (1990), Security Council Resolution 787 (1992).

In the past, the United Nations, and particularly the Security Council, has only supervised the application of the respective resolutions. In fact, Resolution 665 and Resolution 787 oblige States to report to the Security Council concerning enforcement measures undertaken.[447] The Security Council took account of these reports, but did not discuss them. The Security Council may have had the ultimate control over the interdiction measures since it was always able to modify and terminate the embargo, but this did never amount to an effective control.[448] Such control could only be admitted if the Security Council had made use of Articles 42 *et seq.* UN Charter.[449] Even though the relevant resolutions have been taken on the basis of Chapter VII of the UN Charter and therefore have been binding upon member States, they did not oblige them to undertake any interdiction measures. Member States thus enjoyed a certain liberty in their decision whether to board a certain vessel or not. The interdiction measures are thus not attributable to the United Nations.

The case may well be different regarding United Nations peacekeeping operations where the United Nations Secretariat has acknowledged and adopted the conduct of these operations as one attributable to the organization.[450] These operations have nevertheless not involved any maritime interdiction measures and are thus not of great relevance for this study.

One might argue that the authorization by the Security Council as such may be sufficient to entail a (vicarious) responsibility comparable to the responsibility of one State assisting another.[451] However, if the resolution has been legal, then also one ought to presume that the implementing measures within the limits imposed by the resolution have been lawful. As far as it concerns interdiction measures outside the framework of the authorizing resolution, responsibility should be borne by the implementing State or regional organization alone and not the United Nations.[452] Therefore, only if the authorizing resolution itself had been illegal,[453]

---

447 *Cf. Koskenniemi*, Martti, "Le Comité des Sanctions (créé par la résolution 661 (1990) du Conseil de sécurité)", 37 AFDI (1991), pp. 119 *et seq.*, at 132.

448 *Pagani*, Fabrizio, "Le misure di interdizione navale in relazione alle sanzioni adottate dall'ONU", 76 Rivista di diritto internazionale (1993), pp. 720 *et seq.*, at 755; *UN* Doc. A/51/389 (20 September 1996), "Report on the administrative and budgetary aspects of the financing of the United Nations peacekeeping operations", at para. 17.

449 *Cf. Lavalle*, Roberto, "The Law of the United Nations and the Use of Force, under the relevant Security Council Resolutions of 1990 and 1991, to resolve the Persian Gulf Crisis", 23 Netherlands Ybk. Int'l L. (1992), pp. 3 *et seq.*, 27.

450 *UN* Doc. A/CN.4/541 (2 April 2004), *Gaja*, Giorgio, "Second Report on the Responsibility of International Organizations", at 17, para. 35.

451 *Cf.* Draft Article 16, para. 2 of the ILC's Draft Articles on the Responsibility of International Organizations, reprinted in *UN* Doc. A/60/10 (2005), "Report of the International Law Commission on the Work of its Fifty-Seventh Session, at 77.

452 *Cf. ibid.*, at 104 (citing a letter of 11 November 1996 by the United Nations Secretary-General to the Prime Minister of Rwanda).

453 On the legal limits imposed on the Security Council adopting resolutions see *Zimmermann*, Andreas/*Elberling*, Björn, "Grenzen der Legislativbefugnisse des Sicherheitsrats", 52 Vereinte Nationen (2004), pp. 71 *et seq.*, at 71; *Bothe*, Michael, "Les limites des pouvoirs du Conseil de securité", in *Dupuy*, René-Jean (ed.), "The Develop-

the United Nations may bear responsibility for operations to enforce the embargo. Since, due to the discretion available to the Security Council, the illegality of its resolution will be hard to obtain[454] and since the degree of control exercised by the Security Council was so low, responsibility for the enforcement of the respective embargo will either rest with the States or the regional organization implementing the embargo.

b) Regional organizations enforcing embargoes on the seas

All of the naval interdiction operations under the mandate of the Security Council except Southern Rhodesia have been enforced by regional organizations. Only in the case of Southern Rhodesia, one State (the United Kingdom) exclusively enforced the embargo and thus represents the only likely liable entity in that scenario.

In the case of Iraq, the Western European Union only coordinated some measures, but left the effective control and particularly the decision which vessel was to be boarded where and when to the allied powers fighting against Iraq. These powers were led by the United States and, even though the Rules of Engagement are confidential, it may be presumed that the United States had such a large degree of command and control that it bore the main responsibility for interdictions within the framework of the so-called Operation Desert Storm.[455]

In the second phase of the conflict in Yugoslavia, however, there was a unified command center for the combined naval enforcement operation "Sharp Guard" of WEU and NATO.[456] This center determined the composition of the fleets, the techniques of intervention, the rules of engagement and most often even the particular measure of interdiction in individual cases.[457] The international legal personalities of WEU[458] and NATO[459] are widely accepted. Therefore, these

---

ment of the Role of the Security Council" (Dordrecht: Nijhoff, 1993), pp. 67 *et seq.*, at 69-70.

454 *Dominicé*, Christian, "The International Responsibility of the United Nations for Injuries Resulting from Non-Military Enforcement Measures", in *Ragazzi*, Maurizio (ed.), "International Responsibility Today – Essays in Memory of Oscar Schachter" (Leiden: Nijhoff, 2005), pp. 363 *et seq.*, at 366.

455 *Cf. Cushman*, John H., "Command and Control in the Coalition", 117 Naval Institute Proceedings (May 1991), pp. 74 *et seq.*, at 74-75.

456 *UN* Doc. S/1996/946 (15 November 1996), "Final Report of the Security Council Committee established pursuant to resolution 724 (1991) concerning Yugoslavia", at 32, para. 79b).

457 *Scholz*, Oliver, "Die Durchsetzung von Zwangsmaßnahmen nach Art. 41 der Satzung der Vereinten Nationen, insbesondere mit militärischen Mitteln" (Frankfurt am Main: Lang, 1998), at 44-45.

458 *Cremer*, H.C., "Art. 17 EUV", para. 2, in *Calliess*, Christian *et al.* (eds.), "Kommentar des Vertrages über die Europäische Union und des Vertrages zur Gründung der Europäischen Gemeinschaft" (2nd ed., Neuwied: Luchterhand, 2002), pp. 186 *et seq.*, at 188-189, para. 2. But see *Gerteiser*, Kristina, "Die Sicherheits- und Verteidigungspolitik der Europäischen Union" (Frankfurt am Main: Lang, 2002), at 29-30.

organisations were probably responsible for most of the interdiction measures in the Adriatic Sea.[460] However, NATO and its member States may also conclude so-called Status of Force Agreements (SOFA) according to which the sending States retains the exclusive responsibility for conduct of their troops even when they are acting on the command of NATO.[461] Lacking such exemptions, NATO is solely responsible and member States only grant compensation *ex gratia*, without any *opinio juris*.[462]

The embargo against Haiti was enforced by naval vessels of the United States, Canada, France, the Netherlands and the United Kingdom.[463] The relationship between the naval commands remained quite lose which is why the responsibility for interferences during these operations was probably borne by the individual States.

As far as it concerns Sierra Leone, the Security Council in Resolution 1132 only authorized ECOWAS to enforce the embargo. Such authorization presumably limits lawful enforcement actions to those undertaken under the ECOWAS command structure, the so-called ECOMOG (Economic Monitoring Group).[464] Since 1999, the ECOMOG force commander has complete control of the various forces[465] and therefore ECOWAS most likely bears responsibility for the enforcement actions by ECOMOG forces. However, apparently the enforcement of the embargo, due to a lack of naval resources of ECOWAS member States, has not played a significant role in the conflict since merchant ships continued to enter Sierra Leone ports[466] and since no maritime interdiction activities are mentioned in the Reports of the Security Council Committee monitoring the enforcement of Resolution 1132.[467] This is probably due to the fact that maritime transport was

---

459 *Schmalenbach*, Kirsten, "Die Haftung Internationaler Organisationen" (Frankfurt am Main: Lang, 2004), at 535-536.

460 *Pagani*, Fabrizio, "Le misure di interdizione navale in relazione alle sanzioni adottate dall'ONU", 76 Rivista di diritto internazionale (1993), pp. 720 *et seq.*, at 756, n. 146.

461 *Cf., e.g.,* Art. VIII, para. 5, lit. e of the North Atlantic Treaty Organization Status of Forces Agreement, adopted on 4 April 1949, UNTS, Vol. 34, pp. 243 *et seq.*

462 *Cf. Schmalenbach*, Kirsten, "Die Haftung Internationaler Organisationen" (Frankfurt am Main: Lang, 2004), at 558-559.

463 *Pagani*, Fabrizio, "Le misure di interdizione navale in relazione alle sanzioni adottate dall'ONU", 76 Rivista di diritto internazionale (1993), pp. 720 *et seq.*, at 721, n. 1.

464 *Soons*, Alfred H.A., "Enforcing the economic embargo at sea", in *Gowlland-Debbas*, Vera (ed.), "United Nations Sanctions and International Law" (The Hague: Kluwer Law International, 2001), pp. 307 *et seq.*, at 319.

465 "Profile: ECOMOG", BBC News, 17 June 2004, available at <http://news.bbc.co.uk/2/hi/africa/country_profiles/2364029.stm>.

466 *UN* Doc. S/1997/895 (17 November 1997), "First Report of the Economic Community of West African States Committee of Five on Sierra Leone to the Security Council", pp. 3 *et seq.*, at 15-16, para. 41.

467 *UN* Doc. S/1998/1236 (31 December 1998), "Report of the Security Council Committee established pursuant to resolution 1132 (1997) concerning Sierra Leone (1997 Report)", at 2; *UN* Doc. S/1999/1300 (31 December 1999), "1999 Report"; *UN* Doc. S/2000/1238 (26 December 2000), "2000 Report"; UN Doc. S/2002/50 (14 January 2002), "2001 Report"; *UN* Doc. S/2002/1414 (24 December 2002), "2002 Report"; *UN*

scared off by military aircraft and that after the oil embargo was lifted on 15 March 1998,[468] arms falling under the arms embargo were mainly transport by civil aircraft.[469]

c) Operation Enduring Freedom

In the case of Operation Enduring Freedom, the relevant resolutions by the Security Council have been extremely vague because China opposed any new authorization for maritime interdictions on the high seas.[470] Their general terms[471] are not sufficiently explicit as compared to the enforcement of the aforementioned embargoes to cover any interdiction measures against foreign vessels on the high seas[472] and the United Nations should not bear any responsibility if a regional organization or a State claims the resolution as legal basis for an interference with the navigation of a foreign vessel. Neither is the North Atlantic Treaty Organization (NATO) directly involved in Operation Enduring Freedom. Instead, the United States lead the operation from the U.S. Central Command in Tampa Bay, Florida. The multinational naval forces at the Horn of Africa are then led by one commander on a rotating basis for a period of four to six months, but each State also exercises a considerable degree of control over its own naval forces. Hence, the issue of effective control and thus also the issue of international responsibility is extremely complex in the case of Operation Enduring Freedom. The Rules of Engagement might bring some light to these questions, but they are still kept confidential. To determine the responsible entity for an interdiction measure within the framework of Operation Enduring Freedom, it is submitted that for each boarding or interference, one needs to find out whether the decision to board had been taken by the Central Command (responsibility of the United States), the command of the multinational forces (responsibility of the leading State) or a national authority (responsibility of the individual boarding State). Since no legal obligation of the boarding State to follow orders by the Central Command or by the command of the multinational forces is apparent, the responsibility of the individual boarding State is most likely.

Doc. S/2004/166 (27 February 2004), "2003 Report"; *UN* Doc. S/2005/44 (25 January 2005), "2004 Report"; *UN* Doc. S/2005/843 (30 December 2005), "2005 Report".

468 Security Council Resolution 1156 (15 March 1998).

469 *Cf. UN* Doc. S/1999/1300 (31 December 1999), "Report of the Security Council Committee established pursuant to resolution 1132 (1997) concerning Sierra Leone", at 4.

470 *Bergin*, Anthony, "The Proliferation Security Initiative – Implications for the Indian Ocean", 20 Int'l J. Mar. & Coast. L. (2005), pp. 85 *et seq.*, at 91.

471 "Take the necessary steps to prevent the commission of terrorist acts [...]; Ensure that any person who participates in the financing, planning, preparation or perpetration of terrorist acts or in supporting terrorist acts is brought to justice [...]." Security Council Resolution 1373 (2001), para. 2, lit. a and c.

472 *Schmidt-Radefeld*, Roman, "Enduring Freedom – Antiterrorkrieg für immer?", 18 HVR (2005), pp. 245 *et seq.*, at 248; but see *Heintschel von Heinegg*, Wolff, "Der Einsatz der Deutschen Marine im Rahmen der Operation 'Enduring Freedom'", 40 AVR (2002), pp. 145 *et seq.*, at 172-173.

d) Conclusion

Concluding, in joint operations, international responsibility for the conduct of the crews of naval vessels lies where operational command and control is vested according to the arrangements establishing the modalities of cooperation between the State, regional organizations and the United Nations. In the absence of formal arrangements between the United Nations and the States or regional organizations providing troops, responsibility would be determined in each and every case according to the degree of effective control exercised by either party in the conduct of the operation. While one may reasonably exclude such control on the part of the United Nations, one nevertheless has to analyze on a case-by-case basis whether a particular interdiction was under the effective control by a regional organization or by a State enforcing an embargo.

3. Responsibility of member States for wrongful acts by an International Organization

Under certain circumstances, an International Organization may thus be responsible for interdiction measures on the high seas. However, comparable to the situation when two States incur liability for a multilateral boarding (*supra*), one might ask whether a member State may also concurrently bear responsibility for the conduct of an International Organization.

This issue was debated in two important domestic court cases before British and Swiss courts. In these two cases, the claimants failed to establish the liability of member States for acts committed by an International Organization.[473]

The main argument of the court decisions was that the separate legal personality of the organization makes it impossible to hold the members liable for the organization's acts.[474] This argument raises some doubts because the recognition of legal personality by a third State does not necessarily include the acceptance that from the moment of recognition, the International Organization will bear exclusive responsibility for its conduct.

Another argument was that an organization may, if its constitutive treaty so provides, act on its own account and not as agent of the member States.[475] Hence, the conduct of the organization usually is not directly imputable to member States. However, an International Organization may also act as its members' agent if its actions are imputable to the latter according to the general rules on attribution,[476]

---

[473] *Maclaine Watson v. Dept of Trade*, High Court, Chancery Division. 13 May 1987, 77 ILR 45; *Westland Case*, Swiss Federal Tribunal, 19 July 1988, 80 ILR 658.

[474] *Maclaine Watson v. Dept of Trade*, High Court, Chancery Division. 13 May 1987, 77 ILR 45.

[475] *Maclaine Watson & Co. Ltd. v. International Tin Council (No. 2)*, Court of Appeal, 27 April 1988, 80 ILR, pp. 110 *et seq.*, at 114; *Seidl-Hohenveldern*, Ignaz/*Loibl*, Gerhard, "Das Recht der internationalen Organisationen einschließlich der supranationalen Gemeinschaften" (7th ed., Köln: Heymanns, 2000), at 91, para. 0709.

[476] *Cf. Sienho Yee*, "The Responsibility of States Members of an International Organization for its Conduct as a Result of Membership or their Normal Conduct associated with

even though there may exist a presumption that its conduct has been on its own account.[477] Furthermore, the member States might be significantly involved in the decision-making process within the International Organization. This involvement might have amounted to assistance under the general law on State responsibility. Thus, the mere fact that the International Organization constitutes a separate legal personality does not as such exclude the responsibility of its member States or lead to the subsidiarity of the latters' responsibility.[478]

The fact that the constituent instrument of an International Organization does not explicitly exempt the responsibility of member States for conduct of the organization does not by itself imply such responsibility. Some constituent instruments of international financial institutions or of commodity organization do indeed contain such an exemption,[479] but the practice is not sufficiently consistent to show the existence of a rule of customary international law.[480] Furthermore, the constituent instrument as a treaty between the member States may not affect the rights of third States such as the right to invoke the responsibility of a member State for certain conduct.[481] Therefore, such constituent instrument also cannot limit the extent of responsibility of the organization vis-à-vis third States.[482] Exceptionally, such limitation may apply in relations to third States which have voluntarily contracted with the International Organization.[483] This study, though,

---

Membership", in *Ragazzi*, Maurizio (ed.), "International Responsibility Today – Essays in Memory of Oscar Schachter" (Leiden: Nijhoff, 2005), pp. 435 *et seq.*, at 437.

477 *Klein*, Pierre, "La responsabilité des organisations internationales" (Bruxelles: Bruylant, 1998), at 504. Sienho Yee nevertheless strongly rejects such a presumption. *Cf. Sienho Yee*, "The Responsibility of States Members of an International Organization for its Conduct as a Result of Membership or their Normal Conduct associated with Membership", in *Ragazzi*, Maurizio (ed.), "International Responsibility Today – Essays in Memory of Oscar Schachter" (Leiden: Nijhoff, 2005), pp. 435 *et seq.*, at 443.

478 *Ibid.*, at 442; but see *Klabbers*, Jan, "An Introduction to International Institutional Law" (Cambridge: Cambridge University Press, 2002), at 302.

479 Art. II, Section 6 and Art. IV, Section 9 of the International Bank for Reconstruction and Development Articles of Agreement, UNTS, Vol. 2, pp. 134 *et seq.*; Art. 6, para. 5 of the Statute of the African Development Bank, adopted on 4 August 1963, UNTS, Vol. 510, pp. 3 *et seq.*; Art. 6 of the Statute of the Common Fund for Commodities, adopted on 27 June 1980, UNTS, Vol. 1538, pp. 3 *et seq.*

480 *Maclaine Watson & Co. Ltd. v. International Tin Council (No. 2)*, Court of Appeal, 27 April 1988, 80 ILR, pp. 110 *et seq.*, at 174; *J.H. Rayner v. Dpt of Trade*, House of Lords, 26 October 1989, 81 ILR, pp. 704 *et seq.* But see *Hartwig*, Matthias, "Die Haftung der Mitgliedstaaten für Internationale Organisationen" (Berlin: Springer, 1993), at 290-291.

481 *Sienho Yee*, "The Responsibility of States Members of an International Organization for its Conduct as a Result of Membership or their Normal Conduct associated with Membership", in *Ragazzi*, Maurizio (ed.), "International Responsibility Today – Essays in Memory of Oscar Schachter" (Leiden: Nijhoff, 2005), pp. 435 *et seq.*, at 440.

482 *Ibid.*, at 447; *Brownlie*, Ian, "The Responsibility of States for the Acts of International Organizations", *ibid.*, pp. 355 *et seq.*, at 359.

483 *Sienho Yee*, "The Responsibility of States Members of an International Organization for its Conduct as a Result of Membership or their Normal Conduct associated with

mainly concerns situations where an International Organization orders interferences on the high seas against the will of the flag State and one therefore cannot presume any limitation of responsibility on the basis of the constituent instrument of the organization.

If the recognition of the International Organization and its constituent instruments are of little or no relevance, the issue needs to be resolved by an application of the general law on State responsibility. Here, the above-mentioned principles on attribution and participation play a major role.

Even though most International Organizations require unanimous decisions, the member States do not have at their disposal such a degree of control over the organization that its conduct is directly imputable to the member States.[484] They are only able to prevent certain decision, but not to control the entire decision-making.[485] Exceptionally, such control may however be determined if the claimant proves the actual authority of a member State over the disputed act of the organization.[486] Nevertheless, there does not seem to exist a general rule providing that member States may be responsible for their voting in an International Organization to third States.[487]

In State practice, France, Italy, Portugal and Canada have claimed that they are not responsible as member States for decisions taken by NATO in the conflict with Serbia and Montenegro.[488] Serbia and Montenegro strongly opposed these claims, but argued that the member States were responsible for their own acts and not for the decisions taken by NATO.[489] The International Court Justice was not able to rule on any of the preliminary objections because Serbia and Montenegro was not a party to the Statute of the Court when the application was filed and thus

Membership", in *Ragazzi*, Maurizio (ed.), "International Responsibility Today – Essays in Memory of Oscar Schachter" (Leiden: Nijhoff, 2005), pp. 435 *et seq.*, at 449-450.

484 *Westland Case*, Swiss Federal Tribunal, 19 July 1988, 80 ILR 658.

485 *Hartwig*, Matthias, "Die Haftung der Mitgliedstaaten für Internationale Organisationen" (Berlin: Springer, 1993), at 292.

486 *Maclaine Watson v. Dept of Trade*, High Court, Chancery Division. 13 May 1987, 77 ILR 46.

487 *Higgins*, Rosalyn, "Preliminary Report of the Institut de Droit International", 66 Annuaire de l'Institut de Droit International (1996-I), at 415-416.

488 *Legality of Use of Force (Serbia and Montenegro v. France)*, Preliminary Objections of the French Republic (5 July 2000), at paras. 23-24, available at <www.icj-cij.org/icjwww/idocket/iyfr/iyfrframe.htm>; *Legality of Use of Force (Serbia and Montenegro v. Portugal)*, Preliminary Objections of the Portuguese Republic (5 July 2000), at paras. 130-141, available at <www.icj-cij.org/icjwww/idocket/iypo/iypoframe.htm>; *Legality of Use of Force (Serbia and Montenegro v. Italy)*, Preliminary Objections of the Italian Republic, at 19, available at <www.icj-cij.org/icjwww/idocket/iyit/iyitframe.htm>; *Legality of Use of Force (Serbia and Montenegro v. Canada)*, Provisional Measures, Oral Pleading of Canada (12 May 1999), *ICJ* Doc. CR 99/27.

489 *Higgins*, Rosalyn, "The International Court of Justice: Selected Issues of State Responsibility", in *Ragazzi*, Maurizio (ed.), "International Responsibility Today – Essays in Memory of Oscar Schachter" (Leiden: Nijhoff, 2005), pp. 271 *et seq.*, at 274.

did not have access to the Court.[490] In total, the existing State practice therefore seems inconclusive.

It is submitted, however, that the requirements for the responsibility of member States for the conduct of an International Organization are quite strict. The International Organization must either lack international legal personality, or the International Organization must have acted on the account of a member State. A member State is generally not liable solely due to its membership for the obligations of an International Organization of which it is a member.[491] An alternative source of responsibility would exist if the member State had controlled the International Organization to such a degree that one could talk of "effective control". The conditions under which a member State has gained such "effective control" are still quite uncertain and probably equity will play a great part in the determination whether or not such control was exercised.[492]

However, since the general law on State responsibility adheres to the principle of independent responsibility, some authors submit that a member State may also be separately liable for its involvement in the conduct of the International Organization as co-author or participant.[493] Since such liability might easily circumvent the strict "effective control" requirement, it is proposed here that extreme care be applied when determining this issue and that liability for participation could only come up for a part of the damage, depending on the degree of participation. Furthermore, the mere voting in a body of the regional organization could be attributed as well to the regional organization as to the member State and therefore should not suffice as participatory act.

Finally, member States need to carefully question whether already the transfer of competences to an International Organization might entail their responsibility and they need to continuously and diligently control the organization in order to prevent the violation of international law by the latter.[494] However, in order to establish the responsibility of a member State, one needs to show that the transfer

---

490 See, *e.g.*, *Legality of Use of Force (Serbia and Montenegro v. France)*, Judgment of 15 December 2004, at para. 114, available at <www.icj-cij.org/icjwww/idocket/iyfr/iyfrframe.htm.

491 Article 6 of the Resolution "The Legal Consequences for Member States of the Non-fulfilment by International Organizations of their Obligations toward Third Parties", 66 Annuaire de l'Institut de Droit International (1996-II), at 449.

492 *Hartwig*, Matthias, "Die Haftung der Mitgliedstaaten für Internationale Organisationen" (Berlin: Springer, 1993), at 297.

493 *Sands*, Philippe/*Klein*, Pierre, "Bowett's Law of International Institutions" (London: Sweet & Maxwell, 2001), at 524; UN Doc. A/51/389 (20 September 1996), "Report on the administrative and budgetary aspects of the financing of the United Nations peacekeeping operations", at para. 6; *cf.* also *Sienho Yee*, "The Responsibility of States Members of an International Organization for its Conduct as a Result of Membership or their Normal Conduct associated with Membership", in *Ragazzi*, Maurizio (ed.), "International Responsibility Today – Essays in Memory of Oscar Schachter" (Leiden: Nijhoff, 2005), pp. 435 *et seq.*, at 443, at 452.

494 *Matthews v. The United Kingdom*, European Court of Human Rights (18 February 1999), Application 24833/94, at para. 32.

of competences as such or the lack of control has amounted to an independent internationally wrongful act.

In the situations where regional organizations and their member States enforce an embargo imposed by the United Nations Security Council, the member States may thus be responsible for certain conduct of the regional organization. This requires first that the regional organization does indeed bear some responsibility for the interference. As has been shown in the previous part of this study (*supra*), such responsibility will only arise when the regional organization was in command of the forces which interfered with the navigation of a foreign vessel. When such command by the regional organization exists, any effective control by one member State will be extremely hard to show.

Thus, it is submitted here that once the responsibility of a regional organization has been shown, member States may only incur own liability if the organization has acted as agent of the member State or if the member State was a participant in the conduct of the regional organization. The latter liability is limited to the extent in which the individual member State has contributed to the violation of international law by the regional organization.

Suffice it to add that the responsibility of the regional organization is generally not limited. If this organization does not have the financial resources to compensate for the damage, then the member States need to contribute the necessary assets. This contribution, however, is not equivalent to a responsibility of the member States vis-à-vis the claimant.

4. The applicability of the compensation provisions to International Organizations

This study has shown that the application of the general law on State responsibility may lead to the responsibility of an International Organization for interferences with navigation on the high seas. However, it is not yet clear whether compensation provisions such as Art. 110, para. 3 LOSC with their own particularities may apply to such cases.

Only one International Organization, namely the European Community, has ratified the Law of the Sea Convention.[495] The European Community, as a non-member due to Art. 5 of the Convention on the International Maritime Organization,[496] has not become a party to any of the IMO Conventions such as the Intervention Convention or the SUA Convention and its 2005 Protocol. It has signed the Migrant Smuggling Protocol[497] and ratified the Fish Stocks Agree-

495 <www.un.org/Depts/los/reference_files/status2006.pdf>.

496 "Membership in the Organization shall be open to all States…", Art. 5 of the Convention on the International Maritime Consultative Organization, adopted on 6 March 1948, reprinted in 53 AJIL (1959), at 516.

497 "Signatories – Protocol against the Smuggling of Migrants", available at <www.unodc.org/unodc/crime_cicp_signatures_migrants.html>.

ment.[498] Even as far as it concerns the Law of the Sea Convention, the European Community is only bound "to the extent that it has competence in accordance with" a separate declaration submitted according to Art. 5 of Annex IX to the Law of the Sea Convention.[499] While the European Community has significant competences in matters of fisheries[500] and maritime transport,[501] this declaration explicitly states that "in respect of measures relating to the exercise of jurisdiction over vessels, flagging and registration of vessels and the enforcement of penal and administrative sanctions, competence rests with the Member States whilst respecting Community law."[502] Thus, it is not likely that the provisions dealing with interferences on the high seas (measures of law enforcement) will directly apply to the European Community with its current status of integration. If however, the European Community, particularly after the establishment of the European Maritime Safety Agency (EMSA), starts interdiction operation with its own vessels, the letters of the mentioned declaration might become irrelevant.

All of the other International Organizations which have been involved in multilateral interdiction operations, such as NATO, have not ratified any international convention dealing with the Law of the Sea.

The major issue thus becomes whether a treaty provision would nevertheless apply to an International Organization because (1) all of the member States have ratified the relevant international convention or (2) because the provision has become part of customary international law. As far as it concerns the first alternative, one ought to consider that if the International Organization were not bound by obligations of their member States and if the latter were not concurrently responsible for conduct of the International Organization, then they could easily circumvent their obligations by transferring competences to an International Organization. Sound logic and probably also the prohibition of an abuse of rights thus oblige to apply the treaty obligations of member States to the International Organization.

The issue becomes much more complicated if only some member States of an International Organization have ratified an international convention. If one or more member States have denied ratifying a certain convention, it would seem

498 "Chronological lists of ratifications of, accessions and successions to the Convention and the related Agreements as at 28 April 2006", available at <www.un.org/Depts/los/reference_files/chronological_lists_of_ratifications.htm#Agreement%20for%20the%20implementation%20of%20the%20provisions%20of%20the%20Convention%20relating%20to%20the%20conservation%20and%20management%20of%20straddling%20fish%20stocks%20and%20highly%20migratory%20fish%20stocks>.

499 Art. 4, para. 2 of Annex IX of the Law of the Sea Convention.

500 Arts. 32 *et seq.* of the Treaty establishing the European Community, adopted on 25 March 1957, Consolidated Version, OJ C 325 (24 December 2002).

501 Arts. 70 *et seq.* of the Treaty establishing the European Community, adopted on 25 March 1957, Consolidated Version, OJ C 325 (24 December 2002).

502 "Declarations made pursuant to article 5, para. 1 of Annex IX to the Law of the Sea Convention", available at <www.un.org/Depts/los/convention_agreements/convention_declarations.htm#European%20Community%20Declaration%20made%20upon%20formal%20confirmation>.

unreasonable to apply provisions of this convention to an International Organization of which they are members. If however all member States, though not parties to a particular convention, have accepted the relevant rules embodied in the convention, then one may cautiously consider the applicability of the convention to the international convention. Such may be the case with the membership of the United States in NATO. The United States has thus far refrained from ratifying the Law of the Sea Convention because of various reasons, which nevertheless do not involve any of the rules contained in Part VI of the Convention, such as Art. 110, para. 3 LOSC.[503]

Similar considerations may apply concerning the status of the compensation provisions as customary international law. In fact, the United States has accepted all provisions of the Law of the Sea Convention dealing with the "traditional uses of the oceans" as customary international law.[504] Presumably, this includes Part VI of the Law of the Sea Convention. In fact, the United States is still a party to the Convention on the High Seas which contains provisions basically identical to Art. 110, para. 3 and Art. 106 LOSC. However, one also needs to recognize that some of the relevant conventions (such as the 2005 SUA Protocol) have established new grounds for interferences and, as a safeguard, created a right to compensation. Instead of cherrypicking certain convention provisions, it is thus always necessary to consider the whole balance between rights and obligations of a certain convention before applying it to non-parties.

A detailed study of the relevant conventions and their compensation provisions as to their status as customary international law would exceed the scope of this thesis and, regarding some newer provisions like Art. 8bis, para. 10, lit. b of the 2005 SUA Protocol, might be outdated by the time this study is published.

The application of treaty provisions to International Organizations thus proves to be a complicated issue in desperate need of clarification and maybe codification.[505] A separate part of this study will deal with the issue whether the compensation provisions of the Law of the Sea apply in situations of international conflicts, the most common scenario where International Organizations are involved in maritime interdiction operations (*infra*).

503 *Cf., e.g., Duff*, John A., "A Note on the United States and the Law of the Sea: Looking Back and Moving Forward", 35 ODIL (2004), pp. 195 *et seq.*, at 197 (citing the ultimatum by President Reagan "regarding six specific issues which required resolution if the United States were to become a party to the Treaty").

504 *Oxman*, Bernard H., "Testimony before the Senate Committee on Foreign Relations" (14 October 2003), available at <http://foreign.senate.gov/testimony/2003/Oxman Testimony031014.pdf (citing a declaration of President Ronald Reagan).

505 The International Law Commission has thus far only drafted the following provision without major comments: "An act of an International Organization does not constitute a breach of an international obligation unless the International Organization is bound by the obligation in question at the time the act occurs." *UN* Doc. A/60/10 (2005), "Report of the International Law Commission on the Work of its Fifty-Seventh Session", at 91.

5. Conclusion

Even though the applicable law remains to be quite uncertain, this study has elaborated that both International Organizations and their member States may under certain circumstances be responsible for maritime interdiction operations. Most important in this respect are the general rules on attribution in the law on State responsibility. If these rules lead to a liability of the International Organization, then a potential responsibility of its member States will be very unlikely and subject to strict conditions.

F. The effect of conduct by the boarded party

Every domestic legal system assesses the conduct of the claimant before he is granted a compensation award. Such conduct might bar his claim in total (clean hands doctrine) or may at least reduce the compensation award (contributory negligence). Needless to say whether as "general principles of international law" or as customary international law, the general law of State responsibility may more or less have absorbed this approach into public international law.

This study will first analyze the status of the clean hands doctrine in the general law of State responsibility (1.) and its applicability to the compensations provisions most relevant to this study (2.). Then, the principle of contributory negligence will be elaborated upon (3.), particularly with regard to the Law of the Sea (4.).

I. Clean Hands Doctrine

As early as 1810, the U.S. vessel *The Amédie*, which was carrying slaves, was seized on the high seas by an English captor. The shipowner, before a British court, claimed this interference to be unlawful. Even though interferences on the high seas on the grounds of suspicion of slave trade were prohibited at the time, the Lords Commissioners decided that the fact that the slave trade was forbidden by U.S. and by British laws would defeat a claim to restitution.[506] One might consider this to be an application of the clean hands doctrine according to which a claimant may not benefit from its own behaviour. This doctrine is also known

[506] *The Amédie*, cited in *Moore*, John Bassett, "Digest of International Law", Vol. 2 (Washington: Government Printing Office, 1906), at 914-5. *Cf.* also *The Fortuna*, 1 Dods. 81 (12 March 1811). One ought to bear in mind that these cases occurred during the Napoleonic wars and therefore might have applied the rules of naval warfare. However, at least in the case of *The Amédie*, the decision is formulated in more general terms. The rule that a vessel violating the law of the flag State is liable to capture by other States has nevertheless also been expressed in times of peace, cf. *Madrazo v. Willes*, 3 Barn. & Ald. 353 (1820). But then see *The Antilope*, 10 Wheaton 66, at 116 (1825).

under the following Latin terms: "Ex delicto non oritur actio", "Nemo ex suo delicto meliorem suam conditionem facit", "Ex turpi causa non oritur" or "Inadimplenti non est adimplendum".

However, it is very dubious whether this principle of common law is applicable in the general law of state responsibility. The International Law Commission has not explicitly included the principle in its Articles on State Responsibility.[507]

Both the Permanent Court of International Justice (PCIJ) and the International Court of Justice (ICJ) have nevertheless applied the clean hands doctrine as far as it concerns the conduct of the claiming State.[508] In the *Chorzów Factory Case*, the PCIJ held that it is "a principle generally accepted in the jurisprudence of international arbitration, as well as by municipal courts, that one party cannot avail himself of the fact that the other has not fulfilled some obligation or has not had recourse to some means of redress, if the former party has, by some illegal act, prevented the latter from fulfilling the obligation in question, or from having recourse to the tribunal which would have been open to him."[509] The ICJ explicitly referred to this holding when it considered Hungary's conduct and its effect on the right to terminate the treaty with Slovakia in the *Gabcíkovo-Nagymaros Case*.[510]

Judge *Schwebel* in his dissenting opinion in the *Nicaragua Case*, referring to much valuable authority, considered Nicaragua's "hands", due to its aggressive acts in El Salvador, so "odiously unclean" that it could not claim the violation of international law by the United States.[511] However, the Court in that case did not follow this line of argument. Considering the whole jurisprudence of the PCIJ/ICJ, one must nevertheless admit that in inter-State relations, the conduct of the claiming State, if unlawful, might lead to a denial of its claim.[512]

These cases only concerned the prior conduct of the claiming State, but the application of the doctrine is also discussed if the individual for whom the claiming State exercises diplomatic protection has acted illegally.

---

507 Commentary on Chapter V, para. 9, in: *Crawford*, James, "The International Law Commission's Articles on State Responsibility" (Cambridge: Cambridge University Press, 2002), at 162.

508 *Case concerning the Factory at Chorzów (Germany/Poland)*, *Jurisdiction*, Judgment of 26 July 1927, (1927) PCIJ Series A, No. 9, pp. 1 *et seq.*, at 31; *Gabcíkovo-Nagymaros (Hungary/Slovakia)*, Judgment of 25 September 1997, ICJ Reports 1997, pp. 7 *et seq.*, at 67, para. 110.

509 *Case concerning the Factory at Chorzów (Germany/Poland)*, *Jurisdiction*, Judgment of 26 July 1927, (1927) PCIJ Series A, No. 9, at 31. See also *Diversion of Water from the River Meuse (Netherlands/Belgium)*, Dissenting Opinion Judge Hudson, (1937) PCIJ Series A/B No. 70, pp. 73 *et seq.*, at 77.

510 *Gabcíkovo-Nagymaros (Hungary/Slovakia)*, Judgment of 25 September 1997, ICJ Reports 1997, pp. 7 *et seq.*, at 67, para. 110.

511 *Military and Paramilitary Activities in and against Nicaragua (Nicaragua v. United States of America)*, Dissenting Opinion Judge Schwebel, ICJ Reports 1986, pp. 14 *et seq.*, at 392-394. See also *Arrest Warrant of 11 April 2000 (Democratic Republic of the Congo v. Belgium)*, Dissenting opinion of Judge *ad hoc* Van den Wyngaert, ICJ Reports 2002, at para. 35.

512 *Cf. UN* Doc. A/CN.4/546 (11 August 2004), *Dugard*, John, "Sixth report on diplomatic protection", at 5, para. 6.

A multitude of arbitral awards[513] have led *Rousseau* and *Witenburg* to the conclusion that a claim is inadmissible if the occurrence was provoked by an individual's breach of either domestic or public international law.[514] *Hackworth* also argued that the conduct can be a reason for a tribunal to reject the claim.[515] Professor *Reuter* in the *Barcelona Traction Case*, proposed that the Barcelona Traction company had so manifestly breached Spanish law that they were no more entitled to diplomatic protection by Belgium.[516]

Could one reasonably apply the doctrine to the case where the shipowner or the crew of a vessel has broken the domestic law of its flag State or international law?

There is a great variety of arguments against such an application of the doctrine. First, one might consider the rationale behind the clean hands doctrine to be that an individual always has to act correctly in the territory of another State.[517] In fact, most cases that have applied the doctrine dealt with the conduct of an individual in a foreign State. In the case of a vessel on the high seas, however, no other State has any jurisdiction over the "territory". Instead, only the law of the flag State and public international law apply.

Secondly, one might wonder how far a violation by an individual of the law of its national or flag State would influence the relations to a third State. The violation of a domestic law does not necessarily justify the breach of an obligation under public international law because the two legal systems remain to be distinct.[518]

Thirdly, there are very few cases how an individual may breach public international law. As far as it concerns the Law of the Sea, the trade of slaves, piracy and unauthorized broadcasting are such international crimes. However, interferences with navigation by other States than the flag State are only allowed under very limited circumstances.[519] If a third State does board a vessel, it usually faces the risk of paying compensation.[520] As elaborated, the compensation provisions serve the purpose of deterring abusive interferences. Except where explicitly provided for in an international convention, no State has a right to interdict foreign vessels on the high seas. *A fortiori*, no State should be able to claim the unlawful conduct

513 For a list of cases see *Salmon*, Jean J.A., "Des 'Main Propres' comme condition de recevabilité des réclamations internationales", 10 AFDI (1964), pp. 225 *et seq.*, at 237-258.

514 *Rousseau*, Charles, "Cours de droit international public: La responsabilité internationale" (1959-60), at 184.

515 *Hackworth*, Green Haywood, "Digest of International Law", Vol. 5 (Washington: Government Printing Office, 1943), at 709.

516 *Salmon*, Jean J.A., "Des 'Main Propres' comme condition de recevabilité des réclamations internationales", 10 AFDI (1964), pp. 225 *et seq.*, at 225.

517 *Garcia-Arias*, Luis, "La doctrine des 'clean hands' en droit international public", 30 Annuaire des anciens Auditeurs de l'Académie de droit international (1960), pp. 14 *et seq.*, at 17.

518 *Salmon*, Jean J.A., "Des 'Main Propres' comme condition de recevabilité des réclamations internationales", 10 AFDI (1964), pp. 225 *et seq.*, at 246.

519 See, e.g., Arts. 110, para. 1, 105 LOSC.

520 See, e.g., Arts. 110, para. 3, 106 LOSC.

of the shipowner or the ship's crew as a circumstance precluding the wrongfulness of the interference if the State cannot base its claim on an authorization to interfere with navigation.

Quite apart from these considerations, it is rather doubtful whether the clean hands doctrine as far as it concerns the conduct of private individuals has become a general principle of public international law at all. There are many cases where States have successfully claimed diplomatic protection for their nationals who have manifestly breached the domestic law of the State of their residence.[521] In the *LaGrand Case*, the United States never claimed the objection of the unclean hands of the detained individuals, but rather invoked the unclean hands of the applicant State.[522] Furthermore, the doctrine has been firmly rejected by some authors,[523] at least as far as it concerns its application to issues of admissibility.[524] States have often abstained from exercising diplomatic protection on behalf of nationals who have by their own illegal conduct provoked a disputed act of a third State.[525] They have done so, however, not because they felt obliged by international law, but simply because of a political decision in the exercise of discretion at hand in cases of diplomatic protection.[526] This State practice therefore does not result from an *opinio juris* and, hence, is not sufficient to establish a rule of customary international law.[527] This might have been the reason why the ILC decided not to include an article on the clean hands doctrine in its Articles on State Responsibility.

---

521 See, *e.g.*, *Case Concerning Avena and Other Mexican Nationals (Mexico v. United States of America)*, Judgment of 31 March 2004, reprinted in 43 ILM (2004), pp. 581 *et seq.*; *LaGrand (Germany v. United States)*, Judgment of 27 June 2001, ICJ Reports 2001, pp. 466 *et seq.*, at para. 15; *Vienna Convention on Consular Relations (Paraguay v. United States of America)*, Application of Paraguay, at paras. 5 *et seq.*, available at <www.icj-cij.org/icjwww/idocket/ipaus/ipausframe.htm>.

522 *LaGrand (Germany v. United States)*, Counter-Memorial by the United States, at paras. 92-94, available at <www.icj-cij.org/icjwww/idocket/igus/igusframe.htm>; *ibid.*, Oral Argument by the United States (14 November 2000), Verbatim Record 2000/28, at paras. 3.43-3.53.

523 *Fitzmaurice*, Gerald, "The case of the I'm Alone", 17 BYIL(1936), pp. 82 *et seq.*, at 102; *Rousseau*, Charles, "Droit international public", Vol. 5 (Paris: Sirey, 1983), at 177.

524 *Salmon*, Jean J.A., "Des 'Main Propres' comme condition de recevabilité des réclamations internationales", 10 AFDI (1964), pp. 225 *et seq.*, at 236.

525 For example, in the case of the *Deerhound*, the United Kingdom did not claim compensation on behalf of the shipowner because his vessel had attempted to convey arms to Spain. However, the United Kingdom nevertheless demanded and achieved the acquittal of the vessel which had been wrongfully seized by Spain. *Moore*, John Bassett, "Digest of International Law", Vol. 2 (Washington: Government Printing Office, 1906), at 979-980.

526 *Salmon*, Jean J.A., "Des 'Main Propres' comme condition de recevabilité des réclamations internationales", 10 AFDI (1964), pp. 225 *et seq.*, at 236.

527 But see *Miaja de la Muela*, Adolfo, "Le role de la conditions des mains propres de la personne lésée dans les réclamations devant les tribunaux internationaux", in *Ibler*, Vladimir (ed.), "Mélanges offerts à Juraj Andrassy" (The Hague: Nijhoff, 1968), pp. 189 *et seq.*, at 207; *The Mary Lowell*, in *Moore*, John Bassett, "Digest of International Law", Vol. 2 (Washington: Government Printing Office, 1906), at 983-984.

During the discussion of its Articles on Diplomatic Protection, the ILC followed the reasoning of its special rapporteur and held the case law to be insufficient to prove a rule of customary international law.[528] The special rapporteur *John Dugard* used strong words to question the existence of the clean hands doctrine. The authority for the doctrine was "uncertain and of ancient vintage, dating mainly from the mid-nineteenth century" and the inclusion of an article "would clearly not be an exercise in codification [of international law] and is unwarranted as an exercise in [its] progressive development."[529]

Even as far as it concerns the Law of the Sea as applied by anglo-saxon domestic courts, one must question the applicability of the doctrine. As early as 1816, Lord Stowell held that, even though the vessel *Le Louis* was engaged in "malign" transport, there was no right for other States than the flag State to seize her and that therefore, the vessel had to be acquitted.[530] Hence, the conduct of the ship did not bar the ship's owner from claiming the release before the court in a jurisdiction where the clean hands doctrine was well-founded.

Furthermore, if one were to accept the clean hands doctrine as a circumstance precluding wrongfulness, any illicit conduct of an individual would lead to the loss of his diplomatic protection. Any international tribunal would be barred from deciding a case on the merits and thus from declaring the conduct of the respondent State as unlawful. Hereby, the respondent State might get the impression that in public international law, the end (*e.g.*, interdiction of unlawful maritime transport) justifies the means (*e.g.*, violation of the freedom of navigation and the exclusive jurisdiction of the flag State). Such a perception would undermine well-founded principles of the Law of the Sea, and probably of public international law in general.

The inapplicability of the clean hands doctrine nevertheless does not mean that the conduct of individuals is irrelevant to the ruling by an international tribunal.[531] However, the international tribunal should assess this conduct in the calculation of the damages to be awarded under the principle of contributory negligence.[532] A later part of this study will be devoted to this principle.

---

528 *UN* Doc. A/60/10 (2005), "Report of the International Law Commission, Fifty-seventh session", at 112, para. 231.

529 UN Doc. A/CN.4/546 (11 August 2004), *Dugard*, John, "Sixth report on diplomatic protection", at 9, para. 18.

530 *Le Louis*, 2 Dods. 210; cited and commented by *Kern*, Holger Lutz, "Strategies of Legal Challenge: Great Britain, International Law, and the Abolition of the Transatlantic Slave Trade", 6 Journal of the History of International Law (2004), pp. 233 *et seq.*, at 239-240.

531 But see *Lambie*, Margaret, "Presumption of cessation of citizenship: its effect on international claims", 24 AJIL (1930), pp. 264 *et seq.*, at 271-2.

532 The ILC seems to prefer this approach, see *UN* Doc. A/60/10 (2005), "Report of the International Law Commission, Fifty-seventh session", at 112, para. 231; *UN* Doc. A/CN.4/546 (11 August 2004), *Dugard*, John, "Sixth report on diplomatic protection", at 8, para. 16.

II. The limited reception of the doctrine in international maritime conventions

In spite of this scepticism concerning the applicability of the clean hands doctrine in the general law on State responsibility and diplomatic protection, the relevant compensation provisions all seem to have codified it, to a limited extent. According to Art. 110, para. 3 LOSC, a compensation claim requires "that the ship boarded has not committed any act justifying [the suspicions]". Therefore, certain conduct, which would give rise to suspicions of being engaged in an activity that would allow an interference, renders the hands of the vessel unclean and bars a compensation claim. For example, a ship without name and port of origin painted on the hull and that is not answering radio calls would probably raise the suspicion of being without nationality and could not claim compensation for a boarding even if it was lawfully registered in its flag State.

Art. 9, para. 2 Migrant Smuggling Protocol and Art. 8bis, para. 10, lit. b SUA Protocol use the same terminology as Art. 110, para. 3 LOSC and therefore follow a comparable approach.

Likewise, a compensation claim under Art. 106 LOSC requires that the seizure occurred "without adequate grounds" and a precondition for a compensation award under Art. 111, para. 8 LOSC is that the interference took place in "in circumstances which do not justify the exercise of the right of hot pursuit".

Art. 21, para. 18 Fish Stocks Agreement requires that the "action is unlawful or exceeds that reasonably required *in the light of available information* to implement the provisions of this article" (emphasis added). Here, the terms "in the light of available information" probably mean that the perspective of the boarding State before the boarding is determinative and that the conduct of the boarded party could represent such information which might then bar a compensation claim.

All the mentioned provisions thus seem to apply the clean hands doctrine. However, not every unlawful conduct of the boarded party will *per se* bar an eventual compensation claim. The violation of any domestic law, for example, is not at all relevant. The hands of the ship will only be "unclean" if its conduct raised the suspicion of being engaged in exactly that kind of activity which the complementary boarding provision attempts to combat (*e.g.*, migrant smuggling in Art. 9, para. 2 Migrant Smuggling Protocol). Furthermore, the conduct needs to have occurred before the interference took place. Finally, it seems justified to require that the conduct needs to have caused the interference and that the interfering State may not *ex post* try to find some more causes of suspicion after the first cause proved to be wrong.

If one thus conditions the clean hands doctrine by these three limitations, then it is very well applicable to the mentioned compensation provisions.

Hence, contrary to the general law on State responsibility, the conduct of a private entity might exclude the liability of a State party to these conventions. But whose conduct is relevant to bar the compensation claim? Three of the provisions explicitly mention the conduct of the ship or vessel (Art. 110, para. 3 LOSC; Art. 9, para. 2 Migrant Smuggling Protocol; Art. 8bis, para. 10, lit. b SUA Protocol).

Needless to say that a ship or a vessel cannot commit acts herself,[533] but that rather the conduct of the shipowner or the ship's crew will be relevant in this respect. Why were the provisions drafted in such an atypical way? It seems very likely that the drafting must have been linked to the special status of private entities being able to claim compensation. If the compensation provisions establish legal relations between the boarding State and private entities, then the natural consequence must be that the conduct of the private entities will be as relevant to the regal relationship as the measures undertaken by the boarding State. Therefore, the nature of the application of the clean hands doctrine, at least in the three mentioned compensation provisions underlines the entitlement of private entities to claim compensation under these provisions of public international law.

Finally, Art. VI of the Intervention Convention is very different in this respect. The Intervention Convention permits interferences with navigation even amounting to the destruction of vessels on the high seas if these vessels constitute threats to the environment of a coastal State. Here, the conduct of the ship's crew or her owner is not relevant to the lawfulness and the consequences of the interference. Instead, the coastal State acts to protect itself against a threat that might even have been caused by lawful navigation. The justification for the interference is similar to a state of necessity and the different wording of Art. VI Intervention Convention therefore not surprising. Lacking the status of customary international law and codification in the Intervention Convention, the clean hands doctrine does not find any application to situations covered by the Intervention Convention.

III. Contributory negligence in the general law on State responsibility

Apart from the mentioned cases where the conduct of private entities may bar a compensation claim in certain cases, one may wonder what the role of other reprehensible conduct of the flag State, the shipowner and the ship's crew in the determination of State responsibility might be. *Michael Byers*, for example, argues that the mere transport of weapons of mass destruction and related material by itself could constitute contributory negligence and could thereby reduce the liability of the boarding State.[534]

It seems well-established in State practice that the conduct of the State claiming compensation is relevant for the determination of State responsibility of another State and for the amount of compensation due.[535] Hence, a flag State not control-

---

533 *Cf. IMO* Doc. LEG 88/3/3 (19 March 2004), "Comments on draft article 8bis submitted by the International Chamber of Shipping (ICS), the International Shipping Federation (ISF) and the International Confederation of Free Trade Unions (ICFTU)", at para. 19.

534 *Byers*, Michael, "Policing the High Seas: The Proliferation Security Initiative", 98 AJIL (2004), pp. 526 *et seq.*, at 543.

535 *Graefrath*, Bernhard, "Responsibility and Damage Caused: relations between responsibility and damages", 185 RdC (1984-II), pp. 95 *et seq.*; *Bollecker-Stern*, Brigitte, "Le prejudice dans la théorie de la responsabilité internationale" (Paris: Pedone, 1973), at 265-300; *Delagoa Bay Railway (Great Britain and United States/Portugal)*, Martens

ling the vessels under its flag according to Art. 94 LOSC and thereby unable to inform other States about security conditions, ownership and cargo on a particular vessel could contribute to the suspicion that the vessel violates public international law and the vessel could thus be subject to a boarding. In such a case, the lack of control by the flag State might reduce the liability of the boarding State. Such reduction, however, only applies to relations between the two States and since the conduct of the flag State is not imputable to private entities like the shipowner, their compensation claim against the interfering State should remain unaffected.

However, the situation is not as clear if the shipowner or the ship's crew has acted negligently. Usually, in the general law of State responsibility, only the conduct of State organs is attributable to a State to entail its responsibility (Art. 4 ASR). At first sight, there does not seem to be a sound reason to follow a different course concerning the conduct of the State claiming responsibility since the law on State responsibility governs the obligations and rights between States only. On the other hand, one must take into account that in cases of diplomatic protection, the damage on the part of an individual triggers the responsibility of a State. Fairness therefore dictates that the conduct of this individual is not ignored in the assessment of responsibility.[536] Furthermore, neglecting this conduct would render the situation of the individual more favourable if his State of nationality exercised diplomatic protection than if it brought his claim individually before a domestic court.[537] The issue also arose in the case of the *S.S. Wimbledon* when a vessel was refused passage through the Kiel Canal and the captain decided to harbour in Brunsbüttel for some time instead of using the Kattegat as an alternative route. The Permanent Court of International Justice implicitly ruled that negligent conduct of the captain would have reduced liability of Germany, but denied negligence in the case at hand.[538] Another example is the *Costa Rica Packet Case*, in which the shipowners did not take all efforts to continue to whale even though the captain was detained and thereby missed a whole whaling season. The arbitrator hence only allowed a reduced amount of damages.[539] Furthermore, an arbitrator reduced the award of damages for passengers negligently violating the laws of neutrality in the case of *Craig, Ballantine and Mc Curdy v. Mexico*.[540] In the case

Nouveau Recueil, 2nd series, vol. 30 (1900), pp. 329 *et seq.*; *LaGrand (Germany v. United States)*, Judgment of 27 June 2001, ICJ Reports 2001, at paras. 57, 116.

536 Commentary on Art. 39 ASR, para. 2, in *Crawford*, James, "The International Law Commission's Articles on State Responsibility" (Cambridge: Cambridge University Press, 2002), at 240.

537 *Ibid.*

538 *The S.S. Wimbledon (United Kingdom, France, Italy and Japan v. Germany, Poland intervening)*, Judgment of 28 June 1923, (1923) PCIJ Series A, No. 1, at 31.

539 *Costa Rica Packet (United Kingdom/Netherlands)*, reprinted in *Moore*, John Bassett, "History and digest of the international arbitrations to which the United States has been a party", Vol. 5 (Washington: Government Printing Office, 1898), pp. 4948 *et seq.*, at 4953.

540 *Craig, Ballantine and Mc Curdy v. Mexico*, reprinted in *Moore*, John Bassett, "History and digest of the international arbitrations to which the United States has been a party", Vol. 3 (Washington: Government Printing Office, 1898), pp. 2768 *et seq.*

of *Waydell & Co.*, the Spanish Claims Commission did not allow indemnity for losses sustained on account of suspension of work, or delay, or damage brought about by the mismanagement of the owners or their agents.[541]

Bearing in mind this case law, the International Law Commission has drafted its Article 39 ASR according to which "account shall be taken of the contribution to the injury by wilful or negligent conduct or omission of the injured State or any person or entity in relation to whom reparation is sought".

In the case of the interference of a vessel in international waters, the "person or entity in relation to whom reparation is sought" could definitely be the shipowner who asks his flag State to claim compensation of the damage suffered by him as a result of interference by a boarding State. Any order or negligent conduct by the shipowner leading to suspicions about the cargo of the vessel might constitute a contribution to the injury falling under Art. 39 ASR. Furthermore, the crew and the captain are subject to the directions of the shipowner and their conduct is usually attributable to him. Therefore, even if they do not suffer damages themselves by the interference (as in the case of a detention or maltreatment), their conduct is nevertheless relevant for the determination of responsibility as conduct attributed to the shipowner.

One ought not to forget that the captain usually has a dual role exercising jurisdiction of the flag State[542] and following directives of the shipowner. If the captain exercises jurisdiction of the flag State, his conduct is directly attributable to the flag State as State agent. This could be the case if the captain authorized the boarding of the vessel and hereby allowed law enforcement by a State other than the flag State. If the captain followed an order by the shipowner, then the above considerations concerning crew members would find application.

Therefore, the conduct of the claiming flag State, the shipowner, the ship's crew, her captain or anybody else who suffered damage or who was employed by a person suffering damages could lead to a reduction of the responsibility of the boarding State through contributory negligence.

IV. Contributory negligence in cases codified by maritime conventions

If the principle of contributory negligence is thus applicable in the general law of State responsibility, what is its role in cases covered by the compensation provisions relevant for this study? It has already been elaborated that, apart from situa-

---

541 *Waydell & Co. (United States/Spain)* (1937), cited by *Whiteman*, Marjorie M., "Damages in International Law", Vol. 2 (Washington, U.S. Government Printing Office, 1937), at 1018.

542 Most States delegate the exercise of jurisdiction on vessels flying their flag to the captain of the vessel. *Cf. Colombos*, Constantin John, "Internationales Seerecht" (München: Beck, 1963), at 244; *Pearce Higgins*, Alexander, "Le régime juridiqe des navires de commerce en haute mer en temps de paix", 30 RdC (1929-V), pp. 8 *et seq.*, at 18.

tions under the Intervention Convention, the clean hands doctrine may, under certain conditions, lead to an exemption of responsibility under the other compensation provisions.

If the conduct of private entities involved in the navigation of the ship (1) raises the suspicion of being engaged in an activity to be prevented by the provision authorizing an interference, (2) occurs before the boarding and (3) directly causes the boarding, the boarding State will not bear responsibility (*supra*).

The provisions cover these situations explicitly and should therefore supersede as *lex specialis* any general principle of contributory negligence. Most likely, the drafters also intended to limit conduct with effect on the compensation award to the situations covered by the respective compensation provision. Hence, it is submitted that any other conduct of the "ship" before the interference, *e.g.*, raising suspicion of a criminal activity not covered by the provision, will not affect the liability of the boarding State.

However, it seems justified to oblige all parties to a dispute involving such an interference to act in *bona fides* after the interference took place. For example, one could require all private entities to minimize the damage caused by the interference[543] and to adequately inform the other party during the resolution of the dispute. If a private claimant omits to do so, then according to general international law, he should bear an equitable part of his own damage and the compensation award should be reduced accordingly. Art. 304 LOSC recognizes that the general international law on State responsibility remains applicable and also shows that the general law on State responsibility is not static, but open to progressive development as with the strengthened status of the individual.[544]

Thus, the principle of contributory negligence only applies to conduct of private entities after the interference with navigation took place in cases covered by the relevant compensation provisions.

G. Consensual boardings

The fact that the flag State authorizes another State to board a vessel flying the flag of the former, precludes the wrongfulness of the boarding in relation to the flag State.[545] Since the freedom of navigation and the exclusive right to exercise jurisdiction on its vessel are traditionally construed to represent rights of the flag State only, the boarding as such is rendered lawful by the consent of the flag

[543] *Cf.* Commentary on Art. 39 ASR, para. 4, in *Crawford*, James, "The International Law Commission's Articles on State Responsibility" (Cambridge: Cambridge University Press, 2002), at 239. *Cf.* also Art. 300 LOSC.

[544] *Cf.* also Nordquist, Myron H. (ed.), "United Nations Convention on the Law of the Sea 1982 – A Commentary", Vol. 5 (Dordrecht: Nijhoff, 1989), at 163-164, para. 304.3.

[545] *Cf.* Art. 20 ASR.

State.[546] Even though the freedom of navigation, as Art. 110, para. 3 LOSC shows, contains a dual protection of the flag State and of private entities involved in the navigation of the ship, the exclusive jurisdiction remains with the flag State and it is generally the flag State who may authorize intrusions by other States into this jurisdiction.

Even though a State may not validly consent to a derogation from a norm of *ius cogens*,[547] the freedom of navigation and the exclusive right of a State to exercise jurisdiction on its vessels have not acquired the status of such norms.[548]

The consent of the flag State to a boarding does not justify an intrusion into the human rights of individuals concerned with the navigation of the vessel. It is strictly limited to allow access to the vessel. The State of nationality of crew members or cargo owners and probably also the flag State may therefore still claim the violation of human rights of these individuals in cases of, *e.g.*, personal injury or damage to property. Art. 110, para. 3 LOSC and similar compensation provisions may also constitute individual rights, but they are nevertheless very much linked to the freedom of navigation and the exclusive jurisdiction of the flag State. Therefore, contrary to human rights, the consent of the flag State to a boarding in this respect limits the individual right to claim compensation from the boarding State.

Also, the flag State may subject its consent to certain conditions. Then, the boarding is only lawful if it remains within these limits. Thus, for example, the flag State may give consent to a boarding if it is undertaken in a certain area of the sea, within a certain period of time or if the delay of the vessel does not exceed a certain time. The flag State may also condition its authorization on certain responsibility requirements. Art. 8bis, para. 7 of the 2005 SUA Protocol explicitly recognizes this possibility.

Furthermore, the consent of the flag State has to be valid to preclude the wrongfulness of the boarding. Such validity requires that the person giving consent was authorized to do so on behalf of the flag State and that the consent did not result from coercion[549] or misrepresentation.[550] Answering the question who is the authorized person depends on the rules of international law relating to the ex-

---

546 Cf. *Ronzitti*, Natalino, "The Law of the Sea and the Use of Force Against Terrorist Activities", in *id.* (ed.), "Maritime Terrorism and International Law" (Dordrecht: Nijhoff, 1990), pp. 1 *et seq.*, 8.

547 *Cf.* Art. 26 ASR.

548 *Wolfrum*, Rüdiger, "Die Internationalisierung staatsfreier Räume: die Entwicklung einer internationalen Verwaltung für Antarktis, Weltraum, Hohe See und Meeresboden" (Berlin: Springer, 1984), at 134. But see *von Münch*, Ingo, "Freedom of Navigation and the Trade Unions", 19 GYIL (1976), pp. 129 *et seq.*, at 129.

549 Commentary on Art. 20 ASR, para. 4, in *Crawford*, James, "The International Law Commission's Articles on State Responsibility" (Cambridge: Cambridge University Press, 2002), at 163.

550 *Gilmore*, William C., "Drug Trafficking at Sea: The Case of R. v. Charrington and Others", 49 ICLQ (2000), pp. 477 *et seq.*, at 483-484.

pression of the will of the State, as well as rules of internal law.[551] The competent authority may be any kind of "minor" or "petty" official.[552] The answer may also depend on the rule otherwise breached.[553]

In some cases, an international convention obliges the flag State to name the authority competent to authorize boardings of vessels flying its flag.[554] Other States parties to the convention may then exclusively board vessels if they are authorized by this particular authority. In the case of *R. v. Charrington and Others*, the British Customs Service tried to reach the authority named by Malta, but this authority had become defunct. In fact, the Maltese Attorney General in consultation with the Maltese Prime Minister had become the new competent authority. The British Customs Service, however, could not prove that the Attorney General had been contacted and only showed an authorization by the Malta Maritime Authority. The judge ruling on the case favoured the view of the defence that lacking a valid authorization, the boarding had been unlawful.[555]

It is not quite clear whether the captain of a vessel may also be a competent authority as regards the consent to a boarding by another State. The flag State usually designates some jurisdiction to the captain, for example, as far as it concerns a certain degree of criminal jurisdiction over acts committed on the vessel (usually limited to investigatory powers). Furthermore, the captain has the final responsibility for letting other persons on board while the vessel is in port or on sea.[556] It may be fair to say that on the high seas, the captain represents the flag State in exercising this exclusive jurisdiction. The right to deny boarding usually does not exist vis-à-vis authorities of the flag State.[557]

No case is known to the author where a flag State claimed the unlawfulness of a boarding by another State authorized by the captain of the boarded vessel. In fact, States have for long considered the consent of the captain to be relevant for the legality of the boarding.[558] The Danish government, *e.g.*, admits that a captain may

551 Commentary on Art. 20 ASR, para. 5, in *Crawford*, James, "The International Law Commission's Articles on State Responsibility" (Cambridge: Cambridge University Press, 2002), at 164; *Abass*, Ademola, "Consent Precluding State Responsibility: A critical analysis", 53 ICLQ (2004), pp. 211 *et seq.*, at 215.

552 *Massey (U.S. v. Mexico)*, 4 RIAA 155, 157 (1927).

553 Commentary on Art. 20 ASR, para. 6, in *Crawford*, James, "The International Law Commission's Articles on State Responsibility" (Cambridge: Cambridge University Press, 2002), at 163.

554 *Cf., e.g.,* Art. 17, para. 7 of the United Nations Convention Against Illicit Traffic in Narcotic Drugs and Psychotropic Substances.

555 *Gilmore*, William C., "Drug Trafficking at Sea: The Case of R. v. Charrington and Others", 49 ICLQ (2000), pp. 477 *et seq.*, at 478-480.

556 *Prüssmann*, Heinz/*Rabe*, Dieter, "Seehandelsrecht" (3rd ed., München: Beck, 1992), at 220; *Segelken*, Hans, "Kapitänsrecht" (2nd ed., Hamburg: Verlag Weltarchiv, 1974), at 488.

557 *Cf. Bemm*, Wilfrid/*Lindemann*, Dierk, "Seemannsgesetz" (4th ed., Uelzen: Becker, 1999), at 190.

558 *Cf.* Mr. Webster, Secretary of State, to Mr. Everett, minister to England (28 March 1843), reprinted in *Moore*, John Bassett, "Digest of International Law", Vol. 1 (Washington: Government Printing Office, 1906), at 935, 937.

lawfully permit boardings and thereby render it "consensual".[559] The United States Coast Guard has published a memorandum according to which "the master of a foreign-flagged vessel can verbally consent to the U.S. Coast Guard boarding his or her vessel."[560] Within the framework of the U.S.-led and UN-mandated "Operation Enduring Freedom", the German Rules of Engagement provide that the consent of the boarded vessel's captain is sufficient to render the presence of German naval officers on board of the vessel lawful until the vessel can be searched in its next port.[561] Therefore, it is suggested that the ship's captain or another designated crew member may validly give consent to a boarding by a State other than the flag State and hereby preclude the wrongfulness of the boarding under public international law. Most often, the captain will also be able to contact the shipowner or bareboat charterer before he grants approval to a boarding. In such a case, the unconditioned permission by the shipowner or bareboat charterer will render a later claim for compensation impossible.

However, where the States parties to a convention have laid down the procedures for the boarding of foreign vessels and where such procedures require the consent of some designated authority of the flag State other than the captain,[562] then the latter's consent ought to be without legal consequences. Otherwise, the codified procedures would become meaningless which definitely would contradict the intentions of the States parties.

Furthermore, one needs to notice that there is a significant risk of abusive interferences because naval officers, simply by showing force, may easily put pressure on the captain in order to be granted consent. International lawyers therefore need to analyze with scrutiny whether the captain had freely authorized the interference or whether his consent had been the result of coercion by the interfering State.

Even more obscure is the issue whether a captain may also consent to the seizure, diversion and arrest of his vessel. Does his consent to the boarding entail an authorized seizure? *Liljedahl* claims that arrest of persons or seizure of the ship

---

559 *Liljedahl*, John, "Transnational and international crimes: jurisdictional issues", in *Mukherjee*, Proshanto K. *et al.* (eds.), "Maritime violence and other crimes at sea" (Malmö: WMU, 2002), pp. 115 *et seq.*, at 123.

560 *Kramek*, Joseph E., "Bilateral Maritime Counter-Drug and Immigrant Interdiction Agreements: Is this the world of the Future?", 31 U. Miami Inter-Am. L. Rev. (2000), pp. 121 *et seq.*, at 132.

561 „Was darf die Bundeswehr im Kampf gegen den Terror?", Frankfurter Allgemeine Sonntagszeitung, 22 January 2005, p. 2.

562 For example, Art. 8bis, para. 15 SUA Protocol stipulates that "Upon or after depositing its instrument of ratification, acceptance, approval or accession, each State Party shall designate the authority, or, where necessary, authorities to receive and respond to requests for assistance, for confirmation of nationality, and for authorization to take appropriate measures. Such designation, including contact information, shall be notified to the Secretary-General within one month of becoming a Party, who shall inform all other States Parties within one month of the designation. Each State Party is responsible for providing prompt notice through the Secretary-General of any changes in the designation or contact information." Very similar to this provision: Art. 8, para. 6 Migrant Smuggling Protocol; Art. 17, para. 7 of the United Nations Convention against Illicit Traffic in Narcotic Drugs and Psychotropic Substances.

may only be done with express permission by the flag State.[563] The jurisdiction delegated by the flag State to the captain is temporary only and definitely subsidiary to the powers of official authorities of the flag State. A seizure may usually only take place after a vessel has been inspected. Usually, once a vessel has been stopped on the high seas, time remains to contact the flag State and to ask for the authorization of further measures. Therefore, exercise of authority by the captain in such cases should not be necessary. A seizure or diversion may thus only be authorized by the flag State.

In any case, consent must be actually expressed by the flag State or individuals representing it rather than merely be presumed on the basis that the State would have consented if it had been asked.[564]

Even if a flag State has consented to a boarding and thus rendered it lawful, it may still, under certain circumstances, be entitled to compensation for material losses.[565] "Without the possibility of such recourse the State whose conduct would otherwise be unlawful might seek to shift the burden of the defence of its own interests or concerns on to an innocent State."[566] For example, in the *Gabcikovo-Nagymaros Case*, Hungary invoked a state of necessity as a circumstance precluding wrongfulness, but "acknowledged that, in any event, such a state of necessity would not exempt it from its duty to compensate its partner."[567]

However, it is not quite sure whether Hungary did not derive this obligation from the treaty[568] with Slovakia instead of the general law on state responsibility. Furthermore, States may sometimes have compensated other States because of comity and lacking *opinio juris*. It seems a little overhasty of the ILC to draft a principle relying solely on Hungary's state practice. Also, it seems contradictory to preclude the wrongfulness of a conduct, but then "to relieve a State from its responsibility to compensate for the material loss caused by its conduct."[569]

The better solution seems requiring an authorization granted under certain conditions relating to responsibility. If the flag State has such an opportunity to impose conditions relating to responsibility when granting consent to a boarding, then it should no longer be able to claim compensation in respect of a boarding undertaken after an unconditioned authorization.

---

563 *Liljedahl*, John, "Transnational and international crimes: jurisdictional issues", in *Mukherjee*, Proshanto K. *et al.* (eds.), "Maritime violence and other crimes at sea" (Malmö: WMU, 2002), pp. 115 *et seq.*, at 124.

564 *Ibid.*

565 *Cf.* Art. 27(b) ASR.

566 Commentary on Art. 27 ASR, para. 5, in *Crawford*, James, "The International Law Commission's Articles on State Responsibility" (Cambridge: Cambridge University Press, 2002), at 190.

567 *Gabcíkovo-Nagymaros (Hungary/Slovakia)*, Judgment of 25 September 1997, ICJ Reports 1997, pp. 7 *et seq.*, at 39, para. 48.

568 Hungary in fact considered itself still bound by the treaty. *Cf. ibid.*

569 *Yamada*, Chusei, "Revisiting the International Law Commission's Draft Articles on State Responsibility", in *Ragazzi*, Maurizio (ed.), "International Responsibility Today – Essays in Memory of Oscar Schachter" (Leiden: Nijhoff, 2005), pp. 117 *et seq.*, at 123.

Finally, the consent by the flag State needs to be expressed before the boarding takes place. In the mentioned case of *R. v. Charrington and Others*, no competent authority had declared its consent to the boarding, but the Maltese Attorney General declared in the court proceedings that he had no objections to the boarding. The judge did not accept such *ex post* consent as justification of the boarding,[570] presumably because such reasoning would offer little protection to private entities with an interest in the navigation of the vessel.

H. The extent of responsibility

Having thus laid down the major preconditions and exclusions of State responsibility under the relevant compensation provisions, this study will now analyze the consequences of State responsibility. This part will start with a brief examination of the differences between the analyzed compensation provisions (I.). It will then continue with a comparison between the compensation provisions and the general law on State responsibility (II.) before finally describing some damages which may be claimed under the provisions (III).

I. A comparison of the different provisions

All of the analyzed compensation provisions more or less qualify the nature of the damage covered and also establish the requirement of a certain link between the damage and the conduct of the responsible State. This part will attempt to determine whether any substantial differences exist in this respect between the different compensation provisions. Due to its anomaly, the compensation provision of the Intervention Convention will be analyzed in a separate part (IV.).

1. The link between the conduct by the responsible State and the damage

All of the compensation provisions[571] impose the requirement of a certain link between the damage and the conduct of the responsible State. In this regard, however, the wording of the relevant provisions differs to a certain degree. Art. 110, para. 3 LOSC and Art. 9, para. 2 Migrant Smuggling Protocol simply stipulate that the vessel "shall be compensated for any loss or damage that may have been sustained"/"indemnizado por todo perjuicio o daño sufrido"/"возмещены любые причиненные убытки или ущерб" and thus at first sight do not seem to limit the damages covered at all. The French text, however, at least limits the covered

570 *Gilmore*, William C., "Drug Trafficking at Sea: The Case of R. v. Charrington and Others", 49 ICLQ (2000), pp. 477 *et seq.*, at 480.

571 Due to its anomaly, Art. VI of the Intervention Convention will not be analyzed here, *cf. infra*.

damages to "toute perte ou ... tout dommage *éventuels*" (emphasis added). The link between the boarding and the damage nevertheless remains quite imprecise.

Art. 106 LOSC, however, covers only the damage "caused by the seizure"/"causé de ce fait". Hence, the provision at least requires a causal link. Likewise, Art. 111, para. 8 LOSC only provides for an obligation to compensate for damages "that may have been *thereby* sustained" (emphasis added). The term "thereby" here most likely refers to the stoppage or arrest of the vessel. Most detailed are Art. 21, para. 18 Fish Stocks Agreement and Art. 8bis, para. 10, lit. b of the 2005 SUA Protocol. According to these provisions, States shall be liable for damage "attributable to them arising from action taken pursuant to this article". The term "attributable" indicates that mere causation does not suffice, but that lawyers and judges need to apply additional factors in weighing whether the link in the case at hand suffices. Furthermore, the provisions clearly describe the conduct of the responsible party which needs to be the origin of the damage.

Do these differences in drafting also lead to a difference in the substantial meaning of the provisions? In particular, are the damages covered under Art. 110, para. 3 LOSC wider than under, *e.g.*, Art. 21, para. 18 Fish Stocks Agreement because the latter regulates the link between the conduct of the responsible State and the damages covered in a more explicit way?

Since the general law on State responsibility is applicable to all issues not explicitly dealt with by provisions of the Law of the Sea Convention (*cf.* Art. 304 LOSC) and since these provisions are the least precise concerning the link between the conduct of the responsible State and the damage, one may recur to these general principles in order to clarify this link. According to the general law on State responsibility, only the injury caused by an internationally wrongful act needs to be repaired by the responsible State.[572] Mere causation, however, does not suffice because remote damages need to be excluded from the coverage.[573] Since all domestic legal systems require some sort of "directness", "foreseeability" or "proximity" of the damage, there is a strong argument that such link requirement represents a general principle of international law.[574] Moreover, a great number of arbitral tribunals have applied these criteria to cases of public international law.[575] The precise nature of this link nevertheless remains a

[572] *Cf.* Art. 31, para. 2 ASR; *Verzijl*, Jan Hendrik Willem, "International Law in Historical Perspective", Vol. 6, (Leiden: Sijthoff, 1973), at 735-736.

[573] Commentary on Art. 31 ASR, para. 10, in *Crawford*, James, "The International Law Commission's Articles on State Responsibility" (Cambridge: Cambridge University Press, 2002), at 204-205.

[574] *Zweigert*, Konrad/*Kötz*, Hein, "Einführung in die Rechtsvergleichung" (3rd ed., Mohr: Tübingen, 1996), at 603, 612-613, 621; *Honoré*, A.M., "Causation and Remoteness of Damage", in *Tunc*, André (ed.), "International Encyclopedia of Comparative Law", Vol. 11, Part 1 (Tübingen: Mohr, 1983), at 40-46, 49-60; *Bin Cheng*, "General Principles of Law as applied by International Courts and Tribunals" (London: Stevens, 1953), at 253.

[575] *Trail Smelter Arbitration (United States/Canada)* (16 April 1938), 3 RIAA, pp. 1905 *et seq.*, at 1938, 1941; *Responsibility of Germany for Damage Caused in the Portuguese Colonies in the South of Africa (Portugal/Germany)* (1928), 2 RIAA, pp. 1011 *et seq.*,

controversial issue in public international law.[576] Closest to a feasible definition of the criterion is probably the description by *Bin Cheng*: "[T]he duty to make reparation extends only to those damages which are *legally* regarded as the consequences of an unlawful act. These are damages which would normally flow from such an act, or which a reasonable man in the position of the wrongdoer at the time would have foreseen as likely to result, as well as all intended damages" (emphasis added).[577]

Thus, the general law on State responsibility is much more elaborated than the imprecise terms used in some of the different conventions. The desire to nevertheless mention some qualified link between the conduct of the responsible State and the damage to be covered is probably a consequence of the fact that "losses" are also covered by the provisions. Such losses, in the early years of public international law, had once been regarded as indirect damages[578] and it became a controversial issue whether they should be covered by the general duty to repair in the law of State responsibility. Apparently, the inclusion of the term "losses" evoked certain concerns among delegates that even remote damages might be covered by the new provisions and led to an increased regulation of the principle of proximate causality in the provisions.

Since this regulation has nevertheless remained imprecise compared to the general law on State responsibility and since the latter still applies to issues unresolved by the compensation provisions as such, it is submitted that in this regard, the relevant compensation provisions do not differ from each other and from the general law on State responsibility to a significant degree.

Whatever State party to any of these conventions is considering the boarding and inspection of a foreign vessel thus needs to be aware that it may have to bear those damages suffered by private interests related to the vessel which could be foreseen before the boarding and which are a typical consequence of the interference.

Finally, one ought to add that the principle of proximate cause and similar principles have been developed for criminal and tort actions in domestic law and there is a certain reluctance to apply them to torts not involving negligence.[579] Some of the analyzed compensation provisions provide for liability for lawful conduct and thus follow a similar, but not identical pattern compared to the principle of strict liability. Could one allege, in analogy to domestic legal systems, that the principle of proximate cause or the foreseeability criterion would not apply to cases where a

---

at 1031; *Administrative Decision No. II*, United States-Germany Mixed Claims Commission (1923), 7 RIAA pp. 23 *et seq.*, at 30; *Dix Case*, United States-Venezuela Commission (1903), 9 RIAA, pp. 119 *et seq.*; *Lusitania Cases*, United States-Germany Commission (1922), 7 RIAA, pp. 23 *et seq.*

576 *Cf. Atiyah*, Patrick Selim, "An Introduction to the Law of Contract" (5th ed., Oxford: Clarendon Press, 1995), at 466; *Verzijl*, Jan Hendrik Willem, "International Law in Historical Perspective", Vol. 6, (Leiden: Sijthoff, 1973), at 736.

577 *Bin Cheng*, "General Principles of Law as applied by International Courts and Tribunals" (London: Stevens, 1953), at 253.

578 *Brownlie*, Ian, "State Responsiblity" (Oxford: Clarendon Press, 1983), at 225.

579 *Cf. Wagon Mound* [1961] A.C. 388, 426-7.

State is liable for lawful conduct? Such analogy seems more than questionable. First, due to heterogeneous practice of domestic courts, one must doubt that a general principle limiting the principle of proximate cause to unlawful or negligent conduct has emerged. Secondly, the compensation provisions have for object and purpose to deter abusive interferences with navigation and to protect maritime transport (*supra*). A boarding State hereby becomes aware that each boarding is associated with a considerable risk of triggering its liability. However, when doing this assessment the boarding State needs a certain degree of security and cannot include any unforeseeable damage. Thirdly, one may argue that if a State is responsible only for damage proximately caused by its internationally wrongful act, then, *a fortiori*, it should not be responsible for other, additional types of damages in cases of liability for lawful conduct.

2. Qualification of the damage

While the necessary link between damage and conduct of the responsible State seems to be the same under each of the mentioned compensation provisions, their coverage may nevertheless differ. At first sight, the compensation provisions, as far as it concerns the extent of responsibility, may be divided into two types.

a) "Any loss or damage"

The first type, which is by far the most common, provides that the vessel shall be compensated "for any loss or damage"/"toute perte ou ... tout dommage"/"todo perjuicio o daño"/"убытки или ущерб". These terms are common to Art. 110, para. 3 LOSC, Art. 106 LOSC, Art. 111, para. 8 LOSC, Art. 21, para. 18 Fish Stocks Agreement and Art. 9, para. 2 Migrant Smuggling Protocol. These provisions thus explicitly distinguish between "loss" and "damage". Such a distinction is unknown to the general law of State responsibility according to which the responsible State has to compensate for the damage caused by its internationally wrongful act.[580] Damage here includes any material or moral damage, the former embracing any "damage to property or other interests … which is assessable in financial terms".[581] Material damage, among others, also includes lost profits when financially assessable.[582] As far as it concerns interferences in the high seas, it would also include *e.g.*, demurrage, additional harbour fees and contractual penalties.

The drafters of the compensation provisions nevertheless deemed it necessary to distinguish between "losses" and other damage. The terms find their origin in the negotiations within the International Law Commission drafting the Convention on the High Seas. In the sixth report by *J.P.A. François*, draft article 21 (the

[580] Art. 36, para. 1 ASR.

[581] Commentary on Art. 31 ASR, para. 5, in *Crawford*, James, "The International Law Commission's Articles on State Responsibility" (Cambridge: Cambridge University Press, 2002), at 202.

[582] *Cf.* Art. 36, para. 2 ASR.

predecessor to Art. 110, para. 3 LOSC) provided that the vessel shall be compensated for the "dommage subi".[583] Likewise, draft article 23 (the predecessor to Art. 106 LOSC) stipulated that the seizing State is responsible for "tout dommage causé par la capture".[584] As the explanation by *J.P.A. François* in the discussion shows, it was his intention to compensate for "damages".[585] After a drafting committee amended draft article 21, the International Law Commission adopted a provision according to which the vessel should be compensated "for the loss sustained".[586] In its commentary, the ILC stated that the responsible State "must compensate the merchant vessel for any delay caused by the warship's action."[587] Thus, it seems as if the members of the International Law Commission wanted to limit the extent of responsibility under the provision to lost profits. However, the United Kingdom, in a comment on the draft articles, proposed to replace the terms "for the loss sustained" by the terms "for any loss sustained" in order to include even losses suffered as a consequence of rather short delays.[588] Furthermore, the United Kingdom proposed to add the word "damage".[589]

The special rapporteur had no objections to these proposals and accordingly amended its final draft both in regard to the predecessor of Art. 110, para. 3 LOSC and the predecessor of Art. 106 LOSC.[590] Thus, the International Law Commission had a comprehensive compensation provision in mind covering both the slightest lost profits and other kinds of financially assessable damage. During the First Conference on the Law of the Sea, the same terms were then also adopted for Art. 23, para. 7 CHS, the predecessor of Art. 111, para. 8 LOSC. The issue of the extent of responsibility was not discussed during the Third Conference on the Law

583 *UN* Doc. A/CN.4/79, "Sixième rapport de J.P.A. François", reprinted in Yearbook of the International Law Commission (1954-II), pp. 7 *et seq.*, at 14-15.

584 *Ibid.*, at 16.

585 "Summary Records of the Seventh Session of the International Law Commission, 288th meeting" (10 May 1955), reprinted in Yearbook of the International Law Commission (1955-I), at 27.

586 "Summary Records of the Seventh Session of the International Law Commission, 321st meeting" (28 June 1955), reprinted in Yearbook of the International Law Commission (1955-I), at 229; *UN* Doc. A/2934, "Report of the International Law Commission covering the work of its seventh session", reprinted in Yearbook of the International Law Commission (1955-II), pp. 19 *et seq.*, at 26.

587 Commentary on draft article 21, in *UN* Doc. A/2934, "Report of the International Law Commission covering the work of its seventh session", reprinted in Yearbook of the International Law Commission (1955-II), pp. 19 *et seq.*, at 27.

588 *UN* Doc. A/CN.4/99/Add.1 (15 March 1956), "Note verbale by the United Kingdom", reprinted in Yearbook of the International Law Commission (1956-II), pp. 80 *et seq.*, at 81.

589 *Ibid.*

590 *UN* Doc. A/CN.4/97/Add.1 to 3, "Summary of replies from Governments and conclusions of the Special Rapporteur", reprinted in Yearbook of the International Law Commission (1956-II), pp. 13 *et seq.*, at 20, para. 147; UN Doc. A/3159, "Report of the International Law Commission covering the work of its eighth session", reprinted in Yearbook of the International Law Commission (1956-II), pp. 253 *et seq.*, at 261.

of the Sea (UNCLOS III). The same is true for the negotiations leading to Art. 21, para. 18 Fish Stocks Agreement and Art. 9, para. 2 Migrant Smuggling Protocol.

All one may thus conclude from the *travaux préparatoires* is that these compensation provisions targeted a wide-ranging obligation to compensate for lost profits and other kinds of damage. They do not explain, however, why such strange distinction between "loss", on the one hand, and "damage", on the other, was used. There may be two reasons for this awkward drafting procedure. First, at the time the original provisions (Art. 22, para. 3 and Art. 20 CHS) were drafted, there was still some confusion in the law of State responsibility, particularly regarding the obligation to compensate for lost profits. The drafters thus might have found it necessary to clarify the content of the obligation of the liable State. Secondly, the deterrent effect of the provision gains significantly when strong words are used even though their substantial effect may be rather declaratory. Generally, it seems fair to say that the older the provision, the more important has been the first consideration, while the second consideration has been more relevant for the later provisions. Thirdly, one ought not to forget that the drafters of the younger provisions might have had a certain consistency with the Law of the Sea Convention in mind and therefore were reluctant to change some of the terms.

b) "Any damage, harm or loss"

The most recent of all analyzed compensation provisions, Art. 8bis, para. 10, lit. b of the 2005 SUA Protocol, stipulates, *inter alia*, that "States Parties shall be liable for any damage, harm or loss". Thus, compared to the other provisions, the term "harm" has been added to the liability coverage. In regard of the fact that the previously analyzed provisions already provide for a comprehensive coverage, one may seriously question why such a new term needed to be added to the provision. More confusion even comes up if one considers the French and the Spanish texts. The French version in this respect simply copies the text of Art. 110, para. 3 LOSC. The Spanish version, however, was enriched by the term "perdidas". Surprisingly, this term comes closest to a translation of the English "losses", while "perjuicios" (already in Art. 110, para. 3 LOSC) may be translated by "harm".

In the English language, the term "harm" has a rather wide meaning and could be used for any physical and financial suffering. However, it is more common in the context of physical harm.[591]

The history of the provision nevertheless at least sheds some light on the confusing terms used in the different versions. During the negotiation of the 2005 SUA Protocol, the draft provision had in this respect from the very start adhered to the terms used by Art. 110, para. 3 LOSC: "loss or damage".[592] Quite late in the negotiations, however, the Greek delegation proposed the addition of the word "harm" to the provision.[593] There was also another delegation which proposed the

[591] *Cf.* "Black's Law Dictionary" (7th ed., St. Paul, West Group, 1999), at 722.

[592] *Cf. IMO* Doc. LEG 86/5 (26 February 2003), "Draft amendments to the SUA Convention and Protocol Submitted by the United States", at 11.

[593] *IMO* Doc. LEG/SUA/WG.2/WP.5 (1 February 2005), "Submission by Greece".

inclusion of terms such as "harm" and "delay" in the provision. The Working Group, where the negotiations at this stage took place, agreed to the inclusion of the term "harm" in the text of draft article 8bis, para. 8, lit. b of the 2005 SUA Protocol.[594] With respect to the word "delay", however, the Working Group agreed that there was no need to include it, as delay should be considered within the scope of damages and losses.[595]

It is submitted that "harm" is also within this scope since under the general law of State responsibility, the responsible State has to compensate for, *inter alia*, personal injury.[596] The main reason behind the inclusion of the term "harm" has probably been to facilitate the application of the provision before domestic courts. Some domestic legal systems might have developed sophisticated distinctions between different types of damages and "harm" may represent a separate category. Together with some potential deterrent effect on States willing to interfere with navigation, the inclusion of the term "harm" in Art. 8bis, para. 10, lit. b of the 2005 SUA Protocol thus helps to guarantee a comprehensive protection of shipping interests against sufferings caused by interferences on the high seas before domestic tribunals.

As far as it concerns the meaning of the provision in public international law, though, the modification has been rather unsubstantial.

II. The provisions and the general law on State responsibility

Art. 110, para. 3 LOSC and the other compensation provisions provide for "compensation for any loss [, harm] or damage sustained". Under the general law on State responsibility, however, the major consequence of State responsibility is an obligation to provide reparation which can have the three forms of restitution, compensation and/or satisfaction (Art. 34 ASR). Articles 28-39 ASR have been widely accepted to constitute customary international law.[597] It therefore seems necessary to determine in how far and under what conditions, these forms of reparation may be available in cases of interference with navigation on the high seas. Some authors claim that according to the Articles on State Responsibility, the responsible State would be faced with a bundle of obligations (*e.g.*, the obligation to be exposed to lawful countermeasures), of which the duty to repair the injury

594 *IMO* Doc. LEG/SUA/WG.2/4/Corr.1 (24 February 2005), "Report of the Working Group, Corrigendum".

595 IMO Doc. LEG/SUA/WG.2/4/Corr.1 (24 February 2005), "Report of the Working Group, Corrigendum".

596 Commentary on Art. 36 ASR, para. 16, in *Crawford*, James, "The International Law Commission's Articles on State Responsibility" (Cambridge: Cambridge University Press, 2002), at 223.

597 *Dominicé*, Christian, "The International Responsibility of the United Nations for Injuries Resulting from Non-Military Enforcement Measures", in *Ragazzi*, Maurizio (ed.), "International Responsibility Today – Essays in Memory of Oscar Schachter" (Leiden: Nijhoff, 2005), pp. 355 *et seq.*, at 368.

was only one element.[598] However, this study will concentrate on issues of reparation solely.

As has been determined *supra*, the scenario of a private entity claiming compensation for an interference with navigation on the high seas may be assimilated to the situation where an individual claims compensation for the violation of a human right. The international law on human rights (at least in some international regimes) is nevertheless more or less comparable to the general law on State responsibility since compensation for all financially assessable damages is awarded, subsidiary to *restitutio in integrum*.[599]

Some of the analyzed compensation provisions (Art. 110, para. 3 LOSC, Art. 9, para. 2 Migrant Smuggling Protocol and Art. 8bis, para. 10, lit. b of the 2005 SUA Protocol), at least partially establish a special form of State responsibility which does not require an internationally wrongful act, but only the occurrence of damage due to a lawful activity (*supra*). The consequence of such a liability is usually solely compensatory.[600] This is probably why the provisions explicitly only mention an obligation to compensate as legal consequence.[601] This may reflect the traditional common law approach, "under which money was taken to be the measure of all things".[602]

However, even the other compensation provisions which definitely require an internationally wrongful act by the interfering State also seem to limit the legal consequence to an obligation to compensate since they do not explicitly oblige the interfering State to provide for restitution of the shipowner's property.

Does this mean that there is no place for other forms of reparation in cases of interferences with navigation on the high seas? According to Art. 304 LOSC, "[t]he provisions of this Convention regarding responsibility and liability for damage are without prejudice to the application of existing rules and the development of further rules regarding responsibility and liability under international

---

598 *Salmon*, Jean, "Dictionnaire de droit international public" (Bruxelles: Bruylant, 2001), at 999; *Stern*, Brigitte, "A Plea for 'Reconstruction' of International Responsibility based on the Notion of Legal Injury", in *Ragazzi*, Maurizio (ed.), "International Responsibility Today – Essays in Memory of Oscar Schachter" (Leiden: Nijhoff, 2005), pp. 93 *et seq.*, at 97.

599 *Cf., e.g., Bernhardt*, Rudolf, "Just Satisfaction under the European Convention on Human Rights", in *Ragazzi*, Maurizio (ed.), "International Responsibility Today – Essays in Memory of Oscar Schachter" (Leiden: Nijhoff, 2005), pp. 243 *et seq.*, at 251. See Art. 63, para. 1 of the American Convention on Human Rights, adopted on 22 November 1969, *OAS* Doc. OEA/Ser.K/XVI/1.1 Doc. 65, Rev. 1, Corr. 1 (7 January 1970); Art. 41 of the European Convention on Human Rights, adopted on 4 November 1950, UNTS, Vol. 213, pp. 221 *et seq.*, amended version available at <www.echr.coe.int>.

600 *Ushakov*, Yearbook of the International Law Commission (1970-I), at 188; *Waldock*, *ibid.*, at 190.

601 See *Graefrath*, Bernhard, "Responsibility and Damage Caused: relations between responsibility and damages", 185 RdC (1984-II), pp. 95 *et seq.*, at 107 (using Art. VII of the Space Treaty as an example).

602 *Crawford*, James/ *Olleson*, Simon, "The Nature and Forms of International Responsibility", in *Evans*, Malcolm D. (ed.), "International Law" (2003), pp. 455 *et seq.*, at 467.

law." Thus, one may follow that the remedies under the general law on State responsibility remain available even in cases where the compensation provisions of the Law of the Sea Convention apply. It is submitted that only if rules of the general regime on State responsibility would contradict object and purpose of a compensation provision, the latter would, as *lex specialis*, bar the application of the general regime.

It seems appropriate to clearly distinguish between rights of the flag State and rights of private entities in this regard. The flag State, exercising diplomatic protection on behalf of its nationals or claiming violation of its own rights, may generally claim all forms of reparation as consequences of an unlawful interference with the navigation of a vessel under its flag by another State. If, however, the interference was lawful, only compensation may be claimed under the requirements of the relevant compensation provisions.

Private entities, on the other hand, do not have a general remedy under public international law and need to rely on their limited recognition awarding them explicit rights. Therefore, private entities such as the shipowner or cargo interests may only avail themselves of those compensation provisions which have granted them individual rights (Art. 110, para. 3 LOSC, Art. 9, para. 2 Migrant Smuggling Protocol and Art. 8bis, para. 10, lit. b of the 2005 SUA Protocol; maybe also Art. 21, para. 18 Fish Stocks Agreement). Under these provisions, which only mention a right to compensation, private entities may thus not claim restitution of their property (*restitutio in integrum*) or satisfaction in order to repair the injuries suffered. These forms of reparation would affect the sovereignty of the responsible State much more than the mere obligation to compensate and would hence require explicit regulation in the compensation provisions. Instead, they will have to rely upon other provisions of the Law of the Sea Convention, *e.g.*, prompt release procedures under Art. 73, para. 2 and Art. 292 LOSC which nevertheless require the involvement of the boarded vessel's flag State.

As far as it concerns those compensation provisions which seem to adhere to the general law on State responsibility, but nevertheless only provide for an obligation to compensate (*cf.*, *e.g.*, Art. 106 LOSC), their effect in respect to the general law on State responsibility is probably clarifying or even declaratory. It is submitted that, as Art. 304 LOSC shows, it has not been the intention of the States parties to the Law of the Sea Convention to limit the consequences of State responsibility to an obligation to compensate, but rather to preserve all other remedies available to States under the general law on State responsibility.

One may thus conclude that the some of the analyzed compensation provisions have added significant remedies available to private entities to the existing general law on State responsibility without seriously limiting the scope of application of the latter. Hence, a flag State is under no obligation to refrain from exercising flag State protection and claiming the restitution of a vessel under its flag to a shipowner, when the latter has claimed compensation under any provision of the Law of the Sea Convention. Evidently, the flag State is nevertheless barred from claiming the compensation of damage which the private entity has already received under its separate claim based on one the compensation provisions entitling private entities.

III. Types of damages which may be claimed and their calculation

This study will now examine what kind of damages can be claimed as compensation for a wrongful interference on the high seas. As a starting point, one must bear in mind that compensation as a form of reparation "must, as far as possible, wipe out all the consequences of the ... act and re-establish the situation which would, in all probability, have existed if that act had not been committed."[603] The only requirements are that the damage has been proximately caused by the relevant conduct and that the damage is financially assessable. Special attention will be paid to the judgment of the International Tribunal for the Law of the Sea (ITLOS) in the case *The M/V "Saiga" (No. 2) (Saint Vincent and the Grenadines v. Guinea)*.

A claim to compensation is "a claim to indemnification [of the whole damage] in terms of money."[604] The notion of damages is generally understood to include material and moral damage, but not merely abstract concerns or general interests of a State unaffected by the breach.[605] While it has been held that "liability as a rule is for material damage only,"[606] even a moral damage is financially assessable and thus does not differ significantly from a so-called material damage. Hence, it is submitted, that even moral damage can be claimed under the relevant compensation provisions.[607]

1. Delay of the vessel

Every interference causes a certain delay of the vessel, ranging from a few minutes to many months if the vessel is seized and brought to a port. In the relationship between shipowner and charterer, delays and detention in port will usu-

---

603 *The Factory at Chorzów (Germany v. Poland), Merits*, Judgment of 13 September 1928, (1928) PCIJ Ser. A No. 17, at 47.

604 *Graefrath*, Bernhard, "Responsibility and Damage Caused: relations between responsibility and damages", 185 RdC (1984-II), pp. 95 *et seq.*, at 90.

605 Commentary on Art 31, para. 5, *UN* Doc. A/56/10 (2001), "Report of the International Law Commission on the work of its Fifty-third session", at 225; *Graefrath*, Bernhard, "Responsibility and Damage Caused: relations between responsibility and damages", 185 RdC (1984-II), pp. 95 *et seq.*, at 95; *Tanzi*, Attila, "Is Damage a distinct Condition for the Existence of a Internationally Wrongful Act?", in *Spinedi*, Marina *et al.* (eds.), "United Nations Codification of State Responsibility" (New York: Oceana Publications), pp. 1 *et seq.*, at 13; *Brownlie*, Ian, "State Responsiblity" (Oxford: Clarendon Press, 1983), at 54, 84.

606 *Handl*, Günther, "Territorial Sovereignty and the Problem of Transnational Pollution", 69 AJIL (1975), pp. 59 *et seq.*, at 60; *Dupuy*, Pierre-Marie, La responsabilité internationale des Etats pour les dommages d'origine technologique et industrielle (Paris: Pedone, 1976), at 56.

607 *Cf.* Commentary on Art. 36, para. 1, in *UN* Doc. A/56/10 (2001), "Report of the International Law Commission on the work of its Fifty-third session", at 244.

ally trigger the demurrage provisions, placing the risks on the charterers.[608] However, if the vessel is stopped on the high seas, then the shipowner will usually need to bear the damage.[609]

There are some older domestic court opinions indicating that a simple delay is not a damage which can be claimed from the interfering State.[610] Furthermore, there is at least one author who believes that "if it is only inconvenience that is caused by visit and search of an innocent ship, there is no compensation payable."[611]

On the other hand, demurrage, which is an allowance or compensation for the delay or detention of a vessel,[612] has since long been a damage which could be claimed for compensation.[613] In the case of the *Sirius*, for example, the Belgian *Cour de Cassation* awarded damages of 1 million Belgian Francs per day of delay to the owner because a Greenpeace vessel had encumbered the ship.[614] Nowadays, the costs for the operation of a vessel can easily be calculated and constitute, even for a few hours of delay, more than a mere "inconvenience". According to some shipping companies, a surprise boarding at sea can cause unnecessary delays which cost up to $40,000 an hour.[615] Furthermore, one can with no major difficulties estimate the proximate arrival time of the vessel at the next destination, compare it to the actual arrival time after the interference and determine the financial damage caused (*e.g.*, contractual penalties, costs for fuel and crew's wages). Thus, any delay caused by an interference with navigation represents a financially assessable damage of the shipowner or other private entities which needs to be compensated under the general law of State responsibility and thus also according to the terms of the analyzed compensation provisions.

Considering this well-established principle, a comment in an explanatory report by the Council of Europe seems quite surprising. The committee of governmental experts under the authority of the European Committee on Crime Problems (CDPC) of the Council of Europe in 1995 discussed compensation issues arising under the European "Agreement on Illicit Traffic by Sea implementing Article 17 of the United Nations Convention against Illicit Traffic in Narcotic Drugs and

---

608 *Cf. Herber*, Rolf, "Seehandelsrecht" (New York: de Gruyter, 1999), at 256-258; on the differences between German and English/U.S. maritime law in this respect see *Rabe*, Dieter, "Seehandelsrecht" (4th ed., München: Beck, 2000), at 477.

609 *Todd*, Paul, "Private Law Aspects and Commercial Concerns associated with Emerging Issues in Maritime Security", in *Mejia*, Max (ed.), "Contemporary Issues in Maritime Security" (2005), pp. 299 *et seq.*, at 302.

610 *Cf. Starrett v. United States.*, 39 Ct.Cl. 34 (1903); *The Nancy*, 37 Ct.Cl. 401 (1902).

611 *O'Connell*, Daniel Patrick, "The International Law of the Sea", Vol. 2 (Oxford: Clarendon Press, 1984), at 802.

612 *The Apollon*, 22 U.S. 362, 378 (1824); *The Lindisfarne*, Anglo-American Arbitration Tribunal, Nielsen's Report (1926), pp. 483 *et seq.*, at 487.

613 See, *e.g., The Lively*, 15 F.Cas. 631, 635 (C.C. D.Mass. 1812). *Cf.*, for an implicit recognition of simple delay as demurrage *U.S. v. The Nuestra Senora De Regla*, 108 U.S. 92, 103 (1883); *The Nancy*, 37 Ct. Cl., 401 (1902).

614 *The Sirius*, Droit européen des transports (1985), pp. 540-543.

615 "Some Ships Get Coast Guard Tip Before Searches", New York Times, 20 May 2006.

Psychotropic Substances". These governmental experts commented the compensation provision of the agreement with the following terms: "at the same time liability to pay compensation does not exist, where suspicions prove to be unfounded, for the mere interference with the freedom of navigation, *regardless of whether or not any actual loss was sustained* / d'autre part, la responsabilité de la réparation financière n'existe pas lorsque les soupçons se révèlent dénués de fondement en cas de simple entrave à la liberté de la navigation, *qu'il y ait eu ou non effectivement perte* (emphasis added)."[616] Thus, the experts seem to distinguish between "mere interferences / simple entraves", for which no compensation is owed no matter whether the shipowner suffered damages, and other, more severe interferences leading to an obligation to compensate. Unfortunately, no definition is given in order to clearly distinguish the two kinds of interferences. One might nevertheless presume that the governmental experts considered the mere delay caused by the boarding of a vessel to represent a "mere interference" since any boarding causes such delay.

The authority of this comment is open to severe doubt. On the one hand, the explanatory report has been approved by experts of all governments representing the States parties to the agreement. The report is also adopted at the same time as the convention and published with it. Thus, it may constitute a guide to the interpretation of the convention and could be seen as part of the 'context' in which the convention was concluded.[617] Furthermore, one might take into account that the organs having concluded the treaty are the most qualified to interpret it.[618] The explanatory report might thus represent a means of interpretation equivalent to the wording of the agreement itself rather than subsidiary *travaux préparatoires* (cf. Art. 31, para. 2 VCLT). On the other hand, the explanatory report explicitly provides that it "does not constitute an instrument providing an authoritative interpetation of the text of the agreement although it may facilitate the understanding of the Convention's provisions / ne constitue pas un instrument d'interprétation authentique du texte de l'accord, bien qu'il puisse faciliter la compréhension des dispositions qui y sont contenues."[619] The governmental experts themselves therefore attributed only subsidiary authority to the explanatory reports. Furthermore, the fact that the report comments the convention with a clear deviation from the general law on State responsibility without any indication why such a deviation

616 Explanatory Report to the Council of Europe Agreement on Illicit Traffic by Sea implementing Article 17 of the United Nations Convention against Illicit Traffic in Narcotic Drugs and Psychotropic Substances, at para. 95, available at <http://conventions.coe.int/Treaty/EN/Reports/Html/156.htm.

617 *Sinclair*, Ian, "The Vienna Convention on the Law of Treaties" (Manchester: University Press, 1984), at 129-130; *Aust*, Anthony, "Modern Treaty Law and Practice" (Cambridge: Cambridge University Press, 2000), at 191.

618 *Reuter*, Paul, "Introduction to the Law of Treaties" (2nd ed., London: Paul Kegan International, 1995), at 95, para. 138 (1995).

619 Explanatory Report to the Council of Europe Agreement on Illicit Traffic by Sea implementing Article 17 of the United Nations Convention against Illicit Traffic in Narcotic Drugs and Psychotropic Substances, at para. 2, available at <http://conventions.coe.int/Treaty/FR/Reports/Html/156.htm.

may be justified evidently shows that the authors of the report inadequately considered the existing state of public international law.

Finally, one ought to consider that the report only concerns a regional agreement implementing an international convention which neither contains any compensation provision nor provides for the boarding of foreign vessels without the consent of the flag State. The States parties therefore dealt with a similar, but not equivalent situation compared to the cases arising under the discussed compensation provisions of international convention. Therefore, it seems doubtful whether their conduct during the negotiations of this agreement can be considered as State practice regarding the interpretation of the other conventions containing compensation provisions.

Notwithstanding these considerations, the practice of the States parties to this European agreement does not seem to be sufficient to provide for an exception of a well-established principle of the law of State responsibility, namely that the responsible State has to compensate all financially assessable damage of the victim. Some States with interests in the Caribbean Sea, for example, have adopted an agreement implementing the United Nations Convention against Illicit Traffic in Narcotic Drugs and Psychotropic Substances which stipulates that "[c]laims against a Party for damage, injury or loss resulting from law enforcement operations pursuant to this Agreement, including claims against its law enforcement officials, shall be resolved in accordance with international law".[620] In doing so, these States presumably intended to adhere to the general law on State responsibility which provides that all financially assessable damage needs to be compensated by the responsible State (*supra*).

2. Expected profits

Similar issues arise with the notion of "expected profits". Some early American cases deny the award of lost profits as damage in cases of interferences with navigation because of the uncertainty in assessing the damage.[621] Thus, it was held that "[t]he probable or possible benefits of a voyage, as yet *in fieri*, can never afford a safe rule by which to estimate damages in cases of a marine trespass. There is so much uncertainty in the rule itself, so many contingencies which may vary or extinguish its application, and so many difficulties in sustaining its legal correctness, that the court cannot believe it proper to entertain it."[622]

However, international arbitral tribunals have usually granted lost profits.[623] In *The Cape Horn Pigeon Case*, the arbitrator applied to an international dispute the

---

[620] Article 28 of the Agreement concerning Co-Operation in suppressing illicit maritime and air trafficking in narcotic drugs and psychotropic substances in the Caribbean Area, February 2003, on file with the author.

[621] *The Apollon*, 22 U.S. 362, 376-7 (1824); *The Lively*, 15 F.Cas. 631, 634-5 (C.C. D.Mass. 1812).

[622] *The Amiable Nancy*, 16 U.S. 546, 560-1 (1818).

[623] *Delagoa Bay Railway Case*, reprinted in *Moore*, John Bassett, "History and digest of the international arbitrations to which the United States has been a party", Vol. 2

principle of civil law according to which one can also claim the gain one could not have made due to the interference, no certitude required, but only under ordinary circumstances.[624] A certain reluctance of other tribunals[625] can only be explained by the problems to determine the expected profits with a reasonable degree of certitude. One can nevertheless no more argue that lost profits are an indirect damage that cannot be recovered.[626] The whole notion of indirect damages is probably overcome.[627]

Various approaches have been undertaken to handle the issue which is particularly relevant in interferences with fishing vessels because their potential catch will be difficult to determine. For example, Umpire *Parker* in a case between the United States and Germany held that Germany was, due to the uncertainty, not obliged to pay the value of any probable catch.[628]

Merchant cargo vessels usually have fixed contracts and damage should be easy to ascertain. Their freight is comparatively uncomplicated to verify and has thus always been a recoverable item.[629] In *The Montijo*, the umpire allowed a sum of money per day for loss of the use of the vessel.[630] In *The Betsey*, compensation was awarded also for the demurrage for the period representing loss of use.[631] As a general rule, in the loss of profits due to the temporary loss of use and enjoyment

(Washington: Government Printing Office, 1898), pp. 1865 *et seq.*; *The William Lee*, reprinted in *Moore*, John Bassett, "History and digest of the international arbitrations to which the United States has been a party", Vol. 4 (Washington: Government Printing Office, 1898), pp. 3405-7; *Yuille Shortridge and Co. (Great Britain v. Portugal)* (1861), in *de la Pradelle*, Albert/*Politis*, Nicolas, "Recueil des arbitrages internationaux", Vol. 2 (1957), pp. 78 *et seq.*; *Sapphire International Petroleums Ltd. v. National Iranian Oil Company* (15 March 1963), 35 ILR, pp. 136 *et seq.*, at 187, 189.

624 *Affaire des Navires Cape Horn Pigeon, James Hamilton Lewis, C.H. White et Kate and Anna (United States/Russia)* (1902), 9 RIAA, pp. 51 *et seq.*, at 65.

625 *Shufeldt (USA/Guatemala)* (1930), 2 RIAA, pp. 1079 *et seq.*, at 1099 (1930); *Amco Asia Corp. and Others v. Republic of Indonesia*, 1 ICSID Reports (1990), pp. 569 *et seq.*, at 612, para. 178.

626 *Graefrath*, Bernhard, "Responsibility and Damage Caused: relations between responsibility and damages", 185 RdC (1984-II), pp. 95 *et seq.*, at 96.

627 *Cf. Brownlie*, Ian, "State Responsiblity" (Oxford: Clarendon Press, 1983), at 225. But see *Rousseau*, Charles, "Droit international public" (Paris: Sirey, 1953), at 384-6.

628 *Administrative Decision No. VII (United States/Germany)* (1937), reprinted in *Whiteman*, Marjorie M., "Damages in International Law", Vol. 2 (Washington, U.S. Government Printing Office, 1937), pp. 1243-1244.

629 *The Lively*, 15 F.Cas. 631, 634 (C.C. D. Mass. 1812).

630 *The Montijo* (1875), reprinted in *Moore*, John Bassett, "History and digest of the international arbitrations to which the United States has been a party", Vol. 2 (Washington: Government Printing Office, 1898), pp. 1421 *et seq.*

631 *The Betsey* (1794), reprinted in *Moore*, John Bassett, "History and digest of the international arbitrations to which the United States has been a party", Vol. 5 (Washington: Government Printing Office, 1898), pp. 47 *et seq.*, at 113.

of an income-producing asset, the loss compensated is the income to which the claimant was entitled by virtue of undisturbed ownership.[632]

If the flag State or shipowner has received compensation for a seized or destroyed vessel, no profits are granted for the period after the adjudication because the property has already been restored in the compensation award.[633] Concerning the period until adjudication, it is assumed that the flag state can expect *restitutio in integrum*, which is why it can claim lost profits for that period.[634]

Even though private entities under the analyzed compensation provisions do not enjoy the right to claim *restitutio in integrum*, one might similarly argue that a private businessman would have invested the sum he was entitled to in order to gain profits and that the denial of compensation has prevented him from gaining such profits. In order to ascertain the amount of profits, one likewise ought to consider the profits he would have gained if his property had remained unaffected by the interference.

3. Value of the vessel and cargo

If the vessel and her cargo are lost (*e.g.* by an unlawful confiscation), the true measure of compensation is the "replacement cost … at the time of the loss."[635] There are some cases where the replacement cost at the commencement of the voyage was taken as measure,[636] but the arbiters in these cases presumably had trouble to determine the deterioration of the vessel's value during her voyage. Nowadays, the "time of the loss" has become the common date of evaluation in cases where the vessel had either been destroyed or confiscated.

This replacement cost is usually the capital value of the property lost assessed on the basis of the "fair market value"[637] at the moment the damage occurs.[638]

---

632 Commentary on Art. 36, para. 29, in UN Doc. A/56/10 (2001), "Report of the International Law Commission on the work of its Fifty-third session", at 261.

633 *Norwegian Shipowners Case (Norway/USA)* (1922), 1 RIAA, pp. 307 *et seq.*; *Factory at Chorzów (Germany v. Poland), Merits,* Judgment of 13 September 1928, (1928) PCIJ Ser. A No. 17, at 47.

634 Commentary on Art. 36, para. 29, in *UN* Doc. A/56/10, "Report of the International Law Commission on the work of its Fifty-third session", at 261.

635 Cf. *Corfu Channel (United Kingdom v. Albania)*, Judgment of 15 December 1949, ICJ Reports 1949, pp. 244 *et seq.*, 249; *Henry James Bethune (Great Britain) v. United States* (1 May 1914), 6 RIAA, pp. 32 *et seq.*, at 34; *Whiteman*, Marjorie M., "Damages in International Law", Vol. 2 (Washington, U.S. Government Printing Office, 1937), at 1022.

636 Danish Indemnity Commission (1832), reprinted in *Moore*, John Bassett, "History and digest of the international arbitrations to which the United States has been a party", Vol. 5 (Washington: Government Printing Office, 1898), pp. 4568 *et seq.*; American Indemnity Commission (1833), *ibid.*, pp. 4585 *et seq.*

637 *American International Group, Inc. v. Government of the Islamic Republic of Iran*, 4 Iran-U.S.C.T.R. (1983), pp. 96 *et seq.*, at 106; *Starrett Housing Corp. v. Government of the Islamic Republic of Iran*, 16 Iran-U.S.C.T.R. (1987), pp. 112 *et seq.*, at 201.

638 *Verzijl*, Jan Hendrik Willem, "Le droit des prises de la Grande Guerre" (Leyde: Sijthoff, 1924), at 1128.

Usually, the value at the location where the damage occurs is decisive or, if the damage occurs on the high seas, at the destination because these are the places where the claimant could have sold the damaged property at the time of the injury. Since there is a world-wide market for almost every kind of vessels and cargo, the determination of the value should not cause as much trouble as it did in the 19th century when arbitrators needed to first assess the original cost and then deduct the depreciation until the loss occurred.[639]

In times of war, the value of certain vessels and cargoes may rise with great speed. A French tribunal has considered such an increase to be a case of *force majeure* and only awarded compensation of the value at the time of the seizure.[640] The claimant thus could not receive the higher amount he would have gained if he had sold the vessel at its destination.

An interesting issue arises if the flag State of a detained vessel claims compensation instead of *restitutio in integrum*. Usually, the latter is the primary form of reparation.[641] However, the only legal consequence under the relevant provisions of the LOSC is compensation. This is probably why the International Tribunal for the Law of the Sea, while upholding the primacy of *restitutio in integrum*, applied both Art. 111, para. 8 LOSC and the general law on State responsibility in the case of the *M/V Saiga (No. 2)*.[642] This implies that only an application of the general law on State responsibility could ensure the restitution of the vessel in that case. Since the applicant, St. Vincent and the Grenadines, had only relied on Art. 111, para. 8 LOSC for its claim,[643] the judgment of ITLOS must be understood to either extend the claim of the applicant or to regard the general law of State responsibility as always applicable through Art. 304 LOSC even when the applicant exclusively refers to Art. 111, para. 8 LOSC for its claim. The latter seems more probable considering the reasoning of ITLOS in its judgment.[644]

---

[639] *Cf. Whiteman*, Marjorie M., "Damages in International Law", Vol. 2 (Washington, U.S. Government Printing Office, 1937), at 1022-1053.

[640] *Insulinde (Nr. 2)*, 28 September 1915, France, reprinted in: *Verzijl*, Jan Hendrik Willem, "Le droit des prises de la Grande Guerre" (Leyde: Sijthoff, 1924), at 1145.

[641] Art. 36, para. 1 ASR; Commentary on Art. 36 ASR, para. 3, in *UN* Doc. A/56/10 (2001), "Report of the International Law Commission on the work of its Fifty-third session", at 245; *Factory at Chorzów (Germany v. Poland)*, *Merits*, Judgment of 13 September 1928, (1928) PCIJ Ser. A No. 17, 47; *Papamichalopoulos v. Greece*, 330-B Eur. Ct. H.R. (ser. A) (1995), at para. 36; *Velásquez Rodríguez v. Honduras*, 1989 Inter-Am.Ct. H.R. (ser. C) No. 4, at 26-7, 30-1; *Tippetts, Abbett, McCarthy, Stratton v. TAMS-AFFA Consulting Engineers of Iran and Others*, 6 Iran-U.S.C.T.R. (1984), pp. 219 *et seq.*, at 225.

[642] *The M/V "Saiga" (No. 2) Case (Saint Vincent and the Grenadines v. Guinea)*, Judgment of 1 July 1999, ITLOS Reports 1999, pp. 10 *et seq.*, at 65, paras. 169-70.

[643] *The M/V "Saiga" (No. 2) Case (Saint Vincent and the Grenadines v. Guinea)*, Oral Argument of St. Vincent and the Grenadines, 19 March 1999, ITLOS Pleadings, pp. 1208 *et seq.*, at 1231.

[644] *Cf. The M/V "Saiga" (No. 2) Case (Saint Vincent and the Grenadines v. Guinea)*, Judgment of 1 July 1999, ITLOS Reports 1999, pp. 10 *et seq.*, at 65, para. 169.

4. Detention and mistreatment of the crew

As the case of the *M/V Saiga (No. 2)* shows, interferences with vessels on the seas are frequently followed by a detention of the crew. The only material damage that occurs in such a case are the financial losses of the crewmembers due to the detention which constitute merely a starting point for the award of compensation.[645] Non-material damages, which are financially assessable and may be subject of a claim of compensation (*e.g.*, mental suffering, injury to feelings, humiliation, shame, degradation, loss of social position),[646] can become very significant in such cases. Traditionally, arbitrators have, in cases of simple deprivation of liberty, awarded a set amount for each day spent in detention.[647] Such awards were often increased when abusive conditions of confinement accompanied the wrongful arrest and imprisonment, resulting in particularly serious physical and psychological injury.[648] Compared to these awards, the amounts granted by human rights tribunals have been fairly modest.[649]

Since already in 1943, awards had varied between 8 dollars a day and 2,000 dollars for one-and-a-half hours of detention, it is hardly possible to establish any general rules concerning the assessment of damages for unlawful detentions.[650]

The relevant compensation provisions of the Law of the Sea Convention and some of the other analyzed provisions only refer to damage sustained by the ship. Taking into consideration the drafting history of these provisions, the meaning of the term "the ship", and the connection of the compensation provisions with the freedom of navigation, it seems doubtful whether an individual such as a seaman or a passenger may claim a violation of his rights under these compensation provisions. It is more likely that the compensation provisions were drafted in order to protect the shipowner and maybe also cargo interests.

However, if the flag State exercises the so-called flag State protection, a different form of diplomatic protection, then it may also act on behalf of crew mem-

---

645 *Graefrath*, Bernhard, "Responsibility and Damage Caused: relations between responsibility and damages", 185 RdC (1984-II), pp. 95 *et seq.*, at 100.

646 *The Lusitania Claims (United States v. Germany)* (1923), 7 RIAA 32. See also *Chevreau (France v. United Kingdom)* (1923), 2 RIAA 1113; *Di Caro (Italy/ Venezuela)* (1903), 10 RIAA 597; *Heirs of Jean Maninat (France/Venezuela)* (1903), 10 RIAA 55.

647 *Topaze (Belgium/Venezuela)* (1903), 9 RIAA 387; *Walter Faulkner v. Mexico* (1926), 4 RIAA pp. 67 *et seq.*, at 71.

648 See, *e.g.*, *William McNeill (United Kingdom/Mexico)* (1931), 5 RIAA pp. 164 *et seq.*, at 168.

649 *Shelton*, Dinah, "Remedies in International Human Rights Law" (Oxford: Oxford University Press, 2000), at 217; *cf. Pellonpää*, Matti, "Individual Reparation Claims under the European Convention on Human Rights", in *Randelzhofer*, Albrecht *et al.* (eds.), "State Responsibility and the Individual: Reparation in Instances of Grave Violations of Human Rights" (The Hague: Nijhoff, 1999), pp. 109 *et seq.*, at 113-114; *Fernandez*, Lovell, "Reparation for Human Rights Violations Committed by the Apartheid Regime in South Africa", *ibid.*, pp. 173 *et seq.*, at 178.

650 *Hackworth*, Green Haywood, "Digest of International Law", Vol. 5 (Washington: Government Printing Office, 1943), at 743.

bers even if these have a nationality different from the flag State itself.[651] The flag State's claim on behalf of the crew members accordingly then needs to be based on the general law on State responsibility in connection with human rights and/or the protection of aliens and not on the analyzed compensation provisions.

The International Tribunal for the Law of the Sea apparently has understood Art. 111, para. 8 LOSC to include damage to individual crewmembers treating the vessel and its crew as a functional unity, but the ambiguous wording of the decision leaves room for the speculation that ITLOS has simply applied the general law on State responsibility.[652] ITLOS did not compute the damages strictly according to days of detention, but awarded lump sums to crew members.[653] Hereby, ITLOS followed the approaches of the Iran-U.S. Claims Tribunal and the United Nations Compensation Commission.[654] Therefore, the Tribunal treated all crew members equally and did not award larger damages on the basis of greater earning capacity, responsibilities and status. According to Governing Council Decision No. 8 of the United Nations Claims Commission,[655] damages of USD 1,500 plus USD 100 for each day of detention beyond three could be awarded in respect of a person illegally detained for more than three days.

The crew members of the *M/V Saiga* were detained on 28 October 1997. Two crew members were allowed to leave Guinea on 1 November 1997. Hence, Guinean authorities detained them for five days. ITLOS awarded exactly USD 1,700 in respect of both detentions and therefore strictly followed Governing Council Decision No. 8. All other crew member had the first opportunity to leave Guinea

---

651 *UN* Doc. A/CN.4/L.647 (24 May 2004), Draft Articles on Diplomatic Protection, Art. 19; *Reparations for Injuries Suffered in the Service of the United Nations*, Dissenting Opinion by Judge Hackworth, ICJ Reports 1949, pp. 174 *et seq.*, at 202; *ibid.*, Dissenting Opinion by Judge Badawi Pasha, at 206; *Hackworth*, Green Haywood, "Digest of International Law", Vol. 3 (Washington: Government Printing Office, 1942), at 417; *Hyde*, Charles Cheney, "International Law – Chiefly as interpreted and applied by the United States", Vol. 2 (2nd ed., Boston: Little, Brown and Company, 1947), at 1179-81; *Borchard*, Edwin Montefiore, "Diplomatic Protection of Citizens Abroad" (New York, 1915), at 475-8; *Brownlie*, Ian, "Principles of Public International Law" (6th ed., Oxford: Oxford University Press, 2003), at 460; *Dolzer*, Rudolf, "Diplomatic Protection of Foreign Nationals", in *Bernhardt*, Rudolf (ed.), "Encyclopedia of Public International Law", Vol. 1 (Amsterdam: North-Holland, 1992), pp. 1067 *et seq.*, at 1068; *Meyers*, Herman, "The Nationality of Ships" (Den Haag: Nijhoff, 1967), at 104; *Weis*, Paul, "Nationality and Statelessness in International Law" (London: Stevens, 1956), at 43.

652 *The M/V "Saiga" (No. 2) Case (Saint Vincent and the Grenadines v. Guinea)*, Judgment of 1 July 1999, ITLOS Reports 1999, pp. 10 *et seq.*, at 65-66, para 172.

653 Crew members detained for five days were granted US$ 1,700 each, while compensation for the detention of all other crew members was held to be US$ 3,300 each even though they were detained 21, 48, 77 or 93 days. *The M/V "Saiga" (No. 2) Case (Saint Vincent and the Grenadines v. Guinea)*, Judgment of 1 July 1999, ITLOS Reports 1999, pp. 10 *et seq.*, at 66-67, 74.

654 *Wolfrum*, Rüdiger, "Billigflaggen – Schadensersatz – Nacheile", 3 ZeuS (2000), pp. 1 *et seq.*, at 11.

655 *UN* Doc. S/AC.26/1992/8 (27 January 1992), reprinted in 92 ILR 591.

on 17 November 1997. Hence, their detention lasted 21 days. The awarded USD 3,300 in respect of these detentions again exactly reflects the approach by the United Nations Claims Commission.

The Tribunal only granted a privileged treatment to the captain of the vessel. He was detained for 124 days until 28 February 1998. Had the Tribunal strictly followed Governing Council Decision No. 8, it would have awarded the amount of USD 13,600 in respect of him. Instead, the Tribunal granted the amount of USD 17,750. This might show that the Tribunal considered the Governing Council Decision No. 8 to be a non-binding guideline and that the Tribunal does indeed make a difference according to the status of the individual concerned. The different treatment may also reflect the fact that the captain was imprisoned in Conakry and subjected to criminal proceedings while the crew members were detained on board of their ship.

Additional damages were awarded when crew members had suffered "[i]njury, pain, suffering, disability and psychological damage." Governing Council Decision No. 8 also contains lump sums for personal injuries. Apparently, ITLOS did not consider the amounts of these sums to be appropriate. According to the Governing Council Decision No. 8, the flag State could only have claimed USD 15,000 in respect of injuries suffered by Mr. *Djibril Niasse* and USD 5,000 in respect of Second Officer *Klyuyev*. Instead, ITLOS granted damages in the amount of USD 25,000 in respect of Mr. *Djibril Niasse* and USD 10,000 in respect of Second Officer *Klyuyev*. This generous award might have been an expression of the Tribunal's concern for the victims and the decision's emphasis on humanitarian values.[656] However, the Tribunal presumably was also aware that due to the sheer amount of claims before the United Nations Claims Commission, that commission had needed to limit the amounts granted in the awards. The situation in the case of the *M/V Saiga* was very different because only two crew members suffered personal injuries. Hence, the Tribunal presumably deemed it necessary to significantly raise these limits.

It is a further interesting question whether the State of nationality of crew members will also be able to exercise diplomatic protection on behalf of them in addition to the flag State[657] and if so, what relationship would exist between these two remedies. The work of the International Law Commission[658] and the existing

---

656 *Cf. Oxman*, Bernard H./Bantz, Vincent, "Case Report: The M.V. "Saiga" (No. 2) (Saint Vincent and the Grenadines v. Guinea)", 94 AJIL (2000), pp. 140 *et seq.*, at 148.

657 Against such a concurrent right see *von Münch*, Ingo, "Der Diplomatische Schutz für Schiffe", in *Ipsen*, Hans Peter *et al.* (eds.), "Recht über See" (Hamburg: Decker, 1980), pp. 231 *et seq.*, at 249; *Vukas*, Budislav, "Droit de la mer et droits de l'homme", in *id.* (ed.), "The Law of the Sea: Selected Writings" (Leiden: Nijhoff, 2004), pp. 71 *et seq.*, at 76-7; *Watts*, Arthur, "The Protection of Merchant Ships", 33 BYIL(1957), pp. 52 *et seq.*, at 66. For a concurrent right see *McDougal*, Myres Smith/*Burke*, William T., "The Public Order of the Oceans" (New Haven: Yale University Press, 1962); *UN* Doc. A/59/10 (2004), "Report of the International Law Commission on the work of its fifty-sixth session", Commentary on Article 19 of the Draft Articles on Diplomatic Protection, at 90, para. 1.

658 *Ibid.*

State practice tends to favour the existence of a concurrent right. The United Kingdom in an exchange of notes with the United States in 1981 agreed "not to object to prosecution by the United States of anyone other than a United Kingdom national … act[ing] on the understanding that questions relating to the prosecution of nationals of other states are of primary concern to their state of nationality."[659] The United Kingdom thus clearly supports the existence of the seaman's home State's right to exercise diplomatic protection. Germany filed a formal protest on behalf of a vessel with the nationality of Panama (but owned by a German shipowner) in September 1984 after the Iraqi air force had sunk the vessel.[660] Only the United States has so far denied their nationals diplomatic protection by referring to the availability of protection by their flag State and also rejected claims by States of nationality other than flag States.[661]

If one accepts a concurrent right to exercise diplomatic protection by the flag State, then the international law on the settlement of disputes obliges the treat the two claims independently since the parties are different. However, if one State has already received compensation in respect of an individual on behalf of whom another State has also filed claim, then this other State will be barred from receiving any compensation and needs to be satisfied with the mere declaration that the respondent State has acted wrongfully and/or an apology by that State.

5. Punitive damages

Punitive damages are "[d]amages awarded in addition to actual damages when the defendant acted with recklessness, malice, or deceit."[662] The special rapporteur of the ILC, *J.P.A. François*, aimed to punish the interfering state by particularly harsh provisions on compensation when he drafted the predecessor to Art. 110, para. 3 LOSC.[663] This might lead to the conclusion that the compensation under

---

[659] *Siddle*, John, "Anglo-American Co-Operation in the Suppression of Drug Smuggling", 31 Int'l & Comp. L. Q. (1982), pp. 726 *et seq.*, at 743.

[660] *Lagoni*, Rainer, "Gewaltverbot, Seekriegsrecht und Schiffahrtsfreiheit im Golfkrieg", in *Fürst*, Walter *et al.* (eds.), "Festschrift für Wolfgang Zeidler" (Berlin: de Gruyter, 1987), pp. 1833 *et seq.*, at 1850.

[661] "Instruction by the Department of State to the consul in Marseille" (23 February 1938), *Hackworth*, Green Haywood, "Digest of International Law", Vol. 4 (Washington: Government Printing Office, 1943), at 885; *Ross v. McIntyre*, 140 U.S. 453, 472-3 (1891); "Foreign Service Regulations" (June 1941), in *Hyde*, Charles Cheney, "International Law – Chiefly as interpreted and applied by the United States", Vol. 2 (2nd ed., Boston: Little, Brown and Company, 1947), at 1180.

[662] Black's Law Dictionary (8th ed., St. Paul: West Group, 2004), at 418.

[663] *Cf.* UN Doc. A/2934 (2005), "Report of the International Law Commission to the General Assembly 1955", Comment on art. 19, reprinted in Yearbook of the International Law Commission (1955-II), pp. 19 *et seq.*, at 26 ("This article *penalizes* the unjustified seizure of vessels suspected of piracy.") (emphasis added) and UN Doc. A/3159 (1956), "Report of the International Law Commission to the General Assembly 1956", Comment on Art. 46, reprinted in Yearbook of the International Law Commission (1956-II), pp. 253 *et seq.*, at 284 ("This *severe penalty* seems justified in order to prevent the right of visit being abused.") (emphasis added).

the relevant provisions of the LOSC and related conventions should include punitive damages. However, what is more important for an interpretation of these provisions than this statement in the *travaux préparatoires* is the understanding of losses and damages in the context of the drafting of the relevant provisions (Art. 31, para. 2 VCLT).

There may be some support for the granting of punitive damages under public international law.[664] *Dominicé*, for example, states that the absence of the distinction between civil and penal responsibility results in a concept of responsibility having a mixed character, where punitive elements may be detected side by side with compensatory aspects.[665]

The common understanding of compensation in public international law, however, is that it is not concerned to punish the responsible State.[666] In fact, the "law of State responsibility has been gradually eliminating all punitive aspects and equating responsibility with reparation."[667] In the cases of the *Carthage* and the *Manouba*, France claimed 100,000 francs to sanction Italy for certain interferences with navigation in addition to the claims on behalf of its nationals.[668] Apparently altruistically, France requested that the 100,000 francs should be set apart for the benefit of some work or institution of international interest to be designated by the Court.[669] The arbitration tribunal nevertheless denied this claim because a pecuniary penalty would be superfluous and beyond the objects of international adjudication.[670]

One might argue that the decision in the case of the *I'm Alone* nevertheless shows that there is some evidence for the availability of punitive damages in public international law. In that case, two commissioners awarded USD 25,000 to Canada because one of the vessels under her flag was sunk by the United States even though Canada did not suffer any material damages.[671] However, this award has been heavily criticized since the commissioners came to their decision *ex aequo et bono* rather than strictly adhered to sources of public international law

---

664 Cf. *The "I'm Alone" (United States/Canada)* (5 January 1935), 3 RIAA pp. 1609 *et seq.*, at 1616; *Janes Claim (United States v. Mexico)* (16 November 1925), 4 RIAA, pp. 82 *et seq.*, at 90; *Rainbow Warrior Arbitration (New Zealand v. France)* (30 April 1990), 82 ILR, pp. 499 *et seq.*, at 575; *Shaw*, Malcolm N., "International Law" (5th ed., Cambridge: Cambridg University Press, 2003), at 718-9.

665 *Dominicé*, Christian, "Droit international – Observations sur les droits de l'état victime d'un fait internationalement illicite", Vol. 2 (Paris: Pedone, 1982), at 57.

666 *UN* Doc. A/56/10 (2001), "Report of the International Law Commission on the work of its Fifty-third session", Commentary on Art. 36, at 245-6, para. 4.

667 *Barboza*, Julio, "Legal Injury: The Tip of the Iceberg in the Law of State Responsibility", in *Ragazzi*, Maurizio (ed.), "International Responsibility Today – Essays in Memory of Oscar Schachter" (Leiden: Nijhoff, 2005), pp. 7 *et seq.*, at 22.

668 *The Carthage (France/Italy)*, 11 RIAA, pp. 449 *et seq.*, at 458; *The Manouba (France/Italy)*, *ibid.*, pp. 463 *et seq.*, at 472.

669 *Ibid.*

670 *The Carthage (France/Italy)*, 11 RIAA, pp. 449 *et seq.*, at 460; *The Manouba (France/Italy)*, *ibid.*, pp. 463 *et seq.*, at 475.

671 *The I'm Alone (Canada/United States)*, 3 RIAA, pp. 1609 *et seq.*, at 1618.

and since they represented counsellors to their governments rather than independent judges.[672] The authority of their decision for an international lawyer hence must be considered to be quite limited.

Reacting to comments by governments, the International Law Commission has struck out all references to punitive damages in their Articles on State Responsibility.[673] One might even say that "[t]he superimposing of a penalty in addition to full compensation and naming it damages … is a hopeless confusion of terms."[674]

The rejection of punitive damages may or may not be justified by referring to the sovereign equality of States and a consequent impossibility to impose a penalty on another State.[675] If at all, punitive damages are awarded "covertly so that they are indistinguishable from compensation in its true sense."[676] Thus, the gravity of the offence is usually considered in the award of compensation.[677] Neither at the time the provisions were drafted nor today has customary international law explicitly known the award of punitive damages.[678] Since few legal systems provide for punitive damages,[679] they also have not become a general principle of international law.

The punishment of the interfering State, which *J.P.A. François* referred to, can thus not be taken literally. The absence of the requirement of an internationally wrongful act in Art. 110, para. 3 LOSC and similar provisions already constitute a sufficient factor of deterrence to imply a penal character of the provision.

Therefore, the compensation covered under the analyzed provisions does not cover any punitive damages. Exceptionally, in cases of flag State or diplomatic protection, the claiming State may also demand satisfaction according to the general law on State responsibility. Such satisfaction, in rare circumstances may

---

672 *Fitzmaurice*, Gerald, "The case of the I'm Alone", 17 BYIL(1936), pp. 82 *et seq.*, at 94-95.

673 *Crawford*, James, "The International Law Commission's Articles on State Responsibility" (Cambridge: Cambridge University Press, 2002), at 19, 36.

674 *The Lusitania Claims (USA v. Germany)* (1923), 7 RIAA, pp. 39 *et seq.*, at 43; *cf.* also *Lewin*, David Bencionovic, "Die Verantwortlichkeit der Staaten im gegenwärtigen Völkerrecht" (Potsdam-Babelsberg: Inst. für Ausländ. Recht und Rechtsvergleichung, Dt. Akad. für Staats- und Rechtswissenschaft, 1969), at 11; *Whiteman*, Marjorie M., "Damages in International Law", Vol. 1 (Washington, U.S. Government Printing Office, 1937), at 717; *Greig*, D.W., "International Law" (2nd ed., London: Butterworth, 1976), at 602; *Bin Cheng*, "General Principles of Law as applied by International Courts and Tribunals" (London: Stevens, 1953), at 235; *Brownlie*, Ian, "State Responsiblity" (Oxford: Clarendon Press, 1983), at 235.

675 *Graefrath*, Bernhard, "Responsibility and Damage Caused: relations between responsibility and damages", 185 RdC (1984-II), pp. 95 *et seq.*, at 101 (1984-II).

676 *Jørgensen*, N., "A Reappraisal of Punitive Damages in International Law", 68 BYIL (1997), pp. 247 *et seq.*, at 266.

677 *Brownlie*, Ian, "Principles of Public International Law" (6th ed., Oxford: Oxford University Press, 2003), at 447.

678 *Cf. Shelton*, Dinah, "Remedies in International Human Rights Law" (Oxford: Oxford University Press, 2000), at 279 (nevertheless demanding punitive damages to satisfy the "deterrence function of tort law").

679 See, *e.g., BMW of North America, Inc. v. Gore*, 517 U.S. 559, 568 (1996).

also consist of an award of "symbolic damages".[680] It is nevertheless not available for cases where the respondent's liability is based on lawful conduct.

If a claimant, whether State or private entity, bases its claim on one of the analyzed compensation provisions, then it will only be awarded damages excluding any punitive damages or symbolic damages as a means of satisfaction.

6. Interest

Claims for interest are not a separate form of reparation, but part of the compensation sought.[681] According to Art. 38 of the Articles on State Responsibility, interest is "payable when necessary in order to ensure full reparation." The award of interests thus becomes necessary when the principal sum is quantified at an earlier date.[682]

While the whole issue of interest is still very controversial in public international law, a few questions have been settled. No compound interest is awarded in international law[683], since other opinions[684] have not been strong enough to establish a custom.[685] Interest is also not awarded if compensation is due under a lump sum settlement since it will be impossible to determine and since it has usually already been taken into consideration in the settlement.[686] Furthermore, the

---

680 Commentary on Art. 37 ASR, para. 5, in *Crawford*, James, "The International Law Commission's Articles on State Responsibility" (Cambridge: Cambridge University Press, 2002), at 233.

681 *Islamic Republic of Iran v. United States of America (Case No. A.19)*, 16 Iran-U.S.C.T.R. (1987), pp. 285 *et seq.*, at 289-90; *The S.S. Wimbledon (United Kingdom et al. v. Germany)*, 17 August 1923, (1923) PCIJ Ser. A No. 1, at 32; *Norwegian Shipowners' Claim (Norway/United States)* (1922), 1 RIAA, pp. 307 *et seq.*, at 341 (1922); *Administrative Decision No. III (United States/Germany)* (1923), 7 RIAA, pp. 64 *et seq.*, at 70, *British Property in Spanish Morocco (United Kingdom/Spain)* (1925), 2 RIAA, pp. 617 *et seq.*, at 657, 697, 735; *Illinois Central Railroad Company Claim v. United Mexican States* (6 December 1926), 4 RIAA, pp. 134 *et seq.*, at 136.

682 *UN* Doc. A/56/10 (2001), "Report of the International Law Commission on the work of its Fifty-third session", Commentary on Art. 38, at 269, para. 2.

683 *R.J. Reynolds Tobacco Co. v. Government of the Islamic Republic of Iran*, 7 Iran-U.S.C.T.R. (1984), pp. 181 *et seq.*, at 191-2; *Whiteman*, Marjorie M., "Damages in International Law", Vol. 3 (Washington, U.S. Government Printing Office, 1943), at 1997; *British Property in Spanish Morocco (United Kingdom v. Spain)* (1924), 2 RIAA, pp. 615, at 650.

684 *Mann*, Frederick Alexander, "Further Studies in International Law" (Oxford: Oxford University Press, 1990), at 377, 383; *Companía des Desarrollo de Santa Elena SA v. Republic of Costa Rica*, I.C.S.I.D. Case No. ARB/96/1, final award of 1 February 2000, at paras. 103-5.

685 UN Doc. A/56/10 (2001), "Report of the International Law Commission on the work of its Fifty-third session", Commentary on Art. 38, at 273-4, para. 9.

686 See "Foreign Compensation (People's Republic of China) Order 1987 (U.K.)", s. 10, giving effect to the Settlement Agreement of 5 June 1987, U.K.T.S. No. 37 (1987).

goal of an award of interest is to replace the generation of profits by the detained property; thus, one cannot claim interest if one is compensated for lost profits.[687]

However, a few questions still seem to be unsettled due to a lack of a uniform approach by international tribunals.[688]

a) Starting date

First, when does the interest start to run? Approaches are to calculate the interest starting on the date of the relevant conduct of the respondent,[689] on the date on which payment should have been made (proposal by the ILC),[690] on the date of the claim or the demand or even on the date of the judgment/award.[691]

In the case of the *M/V Saiga (No. 2)*, the International Tribunal for the Law of the Sea awarded interest with different starting dates in respect of different categories of loss.[692] In order to understand the judgment, it first seems necessary to recollect the relevant dates of the case:

28 October 1997	Arrest of the *M/V Saiga* and her crew
17 November 1997	Day the crew could have possibly left Conakry
19 February 1998	Last bill for medical expenses of Second Officer *Klyuvev*
4 March 1998	*M/V Saiga* returns to Dakar; last bill for medical expenses of crew member Mr. *Niasse*
31 March 1998	ITLOS presumed that the bills for the repairs have been paid on 31 March 1998
01 July 1999	Judgment

While the interest for the compensation of the discharged cargo started to run on 28 October 1997 (the day of the arrest of the vessel), the starting date for the com-

687 UN Doc. A/56/10 (2001), "Report of the International Law Commission on the work of its Fifty-third session", Commentary on Art. 36, at 262, para. 33,; *Graefrath*, Bernhard, "Responsibility and Damage Caused: relations between responsibility and damages", 185 RdC (1984-II), pp. 95 *et seq.*, at 98.

688 *Gotanda*, J.Y., "Supplemental Damages in Private International Law" (1998), at 13.

689 *Cf. The Apollon*, 22 U.S. 362, 377 (1824); *O'Connell*, Daniel Patrick, "International Law", Vol. 2 (2nd ed., London: Stevens, 1970), at 1122.

690 The ILC nevertheless does not regard this rule to be customary international law. *UN* Doc. A/56/10 (2001), "Report of the International Law Commission on the work of its Fifty-third session", Commentary on Art. 38, at 273-4, para. 10.

691 European Court of Justice, Case 64/76, *P. Dumortier Frères SA v. Council*, 1979 E.C.R. 3091; Case 238/78, *Ireks-Arkady GmbH v. Council and Commission*, 1979 E.C.R. pp. 2955 *et seq.*, at 2975; *The S.S. Wimbledon*, Judgment of 17 August 1923, (1923) PCIJ, Ser. A No. 1, at 15, 32.

692 *The M/V "Saiga" (No. 2) Case (Saint Vincent and the Grenadines v. Guinea)*, Judgment of 1 July 1999, ITLOS Reports 1999, pp. 10 *et seq.*, at 66, para. 173.

pensation for detention of and injuries to crew members was set to be 01 October 1999. Interests for the damage to the vessel herself started to run on 31 March 1998 and interest related to lost charter hire and costs related to the detention of the vessel ran from 01 January 1998. Finally, the interest for medical expenses by two crew members also started to run on 01 January 1998.[693]

Unfortunately, the judgment of ITLOS does not provide any explicit reasoning for this different treatment of the specific damages, but if one compares it to the time-line above, one might come to the following assumptions. Generally, the Tribunal seems to consider interest to be payable from the date on which the damage was caused or, as the case may be, the date when the expense was incurred. Thus, for example, interest for the discharged cargo started to run on the day when the vessel was arrested and the cargo confiscated. This approach rejects the reasoning of the Permanent Court of International Justice in the case of the *S.S. Wimbledon* as being moratory instead of compensatory.

Regarding the interest for lost charter hire, one can presume that ITLOS referred to the date when this charter hire was due and when the shipowner thus lost this income. If one considers the documents available to the Tribunal, the date for the interest regarding the costs related to the detention of the vessel seems to be a compromise between the date of the arrest of the vessel and other proposals submitted by the parties. Concerning the interest relating to the costs of repairs of the vessel, the Tribunal presumably chose the date when the repairs should have been paid by the shipowner. As far as it concerns the costs of detention of the vessel, the Tribunal simply chose a date in the middle of the detention period instead of distinguishing each day of detention. The same compromise was achieved concerning the costs for medical treatment where a date between the injury and the last bill was chosen and where the Tribunal did not distinguish between the different injured crew members.

Concerning the compensation for the detention and personal injury to crew members, the Tribunal granted the respondent State three months for payment until interest would start to run. Apparently, the Tribunal considered these amounts to be due after the time it rendered its judgment and not when the mistreatment occurred. Hereby, the Tribunal clearly distinguished between the mistreatment of crew members and other damages. The judgment also indicates that the Tribunal considered the suffering caused by the mistreatment to be moral damages and that for moral damages, no compensatory, but only moratory interest is due.

This treatment by the Tribunal of personal suffering surprises at first sight. It might be explained by the special nature of the flag State protection of foreign crew members. One can assume that the Tribunal intended to refer to the date the payment should have been made since an obligation to compensate a flag State for damages suffered by crew members can only arise when the flag state decides to exercise (diplomatic or functional) protection. This nevertheless does not explain why the tribunal chose such a late starting date after adjudication of the dispute.

---

[693] *Ibid.*, at 66-67, para. 175.

b) When does the interest stop to run?

Another controversial question is whether the interest stops to run on the date of the settlement of the award or on the date of actual payment of compensation.[694] The latter is proposed by the ILC and by ITLOS which in the case of *The M/V Saiga* did not determine a fixed terminal date for the interest and hence implied that the interest does not stop to run until the compensation is paid.[695] This approach definitely has the advantage of exerting a considerable degree of pressure on the responsible State and may have become part of the general law on State responsibility.

c) The interest rate

Finally, it has also become quite controversial what interest rate should be applied to provide for full reparation. One could think of the rate currently applicable in the respondent State, in the applicant State or an international lending rate.[696] Traditionally, this rate had been agreed upon by the parties to the dispute either in their compromise or in a settlement. The rate was often set at six or four percent.[697] ITLOS, in the *M/V Saiga (No. 2)* Case took into consideration "the commercial conditions prevailing in the countries where the expenses were incurred or the principal operations of the party being compensated are located" and fixed the general interest rate at six percent.[698] This rate was closest to the interest rates applicable in the United Kingdom (where a lot of financial transactions dealing with the *M/V Saiga* had taken place), St. Vincent and the Grenadines (the flag State) and Senegal (where the vessel was repaired). Therefore, not only the States parties to the dispute, but also the origin and the location of the private and juridical persons involved were relevant in the determination of the interest rate. Concerning the discharged cargo of oil, ITLOS fixed a higher interest rate of eight percent to include lost profits.[699] But the higher interest rate also reflects the interest rate in Guinea at the date of the arrest (7.50 %). Furthermore,

---

[694] Commentary on Art. 38 ASR, para. 10, in *Crawford*, James, "The International Law Commission's Articles on State Responsibility" (Cambridge: Cambridge University Press, 2002), at 238.

[695] *Cf.* also *American Cast Iron Pipe Company Claim* (16 October 1966), 40 ILR, pp. 169 *et seq.*, at 173-4.

[696] *Cf. The S.S. Wimbledon (United Kingdom et. al. v. Germany)*, Judgment of 17 August 1923, (1923) PCIJ Ser. A No. 1, at 32.

[697] *Affaire des Navires Cape Horn Pigeon, James Hamilton Lewis, C.H. White et Kate and Anna (United States/Russia)* (29 November 1902), 9 RIAA, pp. 51 *et seq.*, at 65, 71, 76 (six percent); *Henry James Bethune (Great Britain) v. United States* (1914), 6 RIAA, pp. 32 *et seq.*, at 34 (four percent); *Owner, Officers and Men of The Wanderer (Great Britain) v. United States* (1921), 6 RIAA, pp. 68, *et seq.*, at 77 (four percent); *Charterers and Crew of The Kate (Great Britain) v. United States* (1921), 6 RIAA, pp. 77 *et seq.*, at 82 (four percent).

[698] *The M/V "Saiga" (No. 2) Case (Saint Vincent and the Grenadines v. Guinea)*, Judgment of 1 July 1999, ITLOS Reports 1999, pp. 10 *et seq.*, at 66, para. 173.

[699] *Ibid.*

one might comment that an interest always considers lost profits, but may be higher for assets of great economic value such as crude oil.

The interest rate for the detention of and injury to crew members was, on the other hand, considerably lower (three percent) for which ITLOS did not provide any reasoning. ITLOS has probably applied a lower interest rate to these damages to be considerate of the controversial argument that such damages should not be awarded in excess of the more or less arbitrary pecuniary satisfaction awarded in such cases.[700] However, one might also presume that the fact that interest in respect of these injuries only started to run three months after the judgment was relevant in the determination of the interest rate. It seems that the Tribunal has considered these interests to be moratory rather than compensatory because it viewed the damage caused by the personal injury to be moral and thus not really open to compensation. Finally, the low interest rate for personal injury may be explained by the questionable argument that personal freedom and health are not used to gain profits to the same degree as merchandises such as valuable cargo of a vessel.

Nevertheless, the decision of ITLOS makes clear that interest is a form of compensation, that lost profits can be claimed and that they may be included in the awarded interest.

7. Currency of the compensation

An interference with navigation on the high seas will often lead to damages suffered by private entities based in different States. Each of them might have an interest to receive the compensation and to have it calculated in a particular currency. The issue for a competent tribunal might thus become in which currency the award is to be calculated and then granted to the claimant.

As far as it concerns the calculation of the compensation, it seems most adequate to apply the currency of the place where the damage occurred since this would come closest to a restitution in kind. Since in maritime matters, the damage might occur on the high seas and since actors involved in maritime trade usually calculate in U.S. dollars, such calculation seems appropriate to the majority of cases relevant to this study.

The final payment of the compensation, however, is subject to the procedural law of the forum where the litigation takes place. Domestic courts, on which private entities currently need to rely when acting without a protecting State, will usually only grant compensation in the currency of their jurisdiction.[701] If the damage occurred in a different currency, it might become very relevant for the parties whether the court uses the exchange rate of the day the damage occurred or of the day of the judgment. German prize courts used the exchange rate on the day

---

700 *Administrative Decision No. III* (1923), 7 RIAA, pp. 64 *et seq.*, at 65 (U.S.-Germany Mixed Claims Commission); *Subilia*, Jean-Luc, "L'allocation d'interêts dans la jurisprudence internationale" (Lausanne, 1972), at 44.

701 *Cf. The Helicon (Nr. 2)*, reprinted in: *Verzijl*, Jan Hendrik Willem, "Le droit des prises de la Grande Guerre" (Leyde: Sijthoff, 1924), at 1140-1141.

of the damage.[702] Generally, there is no convincing reason to do so. Since exchange rates fluctuate quite randomly in either direction, neither the claimant nor the respondent has an advantage by such a general rule. Furthermore, as the case of the *M/V Saiga* shows, damages may easily increase until the day of the final award. Instead of applying different exchange rates for each kind of damage the claimant has suffered, it seems much more reasonable to simply base the final award on the exchange rate of the day of the decision.

International tribunals are often bound by the compromis to grant potential compensation in an internationally frequent currency such as the U.S. dollar. If an international tribunal is not bound by a compromis or its own rules, it will most likely rule that the payment is to be effected in the currency of the applicant which would come closest to a restitution in kind.[703] As far as it concerns the exchange rate, the above-mentioned considerations apply to international tribunals to the same degree.

8. Damage to the flag state

Attempts have been undertaken by flag states exercising flag State protection to claim compensation because they have suffered own damage due to an interference with the navigation of one of their vessels on the high seas. In the case of the *M/V Saiga*, the applicant claimed compensation for a violation of its rights in respect of ships flying its flag. The International Tribunal for the Law of the Sea nevertheless considered its decision on the illegality of the arrest and subsequent detention to constitute adequate reparation.[704] Similarly, the Permanent Court of Arbitration held that the establishment of a violation of public international law plus the payment of compensation for material losses appear to be sufficient “as a general rule” and denied a French claim to grant compensation of one franc nominal damage to the flag State.[705]

It would indeed be very hard to assess any damage in general to the flag State in cases of interference with navigation. Instead, the flag State needs to rely on other forms of reparation such as satisfaction including, *e.g.*, an apology or merely

---

702 *Trudvang*, reprinted in: *Verzijl*, Jan Hendrik Willem, “Le droit des prises de la Grande Guerre” (Leyde: Sijthoff, 1924), at 1141.

703 *The S.S. Wimbledon (United Kingdom, France, Italy & Japan v. Germany)*, Judgment of 17 August 1923, (1923) PCIJ Ser. A, No. 1, at 32; *Lighthouses Case (France/ Greece)*, 12 RIAA, pp. 250 *et seq.*. But see *In re Jessie Watson (United Kingdom/ Mexico)*, 5 RIAA, pp. 162 *et seq.* (award based upon the national money of the State to be held liable).

704 *The M/V “Saiga” (No. 2) Case (Saint Vincent and the Grenadines v. Guinea)*, Judgment of 1 July 1999, ITLOS Reports 1999, pp. 10 *et seq.*, at 67, para. 176.

705 *The Carthage (France/Italy)*, Permanent Court of Arbitration, 6 May 1913, reprinted in 7 AJIL (1913), pp. 623 *et seq.*, at 627-628; *cf.* also *The Manouba (France/Italy)* (6 May 1913), 11 RIAA, pp. 463 *et seq.*, at 474-475.

a decision by an international tribunal. In most cases, an authoritative finding by an international tribunal constitutes such sufficient satisfaction.[706]

The holding by ITLOS moreover once more shows that other forms of reparation besides compensation are available under the Law of the Sea Convention as legal consequences of wrongful interferences because of the safeguard clause in Art. 304 LOSC.

9. Costs and expenses

The claimant, in order to pursue his claim, often needs to incur considerable expenses for lawyers, the collection of evidence etc. One might argue that, if these costs are necessary to gain a compensation award, then they should be borne by the liable respondent which has to "wipe out all consequences of its conduct."

However, international tribunals have been reluctant to award such costs and expenses to the claimant. In the case of *The M/V Saiga (No. 2)*, the applicant state, Guinea, claimed expenses resulting from the time lost by officials in dealing with the arrest and detention of the ship and its crew. ITLOS held that these expenses were incurred in the exercise of the normal functions of a flag State and thus could not be recovered.[707] Hence, while in most domestic laws, at least lawyers' fees can be claimed by the winning party,[708] each party has to bear its own costs in a dispute between States, probably a characteristic having its origin in the diplomatic function of the settlement of disputes under public international law.[709] The decision of ITLOS was nevertheless controversial (13:7 majority) and at least one judge supposes that ITLOS will deviate from the practice once corresponding internal rules have been adopted.[710] The seven dissenting judges submitted an explicit joint declaration in favour of an award of costs and expenses to the applicant.[711]

The case may well be different though if a private entity bases its claim on one of the relevant compensation provisions before a domestic court or even an inter-

706 *Crawford*, James/ *Olleson*, Simon, "The Nature and Forms of International Responsibility", in *Evans*, Malcolm D. (ed.), "International Law" (2003), pp. 455 *et seq.*, at 467-8.

707 *The M/V "Saiga" (No. 2) Case (Saint Vincent and the Grenadines v. Guinea)*, Judgment of 1 July 1999, ITLOS Reports 1999, pp. 10 *et seq.*, at 67, para. 177.

708 See, *e.g.*, *The Apollon*, 22 U.S. 362, 379 (1824); *Shelton*, Dinah, "Remedies in International Human Rights Law" (Oxford: Oxford University Press, 2000), at 307.

709 *Cf.* Article 9 of the Agreement between the United Kingdom and the United States of America for the settlement of certain pecuniary claims outstanding between the two countries, signed on 18 August 1910, in Martens Nouveau Recueil Général de Traités, Troisième Série, Vol. VI, pp. 361 *et seq.*: „Each government shall bear its own expenses."

710 *Wolfrum*, Rüdiger, "Billigflaggen – Schadensersatz – Nacheile", 3 ZeuS (2000), pp. 1 *et seq.*, at 12.

711 *The M/V Saiga (No. 2) (St. Vincent and the Grenadines)*, Joint Declaration by Judges Caminos, Yankov, Akl, Anderson, Vukas, Treves and Eiriksson on the Question of Costs, ITLOS Reports 1999, pp. 77-78.

national tribunal. It has become common practice for human rights tribunals to award costs and damages to the successful claimant if these expenses have been reasonable.[712] Furthermore, most domestic courts award costs and expenses as part of damages (*supra*). Presumably, lacking substantial and definitive international rules on the issue, a domestic court will be inclined to apply its own procedural law and a general principle may develop in the future when provisions of the Law of the Sea find increased application before domestic courts. Furthermore, the mentioned reasoning derived from diplomatic practice is not directly applicable to disputes between private entities and States where the litigation costs might represent a strong disincentive for the private litigant.

10. The ability of the respondent State to compensate

Damages caused by a single interference with navigation will usually be quite limited and compensation does not create a major challenge for the responsible State which is to compensate these damages. However, an international tribunal may in the future be faced with a multitude of compensation claims by private entities assembled in a single State. Thus, an important flag State may bring forward the claims dealing with interferences with the navigation of its entire merchant fleet and demand compensation by a single State which has initiated a global interdiction campaign. In the latter case, the damages caused by the responsible State might reach extensive amounts with severe strains on its budget.

One might therefore question whether the general law on State responsibility provides for any limit in the amount that compensation may be granted. Does the general law on State responsibility need to consider the capacity of the responsible State to compensate the damage for which it is responsible? Furthermore, most domestic statutes and international conventions which provide for liability for lawful conduct of private entities also establish upper limits of liability. Would it be appropriate to provide for similar limits at least in cases where a State is held responsible for lawful conduct?

As of now, such limitation is unknown to the general law on State responsibility. The case concerning *Armed activities on the territory of the Congo (Democratic Republic of the Congo v. Uganda)* shows that even a poor State such as Uganda may incur liability in an amount well exceeding its own Gross Domestic Product.[713] Furthermore, the negotiations leading to the 1969 Intervention Convention clearly confirm an unlimited State responsibility. In these negotiations, Canada submitted a proposal limiting State responsibility to the same amounts as the liability of shipowners for oil pollution,[714] but evidently found no support

[712] *Bernhardt*, Rudolf, "Just Satisfaction under the European Convention on Human Rights", in *Ragazzi*, Maurizio (ed.), "International Responsibility Today – Essays in Memory of Oscar Schachter" (Leiden: Nijhoff, 2005), pp. 243 *et seq.*, at 248.

[713] *Cf.* "World Court rules Uganda violated rights in Congo", Reuters, 19 December 2005.

[714] *IMCO* Doc. LEG/CONF/3 (September 1969), "International Conference on Marine Pollution Damage, Observations submitted by Governments on draft articles on the

during the Diplomatic Conference in 1969.[715] Therefore, the responsible State usually bears responsibility for all damages caused by attributable conduct.

In order to ensure payment by the respondent, the claimant may well enter into negotiations and thereby offer a reduction of the compensation. However, the claimant in such a case does not act on the basis of *opinio juris*, but rather pursues his own interests in getting the maximum available award.

Some argument has been raised that in limited circumstances, a State should be freed of its obligations, justified by application of the general principle concerning the state of necessity.[716] However, these are rather proposals for the future (*de lege ferenda)*, similar to the ongoing discussion about a law on insolvency of States.

IV. The Intervention Convention: distinction between disproportionate and proportionate damages?

The above considerations have deliberately left out Art. VI Intervention Convention. This provision differs significantly from the other compensation provisions in respect of the extent of responsibility. According to its wording, the responsible State shall only pay compensation "to the extent of the damage caused by measures which exceed those reasonably necessary to achieve the end mentioned in Article I." However, not only disproportionate measures, but also any measure in contravention of the provisions of the Intervention Convention entails the responsibility of the interfering State under Art. VI Intervention Convention.

For example, a coastal State might have proceeded to take measures against a foreign vessel without having consulted the flag State and thereby have violated Art. III, lit. a Intervention Convention. Such a contravention of the convention would usually lead to the responsibility of the coastal State. If, however, the measures have been proportionate, then the coastal State, if one strictly applied the terms of Art VI Intervention Convention, would not have to compensate any damage. Seemingly, the coastal State could thus circumvent requirements of the convention (except the principle of proportionality) without risking its own liability.

Could this have been the intention of the States parties? Could at least the general law on State apply to violations of the convention? The wording of the provision might lead to a denial of the second question since the drafters could have limited the scope of application of the provision to violations of the principle of proportionality. Instead, they seem to have preferred an application of Art. VI Intervention Convention to all violations of the convention. *Prima facie*, Art. VI

---

right of a coastal State to intervene when a casualty which causes or might cause pollution of the sea [by oil] occurs on the High Seas", at 39.

715 *IMCO* Doc. LEG/CONF/C.1/SR.16 (7 May 1971), "Committee of the Whole I, Summary Record of the Sixteenth Meeting", at 8, 13.

716 *ILA*, "Resolution on International Monetary Law", Report of the Sixty-Third Conference (1988), at 20-23.

Intervention Convention therefore seems to constitute *lex specialis* in the relationship with the general law on State responsibility.

The object and purpose of the provision, however, was probably to prevent and deter abusive interferences with navigation. The mentioned scenario with a strict application of the wording of the provision would probably contradict this object and purpose.

Furthermore, a systematic interpretation of Art. VI Intervention Convention taking into consideration the general law on State responsibility and the Law of the Sea at least leaves the international lawyer puzzled in a certain way. Compared to the Law of the Sea, the coastal State gains significant interference rights on the high seas by ratifying the convention. One would thus expect a strict liability regime as safeguard against abusive interferences. Art. VI Intervention Convention, however, seems to be more favourable to the coastal State than the general law on State responsibility. The coastal State would thus gain in two respects, an unlikely result of negotiations between independent sovereign States.

The negotiations toward the Intervention Convention in the beginning focused on the principle of proportionality. It came as no surprise that the first proposal of a compensation provision only mentioned an obligation to compensate in cases where the principle of proportionality had been violated.[717] However, within the course of the negotiations, the provision became more general and sounded like a mere restatement of the general law on State responsibility.[718]

The Spanish delegate therefore commented that "the article was unnecessary since it merely repeated the principle of international liability of States under international law… and favoured deletion of the whole of Article VI."[719] Even the chairman of the Working Group, *Riphagen* stated that "he personally felt there was no need to have [the provision]". On the other hand, he had "no concrete objection to the article and believed that the difficulties it gave rise to were overrated."[720] According to the United Kingdom, there were presentational rather than legal reasons for the article since it made ratification more acceptable for States with large mercantile fleets.[721] Finally, some delegates even put forward the idea that compensation should not be payable only for damage caused by measures which contravene the provisions of the proposed Convention but that compensation should also be payable for damage caused by measures which are taken in

---

[717] *IMCO* Doc. LEG/WG(I).I/2 (18 September 1967), "Legal Committee Working Group I, First Session, Report to the Legal Committee", at 4, 6; *IMCO* Doc. LEG II/4 (11 December 1967), "Legal Committee, Second Session, Conclusions reached and Future Work Programme Proposed", pp. 2 *et seq.*, at 3.

[718] *Cf.* Draft Article VI: "A State which takes measures or purports to take measures falling within the scope of this Convention, which are not justified by its provisions, shall pay compensation for any financial loss suffered thereby." *IMCO* Doc. LEG/WG(I).III/3 (31 May 1968), "Legal Committee Working Group I, Report to the Legal Committee by Working Group I on the work of its second and third sessions", Annex I, at 4.

[719] *IMCO* Doc. LEG III/SR.7 (1 August 1968), "Legal Committee, Third Session, Summary Record of the Seventh Meeting", at 21-22.

[720] *Ibid.*

[721] *Ibid.*, at 23.

contravention of other rules of (general and conventional) international law, if any.[722] The views among the delegates thus differed regarding the compensation provision, but the draft articles were nevertheless sent to the diplomatic conference.

On that conference, there were a great number of proposals to limit the scope of the compensation provision. Canada proposed to apply the provision only to cases of violation of the principle of proportionality[723] and to compensate only "to the extent that measures taken went beyond what was reasonably necessary to achieve the end mentioned in Article I."[724] The United States agreed with the second proposal.[725] Similarly, Australia proposed that "[i]n determining the compensation, regard shall be had to the gravity of the contravention of the Convention."[726]

On 18 November 1969, the Committee of the Whole I of the Diplomatic Conference agreed that the compensation provisions should only cover those damages due to actions in excess of the action permitted under the Convention and thus adopted the second Canadian and the United States proposal.[727] The Spanish delegate still regarded the draft article to merely repeat general international law.[728] However, the United States had clearly argued that the coastal State should be liable only for that part of the damage caused by its actions in excess of action permitted under the Convention and not for any damage resulting from unlawful action.[729] This was evidently a departure from the general law on State responsibility and the delegates should have known of this special character of the provision.

---

[722] *IMCO* Doc. LEG IV/6 (15 November 1968), "Legal Committee, Fourth Session, Report to the Council on the work of its third and fourth Sessions", at 3, para. 9(b).

[723] *IMCO* Doc. LEG/CONF/C.1/SR. 11 (7 May 1971), "Committee of the Whole I, Summary Record of the Eleventh Meeting", at 12.

[724] *IMCO* Doc. LEG/CONF/C.1/SR. 11 (7 May 1971), "Committee of the Whole I, Summary Record of the Eleventh Meeting", at 13.

[725] *IMCO* Doc. LEG/CONF/3 (September 1969), "International Conference on Marine Pollution Damage, Observations submitted by Governments on draft articles on the right of a coastal State to intervene when a casualty which causes or might cause pollution of the sea [by oil] occurs on the High Seas", at 40; *cf.* also *IMCO* Doc. LEG/CONF/3/Corr.3 (12 November 1969), "Proposed text of Article VI submitted by Canada".

[726] *IMCO* Doc. LEG/CONF/3/Add.1 (15 October 1969), "Observations and Proposals of Governments concerning Draft Articles on the Right of a Coastal State to intervene when a Casualty which causes, or might cause, pollution of the sea [by oil] occurs on the High Seas", at 3.

[727] *IMCO* Doc. LEG/CONF/C.1/SR. 11 (7 May 1971), "Committee of the Whole I, Summary Record of the Eleventh Meeting", at 13-14.

[728] *IMCO* Doc. LEG/CONF/C.1/SR.16 (7 May 1971), "Committee of the Whole I, Summary Record of the Sixteenth Meeting", at 13.

[729] *IMCO* Doc. LEG/CONF/3 (September 1969), "International Conference on Marine Pollution Damage, Observations submitted by Governments on draft articles on the right of a coastal State to intervene when a casualty which causes or might cause pollution of the sea [by oil] occurs on the High Seas", at 40.

Therefore, the *travaux préparatoires* generally confirm some of the previous considerations. Under Art. VI Intervention Convention, a violation of any part of the convention only leads to a duty to compensate if the violation has caused damage in excess of what a proportionate measure would have caused. The general law on State responsibility does not apply at all to situations covered by the convention.

The Intervention Convention thus has only deteriorated the situation for flag States (and shipowners) without providing them with adequate safeguards. This particularity is probably due to the urgent situation in the aftermath of the *Torrey Canyon* incident when public opinion was extremely critical of open registers and tanker owners and when time was pressing for an international convention in order to prevent future oil spills.

Article I of the Intervention Convention has nevertheless found great acceptance and acquired the status of customary international law.[730] The compensation provision in Art. VI Intervention Convention, on the other hand, has found very little attention and no application in State practice. Therefore, States which are not bound by the Intervention Convention, but rely on a customary right similar to Art. I Intervention Convention, are subject to the rules of the general law on State responsibility instead of Art. VI Intervention Convention.

J. Some procedural issues

International litigation raises a plethora of procedural issues being the subject of long-lasting deliberations before international tribunals. The law of procedure before international tribunals is rapidly evolving and this study does not follow the ambition to provide for a handbook on how to bring a claim for compensation based on public international law before an international tribunal or a domestic court. However, there are a few procedural issues raised by the compensation provisions which deserve a brief analysis here: namely, the burden of proof (1.), competing claims of protection (2.) and a potential obligation of the protecting State to forward the awarded compensation (3.).

I. The onus of proof

After the examination of the requirements and consequences of State responsibility under the analyzed compensation provisions, it finally seems necessary to find out whether the claimant or the respondent needs to prove the existence or the absence of certain of these requirements. Due to the practice of international tribunals and due to rules in domestic legal systems, it has generally been accepted as a general principle of international law that the claimant bears the burden of

---

[730] *Cf.* Art. 221 LOSC; *Churchill*, Robin R./*Lowe*, Alan Vaughan: "The Law of the Sea" (3rd ed., Manchester: Juris Publications, 1999), at 355.

proof, *i.e.* the claimant needs to prove the existence of all preconditions for his claim (*actori incumbit probatio* or *onus probandi actori incumbit*).[731] Thus, for example, the United States in the *Oil Platforms* case had to prove that the missile which hit one of its vessels had been fired by Iran and that the use of force was thus attributable to the latter.[732] However, depending on the applicable substantial rules, the claimant may also be the defendant of a case claiming a defence, counter-claim or exclusion. More generally speaking, any party to an international dispute needs to prove the existence of facts in its favour (*ei incumbit probation qui dicit, non qui negat*[733] or *actori incumbit probatio, reus in excipiendo fit actor*[734]).[735] If applied to the general law on State responsibility, the claimant needs to prove the commission of an internationally wrongful act attributable to the respondent and the proximate causation of an injury to him, while the respondent may exonerate himself from liability by proving the existence of a circumstance precluding wrongfulness.[736]

The other party in proceedings between sovereign States nevertheless is under an obligation "to co-operate in placing material evidence before the tribunal" thus facilitating in a certain way the burden on the claimant.[737] Therefore, scholars of public international law tend to distinguish between a duty of both parties to produce evidence and the burden of proof which usually is borne by one party only.[738] It seems doubtful whether this obligation applies as well to cases where a private entity claims compensation against an interfering State before a domestic court or an international tribunal. In such cases, due to principles of State immunity, the procedure tends to be rather adversarial than investigatory and one could argue that the party bearing the burden of proof needs to produce the necessary evidence and persuade the court that the requirement for its claim are met. On the other hand, the comparability of a compensation claim after an interference on the high seas and the claim of a violation of human rights has already been asserted (*see supra*). The latter claims, however, at least as far as it concern international tri-

---

[731] *Kazazi*, Mojtaba, "Burden of proof and related issues" (The Hague: Kluwer Law International, 1996), at 116-117; *Bin Cheng*, "General Principles of Law as applied by International Courts and Tribunals" (London: Stevens, 1953), at 330.

[732] *Oil Platforms (Islamic Republic of Iran v. United States of America)*, Judgment of 6 November 2003, ICJ Reports 2003, pp. 161 *et seq.*, 189, para. 57.

[733] *Lasok*, K.P.E., "The European Court of Justice, Practice and Procedure" (2nd ed., London: Butterworths, 1994), at 420 *et seq.*

[734] *Iran v. United States*, Cases A/1 (Issues I, II and IV) of 30 July 1982, Separate Opinion Kashandi/Shafeiei, 1 Iran-U.S.C.T.R. 189, 203, 209 (1981-1982).

[735] *Cf. Bin Cheng*, "General Principles of Law as applied by International Courts and Tribunals" (London: Stevens, 1953), at 332.

[736] Commentary on Chapter V ASR, para. 8, in *Crawford*, James, "The International Law Commission's Articles on State Responsibility" (Cambridge: Cambridge University Press, 2002), at 162.

[737] *Kazazi*, Mojtaba, "Burden of proof and related issues" (The Hague: Kluwer Law International, 1996), at 148-149.

[738] *Cf. Kokott*, Juliane, "The Burden of Proof in Comparative and International Human Rights Law" (The Hague: Kluwer, 1998), at 148-156.

bunals, are generally regarded to be dealt with in investigatory rather than adversarial proceedings.[739] This is due to the subordinate position of the individual in human rights actions. Therefore, one may also argue that only the burden of persuasion falls upon the party which bears the burden of proof. It is submitted that, since uniform rules are lacking, an international tribunal would most likely adhere to this second view, while a domestic tribunal would rather apply domestic law of procedure concerning the obligation to produce evidence.

International conventions have been concerned mostly with the burden of persuasion. In matters of port State control, for example, principles of the general law on State responsibility have remained largely unaffected. The burden of persuasion in instances of alleged undue detentions or delay generally lies with the owner or operator of the ship claiming compensation.[740]

As far as it concerns interferences with navigation on the high seas in times of peace, however, the case may well be different. As early as 1873, the United States and Spain agreed that Spain, which had seized the vessel *Virginius* on the high seas, had to prove that the *Virginius* did not rightfully carry the U.S. flag even though the United States was the applicant in this case. Otherwise, Spain would have to salute to the flag of the United States.[741]

In the case of the *Wanderer*, the United States had seized and detained a British vessel on the high seas on 10 June 1894. The United Kingdom claimed damages on behalf of the owner of the vessel before an arbitral tribunal. This tribunal on 9 December 1921 held that the United States had "to show that its naval authorities acted under special agreement."[742]

These cases have led authors to conclude that "in the case of visit and search of vessels on the high seas in time of peace, the burden lies upon the respondent State to show that its naval authorities acted under [a special interference right]."[743] This reversal of the burden of proof definitely represents an outflow of the importance granted to the freedom of navigation as opposed to the wide-ranging jurisdiction exercised by coastal States within their waters. The reversal also finds some reflection in provisions of important conventions of the Law of the Sea.

Thus, Art. 110, para. 1 LOSC establishes a certain presumption of wrongfulness of any boarding of a foreign vessel on the high seas: "a warship … is not justified in boarding it unless there is reasonable ground for suspecting that…"/ "un navire de guerre … ne peut l'arraisonner que s'il a de sérieuses raisons de soupçonner que ce navire…"/" un buque de guerra … no tendrá derecho de visita, a menos que haya motivo razonable para sospechar que el buque...". Hence, it

[739] *Ibid.*, at 194-195.

[740] *Özcayir*, Z. Oya, "Port State Control" (2nd ed., London: LLP, 2004), at 147; *cf.* also *Hoff Claim*, 4 RIAA, pp. 444 *et seq.*; *The Coquitlam Claim*, 6 RIAA, pp. 45 *et seq.*; *The Lottie May Incident*, 15 RIAA, pp. 23 *et seq.*

[741] "Protocol of the Conference held at the Department of State" (29 November 1873), reprinted in *Moore*, John Bassett, "Digest of International Law", Vol. 2 (Washington: Government Printing Office, 1906), at 896-7.

[742] *The Wanderer (United Kingdom/United States)* (9 December 1921), 6 RIAA, pp. 68 *et seq.*, at 71.

[743] *Brownlie*, Ian, "State Responsiblity" (Oxford: Clarendon Press, 1983), at 78-9.

seems rather easy to prove an unlawful interference on the high seas and, as a consequence, the responsibility of the interfering State. This reversal of the burden of proof also makes sense because the view of the interfering State is most relevant in the issue whether a reasonable ground for suspicion was present. The possibilities of the shipowner, cargo interests or even the flag State to show that such a reasonable ground existed from the perspective of the interfering State are very limited and the burden of proof should therefore be borne by the interfering State as envisaged in Art. 110, para. 1 LOSC.

Art. 110, para. 3 LOSC then even avails the claimant with a privileged burden of proof in cases of compensation for lawful interferences. The claimant merely has to prove that the boarding did not lead to the discovery of any criminal activity which could be a ground for an interference, and that the claimant suffered damages as a consequence. The respondent State may then only exonerate itself by proving that "the ship boarded has not committed any act justifying them". The fact that the burden of proof of this exoneration falls on the interfering State follows from the general principles mentioned above, but also from the (in this respect more explicit) French version: "à condition qu'il n'ait commis aucun acte le rendant suspect." This also shows that Art. 110, para. 3 LOSC, which provides for liability for lawful conduct, has certain aspects in common with the concept of strict liability where the defendant usually has the burden of exculpation.[744]

The other relevant compensation provisions of the Law of the Sea Convention follow a different pattern. According to Art. 105 LOSC, "every State may seize a pirate ship ... and arrest the persons and seize the property on board". Liability of the seizing State under Art. 106 LOSC then requires a seizure "without adequate grounds". The claimant therefore needs to show that the affected vessel was not a pirate ship and that no adequate grounds for the seizure existed.

The provisions on hot pursuit are very similar in this respect. To prove the unlawfulness of a hot pursuit, the claimant, *e.g.*, needs to show that the coastal State had no "good reason to believe that the ship has violated the laws and regulations of that State" (Art. 111, para. 1 LOSC). The compensation provision in Art. 111, para. 8 LOSC then simply requires "circumstances which do not justify the exercise of the right of hot pursuit". The claimant therefore, just like in the general law on State responsibility, needs to show the commission of an internationally wrongful act by the coastal State.

Art. 21, para. 18 Fish Stocks Agreement more or less adheres to the same approach: the claimant needs to show an unlawful or disproportionate measure attributable to the respondent State.

Art. 9, para. 2 Migrant Smuggling Protocol, however, closely follows Art. 110, para. 3 LOSC, while Art. 8bis, para. 10, lit. b of the 2005 SUA Protocol provides the claimant with two alternatives. The claimant may either prove an unlawful or disproportionate measure (like in Art. 21, para. 18 Fish Stocks Agreement), or it may simply demonstrate that the interference did not lead to the discovery of criminal activities sanctioned under the SUA Convention or its 2005 Protocol. In the latter case, the respondent State may then, just like in Art. 110, para. 3 LOSC,

[744] *Ibid.*, at 1.

exonerate itself by proving that the boarded "ship has committed [an] act justifying the measures taken."

Finally, Art. VI Intervention Convention seems to be in line with the general law on State responsibility in so far that the claimant needs to prove an unlawful measure attributable to the respondent State proximately causing damage to the claimant. It is submitted though, that the coverage of damages under this provision is so unusual and favourable to the liable State (see *supra*) that the onus of proving the limitation of damages falls upon this State. In particular, this means that the liable State needs to show how much damage a hypothetical proportionate measures would have caused in order to deduct this damage from the actual damage suffered by the claimant.

Thus, the analyzed compensation provisions significantly differ in matters of the burden of proof. Only some provisions like Art. 110, paras. 1 and 3 LOSC adhere to the classic principle that "the burden lies upon the respondent state to show that its naval authorities acted under [a special interference right]".[745] Most provisions rather codify principles well known from the general law on State responsibility and thereby show that the drafters have not been willing to provide for a comprehensive protection of private interests in all respects.

II. Competing claims of protection

A particular problem arises if the vessel or the cargo damaged during an interference on the high seas was owned by nationals of the interfering state. Can the flag state of the damaged vessel then nevertheless exercise its protection under the analyzed compensation provisions? Could the State of nationality claim the diplomatic protection of its nationals in spite of the availability of flag State protection?

The question whether the flag State in the exercise of flag State protection may make claims against the State of nationality of one of the persons on behalf it is acting necessarily involves the issue of prevalence between competing claims. It has been alleged that the prevalence in competing claims to diplomatic protection is not certain.[746]

In *The I'm Alone Case*, the joint Canadian and American Commission held that no compensation ought to be paid by the United States in respect of the loss of the ship or her cargo.[747] One might presume that the commission denied this compensation because the vessel and the cargo were owned and controlled by American

---

745 *Brownlie*, Ian, "State Responsiblity" (Oxford: Clarendon Press, 1983), at 78-9.

746 *Geck*, Wilhelm Karl, "*Diplomatic Protection*", in *Bernhardt*, Rudolf (ed.), "Encyclopedia of Public International Law", Vol. 1 (Amsterdam: North-Holland, 1992), pp. 1045 *et seq.*, at 1055.

747 *Colombos*, Constantin John, "The International Law of the Sea" (6th ed., London: Longman, 1967), at 173. *Cf.* also *Fitzmaurice*, Gerald, "The case of the I'm Alone", 17 BYIL(1936), pp. 82 *et seq.*; *Hyde*, Charles Cheney, "The Adjustment Of The I'm Alone Case", 29 AJIL (1935), pp. 296 *et seq.*, at 298.

nationals.[748] In that case, the commissioners denied the flag State the protection of the *de facto* U.S. shipowners,[749] but awarded damages concerning injuries suffered by the crew members which had other nationalities. The major factor for this distinction, however, was probably that the shipowners were engaged in the illegal conduct of smuggling while the crew was not aware of their illicit cargo. Hence, the decision does neither confirm the flag State's right to exercise protection of individuals against their State of nationality nor does it explicitly renounce the right. It is therefore not sufficient to establish a rule of customary international law.[750]

Quite to the contrary, at least one author contends that the right to exercise diplomatic protection "is an imperfect one, due to the special nature and qualities of ships. It can be made effective so long as it does not conflict with the control which the State to which the vessel legally belongs is, under international law, permitted to effect and does, in fact effect."[751] Due to the special nature of flag State protection, *Rienow* recommends its prevalence over traditional diplomatic protection.

Such prevalence could easily be reconciled with the extensive flag State protection under the relevant compensation provisions and with their interpretation by ITLOS treating the vessel, her cargo and her crew as a unity protected by the flag State. Quite definitely, the holding of *The I'm Alone* could not have been reached on the basis of any of these provisions. Therefore, an interfering State could be obliged to pay compensation to a flag State when the vessel was owned by nationals of the interfering State.

Any implicit superiority of flag State protection, however, was denied by the International Law Commission which, afraid that the former wording would establish a priority of flag State protection, modified Article 19 DADP.[752] Considering the ILC's authority and the inconclusive indication by ITLOS, *Rienow's* statement should therefore be regarded as a proposal *de lege ferenda*. Quite to the

---

748 *Colombos*, Constantin John, "The International Law of the Sea" (6th ed., London: Longman, 1967), at 173. *Cf.* also *Fitzmaurice*, Gerald, "The case of the I'm Alone", 17 BYIL(1936), pp. 82 *et seq.*; *Hyde*, Charles Cheney, "The Adjustment Of The I'm Alone Case", 29 AJIL 296, 298 (1935).

749 *Cf. Watts*, Arthur, "The Protection of Merchant Ships", 33 BYIL(1957), pp. 52 *et seq.*, at 64.

750 *Geck*, Wilhelm Karl, "*Diplomatic Protection*", in *Bernhardt*, Rudolf (ed.), "Encyclopedia of Public International Law", Vol. 1 (Amsterdam: North-Holland, 1992), pp. 1045 *et seq.*, at 1055.

751 *Rienow*, Robert, "The Test of Nationality of a Merchant Vessel" (New York: Columbia University Press, 1937), at 104-5. See also *Dahm*, Georg/*Delbrück*, Jost/*Wolfrum*, Rüdiger, "Völkerrecht", Vol. 1, Part 2 (2nd ed., Berlin: de Gruyter, 2002), at 356; Wolfrum, Rüdiger, "Recht der Flagge und 'Billige Flaggen' – Neuere Entwicklungen im Internationalen Privatrecht und Völkerrecht", 31 Berichte der Deutschen Gesellschaft für Völkerrecht (1990), pp. 121 *et seq.*, at 128.

752 "Statement of the Chairman of the Drafting Committee, Rodriguez-Cedeno" (28 May 2004), at 33, available at <http://untreaty.un.org/ilc/sessions/56/Diplomatic_protection_statement_final.pdf>.

contrary, the ILC, in spite of a strong demand by Mexico,[753] decided not to deal with any issues of prevalence between competing claims.[754]

Furthermore, an analogy to the rules concerning dual nationals as proposed by the ILC's rapporteur *John Dugard* might provide for a solution to this conflict.[755] According to Art. 7 DADP, "[a] State of nationality may not exercise diplomatic protection in respect of a person against a State of which that person is also a national unless the nationality of the former State is predominant, both at the time of the injury and at the date of the official presentation of the claim." This provision represents customary international law,[756] since the rule had been applied by a great number of international tribunals.[757] U.S. practice follows the rule as well.[758] The former rule of non-responsibility according to which one State of nationality must not bring a claim in respect of a dual national against another State of nationality[759] is no more applicable.

An analogy to Art. 7 DADP in cases of flag State protection nevertheless would lead to considerable problems. How is one to decide whether the flag State or an individual's State of nationality has the predominant link to the individual? The factors proposed by the ILC for the distinction between two States of nationality (habitual residence, the amount of time spent in each country of nationality, date of naturalization; place, curricula and language of education; employment and financial interests; place of family life; family ties in each country; participation in social and public life; use of language; taxation, bank account, social security insurance; visits to the other State of nationality; possession and use of passport of

753 *UN* Doc. A/CN.4/561 (27 January 2006), "Diplomatic Protection – Comments and Observations received from Governments", at 48-49.

754 *UN* Doc. A/CN.4/567 (7 March 2006), *Dugard*, John, "Seventh Report on Diplomatic Protection", at 36, para. 90.

755 *UN* Doc. A/CN.4/538 (4 March 2004), *Dugard*, John, "Fifth Report on Diplomatic Protection", at 29.

756 Commentary on Art. 7 DADP, para. 4, in *UN* Doc. A/59/10 (2004), *International Law Commission*, "Report on the work of its fifty-sixth session", at 43; *cf. Bederman*, David J., "Lump Sum Agreements and Diplomatic Protection", in *ILA*, "Report of the Seventieth Conference" (2002), pp. 230 *et seq.*, at 248.

757 See, *e.g.*, *Nottebohm (Liechtenstein v. Guatemala)*, Second Phase, Judgment of 6 April 1955, ICJ Reports 1955, pp. 4 *et seq.*, at 22-3; *Mergé Claim*, Italian-United States Conciliation Commission, 10 June 1955, 22 ILR (1955), pp. 443 *et seq.*, at 455 (1955); *Esphahanian v. Bank Tejarat*, 21 Iran-U.S. C.T.R (1983), pp. 166 *et seq.*; *UN* Doc. S/AC.26/1991/Rev.1, "Governing Council Decision No. 7", United Nations Compensation Commission, at para. 11.

758 *International Law Institute*, "Digest of United States Practice in International Law in 1979", Vol. 7 (Washington, 1983), at 693-4.

759 See, *e.g.*, Article 4 of the 1930 Hague Convention on Certain Questions Relating to the Conflict of Nationality Laws; *Alexander case* (1898), reprinted in *Moore*, John Bassett, "History and digest of the international arbitrations to which the United States has been a party", Vol. 3 (Washington: Government Printing Office, 1898), pp. 2529 *et seq.*; *Frederick Adams and Charles Thomas Blackmore (Great Britain) v. United Mexican States*, British-Mexican Claims Commission Decision No. 64 of 3 July 1931, 5 RIAA, pp. 216 *et seq.*

the other State; and military service)[760] are not suitable to the situation of flag State protection which has a different nature than traditional diplomatic protection and for which these factors are not quite as important.

Due to the lack of practice of States renouncing their right to exercise diplomatic protection of their nationals, no superiority between the two different regimes of protection can be ascertained. Even if there were some State practice, one would have to show that the States felt obliged or deemed it necessary to renounce their right (*opinio juris sive necessitatis*).[761] Hence, it is submitted that in the case of a conflict between the flag State and an individual's State of nationality, one of the protecting States may generally claim the exercise of protection against the other State. This solution also guarantees that no additional formal rule of public international law impedes the protection of individual rights.

III. An obligation to forward the compensation award to the victim?

It might seem questionable whether a State exercising (flag State or diplomatic) protection on behalf of private entities involved in the navigation of a vessel also needs to forward the compensation awarded by an international tribunal to the victims who have suffered damages. Traditionally, in cases of diplomatic and flag State protection, it lies "within the discretion of the claimant State to divide the awarded indemnity among the injured persons whose claims it has espoused."[762] An obligation to forward the compensation award could only be recognized if an international convention between the parties to the dispute so provided or if the parties had established a special distribution commission.[763] These strict principles of the traditional law on diplomatic protection might have their foundation in the common practice of awarding lump sums instead of detailed compensation awards calculated according to the individual damages. It seems doubtful whether this reasoning might justify an absolute withholding of the award vis-à-vis the victims. Another reasoning might consist in the denial of the argument that the individual has become a subject of public international law and in the idea that the claiming State is merely and exclusively asserting own rights when exercising diplomatic protection.

760 Commentary on Art. 7 DADP, para. 6, in *UN* Doc. A/59/10 (2004), *International Law Commission*, "Report on the work of its fifty-sixth session", at 44.

761 *Cf. North Sea Continental Shelf Case (Denmark/Netherlands v. Germany)*, Judgment of 20 February 1969, ICJ Reports 1969, pp. 3 *et seq.*, at 44.

762 *Verzijl*, Jan Hendrik Willem, "International Law in Historical Perspective", Vol. 6, (Leiden: Sijthoff, 1973), at 770; *Heirs of Jean Maninat (France/Venezuela)* (31 July 1905), 10 RIAA, pp. 55 *et seq.*, at 56, 83.

763 *Bederman*, David J., "Lump Sum Agreements and Diplomatic Protection", in *ILA*, "Report of the Seventieth Conference" (2002), pp. 230 *et seq.*, at 237-239.

Recently, this traditional approach has been heavily criticized because it led to a number of contradictions, primarily because the position of the individual regularly plays a great part in cases of diplomatic protection.[764]

Within the last decades, it has become much more common for international tribunals to clearly distinguish between the different kinds of damages and to calculate the damages suffered by each individual. Thus, for example, the International Tribunal for the Law of the Sea in the case of the *M/V Saiga (No. 2)* provided an annex to its judgment in which the amounts of compensation due for each individual crew member were enumerated.[765] The Tribunal did not explicitly oblige the claimant State to forward the compensation to the crew members, but instead only awarded the compensation "computed as specified in the Annex".[766] Considering its particular concern for the rights of the crew members, the decision might nevertheless be interpreted to indicate that the Tribunal favours an obligation of the applicant State to divide the award in the way proposed in the Annex of the judgment and forward the respective amounts to the victims.

The International Law Commission in its codification project on the issue of diplomatic protection has not yet explicitly stated whether an applicant State is obliged to forward the compensation award to the individual on behalf of whom it exercised diplomatic protection. While the first special rapporteur on the topic, *Mohamed Bennouna*, submitted a report manifestly in favour of individual rights,[767] the second special rapporteur *John Dugard*, was more cautious and favoured the view that diplomatic protection is an exclusive right of the State.[768] Without providing any clear preference, *Dugard* elaborated on the different views concerning the discretion of the State in the exercise of diplomatic protection,[769] but did not discuss whether a State needs to forward the compensation award to the victims. The International Law Commission rejected any limitation on the discretion available to the State of nationality.[770]

The comments by governments to this self-restraint by the International Law Commission are most interesting. Austria stated that "it should be ensured that the injured individual in whose interest the claim was raised will benefit from the

---

764 *Cf. Orrego Vicuña*, Francisco, "The Changing Law of Nationality of Claims", in *ILA*, "Report of the Sixty-ninth Conference" (2000), pp. 631 *et seq.*, at 632-633.

765 *The M/V Saiga (No. 2) (St. Vincent and the Grenadines v. Guinea)*, Judgment of 1 July 1999, ITLOS Reports 1999, pp. 10 *et seq.*, at 74. *Cf.* also *The I'm Alone (Canada/ United States)*, Report of 5 January 1935, 3 RIAA, pp. 1609 *et seq.*, at 1618 (enumerating the amounts of compensation "to be paid to" the individual crew members and their relatives).

766 *The M/V Saiga (No. 2) (St. Vincent and the Grenadines v. Guinea)*, Judgment of 1 July 1999, ITLOS Reports 1999, pp. 10 *et seq.*, at 65, para. 175.

767 *UN* Doc. A/CN.4/484, (4 February 1998), *Bennouna*, Mohamed, "Preliminary Report on Diplomatic Protection", at 14-15, para. 49-54.

768 *UN* Doc. A/CN.4/506 (7 March 2000), *Dugard*, John, "First Report on Diplomatic Protection", pp. 22 *et seq.*, at 26, para. 73.

769 *Ibid.*, pp. 27-34, paras. 75-93.

770 Commentary on Art. 2 DADP, para. 2, *UN* Doc. A/57/10 (2002), "Report of the International Law Commission on the work of its fifty-fourth session", at 173.

exercise of diplomatic protection."[771] The French delegate in the Sixth Committee stated that "the reasons given by the Special Rapporteur as to why it was not necessary to deal with the consequences of diplomatic protection were not fully convincing. Even if diplomatic protection constituted an exception with regard to the general law on responsibility, the question whether a State was under an obligation to pay over to an injured individual money that it had received by way of compensation for a claim based on diplomatic protection was fundamental."[772] These comments together with further criticism by prominent authors[773] led the special rapporteur to reconsider the issue.

He noted that there is a clear tendency in constitutional laws to oblige States to exercise diplomatic protection on behalf of their nationals and that furthermore, the progressive development of human rights in public international law have significantly limited the discretion of the State of nationality in the distribution of the compensation award. However, he concluded that in total, State practice has been insufficient to find an established rule of customary international law.[774] Nevertheless, he deemed it necessary for the International Law Commission to participate in the progressive development of public international law and adopt the following provision: "When a State receives compensation in full or partial fulfilment of a claim arising out of diplomatic protection it shall [should] transfer that sum to the national in respect of whom it has brought the claim [after deduction of the costs incurred in bringing the claim]."[775]

If one accepts these conclusions by the special rapporteur, the establishment of an obligation to forward compensation awards to the victims would require first the adoption by the International Law Commission of the rule proposed by the special rapporteur and secondly, its gradual acceptance by States and other subjects of public international law.

Thus, one might conclude that if a flag State bases its claim on one of the compensation provisions which have not created a right of a private entity, it is not yet obliged to pay over any compensation it may have received in respect of the injured national.

However, as far as it concerns the other compensation provisions (Arts. 110, para. 3 and 111, para. 8 LOSC, Art. 9, para. 2 Migrant Smuggling Protocol and Art. 8bis, para. 10, lit. b of the 2005 SUA Protocol), it has been elaborated above that they have created a right of private entities. These provisions clearly mention

---

771 *UN* Doc. A/CN.4/561 (27 January 2006), "Diplomatic protection, Comments and observations received from Governments", at 7-8.

772 *UN* Doc. A/C.6/60/SR.11 (23 November 2005), "Sixth Committee, Summary Record of the 11th meeting", at para. 73.

773 See, *e.g., Milano*, Enrico, "Diplomatic protection and human rights before the International Court of Justice: re-fashioning tradition?", 35 Netherlands Ybk. Int'l L. (2004), pp. 85 *et seq.*, at 108; *Gaja*, Giorgio, "Droits des Etats et droits des individus dans le cadre de la protection diplomatique", in *Flauss*, Jean-François (ed.), "La Protection Diplomatique" (Bruxelles: Nemesis, 2003), pp. 63 *et seq.*, at 69.

774 *UN* Doc. A/CN.4/567 (7 March 2006), *Dugard*, John, "Seventh Report on Diplomatic Protection", at 43, para. 102.

775 *Ibid.*, at para. 103.

the ship rather than the flag State as the recipient of the compensation.[776] Therefore, they might even be regarded to constitute rights of these private entities vis-à-vis their own flag State. If a flag State is obliged to compensate the vessels of its own nationality for certain interferences on the high seas, then *a fortiori* it must forward any compensation award to the private entities involved in the navigation of the vessel.

Thus, these compensation provisions are not only atypical to the general law on State responsibility because they entitle private entities, but also atypical to the law on diplomatic protection because if the flag State exercises its protection and receives a compensation award, then it may not withhold it, but must pay it over to the individuals on behalf of whom the protection was exercised.

---

776 *Oxman*, Bernard H., "Human Rights and the United Nations Convention on the Law of the Sea", 36 Colum. J. Transnat'l L. (1997), pp. 399 *et seq.*, at 420.

Chapter III: The U.S. strategy: 28 bilateral treaties and the Proliferation Security Initiative

Instead of relying on multilateral conventions, the United States has a considerable tradition of concluding bilateral agreements in order to obtain permission to conduct the boarding of foreign vessels on the high seas or even in waters under foreign jurisdiction when the United States deemed such interferences necessary.

This was already the case when, in times of prohibition of liquor in the United States, major smuggling of beverages took place on the seas surrounding the United States. In negotiations with the United Kingdom, the United States achieved that, in the exchange of notes of 23 January 1924, the United Kingdom agreed not to raise any objection to the boarding of private vessels under British flag in order to search for alcoholic beverages on their way to beat the prohibition.[1] Treaties with other important flag States, the so-called Liquor Treaties, followed.

The United States used similar agreements in order to combat the smuggling of drugs and migrant trafficking, particularly in the Caribbean Sea and the Gulf of Mexico, and to prevent the transport of so-called weapons of mass destruction. Nowadays, 28 agreements are in force between the United States and various other States, supporting U.S. drug, migrant and proliferation security interdiction efforts.[2] These agreements quite significantly differ in their sophistication and wording.

As an alternative to bilateral agreements, the United States has also created the Proliferation Security Initiative, a flexible forum in which States cooperate to prevent the transport of weapons of mass destruction, but where they do not underlie any binding rules or dispute settlement procedures.

This study will examine the potential liability of the boarding State under the major types of agreements and under the Proliferation Security Initiative, taking into consideration both public international law and United States domestic law.

---

1 "Exchange of notes between the United Kingdom and the United States" (23 January 1924), reprinted in 18 AJIL Supplement (1924), pp. 127 *et seq.*

2 *Crowley, Jr.*, John E., "U.S. Maritime Law Enforcement Practices", in *Nordquist*, Myron H. *et al.* (eds.), "Recent Decelopments in the Law of the Sea and China" (Leiden: Nijhoff, 2006), pp. 251 *et seq.*, at 258.

A. The 1924 Liquor Treaties

After the so-called Prohibition Laws of January 1919 (the Eighteenth Amendment to the Constitution of the United States and the so-called Volstead Act[3]) proscribed the production, the sale and the transport of alcoholic beverages, the United States encountered increasing problems with the smuggling of these goods, particularly by maritime transport and most often under the flag of the United Kingdom.[4] Since any enforcement powers in the then still comparatively narrow territorial sea did not suffice to efficiently bar maritime smuggling of liquor to the United States, it concluded international conventions with important flag States.[5] The first of these agreements, the exchange of notes with the United Kingdom,[6] served as basis for the negotiation of the other texts and thus has an exemplary role. These "Liquor Treaties" allowed the United States to board private vessels of the other State party to search for alcoholic beverages outside the territorial sea. However, according to Art. II of these treaties, this enforcement power on board of foreign vessels could only be exercised in a distance from the U.S. coastline which could be traversed by the boarded vessel within one hour.

The Liquor Treaties do not contain any explicit compensation provision, but the dispute settlement provisions give some indications concerning the applicable rules to questions of responsibility. Thus, Article IV of the exchange of notes between the United Kingdom and the United States stipulates that "any claim by a British vessel for compensation on the grounds that it has suffered loss or injury through the improper or unreasonable exercise of the rights conferred by Article II … shall be referred for the joint consideration of two persons, one of whom shall be nominated by each of the High Contracting Parties." While the other treaties envisaged different methods of dispute settlement, they all referred to the same kind of compensation claim.[7]

The provisions quite clearly demonstrate the entitlement of the vessel herself to compensation. Thus, these international treaties imply a right of private entities and not necessarily of the flag State. Furthermore, the compensation claim requires an unlawful or unreasonable enforcement measure by the United States. Liability for lawful conduct is not envisaged even though the United States gained

---

3 41 U.S. Statutes at Large 305.

4 307 out of 332 liquor smuggling vessels in 1924 had British nationality. *Cf. Dickinson*, Edwin D., "Les traités américains concernant les spiritueux", 7 Révue de droit international et de législation comparée (1926), pp. 371 *et seq.*, at 372.

5 In 1926, the United States had such conventions in force with the United Kingdom, Norway, Denmark, Germany, Sweden, Italy, Panama and the Netherlands. *Dickinson*, Edwin D., "Treaties for the Prevention of Smuggling", 20 AJIL (1926), pp. 340 *et seq.*, at 344. The U.S.-German agreement is reprinted in Reichsgesetzblatt II (1926), at 233.

6 "Convention between the United States of American and Great Britain to aid in the prevention of the smuggling of intoxicating liquors into the United States" (23 January 1924), reprinted in 18 AJIL Supplement (1924), pp. 127 *et seq.*

7 *Cf. Dickinson*, Edwin D., "Treaties for the Prevention of Smuggling", 20 AJIL (1926), pp. 340 *et seq.*, at 343-344.

the right to board any private vessel of the other State even without reasonable suspicion that the vessel may be smuggling alcoholic beverages. Also, the provisions indicate that not only personal injuries or damage to property, but also lost profits ("loss or injury") could be covered by a compensation claim.

Finally, the United Kingdom was able to draft the provision authorizing interferences by the United States in a way which would clearly exclude any liability of the United Kingdom. According to Art. II of the exchange of notes, the United Kingdom agrees to "raise no objection" to the boarding of private vessels under its flag by authorities of the United States. Instead of actively permitting or authorizing the boardings, the United Kingdom thus simply refrains from exercising its protection for the vessel. Thereby, the United States was to bear the whole responsibility for the individual boarding and no vessel was to claim compensation from the United Kingdom for its alleged "assistance" to the boarding.

This precaution of the United Kingdom also shows how concerned it was about potential compensation claims by private interests related to a vessel flying her flag. Thus, even in 1924, States were aware that in international relations, material rights to compensation were not exclusively held by States, but might potentially be borne by private parties.

The provision was copied in all other Liquor Treaties[8] and thereby presumably also protected the other flag States from potential liability vis-à-vis their own vessels.

B. The 1981 Exchange of Notes

After the Eighteenth Amendment was repealed on 5 December 1933, the Liquor Treaties became mainly irrelevant. However, when the United States encountered increasing problems with the smuggling of drugs in the 1980's, the Liquor Treaties were taken as the basis for the exchange of notes of 13 November 1981 between the United Kingdom and the United States permitting the United States authorities to board private British vessels on the high seas in the Gulf of Mexico, the Caribbean Sea and on the Eastern seaboard to search for drugs destined for unlawful importation into the United States.[9]

In this exchange of notes, the United Kingdom again insisted on the use of the terms that it "will not object to the boarding by the authorities of the United States…" (para. 1). Hereby, the United Kingdom sought to "avoid any implication that the [United States] Coast Guard is acting on behalf of the United Kingdom or that its actions are positively authorised by the United Kingdom Government."[10]

---

8 *Dickinson*, Edwin D., "Les traités américains concernant les spiritueux", 7 Révue de droit international et de législation comparée (1926), pp. 371 *et seq.*, at 379.

9 Reprinted in: *Siddle*, John, "Anglo-American Co-Operation in the Suppression of Drug Smuggling", 31 Int'l & Comp. L. Q. (1982), pp. 726 *et seq.*, at 745.

10 *Siddle*, John, "Anglo-American Co-Operation in the Suppression of Drug Smuggling", 31 Int'l & Comp. L. Q. (1982), pp. 726 *et seq.*, at 740.

Thus, comparable to the 1924 exchange of notes, both parties intended to keep the United States responsible for any boarding under the agreement.

Concerning the whole compensation issue, the entire exchange of notes is much more cautious than the Liquor Treaties. In fact, the 1981 exchange of notes does not place the United States under any explicit obligation to pay compensation. Paragraph 8 of the exchange of notes only stipulates that "[i]f any loss or injury is suffered as a result of any action taken by the United States in contravention of these arrangements or any improper or unreasonable action taken by the United States pursuant thereto, representatives shall meet at the request of either party to decide any question relating to compensation."

This provision may only carry the implication that compensation should be paid in accordance with the general international law on State on responsibility. Contrary to the Liquor Treaties, no reference is made to a "claim by a British vessel". Apparently, the 1981 exchange of notes leaves the question of compensation entirely to the two States parties.[11]

Thus, even though the exchange of notes is based on the Liquor Treaties, its treatment of compensation issues has been cut down significantly as compared to the Liquor Treaties.[12] In particular, the entitlement of a private party is no more recognized.

One may only speculate about the reasons for this development. First, the United States might have been more concerned with potential compensation claims. Secondly, the United Kingdom might have lost some interest in the issue because the Liquor Treaties affected much more vessels under the British flag. Thirdly, the negotiating powers of the two States might simply have shifted toward the United States within sixty years in which the United States has clearly emerged as a dominant global power. Fourthly, however, the United Kingdom has gained some important safeguards in the 1981 exchange of notes as compared to the Liquor Treaties. The United States may only board vessels under the British flag which are reasonably believed to carry drugs for importation to the United States (Paragraph 1 of the exchange of notes).[13] Furthermore, the United Kingdom may after the boarding object to the continued exercise of United States jurisdiction over the vessel and object to the prosecution of any United Kingdom national (Paragraphs. 4 and 5 of the exchange of notes). These safeguards might have been more important to the United Kingdom than a strong compensation provision. Most probably, a combination of these factors led to the terms used in Paragraph 8 of the 1981 exchange of notes.

---

11 *Siddle*, John, "Anglo-American Co-Operation in the Suppression of Drug Smuggling", 31 Int'l & Comp. L. Q. (1982), pp. 726 *et seq*, at 744.

12 Sohn calls the provision "weak". *Cf. Sohn*, Louis B., "International Law of the Sea and Human Rights Issues", in *Clingan*, Thomas A. (ed.), "The Law of the Sea: What lies ahead?" (Honolulu, University of Hawaii, 1988), pp. 51 *et seq.*, at 62.

13 *Cf.* also *Gilmore*, William C., "Narcotics interdiction at sea – UK-US cooperation", 14 Marine Policy (1989), pp. 218 *et seq.*, at 223.

C. Bilateral anti-drugs and migration agreements

Beginning in the 1970's, the United States faced increasing problems with the smuggling of marihuana when Latin America became the chief supplier to the United States.[14] Additionally, Cocaine from Latin America became a popular drug in the 1980's.[15] A major portion of these drugs are transported via maritime routes in the so-called transit zone,[16] particularly cocaine which can easily be hidden on small boats. Furthermore, the Caribbean Sea represents one of the major routes for undocumented migrants with the destination United States.[17] In the first half of 2004, *e.g.*, more than 5,300 undocumented migrants were interdicted by U.S. Coast Guard, especially in the Mona Passage between Puerto Rico and the Dominican Republic.[18]

Traditional maritime law enforcement close to the national shore has proven ineffective in the case of this smuggling and migrant trafficking because the United States coastline with its 8,400 miles is too large to patrol and because interdictions within the own territorial sea cannot occur quick enough to prevent the landing of illegal cargo.[19]

Basically, there are two ways how smugglers can frustrate United States law enforcement efforts. First, due to the geography of the Caribbean Sea with a great stretch of islands coming quite close to the U.S. shoreline, they may transit through foreign territorial seas for the major part of their journey. Secondly, they may use foreign-flagged ships.[20] The Law of the Sea prohibits the United States from undertaking any law enforcement in the territorial sea of other States and (with certain limited exceptions) on foreign-flagged ships on the high seas.[21]

---

14 *Anderson*, Andrew W., "In the wake of the Dauntless: The Background of Maritime Interdictions Operations", in *Clingan*, Thomas A. (ed.), "The Law of the Sea: What lies ahead?" (Honolulu: University of Hawaii, 1988), pp. 11 *et seq.*, at 12.

15 *Ibid.*, at 22.

16 "The transit zone for drug traffic from South America is a six-million square-mile area that includes the Caribbean Sea, the Gulf of Mexico, and the Eastern Pacific." *Hull*, James D./*Emerson*, Michael D., "High 'Seize' Maritime Interdiction Works!", 125 Naval Institute Proceedings (January 1999), pp. 64 *et seq.*, at 65.

17 *Cf. supra. Kramek*, Joseph E., "Bilateral Maritime Counter-Drug and Immigrant Interdiction Agreements: Is this the world of the Future?", 31 U. Miami Inter-Am. L. Rev. (2000), pp. 121 *et seq.*, at 131.

18 *Thorsen*, Howard B., "U.S. Coast Guard in Review", 130 Naval Institute Proceedings (May 2004), pp. 99 *et seq.*, 100.

19 *Hull*, James D./*Emerson*, Michael D., "High 'Seize' Maritime Interdiction Works!", 125 Naval Institute Proceedings (January 1999), pp. 64 *et seq.*, at 65; *Kramek*, Joseph E., "Bilateral Maritime Counter-Drug and Immigrant Interdiction Agreements: Is this the world of the Future?", 31 U. Miami Inter-Am. L. Rev. (2000), pp. 121 *et seq.*, at 131.

20 *Hull*, James D./*Emerson*, Michael D., "High 'Seize' Maritime Interdiction Works!", 125 Naval Institute Proceedings (January 1999), pp. 64 *et seq.*, at 64-65.

21 *Cf.* Arts. 2, 92 and 110, para. 1 LOSC.

In order to overcome these difficulties in the law enforcement in the so-called transit zone where a lot of drug smuggling and undocumented migration takes place, the United States has entered into a series of bilateral maritime agreements with twenty-nine Latin American and Caribbean States.[22] These agreements shall particularly enable U.S. law enforcement in certain "bottlenecks" or "choke-points" in the Caribbean Sea. These are straits maritime smugglers definitely have to pass on their way from South America to the United States, such as the Windward Passage, the Mona Passage or the Yucatan Channel.[23] The limited law enforcement resources are most effective when they use these passages for interdiction efforts.

Based on a Model Agreement,[24] Latin American and Caribbean States have granted the United States Coast Guard the authority for one or more of six different law enforcement operations infringing upon their sovereign rights. First, the "shipboarding" provision allows the U.S. Coast Guard to stop, board and search suspicious vessels under the flag of the other State on the high seas. The "entry-to investigate" provision grants authority to enter the other State's territorial sea and undertake law enforcement there. Thirdly, the "overflight" provisions permit the United States to do surveillance flights in the airspace of the other State. According to the "shiprider" provision, an official of one State party to the agreement regularly embarks onboard the law enforcement plane or ship of the other State party and may then authorize on a case-by-case basis law enforcement in the territorial sea of his State and/or against a vessel on the high seas under the flag of his State. A "pursuit" provision allows, in extension of Art. 111, para. 3 LOSC, hot pursuit in the territorial sea of the States parties to the agreement. Finally, the "order-to-land" provision renders it possible for the U.S. Coast Guard to use airports in the other State for the enforced landing of suspicious aircraft.

The Latin American and Caribbean "partners" of the United States have selected widely different combinations in their agreements with the United States, thus establishing a patchwork of enforcement rights in the transit zone. The most common provision is the shiprider provision (16 agreements in 2000), followed by shipboarding (14 agreements), "entry-to-investigate" and pursuit provisions (each in twelve agreements).[25] Apparently, the Latin American and Caribbean States prefer to retain a considerable degree of control over navigation under their jurisdiction and have thus opted for the shiprider provision. As far as it concerns undocumented migration, most Latin American States have opted to streamline

22 *Kramek*, Joseph E., "Bilateral Maritime Counter-Drug and Immigrant Interdiction Agreements: Is this the world of the Future?", 31 U. Miami Inter-Am. L. Rev. (2000), pp. 121 *et seq.*, at 123.

23 *Anderson*, Andrew W., "In the wake of the Dauntless: The Background of Maritime Interdictions Operations", in *Clingan*, Thomas A. (ed.), "The Law of the Sea: What lies ahead?" (Honolulu: University of Hawaii, 1988), pp. 11 *et seq.*, at 18-19.

24 Reprinted in: *Kramek*, Joseph E., "Bilateral Maritime Counter-Drug and Immigrant Interdiction Agreements: Is this the world of the Future?", 31 U. Miami Inter-Am. L. Rev. (2000), pp. 121 *et seq.*, at 152.

25 *Ibid.*, at 133-135.

the interdiction procedures on an informal basis. In 2000, the only bilateral counter-migration agreement in place for the United States was with Cuba.[26]

In how far does the liability issue play a role at all in interferences under these bilateral agreements? Is Art. 110, para. 3 LOSC applicable to any of the cases covered? The fact that the United States has not become a State party to the Law of the Sea Convention should not become an obstacle to the application of the principles laid down in Art. 110, para. 3 LOSC because the United States has ratified the Convention on the High Seas and is therefore bound by the equivalent principles in Art. 22, para. 3 CHS. However, one might argue that, since the bilateral agreements constitute treaty exceptions to Art. 110, para. 1 LOSC, the compensation provision in Art. 110, para. 3 LOSC is likewise not applicable. Furthermore, any regulation in the bilateral agreement might preclude the applicability of Art. 110, para. 3 LOSC as *lex specialis*.

Since most bilateral agreements copy major parts of it, particularly those concerning the liability of the interfering State, the Model Agreement will be the basis of this study. The text of the Model Agreement is not quite clear-cut in this regard. On the one hand, paragraph 23 of the Model Agreement stipulates that compensation will be available for "any loss or injury … suffered as a result of any action taken by the law enforcement or other officials of one Party *in contravention of this agreement* or any *improper* or *unreasonable* action … taken by a Party pursuant thereto" (emphasis added) and thus indicates that responsibility may, contrary to Art. 110, para. 3 LOSC, be limited to wrongful and disproportionate operations.

On the other hand, the same paragraph safeguards "any other legal rights which may be available". Since this provision has been drafted in the context of dispute settlement, it could also be interpreted as a purely jurisdictional safeguard not dealing with any material rights to compensation. However, para. 24 of the Model Agreement stipulates that "nothing in this agreement is intended to alter the rights and privileges due any individual in any legal proceeding" and finally, para. 25 of the Model Agreement provides that "[n]othing in this agreement shall prejudice the position of either Party with regard to the international Law of the Sea". Finally, the preamble of the Model Agreement contains an explicit reference to Art. 17, para. 9 of the 1988 United Nations Convention against the Illicit Traffic in Narcotic Drugs and Psychotropic Substances. Therefore, the bilateral agreements cannot be regarded as a strictly unilateralist approach of the United States. Instead, they seem to adhere to the general principles of the Law of the Sea.

This consideration, though, does not yet solve the issue as to the applicability of Art. 110, para. 3 LOSC. In fact, the situations covered by the bilateral agreements are so different that they need to be looked at separately. Since this study is strictly confined to the Law of the Sea, situations under the "overflight" and the "order-to-land" provisions will not be analyzed here.

---

26 *Ibid.*, at 138.

I. Shipboarding

Of all the provisions in the agreements, the shipboarding provision comes closest to situations covered by Art. 110 LOSC. The flag State in this case grants a wide consent to the boarding of its vessels on the high seas. The only requirement is that the boarding State has "reasonable grounds to suspect that the vessel is engaged in illicit traffic" (para. 12 Model Agreement). Hence, in the relationship between the States parties to the agreement, the provision adds another exception to the freedom of navigation. Unlike Art. 110, para. 1 LOSC, the exception is not accompanied by a compensation provision. Only the final clauses of the agreement contain some vague references to the rights of individuals and States in the Law of the Sea (*supra*).

The rights under Art. 110, para. 3 LOSC, however, were established only to deter States from abusive reliance on the rights granted under Art. 110, para. 1 LOSC and not for application to any kind of interferences with navigation on the high seas. The international conventions succeeding the Convention for the High Seas and the Law of the Sea Convention took account of this solitary character of Art. 110, para. 3 LOSC and were equipped with own compensation provisions more or less copying Art. 110, para. 3 LOSC.

Thus, the right to obtain compensation under Art. 110, para. 3 LOSC only applies to situations under Art. 110, para. 1 LOSC and is not a "right due any individual" covered by the safeguard clause in the Model Agreement.

The responsibility issue is therefore governed by general international law and the Model Agreement. Paragraph 23 of the Model Agreement provides that "[i]f any loss or injury is suffered as a result of any action taken by the law enforcement or other officials of one Party in contravention of this agreement or any improper or unreasonably action is taken by a Party pursuant thereto, the parties shall consult at the request of either Party to resolve the matter and decide any questions relating to compensation." Even though this provision represents a jurisdictional dispute settlement clause, it nevertheless indicates that a compensation award requires first, an unlawful or disproportionate enforcement action by one of the parties and secondly, a loss or an injury suffered by one of the members or owners of the vessel registered in the other State party to the agreement. A lawful boarding under the Model Agreement particularly requires the existence of reasonable grounds for suspicion that a vessel is engaged in illicit activity prior to the boarding. Bearing in mind that domestic law only has limited significance concerning the interpretation of international treaties, one nevertheless ought to mention that U.S. law defines reasonable suspicion as "particularized and objective basis, supported by specific and articulable facts, for suspecting that someone is engaged in criminal activity."[27] If the United States Coast Guard cannot establish the existence of such reasonable suspicion before the boarding, the United States will thus bear responsibility for the losses incurred by the interdiction measure.

---

27 *Terry v. Ohio*, 392 U.S. 1 (1968).

Since the dispute settlement under the Model Agreement will take place exclusively between the two States, one cannot presume any direct right of private parties involved in the navigation of the ship to claim compensation. Thus, the Model Agreement also in this regard strictly adheres to the traditional law on State responsibility.

II. Shipriders

A different liability regime might exist for interdictions undertaken under the common shiprider provision. Here, the shiprider as agent of the flag State of the boarded vessel permits the interdiction on a case-by-case basis.[28] The decision whether to board or not a certain vessel thus remains under the exclusive control of the flag State. The Model Agreement explicitly provides that "any search and seizure … shall be carried out *by the shiprider*" (emphasis added) (Paragraph 7 Model Agreement). Agents of the other State may only assist and use force in self-defense. Therefore, the flag State of the boarded vessel bears the responsibility for any interdiction operation under the shiprider provision and the other State could only be liable for its contribution as assisting State.

Such liability would nevertheless require an internationally wrongful act by the assisted State. The Law of the Sea, however, does not impose any limitations upon the law enforcement by the flag State on its ship when navigating on the high seas. Quite to the contrary, the Law of the Sea Convention overtly confirms these powers of the flag State in Articles 92, para. 1 and 94 LOSC. Also, the prohibition of interferences in Art. 110, para. 1 LOSC only applies to "foreign ships". These unlimited rights of the flag State nevertheless find a significant limitation in the Model Agreement since its Paragraph 15 stipulates that "[c]ounter drug operations pursuant to this agreement shall be carried out only against vessels … which either of the Parties has *reasonable grounds* to suspect are involved in illicit traffic".

Thus, even interdiction measures of the flag State against its own vessels would violate the agreement if no reasonable grounds were present before the boarding took place. This might indicate a new understanding of the freedom of navigation protecting at least also private entities. Even though no claims or dispute settlement provision is available to any private individual claiming compensation under the bilateral agreement, the shipowner or related interests might, depending on the constitutional system in the flag State, claim the violation of the agreement before domestic courts.

---

28 The United States also deploys Coast Guard officers on board British and Dutch naval vessels in order to authorize law enforcement on U.S. vessels and in U.S. waters. *Kramek*, Joseph E., "Bilateral Maritime Counter-Drug and Immigrant Interdiction Agreements: Is this the world of the Future?", 31 U. Miami Inter-Am. L. Rev. (2000), pp. 121 *et seq.*, at 139.

III. Entry-to-investigate and pursuit

Both the entry-to-investigate and the pursuit provisions have in common that an interfering State acts within the territorial sea of another State. Art. 111, para. 8 LOSC is not applicable to such situations, since the right of hot pursuit under the Law of the Sea Convention "ceases as soon as the ship pursued enters the territorial sea of its own State or of a third State" (Art. 111, para. 3 LOSC). Art. 110, para. 3 LOSC does not apply to neither of the two provisions because its scope of application is confined to boardings on the high seas.

The interfering State under the entry-to-investigate and the pursuit provisions derives its authority from the powers of the coastal State. Hence, the interfering State may only lawfully interfere with the navigation of foreign vessels if it observes the limitations imposed on the exercise of jurisdiction in the territorial sea by the Law of the Sea Convention. Thus, the interfering State needs to abide by the right of innocent passage (Art. 17 LOSC). This protection does not cover the loading and unloading of undocumented migrants and illicit drugs (*cf.* Art. 19, para. 2, lit. g LOSC). The interfering State may hence lawfully board vessels engaged in these activities.

However, the Law of the Sea Convention does not explicitly regulate whether reasonable grounds to suspect that the boarded vessel was engaged in such activity suffices for a lawful interference. The fact that reasonable suspicion represents a sufficient justification under the bilateral agreements does not have any effect to the rights of third States and their vessels enjoying innocent passage (*pacta tertiis non nocent*, cf. Art. 34 VCLT).

Typical for the Law of the Sea, though, is a gradual decline of the coastal State's rights with increasing distance from its shoreline, depending on the maritime zone. If any State may board vessels on the high seas reasonably suspected of being engaged in certain criminal activity, then one could argue that the coastal State may *a fortiori* board those vessels reasonably suspected of being engaged in (and not only those really engaged in) conduct explicitly excluded from the right of innocent passage in Art. 19 LOSC.

Furthermore, the Law of the Sea Convention recognizes a certain margin of appreciation by the coastal State since it strongly refers to the legislative power of the coastal State regarding its own territorial sea (Art. 21 LOSC). Therefore, it has been widely accepted that the coastal State may enforce its immigration and customs laws in the territorial sea against vessels reasonably suspected of infringing these laws as long as the enforcement powers do not render the right of innocent passage meaningless.[29]

---

[29] *Cf. Steinert*, Karl-Friedrich, "Die internationalrechtliche Stellung des Schiffes im fremden Küstenmeer im Frieden" (Frankfurt am Main, 1970), at 105; *O'Connell*, Daniel Patrick, "The International Law of the Sea", Vol. 2 (Oxford: Clarendon Press, 1984), at 953; C. *Colombos*, Constantin John, "The International Law of the Sea" (6th ed., London: Longman, 1967), at 136; *McDougal*, Myres Smith/*Burke*, William T., "The Public Order of the Oceans" (New Haven: Yale University Press, 1962), at 273;

Thus, the reasonable suspicion standard from the bilateral agreements does not violate the right of innocent passage. Nonetheless, the bilateral agreements do no create any rights of third parties (Art. 34 VCLT). The (third) flag State therefore may not claim the violation of the reasonable suspicion standard under the bilateral agreement. Instead, the flag State and the private entities related to the vessel need to rely on domestic legislation of the coastal State and on the Law of the Sea Convention.

This seems particularly problematic because not the coastal State, but the State authorized under the bilateral agreements operates the boarding. In fact, if no shiprider is present, this latter State remains in absolute control over the interference. Due to almost sacrosanct principles of State immunity, this State and its agents may not become subject to the law of State liability of the coastal State.

The Model Agreement took account of this special situation and stipulated in Paragraph 3: "Maritime counter-drug operation in waters [of the coastal State] are the responsibility of, and subject to the authority of, the Government of [the coastal State]." Hence, only the coastal State will be liable for enforcement action under the entry-to-investigae or the pursuit provision.

By this stipulation, the coastal State takes over responsibility for conduct over which it has little, if any control. This may explain why the shiprider provision has generally been quite commonly used in bilateral agreements. It definitely favors the United States because its responsibility for law enforcement under the entry-to-investigate and pursuit provisions is pratically excluded.

IV. Conclusion

The United States have been able to find very favourable conditions in the bilateral agreements with Latin American and Caribbean States. On the one hand, the United States has gained very wide enforcement powers in a region crucial for U.S. security. On the other hand, the liability risk associated with this gain is, compared to the liability regime in Art. 110, para. 3 LOSC, considerably low. Even though the bilateral agreements formally preserve sovereign equality and reciprocity, the political and factual dominance of the United States in the region has thus been transposed to a certain legal dominance as well.

D. Liability under the loose framework of the Proliferation Security Initiative

As a reaction to the *So San* incident when the Spanish navy boarded a North Korean vessel carrying Scud missiles to Yemen, but had to let her continue her voyage, the United States considered it necessary to find new ways how to prevent

Yang, Haijiang, "Jurisdiction of the coastal state over foreign merchant ships in internal waters and the territorial sea" (Berlin: Springer, 2006), at 164-168.

the transport a cargo dangerous to the security of the United States, in particular weapons of mass destruction. A potential multilateral convention authorizing certain interferences with navigation would not be binding upon those States not ratifying it and thus probably upon those most interested in the transport of weapons of mass destruction.[30] Therefore, the *Bush* administration developed a new strategy, the Proliferation Security Initiative (PSI), announced by President *Bush* in Krakow on 31 May 2001. Under this strategy, States cooperate within a very loose organizational framework in order to prevent the maritime transport of weapons of mass destruction. In general, the member States have not signed a formal treaty and thus have not gained any particular right nor incurred strict obligations. There are now more than 60 States supporting the Proliferation Security Initiative.[31]

According to the Statement of Interdiction Principles adopted on 4 September 2003, the supporting States cooperate in the prevention of transportation of weapons of mass destruction and share their information concerning this transport.[32] Moreover, the member States agree to review and strengthen their national laws and undertake a certain number of interdiction measures. These include the cooperation in the search and seizure of suspect vessels flying the flag of a member State and intensive port State control.

Nonetheless, the Proliferation Security Initiative does not enable the member States to board vessels of other States on the high seas. Furthermore, any interdiction under the Statement of Interdiction Principles would still require the *ad hoc* consent by the flag State.

Therefore, any interdiction remains under the exclusive control of the flag State which may initiate, undertake or object to a boarding of one of its vessels. At the same time, the *ad hoc* consent by the flag State justifies any interference. Thus, there is no room for any compensation claim by private interests related to the ship under public international law against any other State than the flag State. Since the flag State bears responsibility for the boarding under the framework of PSI, any private entity claiming compensation would need to address its claim against the flag State and base it on a violation of the laws of the flag State.

Other claims under public international law could only arise if other international obligations such as human rights were violated during the course of an interference.

The loose framework of the Proliferation Security Initiative, in addition to offering the advantage of a certain flexibility, has thus enabled the member States to avoid a strict liability regime as in the more general conventions in the Law of the Sea.

---

30 *Byers*, Michael, "Policing the High Seas: The Proliferation Security Initiative", 98 AJIL (2004), pp. 526 *et seq.*, at 531.

31 *Rademaker*, Stephen G., "The Proliferation Security Initiative – A Record of Success", Testimony before Congress (9 June 2005), available at <www.state.gov/t/ac/rls/rm/47715.htm>.

32 *Department of State*, "Statement of Interdiction Principles" (4 September 2003), available at <http://usinfo.state.gov/products/pubs/proliferation/#statement>.

E. Ship Boarding Agreements within the framework of the Proliferation Security Initiative

The Statement of Interdiction Principles and the cooperation with PSI members has not been sufficient to efficiently prevent any transportation of weapons of mass destruction. In particular, obtaining the consent by the flag State still tends to consume a lot of crucial time in anti-terrorism measures. The United States is therefore seeking to conclude ship boarding agreements with important flag States, based on the experiences gained in the fight against drug smuggling.

In order to gain rapid consent to board vessels suspected of carrying cargoes related to weapons of mass destruction, the United States has today concluded six of these ship boarding agreements. The States parties to these agreements account for more than one third of the world's gross tonnage of merchant ships and the United States is engaged in negotiations with more than 20 additional States.[33]

Most of these agreements contain a compensation provision similar to Art. 13, para. 2 of the United States Draft Agreement[34]: "Any other claim submitted for damage, harm, injury, death or loss resulting from an operation carried out by a Party under this Agreement shall be resolved in accordance with the domestic law of that Party, and in a manner consistent with international law."

This provision is most peculiar since it does not seem to lay down any principles of substantial law, but instead contains vague references to both domestic and international law.

The reference to international law apparently assured some States such as Croatia that a liability regime comparable to Art. 110, para. 3 LOSC would apply.[35] However, serious doubts remain whether the ship boarding agreements really provide for such a guarantee. First, Art. 110, para. 1 LOSC leaves room for bilateral treaties diverging from the principles contained in Art. 110 LOSC. In fact, it is submitted that any treaty providing for exceptions to Art. 110, para. 1 LOSC would *prima facie* exclude the applicability of Art. 110, para. 3 LOSC and require an own regulation of the compensation issue. Secondly, the United States has not yet become a party to the Law of the Sea Convention. Since the status of Art. 110, para. 3 LOSC as customary international law is far less than certain, the provision probably may not represent the applicable international law between the parties to one of the ship boarding agreements. However, one needs to consider that the United States is nevertheless bound by the very similar Art. 22, para. 3 CHS. Thirdly, Art. 13, para. 2 of the Draft Agreement does not quite solve any potential conflict between the domestic law of the interfering State and interna-

33 *Roach*, J. Ashley, "Proliferation Security Initiative (PSI): Countering Proliferation by Sea", in *Nordquist*, Myron H. *et al.* (eds.), "Recent Decelopments in the Law of the Sea and China" (Leiden: Nijhoff, 2006), pp. 351 *et seq.*, at 354.

34 Reprinted in *Roach*, J. Ashley, "Proliferation Security Initiative (PSI): Countering Proliferation by Sea", in *Nordquist*, Myron H. *et al.* (eds.), "Recent Decelopments in the Law of the Sea and China" (Leiden: Nijhoff, 2006), pp. 351 *et seq.*, at 360.

35 *Cf.* also *Valencia*, Mark J., "The Proliferation Security Initiative: Should Malaysia join?", 142 Maritime Studies (May/June 2005), pp. 14 *et seq.*, at 15.

tional law. These two legal systems may have very different rules concerning the responsibility of a State for interferences on the high seas. In the case of such conflict, domestic courts will nevertheless be inclined to apply their domestic law on State liability. Considering the unlikely applicability of Art. 110, para. 3 LOSC, the claimant will thus find it hard to prove before a tribunal of the interfering State that the domestic law of the respondent is in breach of the general international law on State responsibility.

In two respects, the ship boarding agreements seem to restrain the liability of the interfering State as compared to Art. 110, para. 3 LOSC. First, only unlawful conduct of the interfering State entails its liability under the ship boarding agreements. This requirement forms part of the United States law on State liability[36] and represents a general principle in the general law on State responsibility. Secondly, in spite of the fact that "loss" is always mentioned in the compensation provisions of the ship boarding agreements, one must doubt whether United States practice adheres to this wide cover under the compensation claim. According to a high-ranking U.S. official commenting the draft ship boarding agreement, "the United States, as a matter of policy, promptly pays all meritorious claims *for property damage or personal injury*" resulting from law enforcement on the seas (emphasis added).[37] Of the relevant existing U.S. law on State liability, only 33 CFR Section 25.401 allows claims for "Damage to or loss of real property, including damage or loss incident to the use and occupancy or real property by the Coast Guard." Most boardings covered by the ship boarding agreements, however, seem to fall under 33 CFR Section 25.503 because the claimants are foreign citizens or foreign corporations or because the boarding took place outside the United States. Therefore, it does not seem surprising that the Standard Form 95 that is handed over to the ship's crew in any Coast Guard boarding on the high seas does not explicitly mention claims for the loss of profits caused by delay, but is limited to "property damage" and "personal injury/wrongful death".

It might seem quite wise therefore of Panama to have insisted on a reference to Art. 110, para. 3 LOSC, thereby obliging the United States to compensate, under certain circumstances, for the damage caused by lawful boardings and to include the loss of profits caused by mere delay in a potential compensation award. The reference to Art. 110, para. 3 LOSC is nevertheless quite awkward. Art. XXIII, para. 2 of the Panama-United States agreement stipulates that "[i]f responsibility is established, the claim shall be resolved in favor of the claimant by that Party, in accordance with the domestic law of that Party, and in a manner consistent with international law, including paragraph 3 of Article 110 of the Law of the Sea Convention." Thus, one could argue that one needs to establish the responsibility of the boarding party first before one could apply Art. 110, para. 3 LOSC. Such approach would make little sense since Art. 110, para. 3 LOSC embodies the

---

[36] 46 U.S.C., Appendix, Section 746; 46 U.S.C., Appendix, Section 781; 32 CFR 752; 33 CFR 25. See also *infra*.

[37] *Roach*, J. Ashley, "Proliferation Security Initiative (PSI): Countering Proliferation by Sea", in *Nordquist*, Myron H. *et al.* (eds.), "Recent Decelopments in the Law of the Sea and China" (Leiden: Nijhoff, 2006), pp. 351 *et seq.*, at 407.

precondition for the responsibility to exist. Therefore, it is most likely that the rules in Art. 110, para. 3 LOSC represent the applicable law on compensation for the Panama-United States agreement.

The Marshall Islands seem to have been well advised when they included in their ship boarding agreement with the United States the possibility of claims "for loss or damage suffered as a result of a vessel being unduly detained or *delayed* as provided in Regulation XI-2/9.3.5.1 annexed to the International Convention for the Safety of Life at Sea" (emphasis added).[38] The SOLAS provision may have been drafted for law enforcement during port State control, but its wording by reference here as well applies to boardings on the high seas. Probably because the Marshall Islands did not have the same negotiating power as the powerful flag State Panama, they were not able to include in their bilateral agreement a provision comparable to Art. 110, para. 3 LOSC as far as it concerns liability for lawful conduct. Instead, an obligation to compensate under the Marshall Islands-United States agreement requires "undue" and thus probably unlawful conduct by the boarding State.

Finally, it seems important to note that most of the bilateral agreements do not explicitly mention the party entitled to claim compensation. They do however more or less indicate that the claim belongs to a private entity and not to the flag State. All agreements presume that the claim will be brought forward against the boarding State before a domestic court. States as claimants would probably recur to other means of dispute settlement. According to Art. 8, para. 1, lit. f of the Marshall Islands-United States agreement, "[the boarding party shall] ensure that the master of the vessel is, or has been, afforded the opportunity to contact the vessels' owner, manager or Flag State at the earliest opportunity and provided the necessary information to file a claim pursuant to Article 13, paragraph 2." This stipulation seems to recognize potential claims by private entities.

The flag States have thus been able to gain certain safeguards from the United States, particularly in matters of compensation. However, some of the compensation provisions remain quite unclear concerning their substantial meaning and their scope of application. Most peculiar is the common reference to "domestic law". Under most agreements, this domestic law could only be the law of the United States if the case deals with a boarding by the United States Coast Guard or the United States Navy. Therefore, this study will continue with a brief analysis of the domestic United States Law on State Liability.

F. United States law on State Liability

A bilateral agreement concluded between the United States and another State may thus well lead to the applicability of United States law on State liability to a com-

[38] SOLAS Regulation XI-2/9.35.1. stipulates that "[w]hen Contracting Governments exercise control …, all possible efforts shall be made to avoid a ship being unduly detained or *delayed.* If a ship is thereby unduly detained, or delayed, it shall be entitled to compensation *for any loss* or damage suffered" (emphasis added).

pensation claim by a foreign private entity. It may hence seem necessary to provide a brief overview of the existing United States law on State liability. Even though this study is generally confined to public international law, such overview may be interesting first because of its relevance for private interests seeking to claim compensation and secondly because of its potential differences to the analyzed compensation provisions contained in conventions of the Law of the Sea.

In the United States, the Supreme Court has held that "[t]he United States, as sovereign, is immune from suit save as it consents to be sued."[39] This immunity can only be waived if this is "unequivocally expressed in statutory text."[40] The Suits in Admiralty Act, which might be applicable concerning maritime law enforcement, contains the following waiver: "In cases where ... if a private person or property were involved, a proceeding in admiralty could be maintained, any appropriate nonjury proceeding *in personam* may be brought against the United States ...."[41]

However, courts have concluded that the so-called "discretionary function" exception in the Federal Tort Claims Act (FTCA)[42] applies.[43] This exception preserves the United States' sovereign immunity against "[a]ny claim ... based upon the exercise or performance or the failure to exercise or perform a discretionary function or duty on the part of a federal agency or an employee of the [United States], whether or not the discretion involved be abused."[44] The Supreme Court has adopted a two-tier test to determine whether the conduct of a government employee falls within the scope of this exception. First, one must ascertain the nature of the challenged conduct and assess whether it involved an element of judgment or choice.[45] Second, the court decides "whether that judgment is of the kind that the discretionary function exception was designed to shield."[46] Congress has provided both the U.S. Customs Services[47] and the United States Coast Guard[48] with broad grants of authority which leave them a great deal of discretion in deciding which vessels to board and search. One may well argue that the bilateral ship boarding agreements provide similar grants of authority to the United States Coast Guard.[49]

39 *United States v. Sherwood,* 312 U.S. 584, 586 (1941).
40 *Lane v. Pena,* 518 U.S. 187, 192 (1996).
41 46 U.S.C.app. § 742 (2000); see also *Drake Towing Co. v. Meisner Marine Constr. Co.,* 765 F.2d 1060, 1063-64 (11th Cir.1985).
42 28 U.S.C. § 2680(a).
43 See *Tew v. United States,* 86 F.3d 1003, 1005 (10th Cir.1996) (listing cases from the First, Second, Third, Fourth, Fifth, Sixth, Seventh, Ninth, Eleventh, and D.C. Circuits, and joining in their shared holding). *Cf.* also *McMellon v. United States*, 338 F.3d 287, 292 (4th Cir. 2003). See also *Schoenbaum*, Thomas J., "Admiralty and Maritime Law", Vol. 2 (2nd ed., St. Paul: West Publications, 1994), at 454.
44 28 U.S.C. § 2680(a) (2000).
45 See *United States v. Gaubert,* 499 U.S. 315, 322 (1991).
46 *Berkovitz v. United States,* 486 U.S. 531, 536 (1988).
47 19 U.S.C. § 1581(a) (2000).
48 14 U.S.C. § 89(a) (2000).
49 The agreements generally require a "suspect vessel" which is defined as a "vessel used for commercial or private purposes in respect of which there a reasonable grounds to suspect it is engaged in proliferation by sea." *Cf.* Art. 4, paras. 1, 4; Art. 1, para. 7 Draft Agreement, reprinted in *Roach*, J. Ashley, "Proliferation Security Initiative (PSI):

This satisfies the first prong of the *Gaubert* analysis.[50] The purpose of the discretionary function exception "is to prevent judicial 'second guessing' of legislative and administrative decisions grounded in social, economic, and political policy through the medium of an action in tort."[51] The decision to board and search a vessel is the product of the balancing of various compelling policy considerations: enforcement of the U.S. anti-narcotic or other security laws, weighing the costs of implementing such activities against the likelihood of an enforcement success. This was held to be a policy-based decision falling under the scope of the "discretionary function" exception.[52] Thus, the victims of wrongful measures of port State control or high seas interferences by U.S. law enforcement officials generally cannot claim compensation under U.S. law since the remedies of maritime tort law (*e.g.*, negligence) are not available to them.

This may explain why a high-ranking United States official gave the comment to the ship boarding agreement that "[t]he United States, *as a matter of policy* [as opposed to a legal obligation], promptly pays all meritorious claims…" (emphasis added).[53] United States domestic law leaves it largely to the discretion and to political considerations of the government whether a compensation claim against the government for damages caused by law enforcement on the sea should be satisfied or not. From the perspective of the shipowner and other private entities interested in compensation, this level of protection falls well below the rights under, *e.g.*, Art. 110, para. 3 LOSC.

It may also explain why the United States, within its discretion, only pays claims "for property damage or personal injury" and not for lost profits.[54] The Standard Form 95 that is handed over to the ship's crew in any Coast Guard boarding does not explicitly mention claims for the loss of profits caused by delay, but is limited to "property damage" and "personal injury/wrongful death". Presumably, the United States only wants to compensate for exceptional, particularly harsh damages, but not for the most common, economic damages which then have to be borne by the shipping industry.

Finally, one ought to add that the United States law on State liability only permits claims by foreign nationals if their domestic legal systems also allow claims

Countering Proliferation by Sea", in *Nordquist*, Myron H. *et al.* (eds.), "Recent Decelopments in the Law of the Sea and China" (Leiden: Nijhoff, 2006), pp. 351 *et seq.*, at 360.

50 See *Autery v. United States,* 992 F.2d 1523, 1529 (11th Cir.1993); *Mid-South Holding Co., Inc. v. U.S.*, 225 F.3d 1201, 1205 (11th Cir. 2000).

51 *United States v. Gaubert,* 499 U.S. 315, 323 (1991).

52 *B&F Trawlers, Inc. v. United States,* 841 F.2d 626, 631 (5th Cir.1988); *Mid-South Holding Co., Inc. v. U.S.*, 225 F.3d 1201, 1206 (11th Cir. 2000).

53 *Roach*, J. Ashley, "Proliferation Security Initiative (PSI): Countering Proliferation by Sea", in *Nordquist*, Myron H. *et al.* (eds.), "Recent Decelopments in the Law of the Sea and China" (Leiden: Nijhoff, 2006), pp. 351 *et seq.*, at 407.

54 *Roach*, J. Ashley, "Proliferation Security Initiative (PSI): Countering Proliferation by Sea", in *Nordquist*, Myron H. *et al.* (eds.), "Recent Decelopments in the Law of the Sea and China" (Leiden: Nijhoff, 2006), pp. 351 *et seq.*, at 407.

by United States nationals against the State of nationality of the former (reciprocity requirement).[55]

Concluding, the United States law on State liability tends to protect the U.S. government from compensation claims, particularly in matters of maritime law enforcement. In fact, the discretionary function doctrine makes it almost impossible to succeed before United States courts with compensation claims. The United States has therefore carefully guarded its interests when insisting on references to "domestic law" in ship boarding agreements. The "partner States" in these agreements, however, being presumably more or less unaware of the United States law on State liability, seem to have exposed the shipowners under their flags to a considerable risk of suffering losses by an increased number of interdictions on the high seas without adequate remedies.

---

[55] 46 U.S.C. § 785; *Taghadomi v. Extreme Sports Maui*, 257 F.Supp.2d 1262, 1272 (D.Hawai'i 2002); *Pascua v. Astrocielo Neptunea Armandora, S.A.*, 614 F.Supp. 984, 985 (D.C.Tex.,1985).

Chapter IV: Compensation for interferences in international conflicts

A. The law of naval warfare

The classical distinction in public international law between rules applicable in times of peace on the one hand, and rules applicable in times of war on the other hand, also generally applies to the Law of the Sea.[1] Therefore, the Law of the Sea Convention as such does not govern the relations between States in times of war.[2]

A whole separate body of law has developed concerning the Law of the Sea in times of war, the so-called law of naval warfare. For the sake of this study, it thus seems necessary to determine the rules governing the responsibility of States for interferences with navigation in times of war. However, this task has proven to be rather difficult because the law of naval warfare has not been codified in a convention comparable to the Law of the Sea Convention. There have been attempts of codification in the middle of the 19th and at the beginning of the 20th century when western naval powers negotiated and adopted the Paris Declaration of 1856,[3] the Hague Conventions of 1907[4] and the London Declaration of 1909[5]. The status of these texts nevertheless has been questioned due to a lack of ratification,[6] due to the events during World War II[7] and due to the adoption of the United Nations Charter.

---

1 *Dupuy*, René-Jean/*Vignes*, Daniel, "Traité du nouveau droit de la mer" (Paris: Economica, 1985), at 1095.

2 *Churchill*, Robin R./*Lowe*, Alan Vaughan: "The Law of the Sea" (3rd ed., Manchester: Juris Publications, 1999), at 421; *Dalton*, Harvey, "Comments on national security concerns", in *van Dyke*, Jon M. *et al.* (eds.), "International Navigation – Rocks and Shoals ahead?" (Honolulu: University of Hawaii, 1988), pp. 373 *et seq.*, at 373-4.

3 Declaration Respecting Maritime Law, 16 April 1856, reprinted in *Ronzitti*, Natalino (ed.), "The Law of Naval Warfare" (Dordrecht: Nijhoff, 1988), at 64-65.

4 In particular: Convention (X) for the Adaptation to Maritime Warfare of the Principles of the Geneva Convention, 18 October 1907; Convention (XI) relative to certain Restrictions with regard to the Exercise of the Right of Capture in Naval War, adopted on 18 October 1907; Convention (XIII) concerning the Rights and Duties of Neutral Powers in Naval War, adopted on 18 October 1907.

5 Declaration concerning the Laws of Naval War, adopted on 16 February 1909, reprinted in 3 AJIL, Supplement (1909), pp. 179 *et seq.*

6 While the 1856 Declaration had 55 and the relevant Hague Conventions between 28 and 31 States Parties, the 1909 Declaration was signed by only 10 States.

7 In this war, the belligerents did not follow the restrictive approach concerning the definition of contraband as provided in the different conventions on naval warfare. *Cf.*

I. Three views concerning the legality of visit and search of neutral vessels in times of war

The latter event, in particular, has raised doubts concerning the general legality of interferences with navigation in times of war. At first, two schools of thought seem to have emerged. The one school argues that belligerents may only use force against vessels of other States either with the authorization of the Security Council or according to the right of self-defence under Art. 51 of the United Nations Charter.[8] The other view argues that the traditional law of naval warfare is still applicable, though modified by the State practice during World War II and after 1945.[9]

While belligerents, under both views, remain free to search, visit and capture vessels of their enemies, the controversy is substantial as far as it concerns the legality of interferences with the navigation of neutral vessels. Under the more restrictive view, any visit of a neutral vessel would only be legal if it had been authorized by the Security Council or if the neutral vessel constituted at least an imminent threat to the belligerent. The wider view allows the visit and search of all merchant vessels anywhere on the sea with the exception of neutral waters.[10] Because of the hazards of visit and search in a modern armed conflict, these vessels may even be diverted and ordered into port.[11] The traditional law allows a belligerent to capture a neutral vessel if she resists to visit, search and diversions, breaches a blockade, carries contraband or is engaged in other unneutral service.[12]

State practice after 1945 provides arguments for both views. Without going too much into detail, it shall suffice to mention some practice during the Iran-Iraq war of 1980-1988. In that conflict, Iranian naval forces stopped and searched as many as 15 to 20 neutral vessels per day in order to prevent the transport of goods to

Heintschel von Heinegg, Wolff, "Visit, Search, Diversion, and Capture in Naval Warfare: Part I, The Traditional Law", 29 Can. Yb. Int'l L. (1991), pp. 283 *et seq.*, at 325-326; *Levi*, Werner, "Contemporary International Law: A Concise Introduction" (2nd ed., Boulder: Westview, 1991), at 317.

8 *Cf. Churchill*, Robin R./*Lowe*, Alan Vaughan: "The Law of the Sea" (3rd ed., Manchester: Juris Publications, 1999), at 422; *cf.* also *Norton*, Patrick M., "Between the Ideology and the Reality", 17 Harv. Int'l L. J. (1976), pp. 249 *et seq.*, at 250-251; *Lagoni*, Rainer, "Remarks", 82 ASIL Proceedings (1988), pp. 161 *et seq.*, at 162..

9 *de Guttry*, Andrea, "Commentary", in *id. et al.* (eds.), "The Iran-Iraq War (1980-1988) and the Law of Naval Warfare" (Cambridge: Grotius, 1993), pp. 419 *et seq.*, at 427.

10 *Heintschel von Heinegg*, Wolff, "Visit, Search, Diversion, and Capture in Naval Warfare: Part II, Developments since 1945", 30 Can. Yb. Int'l L. (1992), pp. 89 *et seq.*, at 133; A. Pearce Higgins, *Visit, Search and Detention*, 7 BYIL 43 (1926); *The Carthage (France/Italy)*, Permanent Court of Arbitration, 6 May 1913, reprinted in 7 AJIL 623, at 626 (1913).

11 *Heintschel von Heinegg*, Wolff, "Visit, Search, Diversion, and Capture in Naval Warfare: Part II, Developments since 1945", 30 Can. Yb. Int'l L. (1992), pp. 89 *et seq.*, at 133.

12 *Ibid.*, at 135; the Helsinki Principles on the Law of Maritime Neutrality elaborated by the ILA adhere to the traditional law of naval warfare in this respect, *cf.* Principles 5.2.1 and 5.2.2 reprinted in ILA, "Report of the Sixty-Eighth Conference (1998), at 509-510.

Iraq.[13] Only a few flag States made a formal protest against these interferences.[14] The Dutch representative at the United Nations expressly admitted that a belligerent was entitled to restrict navigation to and from ports belonging to the respective enemy.[15] The United Kingdom, however, officially declared that any interference may only be justified as self-defence. Its position was that a party to the conflict may only visit and search neutral vessels if "there is reasonable ground for suspecting that the ship is taking arms or other war material to the other side for use in that conflict."[16] However, one must add that the United Kingdom did not treat the situation as a war.[17] This inconsistent State practice has led to further insecurity concerning the applicable law.

Directly after the Gulf War, and probably due to the uncertainty caused by inconsistent State practice in that conflict, a group of International Lawyers and Naval Experts started their work on the so-called "San Remo Manual on International Law applicable to Armed Conflicts at Sea" (hereinafter San Remo Manual). This group aimed to assemble the existing customary international law taking account of existing conventions, State practice, national navy manuals and judicial decisions.[18] Concerning the controversial issue discussed above, the San Remo Manual came up with a compromise solution. It acknowledged that some traditional rules of naval warfare continue to apply in spite of the adoption of the United Nations Charter, but that the rights of belligerents are also affected by the restraints of the law of self-defence.[19] As a result of these considerations, paragraph 114 of the San Remo Manual provides that "[i]f the commander of a warship suspects that a merchant vessel flying a neutral flag in fact has enemy character, the commander is entitled to exercise the right of visit and search including the right of diversion for search". Likewise, according to paragraph 118, ""[i]n exercising their legal rights in an international armed conflict at sea, belligerent warships and military aircraft have a right to visit and search merchant vessels outside neutral waters where there are reasonable grounds for suspecting

---

13 *Leckow*, Ross, "The Iran-Iraq Conflict in the Gulf: The Law of War Zones", 37 ICLQ (1988), pp. 629, *et seq.*, at 638.

14 See *Gioia*, Andrea/*Ronzitti*, Natalino, "The Law of Neutrality: Third States' Commercial Rights and Duties", in *Dekker*, Ige F. *et al.* (eds.), "The Gulf War of 1980-1988" (Dordrecht: Nijhoff, 1992), pp. 221 *et seq.*, at 226.

15 *UN* Doc. S/PV.2546 (1 June 1984), "Security Council Official Records, 2546th meeting", at para. 31.

16 *House of Commons*, "Third Special Report from the Defence Committee (Session 1986-1987), The Protection of British Merchant Shipping in the Persian Gulf", at 91-92; *Greenwood*, Christopher J., "Remarks", 82 ASIL Proceedings (1988), pp. 158 *et seq.*, at 159.

17 *Lowe*, Alan Vaughan, "Commentary", in *de Guttry*, Andrea *et al.* (eds.), "The Iran-Iraq War (1980-1988) and the Law of Naval Warfare" (Cambridge: Grotius, 1993), pp. 241 *et seq.*, at 244; *cf.* also *Lowe*, Alan Vaughan, "The Impact on the Law of the Sea on Naval Warfare", 14 Syracuse J. Int'l L. & Com. (1988), pp. 657 *et seq.*, at 674.

18 *Doswald-Beck*, Louise, "The San Remo Manual on International Law applicable to Armed Conflicts at Sea", 89 AJIL (1995), pp. 192 *et seq.*, at 193-194.

19 *Ibid.*, at 196-197.

that they are subject to capture." Hence, the San Remo Manual does not provide for an unlimited right of interference. The lawful visit and search always requires some reasonable suspicion. Flying a flag of convenience does not suffice for a suspicion that the vessel is controlled by enemy interests and thus subject to visit and search.[20]

More or less in the same period, a committee of the International Law Association discussed issues of "Maritime Neutrality". This committee was well aware of the developments since 1945 and associated controversies among international lawyers. It nevertheless wanted to contribute to a "restatement or ... development of new law" on maritime neutrality.[21] Contrary to the San Remo Manual, however, this committee came to the conclusion that the traditional law of naval warfare still applies in respect to the legality of visit and search of neutral vessels. According to Principle 5.2.1 of the "Helsinki Principles of the Law of Maritime Neutrality" elaborated by the committee, "belligerent warships have a right to visit and search vis-à-vis neutral commercial ships in order to ascertain the character and destination of their cargo. If a ship tries to evade this control and offers resistance, measures of coercion necessary to exercise this right are permissible. This includes the right to divert a ship where visit and search at the place where the ship is encountered are not practical."[22]

One may preliminarily conclude that three different sets of rules regarding interferences with navigation in times of war may exist: the traditional law of naval warfare, a restrictive view referring particularly to the development of the United Nations Charter and the intermediary opinion of the San Remo Manual. This study shall not in detail elaborate on the issue whether and under which conditions a State is entitled to interfere with navigation, but whether and under which circumstances an interfering State may be liable for its conduct.

Therefore, this thesis will not submit which view is applicable, but will instead analyze the three scenarios separately.

II. Compensation under the traditional law of naval warfare

First, if one applied the traditional law of naval warfare, one clearly needs to distinguish between interferences with navigation on the high seas and captures of vessels after they had been diverted. Since, according to the traditional view, a belligerent would have the right to visit, search and divert neutral vessels on the high seas and the compensation issue would generally not arise for mere interferences with navigation.

---

20 Commentary on paragraph 114, reprinted in *Doswald-Beck*, Louise (ed.), "San Remo Manual on International Law Applicable to Armed Conflicts at Sea" (Cambridge: Cambridge University Press, 1995), at 191.

21 *Bothe*, Michael, "Report of the Committee on Neutrality and Naval Warfare", in *ILA*, "Report of the Sixty-Seventh Conference" (1996), pp. 367 *et seq.*, at 370.

22 "Helsinki Principles on the Law of Maritime Neutrality", reprinted in *ILA,* "Report of the Sixty-Eighth Conference" (1998), pp. 497 *et seq.*, at 509-510.

However, the principle of proportionality and thus the prohibition of unreasonable interferences apply even in the traditional law of naval warfare.[23] Therefore, in cases of unreasonable diversion, undue delay, or unnecessary interference with the ship's voyage, compensation is awarded by the prize court.[24] These prize courts traditionally nevertheless seem to have a very restricted view of the damages to be covered by a compensation award since the fact that the claimants have suffered inconvenience or delay does not by itself afford a valid claim for damages.[25] Since any inconvenience usually causes delays, compensation under the traditional law of naval warfare is not adequate to repair all damages suffered by shipowners in unreasonable interferences. Furthermore, French and German Prize Courts have generally declared themselves incompetent to award compensation in cases where vessels were diverted to their ports for search, but eventually released, because their cargo was neutral.[26] While Anglo-Saxon Prize Courts are generally competent to rule on this matter, the judgment concerning the *Tredegar Hall* seems exemplary for the law on compensation: "Any delay or inconvenience which might occur to a ship as the result of her diversion or detention for the purpose of seizure … is a loss … to the shipowners as a result of the war, and for which, unfortunately, they cannot have any compensation. It is a loss like the losses which have to be submitted to by other citizens in other capacities and other walks of life…"[27] Similarly, the U.S. Commander's Handbook on the Law of Naval Operations provides that "the mere visit and search does not entail an obligation to compensate and the prize court may simply order the release of the vessel if it turns out to be totally neutral."[28] This has led some authors to conclude that the law of naval warfare does not provide for an obligation to compensate even in cases of arbitrary and disproportionate interferences;[29] others claim that a right to compensation for visit, search and diversion in times of war is limited to unreasonable interferences with the presumption for the existence of a probable

23 *Heintschel von Heinegg*, Wolff, "Visit, Search, Diversion, and Capture in Naval Warfare: Part I, The Traditional Law", 29 Can. Yb. Int'l L. (1991), pp. 283 *et seq.*, at 298; *Falk*, 10 Lloyd's Reports of Prize Cases (22 April 1920), pp. 25 *et seq.*, at 49.

24 *Heintschel von Heinegg*, Wolff, "Visit, Search, Diversion, and Capture in Naval Warfare: Part I, The Traditional Law", 29 Can. Yb. Int'l L. (1991), pp. 283 *et seq.*, at 304; *Richards*, Sir Erle, "The British Prize Courts and the war", 1 BYIL(1920/1921), pp. 11 *et seq.*, at 24; *Genet*, Raoul, "Précis de droit maritime pour le temps de guerre", Vol. 1 (Paris: Marchal & Billard, 1939), at 294 *et seq.*

25 *Colombos*, Constantin John, "The International Law of the Sea" (6th ed., London: Longman, 1967), at paras. 893; *Wehberg*, Hans, "Das Seekriegsrecht" (Stuttgart: Kohlhammer, 1915), at 288.

26 *Verzijl*, Jan Hendrik Willem, "Le droit des prises de la Grande Guerre" (Leyde: Sijthoff, 1924), at 1044-1045.

27 Cited in *ibid.*, at 1127.

28 *Cf.* The Commander's Handbook on the Law of Naval Operations, section 7.5 and the footnote in the Annotated Supplement.

29 *Pagani*, Fabrizio, "Le misure di interdizione navale in relazione alle sanzioni adottate dall'ONU", 76 Rivista di diritto internazionale (1993), pp. 720 *et seq.*, at 754, n. 140.

cause for a lawful interference.[30] In practice, prize courts have been extremely reluctant to grant compensation in cases of visit and search.[31]

Even if the interference occurred within the territorial waters of a neutral State and was thus unlawful, the claimant would only be entitled to compensation if there has been a wilful abuse of belligerent rights.[32] If the interfering State had unintentionally violated the sovereignty of the coastal State, the shipowner could not claim compensation even if the vessel was destroyed during the interference, presumably because the entity whose rights had been violated (the coastal State) were not identical to the entity suffering damages (the shipowner or related private entities) or the flag State exercising protection for that entity.[33]

The chances to receive compensation under the traditional law of naval warfare seem to be better in the case of a capture and condemnation. The capture of a vessel is an intermediary step until title passes to the belligerent by condemnation by a prize court.[34] However, if the prize court orders the release of the vessel or if the belligerent releases the vessel before adjudication by a prize court,[35] "the parties interested have the right to compensation, unless there were good reasons for capturing the vessel or goods" (Art. 64 of the 1909 London Declaration). The prize court does not rule on the lawfulness of the capture,[36] but only on the status of the captured vessel as enemy or innocent. The capture remains lawful if the belligerent had good reasons for the capture.[37] Art. 64 of the 1909 London Declaration entitles the "interested parties" a right to compensation in the case of a release, but only "if there were no good reasons for capturing the vessel or goods". Hence, unlike Art. 110, para. 3 LOSC, it links liability to an unlawful capture.

30 *Cf. Colombos*, Constantin John, "The International Law of the Sea" (6th ed., London: Longman, 1967), at 776, para. 893.

31 *Cf. The Patrai*, High Court of Justice (21 May 1952), 19 ILR, pp. 634 *et seq.*, at 636.

32 *Cf. The Anna*, 5 Ch. Rob. 373 (1805).

33 *The Valeria*, 9 Lloyd's Reports of Prize Cases (1923), pp. 32 *et seq.*, at 38-39; *Twee Gebroeders*, 3 Ch. Rob. 162 (1800).

34 *Moore*, John Bassett, "Digest of International Law", Vol. 2 (Washington: Government Printing Office, 1906), at 1001; *The Wilhelmina*, 78 F.Supp. 57 (W.D. Washington, 1948).

35 The German delegation proposed the insertion of this second alternative because a captured vessel may also be released in an administrative procedure as opposed to litigation before a prize court. *Schramm*, Georg, "Das Prisenrecht in seiner neuesten Gestalt" (Berlin: Mittler, 1913), at 537. *Cf.* also General Report to the Naval Conference on Behalf of its Drafting Committee, reprinted in *Scott*, James Brown (ed.), "The Declaration of London – A Collection of Official Papers and Documents" (New York: Oxford University Press, 1919), pp. 130 *et seq.*, at 182.

36 An unlawful capture evidently leads to the liability of the interfering State. *Cf. The Carthage (France/Italy)* (6 May 1913), 11 RIAA, pp. 449 *et seq.*, at 459-460; *The Manouba (France/Italy)* (6 May 1913), 11 RIAA, pp. 463 *et seq.*, at 474-475.

37 *Cf. Heintschel von Heinegg*, Wolff, "Visit, Search, Diversion, and Capture in Naval Warfare: Part I, The Traditional Law", 29 Can. Yb. Int'l L. (1991), pp. 283 *et seq.*, at 307. Verzijl states that "good reason" always justifies wrongful acts and exempts from State responsibility. *Verzijl*, Jan Hendrik Willem, "International Law in Historical Perspective", Vol. 6, (Leiden: Sijthoff, 1973), at 741.

What constitutes a good reason was very controversial among the delegates at the London Conference.[38] The text indicates that the perspective of the captor is relevant and that he must assess the situation before he captures the vessel. Another interpretation, relying particularly on the *travaux préparatoires* only considers the conduct of the crew of the neutral vessel to be relevant.[39] Combining both views, it seems most likely that the perspective of the captor is relevant, but that the basis for his "good reasons" must be a perception of the conduct of the neutral vessel's crew. The facts that a crew member destroyed some of the ship's papers or that false papers were found definitely constitute such good reason.[40]

The provision also clearly entitles "the parties interested". In combination with the availability of prize courts where these private entities appear as parties, one must acknowledge that these parties are granted a right in public international law. The flag State may only play a role in the dispute if the private entities claim a violation of the law of naval warfare by the prize court and then need to rely on the protection by the flag State. Art. 64 of the 1909 London Declaration was included on the proposal of the British delegation which aimed to "obtain the recognition of liberal and equitable rules in respect of payment of compensation to injured neutrals".[41] However, State practice in the two World Wars restrictively interpreted this liberal approach. British prize courts only awarded damages if the claimant was able to prove that the reasonable suspicion on the part of the captor was unfounded and thereby probably reversed the burden of proof as laid down in Art. 64 of the 1909 London Declaration.[42] Some prize courts even limited the responsibility of the belligerent to cases of grave or serious negligence or misconduct on the captor's part.[43] Hence, Art. 64 of the 1909 London Declaration has only acquired the status of customary international law if one interpreted it very restrictively.[44]

If there were "good reasons to capture the vessel" and if the seizure has thus been lawful, but the vessel turned out to be innocent and neutral, then the belligerent must release the vessel and her cargo or, if the vessel or her cargo have

---

[38] *Freiherr Hold von Ferneck*, Alexander, "Die Reform des Seekriegsrechts durch die Londoner Konferenz 1908/1909" (Stuttgart: Kohlhammer, 1914), at 208-210.

[39] *Ibid.*, at 210.

[40] *Cf.* § 8 Deutsche Prisenordnung of 30 September 1909, Reichsgesetzblatt (1914), at 275.

[41] *Kalshoven*, Frits, "Commentary to the 1909 London Declaration Concerning the Laws of Naval Warfare", in *Ronzitti*, Natalino (ed.), "The Law of Naval Warfare" (Dordrecht: Nijhoff, 1988), pp. 257 *et seq.*, at 269; "Report of the British Delegates" (1 March 1909), reprinted in *Scott*, James Brown (ed.), "The Declaration of London – A Collection of Official Papers and Documents" (New York: Oxford University Press, 1919), pp. 235 *et seq.*, at 251.

[42] *The Unitas*, [1948] P. 205 and [1950] A.C. 536.

[43] *Colombos*, Constantin John, "The International Law of the Sea" (6th ed., London: Longman, 1967), at 777, para. 894.

[44] *Cf.* also *Le Louis,* 2 Dods. (1816), pp. 210 *et seq.*, at 243.

already been sold, compensate the shipowner.[45] This rule seems to have some similarities to Art. 110, para. 3 LOSC, but it also grants *restitio in integrum* to private entities. In cases of compensation, prize courts traditionally only either simply forwarded the prize the belligerent gained in the sale[46] or, in the exceptional case that such prize is lower than the market value,[47] the value of the property at the time of the capture without any lost profits or other damages to the shipowner. An innocent vessel for whose capture there were "good reasons" therefore cannot claim any compensation exceeding the value of the vessel from the capturing belligerent. The award thus inadequately reflects the damage the shipowner and other private interests have suffered. However, the shipowner at least does not have to bear expenses incurred in the interest of the captor, such as the costs for loading, shipping and discharging the cargo until requisitioning it.[48] The captor may, nonetheless, deduct the costs for guarding the vessel in port since not the diversion, but only the seizure had been unlawful.[49]

As far as it concerns the burden of proof, there may be further disadvantages for the shipowner and related private interests since it is argued that in time of war, "the question of legality may be raised in general terms and no burden of exculpation is placed upon the respondent state."[50] Hence, both the extent of damages covered and the burden of proof favour the interfering State compared to the regime established by Art. 110, para. 3 LOSC.[51]

Thus far the traditional law of naval warfare. Even though the liability issue was raised during a meeting of the ILA Committee on Maritime Neutrality on 27 May 1998,[52] it was never discussed in detail and not mentioned in either the Helsinki Principles on Maritime Neutrality or its commentary. One may therefore presume that the members of the ILA Committee on Maritime Neutrality intended to leave the existing liability regime in the traditional law of naval warfare largely unaffected.

---

45 German prize courts clearly distinguished this case from an unlawful interference and only granted « Wertersatz » instead of "Schadensersatz". *Cf. Verzijl*, Jan Hendrik Willem, "Le droit des prises de la Grande Guerre" (Leyde: Sijthoff, 1924), at 1127-1160.

46 *Jiul (Nr. 1)* (18 March 1915), printed in: *Verzijl*, Jan Hendrik Willem, "Le droit des prises de la Grande Guerre" (Leyde: Sijthoff, 1924), at 1143.

47 *Apollonia* (24 June 1915), printed in: *ibid.*, at 1144-1145.

48 *In re Compagnie Belge des Mines, Minerais et Métaux*, Conseil des Prises (6 December 1946), 13 ILR, pp. 412 *et seq.*, at 413.

49 *The Manouba (France/Italy)* (6 May 1913), 11 RIAA, pp. 463 *et seq.*, at 474-475.

50 *Brownlie*, Ian, "State Responsiblity" (Oxford: Clarendon Press, 1983), at 78-9 (citing *The Carthage*, 11 RIAA 449 and *The Manouba*, 11 RIAA 463). *Cf.* also *Timandra Shipping Company (United States/Germany)*, cited by *Whiteman*, Marjorie M., "Damages in International Law", Vol. 2 (Washington, U.S. Government Printing Office, 1937) at 1016.

51 *Cf.* also *The Posteiro*, 7 Lloyd's Reports of Prize Cases (1921), pp. 21 *et seq.*, at 41.

52 "Records of Working Session of the Committee on Maritime Neutrality" (27 May 1998), in *ILA* (ed.), "Report of the Sixty-Eighth Conference of the ILA" (1998), pp. 517 *et seq.*, at 518.

III. Liability under the San Remo Manual

Secondly, the law of naval warfare as proposed in the San Remo Manual may apply. Concerning visit, search and diversion under the San Remo Manual, a lawful interference requires well-founded reasons for the suspicion that a neutral vessel may in fact have enemy character.[53] Regarding liability, the San Remo Manual does not contain detailed provisions, but nevertheless seems to adhere to the traditional law on naval warfare. The commentary states that "[i]n cases of unreasonable diversion, undue delay, or unnecessary interference with the ship's voyage compensation should be awarded by the prize court".[54] Doing so, the commentary expressly refers to some authorities of the traditional law of naval warfare.[55] Therefore, even though the commentary does not expressly mention the right of the "interested parties", one can presume that the San Remo Manual aimed to leave the existing law on liability for interferences in naval warfare unaffected. The San Remo Manual hence only modifies the existing law of liability for visit and search in so far, that in the absence of well-founded reasons for suspicion, even a visit and search will be unlawful and entail liability of the belligerent.

The San Remo Manual, in its para. 116, also contains a provision on the capture of neutral vessels. The provision itself does not significantly differ from the traditional law and its commentary indicates that the drafters aimed to maintain the rights of interested parties to compensation as contained in Art. 64 of the 1909 London Declaration. According to the commentary, the order of a prize court to release a captured vessel only entails liability of the capturing State to the shipowner if the prize court ruled that "the grounds put forward by the naval commander to justify capture are not reasonable."[56] Hence, the San Remo Manual is hostile to any liability for lawful conduct and strictly adheres to the London Declaration. One can assume that the San Remo Manual also aimed to maintain the law applicable to lawful captures where the vessel *ex post* turned out to be innocent.

53 Commentary on paragraph 114, reprinted in *Doswald-Beck*, Louise (ed.), "San Remo Manual on International Law Applicable to Armed Conflicts at Sea" (Cambridge: Cambridge University Press, 1995), at 191. *Cf.* also *The Mim*, High Court of Justice (7 July 1947), 14 ILR, pp. 311 *et seq.*, at 316 (holding that a vessel which had come further north than her usual course, raised a reasonable suspicion).

54 Commentary on paragraph 114, *Doswald-Beck*, Louise (ed.), "San Remo Manual on International Law Applicable to Armed Conflicts at Sea" (Cambridge: Cambridge University Press, 1995), at 191, note 158.

55 *Scheuner*, Ulrich, "Durchsuchung von Schiffen", in *Schlochauer*, Hans-Jürgen *et al.* (eds.), "Wörterbuch des Völkerrechts", Vol. 1 (1960), at 407; *Colombos*, Constantin John, "The International Law of the Sea" (5th ed., London: Longman, 1962), at para. 893.

56 Commentary on paragraph 116, reprinted in *Doswald-Beck*, Louise (ed.), "San Remo Manual on International Law Applicable to Armed Conflicts at Sea" (Cambridge: Cambridge University Press, 1995), at 193.

IV. The restrictive view and its consequences for State responsibility

Finally, this analysis will deal with the third scenario, implementing the most restrictive view on the applicable law of naval warfare. According to this view, which is very reluctant to distinguish a war from an international hostility at all, any interference with neutral vessels may only be justified by a Security Council authorization or by self-defence. While it seems obvious that under the first alternative, interferences in the absence of a Security authorization would lead to liability of the interfering State, the issue of self-defence is more unclear due to uncertainties about the requirements of self-defence under public international law.[57] A discussion of these issues would definitely exceed the scope of this study. However, the advice of the British Foreign and Commonwealth Office to British shipping during the Iran-Iraq war seems exemplary of the restrictive view on naval warfare. According to the United Kingdom, the interference of a neutral vessel by a belligerent may be justified under Article 51 of the United Nations Charter if "there is a reasonable ground for suspecting that the ship is taking arms or other war material to the other side for use in that conflict.". Hence, the justification does not require an armed attack by the neutral vessel, but the suspicion of a certain threat caused by the neutral vessel. According to the United Kingdom, the interfering State becomes liable to "the ship" "if the suspicions prove to be unfounded and the ship has not committed acts calculated to give rise to suspicion."[58] These are almost the same terms as in Art. 110, para. 3 LOSC and one could almost suspect that the United Kingdom considers Art. 110, para. 3 LOSC to be applicable in times of war.

It may be questionable whether the position of the United Kingdom is representative for the whole school of thought, but it indicates at least that if one were to restrict justifications for interferences with navigation in times of war to Security Council authorizations and self-defence, one would most likely assimilate the law of naval warfare to the Law of the Sea in times of peace and hereby provide for a better protection of neutral shipping.

V. The development of the damages covered in the law on State responsibility and its consequences for the law of naval warfare

Almost as controversial as the requirements of responsibility for interferences in naval warfare has in the past been the extent of responsibility. During the 1909 London Conference, delegates expressed different views concerning the damages to be compensated by a belligerent. In particular, the issue was whether a

57 *Cf. Bowett*, Derek William, "Self-defence in international law" (Manchester: Manchester University Press, 1958); *Brownlie*, Ian, "International law and the use of force by states" (Oxford: Clarendon Press, 1963); *Dinstein*, Yoram, "War, aggression and self-defence" (3rd ed., Cambridge: Cambridge University Press, 2002).

58 "Answer by the Secretary of State for Foreign and Commonwealth Affairs" (15 February 1988), House of Commons Debates, Vol. 127, Col. 424.

belligerent was obliged to compensate for *damnum emergens*[59] only or also for *lucrum cessans*.[60] France and Japan opposed an obligation to compensate for *lucrum cessans*, while Austria-Hungary supported the inclusion of lost profits.[61] The London Declaration leaves it at the discretion of the prize court to award indirect losses or not.[62] The fact that Austria-Hungary withdrew its proposal because it was afraid the other delegations would instead vote for a stipulation expressly denying *lucrum cessans* indicates that no lost profits are available under the law of naval warfare as codified in the London Declaration.[63] In the beginning of the 20th century, it was much more common for a prize court to deny the award of indirect losses.[64] However, these damages were either not awarded because the claimant could not prove them or because they were deemed not available in the general law on State responsibility. Consequently, prize courts generally denied the award of interest with the exception of procedural interest of 4 percent running from the date the claim was filed.[65] Since then, though, the law of State responsibility has clearly developed an obligation to repair all damages, including *lucrum cessans*[66] and any distinction between these different kinds of damages has become alien to modern public international law. Therefore, it is submitted that even in the law of naval warfare, no matter what theory one follows, *lucrum cessans* is generally available if the claimant can beyond reasonable doubt prove their occurrence and causality by the interference by the respondent belligerent.

---

59 *Damnum emergens* is defined as "actual realized loss" or "positive damage". "Black's Law Dictionary" (7th ed., St. Paul: West Group, 1999), at 398.

60 *Lucrum cessans* is the loss of prospective profits. *Cf. Lauterpacht*, Hersch, "Private Law Sources and Analogies of International Law" (London, 1927), at 149, n. 1.

61 *Schramm*, Georg, "Das Prisenrecht in seiner neuesten Gestalt" (Berlin: Mittler, 1913), at 313-314.

62 General Report to the Naval Conference on Behalf of its Drafting Committee, reprinted in *Scott*, James Brown (ed.), "The Declaration of London – A Collection of Official Papers and Documents" (New York: Oxford University Press, 1919), pp. 130 *et seq.*, at 183.

63 *Freiherr Hold von Ferneck*, Alexander, "Die Reform des Seekriegsrechts durch die Londoner Konferenz 1908/1909" (Stuttgart: Kohlhammer, 1914), at 213-214, n. 1.

64 *Hackett*, Frank Warren, "Reminiscences of the Geneva Tribunal of Arbitration 1872: the Alabama claims" (Boston: Houghton Mifflin, 1911) at 310-325; *Sydney Albert*, Oberprisengericht (25 November 1915), 1 OPGE 62, at 64-65; *Verzijl*, Jan Hendrik Willem, "Le droit des prises de la Grande Guerre" (Leyde: Sijthoff, 1924), at 1150-1152.

65 *Sydney Albert*, Oberprisengericht, 25 November 1915, 1 OPGE 62, at 65; *Arena*, Oberprisengericht, 29 June 1917, 1 OPGE 343, at 346.

66 *Schramm*, Georg, "Das Prisenrecht in seiner neuesten Gestalt" (Berlin: Mittler, 1913), at 314. The lack of doctrine dealing with this issue since then also indicates that the law of naval warfare is no more distinct from the general law on State responsibility on this issue.

VI. Conclusion

This analysis has shown that the international law applicable to interferences in times of war is presently very uncertain and that the controversies of opinions significantly affect the degree of protection of neutral shipping. Even though the recent trend arguing by referring to the United Nations Charter, seems benevolent to maritime trade, a French ordinance of 1584 (!) shows that there is no uniform trend in public international towards better protection of maritime trade which has always found great attention in public international law. According to this ordinance, neutral property could only be condemned if the court ordered full compensation to the owners.[67] Presumably, private interests were not to suffer under conflicts between States under this ordinance.

Be that as it may, future naval conflicts might render the legal situation in naval warfare clearer, probably their only positive consequence and definitely not a reason to sanguinely await new international conflicts.

B. Interdictions authorized by the United Nations Security Council

After this brief elaboration upon the applicable law in cases of naval warfare, this study will now attempt to determine whether the law of naval warfare may also apply to cases where maritime interdictions have been authorized by the United Nations Security Council or whether the general Law of the Sea such as Art. 110, para. 3 LOSC would apply to such situations.

The difference might be quite substantial as far as it concerns compensation issues. If the interdiction measure was unlawful, both the law of naval warfare and the Law of the Sea would generally provide for the responsibility of the interfering State. However, since all Security Council Resolutions authorizing interdiction measures have not imposed any limits on such measures such as "reasonable suspicion",[68] and since the Security Council enjoys a wide margin of appreciation when imposing embargos,[69] an unlawful interference is very unlikely. Instead, all vessels in a certain area are usually indiscriminately subject to an embargo imposed by the Security Council.[70]

If the interdiction measure was lawful, but the cargo of the boarded vessel proves to be innocent, then only an application of Art. 110, para. 3 LOSC would

---

67 *Wheaton*, Henry, "Histoire des progrès du droit des gens en Europe depuis la paix de Westphalie jusqu'au congrès de Vienne" (Leipzig: Brockhaus, 1841), at 82.

68 The sole exception is Security Council Resolution 221 (1966): „Call upon the Government of the United Kingdom of Great Britain and Northern Ireland to prevent, by the use of force if necessary, the arrival at Beira of vessels *reasonably believed to be carrying oil destined for Southern Rhodesia*" (emphasis added).

69 *Ress*, Hans-Konrad, "Das Handelsembargo" (Berlin: Springer, 2000), at 393.

70 *Pagani*, Fabrizio, "Le misure di interdizione navale in relazione alle sanzioni adottate dall'ONU", 76 Rivista di diritto internazionale (1993), pp. 720 *et seq.*, at 753.

provide for the liability of the interfering State. As shown above, the status of the applicable law in times of war may be quite uncertain, but it is at least very questionable that a State would be liable for lawful interdiction measures in times of war.

Most of the embargos by the UN Security Council have not been imposed in the existence of an armed conflict between two or more States, but rather in situations of civil war. On the other hand, some of these conflicts led to the disintegration of the affected State, by which the whole conflict gained international characteristics.[71] The one exception in this regard represents the case of Iraq which had invaded Kuwait. The United States and other naval powers claimed collective self-defence as legal ground for their interdiction measures and the authorization in Resolution 665 (1991) probably did not modify the applicability of the rules of naval warfare in that conflict.[72] However, even the United States refrained from calling the conflict a war, did not declare war against Iraq and even avoided the term "blockade" because it could be interpreted as an act of war.[73]

Thus, a considerable uncertainty exists in international relations as to the applicable law to these new conflicts. One of the earliest authors to recognize this development was *Philip C. Jessup* who asked in 1954 "whether it would not be useful to break away from the old dichotomous approach, acknowledging in law as in fact that there is a third status intermediate between peace and war."[74] *Heintschel von Heinegg* argues that the law of naval warfare is generally applicable to such operations with the exception that the law of neutrality does not apply against operations under a mandate of the Security Council.[75]

Since an explicit codification of this intermediate status is missing, the relevant law may be derived from the Law of the Sea, the law governing the United Nations, customary international law and general principles of international law.

Art. 110, para. 1 LOSC stipulates that "*[e]xcept where acts of interference derive from powers conferred by treaty*, a warship which encounters on the high seas a foreign ship [...] is not justified in boarding it..." (emphasis added). In the case of interferences authorized by the Security Council, the United Nations Charter may well constitute such a treaty exemption to Art. 110, para. 1 LOSC.

---

71 *Bothe*, Michael, "Report of the Committee on Neutrality and Naval Warfare", in *ILA*, "Report of the Sixty-Seventh Conference" (1996), pp. 367 *et seq.*, at 369-370.

72 *Soons*, Alfred H.A., "Enforcing the economic embargo at sea", in *Gowlland-Debbas*, Vera (ed.), "United Nations Sanctions and International Law" (The Hague: Kluwer Law International, 2001), pp. 307 *et seq.*, at 313; *cf.* also *Robertson, Jr.*, H.B., "Interdiction of Iraqi Maritime Commerce in the 1990-1991 Persian Gulf Conflict", 22 ODIL (1991), pp. 289 *et seq.*, at 294-296.

73 *Morabito*, Robert E., "Maritime Interdiction: Evolution of a Strategy", 22 ODIL (1991), pp. 301 *et seq.*, at 307.

74 *Jessup*, Philip C., "Should International Law recognize an intermediate status between peace and war?", 48 AJIL (1954), pp. 98 *et seq.*, at 100. *Cf.* also *Friedmann*, Wolfgang, "The Changing Structure of International Law" (London: Stevens, 1964), at 271.

75 *Heintschel von Heinegg*, Wolff, "Friedliche Nutzung, Seekriegs- und Neutralitätsrecht", in *Graf Vitzthum*, Wolfgang (ed.), "Handbuch des Seerechts" (München: Beck, 2006), pp. 491 *et seq.*, at 596.

Under Chapter VII of the United Nations Charter, the Security Council may determine that a threat to international peace and security exists and may then decide the measures to be taken to restore international peace and security (Art. 39 UN Charter). These decisions are binding upon all States (Art. 25 UN Charter)[76] and may include the interruption of all maritime transport to a State (*cf.* Art. 41 UN Charter).[77] Thus, the law of the United Nations provides for an exemption to the rule expressed in Art. 110, para. 1 LOSC and it seems, *prima facie*, questionable whether Art. 110, para. 3 LOSC should be applied to interferences authorized by the Security Council.

All of the analyzed treaty regimes diverging from Art. 110, para. 1 LOSC contain own compensation provisions indicating the automatic applicability of Art. 110, para. 3 LOSC to them or another regulation of the compensation issue. Furthermore, the fact that Art. 110, para. 3 LOSC provides for liability for lawful conduct and for an entitlement of private entities is so atypical in public international law that an explicit reference seems necessary to guarantee its applicability to other treaty regimes.

The United Nations Charter does not explicitly provide for a compensation provision, but its Art. 50 at least stipulates that "[i]f preventive or enforcement measures against any state are taken by the Security Council, any other state, whether a Member of the United Nations or not, which finds itself confronted with special economic problems arising from the carrying out of those measures shall have the right to consult the Security Council with regard to a solution of those problems." The issue thus becomes whether the United Nations or the Security Council in particular is obliged to offer any assistance to States suffering from the embargo imposed upon a third State. Such an obligation would at least be comparable to a potential responsibility of the United Nations. The wording of the provision does not indicate any solution, but the drafting history of Art. 50 UN Charter is most meaningful. In the negotiations, Venezuela proposed that the Security Council should have the duty to adopt measures helping States which suffered under the consequences from an embargo imposed upon a third State.[78] However, this proposal did not find any success in the Third Committee of the Third Com-

---

76 Concerning the binding effect on non-member States see *Delbrück*, Jost, "Article 25", in *Simma*, Bruno (ed.), "The Charter of the United Nations" (Oxford: Oxford University Press, 1994), pp. 407 *et seq.*, at 414, para. 19; *Cot*, Jean-Pierre /*Pellet*, Alain, "La Charte des Nations Unies" (2nd ed., Paris: Economica, 1991), at 473.

77 It is a controversial issue whether authorizations for maritime interdiction are based on Art. 41 or Art. 42 UN Charter, see *Soons*, Alfred H.A., "Enforcing the economic embargo at sea", in *Gowlland-Debbas*, Vera (ed.), "United Nations Sanctions and International Law" (The Hague: Kluwer Law International, 2001), pp. 307 *et seq.*, at 314; *Scholz*, Oliver, "Die Durchsetzung von Zwangsmaßnahmen nach Art. 41 der Satzung der Vereinten Nationen, insbesondere mit militärischen Mitteln" (Frankfurt am Main: Lang, 1998), at 51-56 with further references.

78 Doc. 2 (FRENCH)/G/7(d)(1) (5 May 1946), "Observations du gouvernement du Venezuela sur les recommandations adoptées à la Conférence de Dumbarton Oaks", at 22, reprinted in 4 Documents de la Conférence des Nations Unies sur l'Organisation Internationale, Vol. 4 (1945), pp. 242 *et seq.*, at 263.

mission negotiating the United Nations Charter.[79] Therefore, the Security Council is not obliged to adopt any specific measures to help these affected States. Likewise, these States do not have any right under Art. 50 to claim compensation for damages caused by an embargo imposed by the Security Council.[80] Quite to the contrary, the provision awards "political discretion" to the Security Council.[81] Hence, one may argue that the drafters of the United Nations Charter decided that States other than the target State (and their citizens) which suffer economic hardship due to the embargo do not have any right to claim compensation from the United Nations and one may even imply that, due to the conclusive regulation in Art. 50 UN Charter, affected States may also not claim compensation from States enforcing the embargo if they remain within the limits of the Security Council resolution authorizing the enforcement measures. Such damages must generally be borne by the affected States and their nationals. At the discretion of the Security Council, such damages may nevertheless be alleviated. The applicability of Art. 110, para. 3 LOSC to measures enforcing an embargo of the Security Council would contradict this decision of the UN Charter and therefore must be denied. Finally, assistance rendered under Art. 50 UN Charter will most likely be limited to some kind of humanitarian aid to alleviate suffering and will probably not be delivered in the form of full monetary compensation.[82] In practice, the Security Council merely calls upon the UN member States to support the States affected by the embargo.[83]

This inapplicability of Art. 110, para. 3 LOSC to interdictions under the authority of the Security Council is confirmed by State practice, particularly in the case of the Iraq conflict. In 1990, the (unsuccessful) official protests by Iraq have

---

79 *Eisemann*, Pierre Michel, "Article 50", in *Cot*, Jean-Pierre *et al.* (eds.), "La Charte des Nations Unies" (2nd ed., Paris: Economica, 1991), pp. 763 *et seq.*, at 764.

80 *Bryde*, Brun-Otto/*Reinisch*, August, "Article 50", in *Simma*, Bruno (ed.), "The Charter of the United Nations", Vol. 1 (2nd ed., München: Beck, 2002), pp. 784 *et seq.*, at 785; *Eisemann*, Pierre Michel, "Article 50", in *Cot*, Jean-Pierre *et al.* (eds.), "La Charte des Nations Unies" (2nd ed., Paris: Economica, 1991), pp. 763 *et seq.*, at 765; *Martin-Bidou*, Pascale, "Les mesures d'embargo prises à l'encontre de la Yougoslavie", 39 Annaire Français de Droit International (1993), pp. 262 *et seq.*, at 281; *Verhoeven*, Joe, "Etats alliés ou nations unies ? L'O.N.U. face au conflit entre l'Irak et le Koweït", 36 Annaire Français de Droit International (1990), pp. 145 *et seq.*, at 167-168; *Tavernier*, Paul, "L'année des Nations Unies", 37 Annaire Français de Droit International (1991), pp. 617 *et seq.*, at 635.

81 *Delbrück*, Jost, "International Economic Sanctions and Third States", 30 AVR (1992), pp. 86 *et seq.*, at 97.

82 In the case of Southern Rhodesia, the United States and the United Kingdom provided an airlift to Zambia for the transport of petroleum products. *Gowlland-Debbas*, Vera, "Collective responses to illegal acts in international law" (Dordrecht: Nijhoff, 1990), at 635.

83 See, *e.g., UN* Doc. S/26056 (8 July 1993), "Letter from the President of the Security Council addressed to the Secretary-General"; *UN* Doc. S/26282 (10 August 1993), "Letter from the President of the Security Council addressed to the Secretary-General".

always been against the lawfulness of the sanctions, none of these States or a private entity has posted a claim under Art. 110, para. 3 LOSC.[84]

Furthermore, the Italian legislator adopted a law concerning the involvement of Italian forces in the enforcement of sanctions against Yugoslavia. This legislation explicitly provided that no damage is owed for the measures adopted by competent authorities executing United Nations Resolutions in matters concerning the embargo against States of the Former Yugoslavia.[85]

Moreover, International Organizations have always refused to bear any responsibility for harmful acts which do not constitute a breach of international law[86] and thus do not seem inclined toward an applicability of Art. 110, para. 3 LOSC to their enforcement of embargos.

Finally, the rationale behind Art. 110, para. 3 LOSC does not seem to cope with the critical situations in which an embargo is authorized by the Security Council. While Art. 110, para. 3 LOSC is meant to protect maritime transport, an embargo, though primarily targeting one particular State, always significantly affects transport business. An effective enforcement of the embargo requires measures against all transport companies in the region whether supporting the target State or not. Furthermore, with the interconnectivity of modern economies, not only the target State, but innocent States as well will often suffer losses due to an embargo imposed upon their neighbours.[87]

Therefore, one needs to follow that Art. 110, para. 3 LOSC or any of the other compensation provisions analysed in this study are not applicable to the enforcement of embargoes under a mandate of the United Nations Security Council.

---

84 *UN* Doc. S/21792 (20 September 1990), "Letter from the Permanent Representative of Iraq to the United Nations addressed to the Secretary-General"; *UN* Doc. S/21861 (19 October 1990), "Letter from the Chargé d'Affaires A.I. of the Permanent Mission of Iraq to the United Nations addressed to the Secretary-General".

85 „Nessun indennizzo è dovuto per i provvedimenti adottati dalle autorità competenti in esecuzione dell risoluzioni dell'ONU, dei regolamenti comunitari e delle decisioni della CECA in material di embargo nei confronti dei Paesi della ex-Iugoslavia". Art. 7, para. 3, d.l. 15 May 1993 n. 144, cited by *Pagani*, Fabrizio, "Le misure di interdizione navale in relazione alle sanzioni adottate dall'ONU", 76 Rivista di diritto internazionale (1993), pp. 720 *et seq.*, at 753.

86 *Sands*, Philippe/*Klein*, Pierre, "Bowett's Law of International Institutions" (London: Sweet & Maxwell, 2001), at 520; *Bowett*, Derek William, "United Nations Forces – A Legal Study of United Nations Practice" (London: Stevens, 1964), at 247; *Salmon*, Jean, "Les accords Spaak-U Thant du 20 février 1965", 11 AFDI (1965), pp. 481 *et seq.*; *UN* Doc. A/51/389 (20 September 1996), "Report on the administrative and budgetary aspects of the financing of the United Nations peacekeeping operations", at para. 6.

87 *Cf. UN* Doc. S/21571 (20 August 1990), "Letter from the Permanent Representative of Jordan to the United Nations addressed to the Secretary-General".

Chapter V: Conclusions and outlook

A. Major conclusions

In spite of their considerable significance in order to maintain a reasonable balance between a great number of security concerns and the freedom of navigation, the compensation provisions analysed in this study have not played a major role in international dispute settlement. Considering the increasing number of interdiction measures, it seems doubtful whether this lack of application is due to the absence of abusive interferences.

Public international law, in particular many international conventions dealing with the Law of the Sea, provides for an extensive protection of maritime transport. Grounds for interferences may have grown in numbers due to rather new safety concerns such as terrorism or drug smuggling. However, each international convention which authorizes interferences with navigation includes a compensation provision as an important safeguard for maritime transport. As this study has shown, some of these provisions differ in favour of maritime transport from the general law on State responsibility in two respects. First, Arts. 110, para. 3 and 111, para. 8 LOSC, Art. 9, para. 2 Migrant Smuggling Protocol and Art. 8bis, para. 10, lit. b of the 2005 SUA Protocol entitle private entities to claim compensation from the interfering State. Art. 21, para. 18 Fish Stocks Agreement may have a similar meaning in this regard. This does not necessarily lead to a potential liability of the flag State vis-à-vis the owner of ships under its flag State since the freedom of navigation continues to be an exclusive right of the flag State. Since private entities generally do not have access to international tribunals in order to claim their rights, they nevertheless primarily still need to rely on domestic courts which apply provisions of public international law. The applicability of these provisions will thus depend on the constitutional framework by which the competent domestic court is bound. Also, the entitlement of private entities necessarily leads to an obligation of the flag State (or State or nationality) to forward any compensation received after it exercised flag State (or diplomatic) protection.

Secondly, Art. 110, para. 3 LOSC, Art. 9, para. 2 Migrant Smuggling Protocol and Art. 8bis, para. 10, lit. b of the 2005 SUA Protocol all provide for liability for lawful conduct. The claimant thus does not need to show that the interfering State has committed an internationally wrongful act as in the general law on State responsibility. As in other cases where public international law provides for liability for lawful conduct, the provisions only oblige the liable entity to compensate the damage suffered by the claimant and thereby exclude other consequences of State responsibility such as satisfaction.

As international relations have become more complex, so have maritime interdictions which nowadays often involve a multitude of State participating in an interference with navigation. Even though hardly any case law or State practice could be obtained, it may be presumed that in the absence of special provisions in international conventions, the principles on attribution and participation of the general law on State responsibility will apply.

As far as it concerns the extent of responsibility, the impact of the judgment of the International Tribunal for the Law of the Sea in the *M/V Saiga (No. 2)* case on the Law of the Sea has been invaluable, but not uncontroversial. The Tribunal seems to have found no substantial difference between Art. 111, para. 8 LOSC and the general law on State responsibility. It nevertheless provided a welcome contribution to the law on the consequences of detention and mistreatment of crew members, an area where outdated arbitral decisions of the 19th and the early 20th century had become irrelevant because of the development of human rights.

Probably bearing in mind these important protections to maritime transport in international conventions, the United States have focused their efforts to be granted authorizations for interdiction measures on bilateral agreements and on the loose framework of the Proliferation Security Initiative. While in some agreements, the United States have been able to significantly limit their own liability by referring to the restricted United States law on State liability, some flag States succeeded in stipulating important references to Art. 110, para. 3 LOSC and thereby widened the scope of application of this important compensation provision.

Due to a considerable degree of imprecision concerning the applicable rules in situations of naval warfare and other international conflicts at sea, the last chapter of this study needed to limit itself to comparing different potential liability regimes depending on the applicable (primary) rules. Hopefully, public international law will find some clarification in this respect in the near future either by decisions of international tribunals, by consistent and uniform State practice or by an international convention.

Finally, this study clarified that if States or regional organization are enforcing an embargo under the mandate of the United Nations Security Council, the analyzed compensation provisions, in particular Art. 110, para. 3 LOSC, are not applicable. Instead, affected flag State and private entities need to rely on the general law on State responsibility and on diplomatic protection.

B. Outlook to the future of the liability regime concerning interferences with navigation on the high seas

The great diversity among compensation provisions dealing with interferences on the high seas is evidence of a certain lack of uniformity. Depending on the ground for the interference, the shipowner either may have own claims against his flag State or other States or needs to depend on his flag State for diplomatic protection. In some cases, the shipowner will profit from beneficial rules regarding liability for lawful conduct, while in other cases, he needs to rely on the rules of the general law on State responsibility. This fragmentation of rules on compensation evidently does not find any convincing explanation in the respective grounds for the interference and seems to represent the result of difficult negotiations leading to the respective international convention. The diversity of compensation provisions thus constitutes an unfortunate situation, but a reality of international law an international lawyer needs to adapt to. Since the different compensation provisions can hardly be interpreted in a uniform way, one can only hope that in the future, delegations on international conferences will "copy & paste" one of the compensation provisions and thereby provide for some more uniform rules.

One might also question whether the responsibility imposed upon interfering States represents an adequate balance between security concerns and freedom of navigation. One could argue that shipping companies are responsible that maritime transport does not create any security risks. Furthermore, one might state that these companies could, by severe security checks, minimize the risks involved with maritime transport. Thus, one might follow that shipping companies at least need to bear a part of the costs caused by maritime interdictions on the high seas.

However, there are considerable counter-arguments against such partial risk-bearing by the maritime industry. First, one must consider that all cases which provide for liability of the interfering State require innocent shipping companies which do not carry any illicit cargo and are not involved in the commission of universal crimes. It would seem unreasonable to hold these companies, which might have undertaken every effort to minimize risks to international security, responsible for a part of the damage caused by the interference. Secondly, the interfering State will in most cases be a State with a special interest in risk minimization, *e.g.*, guarding its own population against terrorist attacks or preventing illicit drugs from entering its territory. Thus, it seems equitable if these States then also are responsible when the pursuit of their own interests causes damage to innocent third parties. Furthermore, one must also take into consideration that shipping companies, shipowners and other private actors in maritime trade already carry a heavy financial burden caused security regimes such as the ISPS code (see *supra*).

Therefore, the liability regime established by some compensation provisions such as Art. 110, para. 3 LOSC or, more recently, Art. 8bis, para. 10, lit. b of the 2005 SUA Protocol provides for a reasonable balance between security concerns and the interests of the maritime industry and represents an equitable result of negotiations between States concerned with their national security and States with great interests in the maritime industry.

Bilateral agreements between interfering and flag States often do not follow this reasonable approach, but rather unilaterally favour the interfering State. One can only hope that in future, flag States will be able to include references to provisions such as Art. 110, para. 3 LOSC in these agreement. Since their partners (the potential interfering States) will most often be States parties to either the Convention on the High Seas or the Law of the Sea Convention, they could easily remind them of the principles they have devoted themselves to in Art. 22, para. 3 CHS and Art. 110, para. 3 LOSC.

Finally, one can only stress that thus far the compensation provisions of multilateral conventions have played a marginal role in the Law of the Sea. It may be presumed that private entities have not yet become aware of their rights under these provisions and, overwhelmed by the naval power of some States, have tacitly accepted the increasing numbers of interdictions on the high seas. Hopefully, this study has contributed to an increasing awareness about these provisions and to a higher frequency of claims before both international and domestic tribunals leading eventually to a greater rule of both law and freedom on the high seas.

Annex 1: Relevant compensation provisions

Art. 110, para. 3 LOSC

"If the suspicions prove to be unfounded, and provided that the ship boarded has not committed any act justifying them, it shall be compensated for any loss or damage that may have been sustained."

Art. 106 LOSC

"Where the seizure of a ship or aircraft on suspicion of piracy has been effected without adequate grounds, the State making the seizure shall be liable to the State the nationality of which is possessed by the ship or aircraft for any loss or damage caused by the seizure."

Art. 111, para. 8 LOSC

"Where a ship has been stopped or arrested outside the territorial sea in circumstances which do not justify the exercise of the right of hot pursuit, it shall be compensated for any loss or damage that may have been thereby sustained."

Art. VI of the 1969 Intervention Convention:

"Any Party which has taken measures in contravention of the provisions of the present Convention causing damage to others, shall be obliged to pay compensation to the extent of the damage caused by measures which exceed those reasonably necessary to achieve the end mentioned in Article I."

Art. 21, para. 18 of the 1995 Straddling Fish Stocks Agreement

"States shall be liable for damage or loss attributable to them arising from action taken pursuant to this article when such action is unlawful or exceeds that reasonably required in the light of available information to implement the provisions of this article."

Art. 9, para. 2 of the 2000 Migrant Smuggling Protocol

"Where the grounds for measures taken pursuant to article 8 of this Protocol prove to be unfounded, the vessel shall be compensated for any loss or damage that may have been sustained, provided that the vessel has not committed any act justifying the measures taken."

Art. 8bis, para. 10, lit. b of the 2005 Protocol to the SUA Convention

"Provided that authorization to board by a flag State shall not per se give rise to its liability, States Parties shall be liable for any damage, harm or loss attributable to them arising from measures taken pursuant to this article when: (i) the grounds for such measures prove to be unfounded, provided that the ship has not committed any act justifying the measures taken; or (ii) such measures are unlawful or exceed that reasonably required in light of available information to implement the provisions of this article. States Parties shall provide effective recourse in respect of such damage, harm or loss."

Annex 2: Bibliography

Abass, Ademola, "Consent Precluding State Responsibility: A critical analysis", 53 International and Comparative Law Quarterly (2004), pp. 211 *et seq.*

Ago, Roberto, "Le délit international", 68 Recueil des Cours (1939-II), pp. 417 *et seq.*

Akehurst, Michael B., "International Liability for injurious consequences arising out of acts not prohibited by international law", 16 Netherlands Yearbook of International Law (1985), pp. 3 *et seq.*

Alexander, Lewis M., "The Changing Nature of the High Seas", in *Crickard*, Frew W. *et al.* (eds.), "Multinational Naval Cooperation and Foreign Policy into the 21st century" (Aldershot: Ashgate, 1998), pp. 30 *et seq.*

de Almeida Nascimento, Adelaida, "El Control de Buques Mercantes en Alta Mar por Parte de los Efectivos de la Armada Española que Participan en la Operación Libertad Duradera: El Episodio del So Sane", 55 Revista española de derecho internacional (2003), pp. 268 *et seq.*

Amerasinghe, Chittharanjan F., "The Essence of the Structure of International Responsibility", in *Ragazzi*, Maurizio (ed.), "International Responsibility Today – Essays in Memory of Oscar Schachter" (Leiden: Nijhoff, 2005), pp. 3 *et seq.*

Ammann, Ulrich, "Der Schutz ausländischer Privatinvestitionen in Entwicklungsländern" (Zürich: Polygraphischer Verlag, 1967)

Anderson, Andrew W., "In the Wake of the DAUNTLESS: The Background and Development of Maritime Interdictions Operations", in *Clingan, Jr.*, Thomas A. (ed.), "The Law of the Sea: What Lies Ahead?, Proceedings of the 20th Annual Conference of the Law of the Sea Institute July 21-24" (Honolulu: University of Hawaii, 1988), pp. 15 *et seq.*

Anzilotti, Dionisio, "Teoria generale della responsabilitá dello stato nel diritto internazionale", Vol. 1 (1902)

Asariotis, Regina, "Implementation of the ISPS Code: an overview of recent developments", 11 Journal of International Maritime Law (2005), pp. 266 *et seq.*

Astley, J./*Schmitt*, M.N., "The Law of the Sea and Naval Operations", 42 Air Force Law Review (1997), pp. 119 *et seq.*

Aust, Anthony, "Modern Treaty Law and Practice" (Cambridge: Cambridge University Press, 2000)

von Bar, "Theorie und Praxis des Internationalen Privatrechts", Vol. 2 (Hannover: Hahn, 1899)

Barry, Ian Patrick, "The right of visit, search and seizure of foreign flagged vessels on the High Seas pursuant to customary international law: A defense of the proliferation security initiative", 33 Hofstra Law Review (2004/2005), pp. 299 *et seq.*

Beck, Michael E., "The Promise and Limits of the PSI", The Monitor (Center for Int'l Trade and Security), Vol. 10, No. 1 (Spring 2004), p. 16.

Bederman, David J., "Lump Sum Agreements and Diplomatic Protection", in *International Law Association*, "Report of the Seventieth Conference" (2002), pp. 230 *et seq.*

Bellayer-Roille, Alexandra, "L'arrêt du Tribunal international du droit de la mer du 1er juillet 1999 – Affaire du navire "Saiga" N° 2", 19 Annuaire de droit maritime et océanique (2001), pp. 111 *et seq.*

Bemm, Wilfrid/*Lindemann*, Dierk, "Seemannsgesetz" (4th ed., Uelzen: Becker, 1999)

Berger, Lee F., "State practice evidence of the humanitarian intervention doctrine: The ECOWAS Intervention in Sierra Leone", 11 Indiana International and Comparative Law Review (2001), pp. 605 *et seq.*

Bergin, Anthony, "The Proliferation Security Initiative – Implications for the Indian Ocean", 20 International Journal of Marine and Coastal Law (2005), pp. 85 *et seq.*

Bergstrand, S.J., "Buy the flag – Developments in the Open Registry Debate" (London: Polytechnic of Central London, 1983)

Bernhardt, Rudolf, "Just Satisfaction under the European Convention on Human Rights", in *Ragazzi*, Maurizio (ed.), "International Responsibility Today – Essays in Memory of Oscar Schachter" (Leiden: Nijhoff, 2005), pp. 243 *et seq.*

Bin Cheng, "General Principles of Law as applied by International Courts and Tribunals" (London: Stevens, 1953)

Bin Cheng, "The Rationale of Compensation for Expropriation", 44 Transactions of the Grotius Society (1958/1959), pp. 267 *et seq.*

Bindschedler, Rudolf L., "La protection de la propriété en droit international public", 90 Recueil des Cours (1956-II), pp. 173 *et seq.*

Böckstiegel, Karl-Heinz, "Die allgemeinen Grundsätze des Völkerrechts über Eigentumsentziehung" (Berlin: De Gruyter, 1963)

Bollecker-Stern, Brigitte, "Le prejudice dans la théorie de la responsabilité internationale" (Paris: Pedone, 1973)

Borchard, Edwin Montefiore, "Diplomatic Protection of Citizens Abroad" (New York, 1915)

Bothe, Michael, "Les limites des pouvoirs du Conseil de securité", in *Dupuy*, René-Jean (ed.), "The Development of the Role of the Security Council" (Dordrecht: Nijhoff, 1993), pp. 67 *et seq.*

Bothe, Michael, "Report of the Committee on Neutrality and Naval Warfare", in *International Law Association*, "Report of the Sixty-Seventh Conference" (1996), pp. 367 *et seq.*

Bouvé, Clement L., "Russia's liability in tort for Persia's breach of contract", 6 American Journal of International Law (1912), pp. 389 *et seq.*

Bowett, Derek William, "Self-defence in international law" (Manchester: Manchester University Press, 1958)

Bowett, Derek William, "United Nations Forces – A Legal Study of United Nations Practice" (London: Stevens, 1964)

Boyle, Alan E., "State Responsibility and International Liability for injurious consequences of acts not prohibited by international law: A necessary distinction?", in *Provost*, René (ed.), "State Responsibility in International Law" (Aldershot: Ashgate, 2002), pp. 141 *et seq.*

Boyle, Alan E., "Further Development of the Law of the Sea Convention: Mechanisms for Change", 54 International and Comparative Law Quarterly (2005), pp. 563 *et seq.*

Briggs, Herbert W., "The travaux préparatoires of the Vienna Convention on the Law of Treaties", 65 American Journal of International Law (1971), pp. 705 *et seq.*

Brown, John Prather, "Toward an Economic Theory of Liability", 2 The Journal of Legal Studies (1973)

Brown Weiss, Edith, "Invoking State Responsibility in the Twenty-First Century", 96 American Journal of International Law (2002), 798 *et seq.*

Brownlie, Ian, "International law and the use of force by states" (Oxford: Clarendon Press, 1963)

Brownlie, Ian, "Principles of Public International Law" (3rd ed., Oxford: Clarendon, 1979)

Brownlie, Ian, "State Responsiblity" (Oxford: Clarendon Press, 1983)

Brownlie, Ian, "Principles of Public International Law" (6th ed., Oxford: Oxford University Press, 2003)

Brownlie, Ian, "The Responsibility of States for the Acts of International Organizations", in *Ragazzi*, Maurizio (ed.), "International Responsibility Today – Essays in Memory of Oscar Schachter" (Leiden: Nijhoff, 2005), pp. 355 *et seq*.

Bryde, Brun-Otto/*Reinisch*, August, "Article 50", in *Simma*, Bruno (ed.), "The Charter of the United Nations", Vol. 1 (2nd ed., München: Beck, 2002), pp. 784 *et seq*.

de Burgh, W., "The Elements of Maritime International Law" (1868)

Byers, Michael, "Policing the High Seas: The Proliferation Security Initiative", 98 American Journal of International Law (2004), pp. 526 *et seq*.

van Bynkershoek, Cornelius, "Quaestionum Iuris Publici Libri Duo", Vol. I (1737).

Cantillon de Tramont, Paul, "De la nationalité des navires" (Montauban, 1907)

Caron, David D., "The ILC Articles on State Responsibility, the Paradoxical Relationship between Form and Authority", 96 American Journal of International Law (2002), pp. 857 *et seq*.

Cavaré, Louis, "Le droit international public positif", Vol. 2, (Paris: Pedone, 1962)

Churchill, Robin R./*Lowe*, Alan Vaughan: "The Law of the Sea" (3rd ed., Manchester: Juris Publications, 1999)

Clayton, Richard/*Tomlinson*, Hugh, "The Law of Human Rights", Vol. 1 (Oxford: Oxford University Press, 2000)

Colombos, Constantin John, "Internationales Seerecht" (München: Beck, 1963)

Colombos, Constantin John, "The International Law of the Sea" (6th ed., London: Longman, 1967)

Cooter, Robert/*Ulen*, Thomas, "Law and Economics" (4th ed., Boston: Pearson Addison-Wesley, 2004)

Cot, Jean-Pierre Cot/*Pellet*, Alain, "La Charte des Nations Unies" (2nd ed., Paris: Economica, 1991)

Cottereau, Gilles, "Système juridique et notion de responsabilité", in *Société française de Droit international* (ed.), "La responsabilité dans le système international" (Paris: Pedone, 1991), pp. 1 *et seq*.

Coulter, Daniel Y./*Goldman*, Alan, "Global Shipping Trends and Implications for Navies", in *Crickard*, Fred W. *et al.* (eds.), "Multinational naval cooperation and foreign policy into the 21st century" (Aldershot: Ashgate, 1998), pp. 46 *et seq*.

Craig, Paul & *de Búrca*, Graínne, "EU Law: Text Cases and Materials" (3rd ed., Oxford, Oxford University Press, 2003)

Crawford, James, "The International Law Commission's Articles on State Responsibility" (Cambridge: Cambridge University Press, 2002)

Crawford, James/ *Olleson*, Simon, "The Nature and Forms of International Responsibility", in *Evans*, Malcolm D. (ed.), "International Law" (2003), pp. 455 *et seq.*

Cremer, H.C., "Art. 17 EUV", in *Calliess*, Christian *et al.* (eds.), "Kommentar des Vertrages über die Europäische Union und des Vertrages zur Gründung der Europäischen Gemeinschaft" (2nd ed., Neuwied: Luchterhand, 2002), pp. 186 *et seq.*

Crowley, Jr., John E., "U.S. Maritime Law Enforcement Practices", in *Nordquist*, Myron H. *et al.* (eds.), "Recent Decelopments in the Law of the Sea and China" (Leiden: Nijhoff, 2006), pp. 251 *et seq.*

Cushman, John H., "Command and Control in the Coalition", 117 Naval Institute Proceedings (May 1991), pp. 74 *et seq.*

de Cussy, Ferdinand, "Phases et Causes Célèbres du Droit Maritime des Nations", Vol. 1 (Leipzig: Bockhaus, 1856)

Dahm, Georg/*Delbrück*, Jost/*Wolfrum*, Rüdiger, "Völkerrecht", Vol. 1, Part 2 (2nd ed., Berlin: de Gruyter, 2002)

Dahm, Georg/*Delbrück*, Jost/*Wolfrum*, Rüdiger, "Völkerrecht", Vol. 1, Part 3 (2nd ed., Berlin: de Gruyter, 2002)

Daillier, Patrick/*Pellet*, Alain, "Droit international public" (7th ed., Paris: L.G.D.J., 2002)

Davidson, Scott, "Dangerous Waters: Combating Maritime Piracy in Asia", 9 Asian Yearbook of International Law (2004), pp. 3 *et seq.*

Degan, Vladimir Duro, "L'interprétation des accords en droit international" (The Hague: Nijhoff, 1963)

Delbez, Louis, "Les principes généraux du Droit international public" (3rd ed., Paris: Pichon et Durand-Auzias, 1964)

Delbrück, Jost, "International Economic Sanctions and Third States", 30 Archiv des Völkerrechts (1992), pp. 86 *et seq.*

Delbrück, Jost, "Article 25", in *Simma*, Bruno (ed.), "The Charter of the United Nations" (Oxford: Oxford University Press, 1994), pp. 407 *et seq.*

Delbrück, Jost, "Proportionality", in *Bernhardt*, Rudolf (ed.), "Encyclopedia of Public International Law", Vol. 3 (Amsterdam: North-Holland, 1997), pp. 1140 *et seq.*

Diaz, Leticia/*Dubner*, Barry Hart, "On the Problem of Utilizing Unilateral Action to Prevent Acts of Sea Piracy and Terrorism: A Proactive Approach to the Evolution of International Law", 32 Syracuse Journal of International Law and Commerce (2004), pp. 1 *et seq.*

Dickinson, Edwin D., "Treaties for the Prevention of Smuggling", 20 American Journal of International Law (1926), pp. 340 *et seq.*

Dickinson, Edwin D., "Les traités américains concernant les spiritueux", 7 Révue de droit international et de législation comparée (1926), pp. 371 *et seq.*

Dinstein, Yoram, "War, aggression and self-defence" (3rd ed., Cambridge: Cambridge University Press, 2002)

Dolzer, Rudolf, "Diplomatic Protection of Foreign Nationals", in *Bernhardt*, Rudolf (ed.), "Encyclopedia of Public International Law", Vol. 1 (Amsterdam: North-Holland, 1992), pp. 1067 *et seq.*

Dominicé, Christian, "Droit international – Observations sur les droits de l'état victime d'un fait internationalement illicite", Vol. 2 (Paris: Pedone, 1982)

Dominicé, Christian, "The International Responsibility of the United Nations for Injuries Resulting from Non-Military Enforcement Measures", in *Ragazzi*, Maurizio (ed.), "International Responsibility Today – Essays in Memory of Oscar Schachter" (Leiden: Nijhoff, 2005), pp. 363 *et seq.*

Domke, Martin, "Foreign Nationalizations – Some Aspects of Contemporary International Law", 55 American Journal of International Law (1961), pp. 585 *et seq.*

Doswald-Beck, Louise, "The San Remo Manual on International Law applicable to Armed Conflicts at Sea", 89 American Journal of International Law (1995), pp. 192 *et seq.*

Doswald-Beck, Louise (ed.), "San Remo Manual on International Law Applicable to Armed Conflicts at Sea" (Cambridge: Cambridge University Press, 1995)

Duff, John A., "A Note on the United States and the Law of the Sea: Looking Back and Moving Forward", 35 Ocean Development and International Law (2004), pp. 195 *et seq.*

Dupuy, Pierre-Marie, "La responsibilité internationale des États pour les dommages d'originie technologique et industrielle" (Paris: Pedone, 1976)

Dupuy, Pierre-Marie, "Le fait générateur de la responsabilité internationale des États", 188 Recueil des Cours (1984-V), pp. 9 *et seq.*

Dupuy, Pierre-Marie, "Responsabilité et légalité", in *Société française pour le droit international* (ed.), "La responsabilité dans le système international" (Paris: Pedone, 1990), pp. 263 *et seq.*

Dupuy, René-Jean / *Vignes*, Daniel, "Traité du nouveau droit de la mer" (Paris: Economica, 1985)

Dalton, Harvey, "Comments on national security concerns", in *van Dyke*, Jon M. *et al.* (eds.), "International Navigation – Rocks and Shoals ahead?" (Honolulu: University of Hawaii, 1988), pp. 373 *et seq.*

Eadie, Edward N., "Relevance of International Criminal Law to Piracy in Asian Waters", Maritime Studies (May/June 2004), pp. 21 *et seq.*

Eagleton, Clyde, "The responsibility of states in international law" (New York City: New York University Press, 1924)

Eberle, Sir James, "Global Maritime Security: What does it mean?", in Crickard, Fred W. *et al.* (eds.), "Multinational naval cooperation and foreign policy into the 21st century" (Aldershot: Ashgate, 1998), pp. 21 *et seq.*

Eisemann, Pierre Michel, "Article 50", in *Cot*, Jean-Pierre et al. (eds.), "La Charte des Nations Unies" (2nd ed., Paris: Economica, 1991), pp. 763 *et seq.*

Elias, Taslim Olawale, "The Modern Law of Treaties" (Dobbs Ferry: Oceana Publications, 1974)

Fatouros, Arghyris A., "Legal Security for International Investment", in *Friedmann*, Wolfgang G. *et al.* (eds.), "Legal Aspects of Foreign Investment" (Boston: Little Brown, 1959), pp. 699 *et seq.*

Fauchille, Paul, "Traité de droit international public", Vol I, part II (Paris: Rousseau, 1925)

Fauteux, Paul, "L'initiative juridique canadienne sur la pêche en haute mer", 31 Canadian Yearbook of International Law (1993), pp. 33 *et seq.*

Fernandez, Lovell, "Reparation for Human Rights Violations Committed by the Apartheid Regime in South Africa", in *Randelzhofer*, Albrecht *et al.* (eds.), "State Responsibility and the Individual: Reparation in Instances of Grave Violations of Human Rights" (The Hague: Nijhoff, 1999), pp. 173 *et seq.*

de Ferron, Olivier, "Le droit international de la mer", Vol. 1 (Geneva: Droz, 1958)

Ficken, Ivan W., "The 1935 Anti-Smuggling Act Applied to Hovering Narcotics Smugglers beyond the Contiguous Zone: An Assessment under International Law", 29 University of Miami Law Review (1974-1975), pp. 700 *et seq.*

Fitzmaurice, Gerald, "The case of the I'm Alone", 17 British Yearbook of International Law (1936), pp. 82 *et seq.*

Fitzmaurice, Gerald, "The Law and Procedure of the International Court of Justice 1951-4: Treaty Interpretation and Other Treaty Points", 33 British Yearbook of International Law(1957), pp. 203 *et seq.*

Fitzmaurice, Malgosia, "The practical working of the Law of Treaties", in *Evans*, Malcolm D. (ed.), "International Law" (2003), pp. 173 *et seq.*

Friedheim, Robert L. "Negotiating the New Ocean Regime" (Columbia: University of South Carolina Press, 1993)

Friedmann, Wolfgang, "The Changing Structure of International Law" (London: Stevens, 1964)

Fulton, Thomas Wemyss, "The Sovereignty of the Sea" (Edinburgh: Blackwood, 1911)

Gaja, Giorgio, "Droits des Etats et droits des individus dans le cadre de la protection diplomatique", in *Flauss*, Jean-François (ed.), "La Protection Diplomatique" (Bruxelles: Nemesis, 2003), pp. 63 *et seq.*

García Amador, F. V., "State Responsibility – Some New Problems", 94 Recueil des Cours (1958-II), pp. 421 *et seq.*

Garcia-Arias, Luis, "La doctrine des 'clean hands' en droit international public", 30 Annuaire des anciens Auditeurs de l'Académie de droit international (1960), pp. 14 *et seq.*

Gardam, Judith Gail, "Proportionality and Force in International Law", 87 American Journal of International Law (1993), pp. 391 *et seq.*

Geck, Wilhelm Karl, "*Diplomatic Protection*", in *Bernhardt*, Rudolf (ed.), "Encyclopedia of Public International Law", Vol. 1 (Amsterdam: North-Holland, 1992), pp. 1045 *et seq.*

Geiß, Robin, "Non-State Actors: Their Role and Impact on the Fragmentation of International Law", in *Zimmermann*, Andreas *et al.* (eds.), "Unity and Diversity in International Law" (Berlin: Duncker & Humblot, 2006), pp. 303 *et seq.*

Genet, Raoul, "Précis de droit maritime pour le temps de guerre", Vol. 1 (Paris: Marchal & Billard, 1939)

Gerteiser, Kristina, "Die Sicherheits- und Verteidigungspolitik der Europäischen Union" (Frankfurt am Main: Lang, 2002)

Gidel, Gilbert, "Le droit international de la mer", Vol. 1 (Paris-Châteauroux: Mellottée, 1932)

Gilmore, William C., "Narcotics Interdiction at Sea: UK-US Cooperation", 13 Marine Policy (1989), pp. 218 *et seq.*

Gilmore, William C., "Drug Trafficking at Sea: The Case of R. v. Charrington and Others", 49 International and Comparative Law Quarterly (2000), pp. 477 *et seq.*

Gioia, Andrea/*Ronzitti*, Natalino, "The Law of Neutrality: Third States' Commercial Rights and Duties", in *Dekker*, Ige F. *et al.* (eds.), "The Gulf War of 1980-1988" (Dordrecht: Nijhoff, 1992), pp. 221 *et seq.*

von Glahn, Gerhard, "Law Among Nations" (New York: MacMillan, 1992)

Gotanda, J.Y., "Supplemental Damages in Private International Law" (1998)

Gowlland-Debbas, Vera, "Collective responses to illegal acts in international law" (Dordrecht: Nijhoff, 1990)

Goy, Raymond, "Le régime international du passager clandestine", 6 Annuaire du droit de la mer (2001), pp. 167 *et seq.*

Goy, Raymond, "Le régime international des migrants illicites par voie de mer", 7 Annuaire du droit de la mer (2002), pp. 249 *et seq.*

Graefrath, Bernhard, "Responsibility and Damage Caused: relations between responsibility and damages", 185 Recueil des Cours (1984-II), pp. 95 *et seq.*

Greig, D.W., "International Law" (2nd ed., London: Butterworth, 1976)

Grotius, Hugo, "The Freedom of the Seas or the Right which belongs to the Dutch to take part in the East Indian Trade" (Translated with a revision of the Latin text of 1633 by Ralph van Deman Magoffin) (New York: Oxford University Press, 1916)

Gureev, S.A., "Jurisdiktion des Flaggenstaats auf Hoher See", in *Akademie der Wissenschaften der UdSSR* (ed.), "Modernes Seevölkerrecht" (translated by *Rauch*, Baden-Baden: Nomos, 1978), pp. 171 *et seq.*

de Guttry, Andrea, "Commentary", in *id. et al.* (eds.), "The Iran-Iraq War (1980-1988) and the Law of Naval Warfare" (Cambridge: Grotius, 1993), pp. 419 *et seq.*

Hackett, Frank Warren, "Reminiscences of the Geneva Tribunal of Arbitration 1872: the Alabama claims" (Boston: Houghton Mifflin, 1911)

Hackworth, Green Haywood, "Digest of International Law", Vol. 3 (Washington: Government Printing Office, 1942)

Hackworth, Green Haywood, "Digest of International Law", Vol. 4 (Washington: Government Printing Office, 1942)

Hackworth, Green Haywood, "Digest of International Law", Vol. 5 (Washington: Government Printing Office, 1943)

Hall, William Edward, "A Treatise on International Law" (Oxford: Clarendon, 1924)

Handl, Günther, "Territorial Sovereignty and the Problem of Transnational Pollution", 69 American Journal of International Law (1975), pp. 59 *et seq.*

Harburger, Heinrich, "Der strafrechtliche Begriff Inland und seine Beziehungen zum Völkerrecht und Staatsrecht" (Nördlingen: Beck, 1882)

Hardin, Garrett, "The Tragedy of the Commons", Science (1938), pp. 1243-1248.

Harndt, Raimundt, "Völkerrechtliche Haftung für die schädlichen Folgen nicht verbotenen Verhaltens" (Berlin: Duncker & Humblot, 1993)

Hartwig, Matthias, "Die Haftung der Mitgliedstaaten für Internationale Organisationen" (Berlin: Springer, 1993)

Hasselmann, Cord-Georg, "Die Freiheit der Handelsschiffahrt" (Kehl am Rhein: Engel, 1986)

Haucke, Michael, "Piratensender auf See" (München: Beck, 1969)

Hautefeuille, Laurent Basile, "Des droits et des devoirs des nations neutres en temps de guerre maritime", Vol. 1 (2nd ed. Paris, 1858)

Heintschel von Heinegg, Wolff, "Visit, Search, Diversion, and Capture in Naval Warfare: Part I, The Traditional Law", 29 Canadian Yearbook of International Law (1991), pp. 283 *et seq.*

Heintschel von Heinegg, Wolff, "Visit, Search, Diversion, and Capture in Naval Warfare: Part II, Developments since 1945", 30 Canadian Yearbook of International Law (1992), pp. 89 *et seq.*

Heintschel von Heinegg, Wolff, "Der Einsatz der Deutschen Marine im Rahmen der Operation 'Enduring Freedom'", 40 Archiv des Völkerrechts (2002), pp. 145 *et seq.*

Heintschel von Heinegg, Wolff, "Friedliche Nutzung, Seekriegs- und Neutralitätsrecht", in *Graf Vitzthum*, Wolfgang (ed.), "Handbuch des Seerechts" (München: Beck, 2006), pp. 491 *et seq.*

Herdegen, Mathias, "Bemerkungen zur Zwangsliquidation und zum Haftungsdurchgriff bei internationalen Organisationen", 47 Zeitschrift für ausländisches öffentliches Recht und Völkerrecht (1987), pp. 537 *et seq.*

Higgins, Rosalyn, "Problems and Process – International Law and How We Use It" (Oxford: Clarendon Press, 1995)

Higgins, Rosalyn, "Some Observations on the Inter-Temporal Rule in International Law", in *Makarczyk* (ed.), "Theory of International Law at the Threshold of the 21st Century" (The Hague: Kluwer Law International, 1996), pp. 173 *et seq.*

Higgins, Rosalyn, "Time and the Law: International Perspectives on an Old Problem", 46 International and Comparative Law Quarterly (1997), pp. 501 *et seq.*

Higgins, Rosalyn, "The International Court of Justice: Selected Issues of State Responsibility", in *Ragazzi*, Maurizio (ed.), "International Responsibility Today – Essays in Memory of Oscar Schachter" (Leiden: Nijhoff, 2005), pp. 271 *et seq.*

Hill, Christopher, "Maritime Law" (6th ed., London: LLP, 2003)

Hinrichs, Ximena, "Measures against smuggling of migrants at sea: A Law of the Sea Perspective", 36 Révue Belge de Droit International (2003), pp. 413 *et seq.*

Freiherr Hold von Ferneck, Alexander, "Die Reform des Seekriegsrechts durch die Londoner Konferenz 1908/1909" (Stuttgart: Kohlhammer, 1914)

Honoré, A.M., "Causation and Remoteness of Damage", in *Tunc*, André (ed.), "International Encyclopedia of Comparative Law", Vol. 11, Part 1 (Tübingen: Mohr, 1983), pp. 40 *et seq.*

Hull, James D./*Emerson*, Michael D. Emerson, "High 'Seize' Maritime Interdiction Works!", 125 U.S. Naval Institute Proceedings (Jan. 1999), pp. 64 *et seq.*

Humphrey, John P., "The International Bill of Rights: Scope and Implementation", 17 William and Mary Law Review (1975-76), pp. 527 et *seq.*

Hunnings, N. March, "Pirate Broadcasting in European Waters", 14 International and Comparative Law Quarterly (1965), pp. 410 *et seq.*

Hyde, Charles Cheney, "The Adjustment Of The I'm Alone Case", 29 American Journal of International Law(1935), pp. 296 *et seq.*

Hyde, Charles Cheney, "International Law – Chiefly as interpreted and applied by the United States", Vol. 2 (2nd ed., Boston: Little, Brown and Company, 1947)

International Law Institute, "Digest of United States Practice in International Law in 1979", Vol. 7 (Washington, 1983)

Ipsen, Knut, "Völkerrechtliche Verantwortlichkeit und Völkerstrafrecht", in *id.*, "Völkerrecht" (5th ed., München: Beck, 2004), pp. 615 *et seq.*

Jacobs, Francis G., "Varieties of approach to treaty interpretation: with special reference to the draft Convention on the Law of Treaties before the Vienna diplomatic conference", 18 International and Comparative Law Quarterly (1969), pp. 318 *et seq.*

Janis, M.W., "Equity in International Law", in: *Bernhardt*, Rudolf (ed.), "Encyclopedia of Public International Law", Vol. 2 (Amsterdam: North-Holland, 1995), pp. 109 *et seq.*

Jennings, Robert/*Watts*, Arthur, "Oppenheim's International Law", Vol. 2 (9th ed., Harlow: Longman, 1992)

Jessup, Philip C., "Should International Law recognize an intermediate status between peace and war?", 48 American Journal of International Law (1954), pp. 98 *et seq.*

Jesus, José Luis, "Protection of Foreign Ships against Piracy and Terrorism at Sea: Legal Aspects", 18 International Journal of Marine and Coastal Law (2005), pp. 363 *et seq.*

Johnson, D.H.N., "Freedom of Navigation", in *Bernhardt*, Rudolf, "Encyclopedia of Public International Law", Vol. 3 (Amsterdam: Elsevier, 1997), pp. 528 *et seq.*

Jørgensen, N., "A Reappraisal of Punitive Damages in International Law", 68 British Yearbook of International Law(1997), pp. 247 *et seq.*

Joyner, C.C., "The 1988 IMO Convention on the Safety of Maritime Navigation: Towards a Legal Remedy for Terrorism at Sea", 31 German Yearbook of International Law (1988), pp. 230 *et seq.*

Kälin, Walter/*Künzli*, Jörg, "Universeller Menschenrechtsschutz" (Basel: Helbing & Lichtenhahn, 2005)

Kalshoven, Frits, "Commentary to the 1909 London Declaration Concerning the Laws of Naval Warfare", in *Ronzitti*, Natalino (ed.), "The Law of Naval Warfare" (Dordrecht: Nijhoff, 1988), pp. 257 *et seq.*

Kazazi, Mojtaba, "Burden of proof and related issues" (The Hague: Kluwer Law International, 1996)

Kelsen, Hans, "Principles of International Law" (2nd ed., New York: Holt, Rinehart, Winston, 1967)

Kern, Holger Lutz, "Strategies of Legal Challenge: Great Britain, International Law, and the Abolition of the Transatlantic Slave Trade", 6 Journal of the History of International Law (2004), pp. 233 *et seq.*

Kieserman, Brad J., "Preventing and Defeating Terrorism at Sea: Practical Considerations for Implementation of the Draft Protocol to the Convention for the Suppression of Unlawful Acts Against the Safety of Maritime Navigation (SUA)", in *Nordquist*, Myron H. *et al.* (eds.), "Recent Developments in the Law of the Sea and China" (Leiden: Nijhoff, 2006), pp. 425 *et seq.*

Klein, Natalie, "Legal Implications of Australia's Maritime Identification System", 55 International and Comparative Law Quarterly (2006), pp. 337 *et seq.*

Klein, Pierre, "La responsabilité des organisations internationales" (Bruxelles: Bruylant, 1998)

König, Doris, "Questionnaire International Law of the Sea", in *Zimmermann*, Andreas *et al.* (eds.), "Unity and Diversity in International Law" (Berlin: Duncker & Humblot, 2006), pp. 27 *et seq.*

Kokott, Juliane, "The Burden of Proof in Comparative and International Human Rights Law" (The Hague: Kluwer, 1998)

Koskenniemi, Martti, "Le Comité des Sanctions (créé par la résolution 661 (1990) du Conseil de sécurité)", 37 Annuaire français de droit international (1991), pp. 119 *et seq.*

Kramek, Joseph E., "Bilateral Maritime Counter-Drug and Immigrant Interdiction Agreements: Is this the world of the Future?", 31 University of Miami Inter-American Law Review (2000), pp. 121 *et seq.*

Krüger, Herbert, "Schiffahrtsfreiheit", in *Schlochauer*, Hans-Jürgen (ed.), "Wörterbuch des Völkerrechts" (2nd ed., Berlin: de Gruyter, 1962), p. 206.

Krugmann, Michael, "Der Grundsatz der Verhältnismäßigkeit im Völkerrecht" (Berlin: Duncker & Humblot, 2004)

Lagoni, Rainer, "Gewaltverbot, Seekriegsrecht und Schiffahrtsfreiheit im Golfkrieg", in *Fürst*, Walter *et al.* (eds.), "Festschrift für Wolfgang Zeidler" (Berlin: de Gruyter, 1987), pp. 1833 *et seq.*

Lagoni, Rainer, "Der Hamburger Hafen, die internationale Handelsschiffahrt und das Völkerrecht", 26 AVR (1988), pp. 261 *et seq.*

Lagoni, Rainer, "Die Abwehr von Gefahren für die marine Umwelt", 32 Berichte der Deutschen Gesellschaft für Völkerrecht (1992), pp. 87 *et seq.*

Lagoni, Rainer, "Zum Recht der Nacheile (Art. 111 SRÜ)", in *Epping*, Volker *et al.* (eds.), "Brücken bauen und begehen – Festschrift für Knut Ipsen" (München: Beck, 2000), pp. 213 *et seq.*

Lagoni, Rainer, "Piraterie und widerrechtliche Handlungen gegen die Sicherheit der Seeschiffahrt", in *Ipsen*, Jörn *et al.* (eds.), "Recht – Staat – Gemeinwohl: Festschrift für Dietrich Rauschning" (Köln: Heymann, 2001), pp. 501 *et seq.*

Lambie, Margaret, "Presumption of cessation of citizenship: its effect on international claims", 24 American Journal of International Law (1930), pp. 264 *et seq.*

Lasok, K.P.E., "The European Court of Justice, Practice and Procedure" (2nd ed., London: Butterworths, 1994)

Lauterpacht, Hersch, "Private Law Sources and Analogies of International Law" (London, 1927)

Lauterpacht, Hersch, "Oppenheim's International Law", Vol. 1 (7th ed., London: Longman, 1948)

Lauterpacht, Hersch, "International Law and Human Rights" (London: Stevens, 1950)

Lauterpacht, Hersch, "Oppenheim's International Law", Vol. 1 (8th ed., London: Longmans, Green, 1955)

Lavalle, Roberto, "The Law of the United Nations and the Use of Force, under the relevant Security Council Resolutions of 1990 and 1991, to resolve the Persian Gulf Crisis", 23 Netherlands Yearbook of International Law (1992), pp. 3 *et seq.*

Leckow, Ross, "The Iran-Iraq Conflict in the Gulf: The Law of War Zones", 37 International and Comparative Law Quarterly (1988), pp. 629, *et seq.*

Lehrman, Thomas D., "Enhancing the Proliferation Security Initiative: The Case for a Decentralized Nonproliferation Architecture", 45 Virginia Journal of International Law (2004), pp. 223 *et seq.*

Levi, Werner, "Contemporary International Law: A Concise Introduction" (2nd ed., Boulder: Westview, 1991)

Lewin, David Bencionovic, "Die Verantwortlichkeit der Staaten im gegenwärtigen Völkerrecht" (Potsdam-Babelsberg: Inst. für Ausländ. Recht und Rechtsvergleichung, Dt. Akad. für Staats- und Rechtswissenschaft, 1969)

Liljedahl, John, "Transnational and international crimes: jurisdictional issues", in *Mukherjee*, Proshanto K. *et al.* (eds.), "Maritime violence and other crimes at sea" (Malmö: WMU, 2002), pp. 115 *et seq.*

Lodge, Michael W./*Nandan*, Satya N., "Some Suggestions Towards Better Implementation of the United Nations Agreement on Straddling Fish Stocks and Highly Migratory Fish Stocks of 1995", 20 International Journal of Marine and Coastal Law (2005), pp. 345 *et seq.*

Lowe, Alan Vaughan, "The Impact on the Law of the Sea on Naval Warfare", 14 Syracuse Journal of International Law and Commerce (1988), pp. 657 *et seq.*

Lowe, Alan Vaughan, "Commentary", in *de Guttry et al.* (eds.), "The Iran-Iraq War (1980-1988) and the Law of Naval Warfare" (Cambridge: Grotius, 1993), pp. 241 *et seq.*

Lucchini, Laurent/*Voelckel*, Michel, "Droit de la mer", Vol. 2, Part. 2 (Paris: Pedone, 1996)

Mahalu, Costa Ricky, "Public International Law and Shipping Practices: The East African Aspirations" (Baden-Baden: Nomos, 1984)

Mann, Frederick Alexander, "The Consequences of an International Wrong in International and National Law", 48 British Yearbook of International Law (1977), pp. 1 *et seq.*

Martin-Bidou, Pascale, "Les mesures d'embargo prises à l'encontre de la Yougoslavie", 39 Annaire français de droit international (1993), pp. 262 *et seq.*

McDorman, Ted L., "Stateless Fishing Vessels, International Law and the U.N. High Seas Fisheries Conference", 25 Journal of Maritime Law and Commerce (1994), pp. 531 *et seq.*

McDougal, Myres Smith/*Burke*, William T., "The Public Order of the Oceans" (New Haven: Yale University Press, 1962)

McLachlan, C., "The Principle of Systemic Integration and Article 31(3)(c) of the Vienna Convention", 54 International and Comparative Law Quarterly (2005), pp. 279 *et seq.*

Lord McNair, Arnold Duncan, "The Law of Treaties" (Oxford: Clarendon Press, 1961)

Medows, Sir Philip, "Observations concerning the dominion and sovereignty of the seas" (1689)

Meyers, Herman, “The Nationality of Ships” (Den Haag: Nijhoff, 1967)

Miaja de la Muela, Adolfo, “Le role de la conditions des mains propres de la personne lésée dans les réclamations devant les tribunaux internationaux”, in *Ibler*, Vladimir (ed.), “Mélanges offerts à Juraj Andrassy” (The Hague: Nijhoff, 1968), pp. 189 *et seq.*

Milano, Enrico, “Diplomatic protection and human rights before the International Court of Justice: re-fashioning tradition?”, 35 Netherlands Yearbook of International Law(2004), pp. 85 *et seq.*

Molenaar, Erik Jaap, “Multilateral Hot Pursuit and Illegal Fishing in the Southern Ocean: The Pursuits of the Viarsa 1 and the South Tomi”, 19 International Journal of Marine and Coastal Law (2004), pp. 19 *et seq.*

Moore, John Bassett, “History and digest of the international arbitrations to which the United States has been a party”, Volumes 2-5 (Washington: Government Printing Office, 1898)

Moore, John F., “The U.S. Navy in 1991”, 118 U.S. Naval Institute Proceedings (May 1992), pp. 133 *et seq.*

Morabito, Robert E., “Maritime Interdiction: Evolution of a Strategy”, 22 Ocean Development and International Law (1991), pp. 301 *et seq.*

Mukundan, Pottengal, “Piracy and Armed Robbery against Ships Today”, 2 WMU Journal of Maritime Affairs (2003), pp. 167 *et seq.*

von Münch, Ingo, “Freedom of Navigation and the Trade Unions”, 19 German Yearbook of International Law(1976), pp. 129 *et seq.*

von Münch, Ingo, “Der Diplomatische Schutz für Schiffe”, in *Ipsen*, Hans Peter *et al.* (eds.), “Recht über See” (Hamburg: Decker, 1980), pp. 231 *et seq.*

Nakatani, Kazuhiro, “Diplomacy and State Responsibility”, in *Ragazzi*, Maurizio (ed.), “International Responsibility Today – Essays in Memory of Oscar Schachter” (Leiden: Nijhoff, 2005), pp. 36 *et seq.*

Nash Leich, Marian, “Contemporary Practice of the USA relating to international law”, 76 American Journal of International Law (1982), pp. 374-377

Nordquist, Myron H. (ed.), “United Nations Convention on the Law of the Sea 1982 – A Commentary”, Vol. 5 (Dordrecht: Nijhoff, 1989)

Norton, Patrick M., “Between the Ideology and the Reality”, 17 Harvard International Law Journal (1976), pp. 249 *et seq.*

Noyes, John E./*Smith*, Brian D., “State Responsibility and the Principle of Joint and Several Liability”, 13 Yale Journal of International Law (1988), pp. 225 *et seq.*

O'Connell, Daniel Patrick, “International Law”, Vol. 1 (2nd ed., London: Stevens, 1970)

O'Connell, Daniel Patrick, "The International Law of the Sea", Vol. 2 (Oxford: Clarendon Press, 1984)

Orrego Vicuña, Francisco, "The Changing International Law of High Seas Fisheries" (Cambridge: Cambridge University Press, 1999)

Orrego Vicuña, Francisco, "The Changing Law of Nationality of Claims", in *International Law Association*, "Report of the Sixty-ninth Conference" (2000), pp. 631 *et seq.*

Orrego Vicuña, Francisco, "The Protection of Shareholders under International Law: Making State Responsibility More Accessible", in *Ragazzi*, Maurizio (ed.), "International Responsibility Today – Essays in Memory of Oscar Schachter" (Leiden: Nijhoff, 2005), pp. 161 *et seq.*

Oxman, Bernard H., "Human Rights and the United Nations Convention on the Law of the Sea", 36 Columbia Journal of Transnational Law (1997), pp. 399 *et seq.*

Oxman, Bernard H./Bantz, Vincent, "Case Report: The M.V. "Saiga" (No. 2) (Saint Vincent and the Grenadines v. Guinea)", 94 American Journal of International Law (2000), pp. 140 *et seq.*

Özcayir, Oya, "The International Ship and Port Facility Security (ISPS) Code", 9 J. Int'l Maritime L. (2003), pp. 578 *et seq.*

Özcayir, Z. Oya, "Port State Control" (2nd ed., London: LLP, 2004)

Pagani, Fabrizio, "Le misure di interdizione navale in relazione alle sanzioni adottate dall'ONU", 76 Rivista di diritto internazionale (1993), pp. 720 *et seq.*

Parameswaran, Benjamin, "The liberalization of maritime transport services: with special reference to the WTO/GATS framework", (Berlin: Springer, 2004)

Partsch, Karl Joseph, "Individuals in International Law", in *Bernhardt*, Rudolf (ed.), "Encyclopedia of Public International Law", Vol. 2 (Amsterdam: North-Holland, 1995), pp. 957 *et seq.*

Pauwelyn, Joost, "The Role of Public International Law in the WTO: How Far Can We Go?", 95 American Journal of International Law (2001), pp. 535 *et seq.*

Pearce Higgins, Alexander, "Le régime juridiqe des navires de commerce en haute mer en temps de paix", 30 Recueil des Cours (1929-V), pp. 8 *et seq.*

Pellonpää, Matti, "Individual Reparation Claims under the European Convention on Human Rights", in *Randelzhofer*, Albrecht *et al.* (eds.), "State Responsibility and the Individual: Reparation in Instances of Grave Violations of Human Rights" (The Hague: Nijhoff, 1999), pp. 109 *et seq.*

Pisillo Mazzeschi, Riccardo, "International Oligations to Provide for Reparation Claims?", in *Randelzhofer*, Albrecht *et al.* (eds.), "State Responsibility and the Individual: Reparation in Instances of Grave Violations of Human Rights" (The Hague: Nijhoff, 1999), pp. 149 *et seq.*

Pisillo Mazzeschi, Riccardo, "The Marginal Role of the Individual in the ILC's Articles on State Responsibility", 14 Italian Yearbook of International Law(2004), pp. 39 *et seq.*

Posner, Richard A., "Economic Analysis of Law" (6th ed., New York: Aspen Publications, 2003)

Poulantzas, Nicholas M., "The Right of Hot Pursuit in International Law" (2nd ed., The Hague: Nijhoff, 2002)

de la Pradelle, Albert, "Maîtres et Doctrines du Droit des Gens" (1939)

de la Pradelle, Albert/*Politis*, Nicolas, "Recueil des arbitrages internationaux", Vol. 2 (1957)

de la Pradelle, Géraud, "Les conflits de loi en matière de nullités" (Paris: Dalloz, 1967)

Prüssmann, Heinz/*Rabe*, Dieter, "Seehandelsrecht" (3rd ed., München: Beck, 1992)

Quéneudec, Jean-Pierre, "La responsabilité internationale de l'Etat pour les fautes personelles de ses agents" (Paris: Pichon et Durand-Auzias, 1966)

Rabe, Dieter, "Seehandelsrecht" (4th ed., München: Beck, 2000)

Ragazzi, Maurizio (ed.), "International Responsibility Today – Essays in Memory of Oscar Schachter" (Leiden: Nijhoff, 2005), pp. 223 *et seq.*

Randelzhofer, Albrecht, "Probleme der völkerrechtlichen Gefährdungshaftung", 24 Berichte der Deutschen Gesellschaft für Völkerrecht (1984), pp. 35 *et seq.*

Raustiala, Kal, "Law, Liberalization & International Narcotics Trafficking", 32 Journal of International Law& Politics (1999), pp. 89 *et seq.*

Rayfuse, Rosemary Gail, "Non-Flag State Enforcement in High Seas Fisheries" (Leiden: Nijhoff, 2004)

Ready, Nigel P., "Ship Registration" (3rd ed., London: Lloyd's of London Press, 1998)

Ress, Hans-Konrad, "Das Handelsembargo" (Berlin: Springer, 2000)

Reuland, Robert C., "The Customary Right of Hot Pursuit onto the High Seas: Annotations to Article 111 of the Law of the Sea Convention", 33 Virginia Journal of International Law (1992-1993), pp. 557 *et seq.*

Reuter, Paul, "Introduction to the Law of Treaties" (2nd ed., London: Paul Kegan International, 1995)

Ricardo, David, "On thc Principles of Political Economy and Taxation" (3rd ed., London, 1817)

Richards, Sir Erle, "The British Prize Courts and the war", 1 British Yearbook of International Law(1920/1921), pp. 11 *et seq.*

Richardson, Michael, "The Threats of Piracy and Maritime Terrorism in Southeast Asia", Maritime Studies (November/December 2004), pp. 18 *et seq.*

Rienow, Robert, "The Test of Nationality of a Merchant Vessel" (New York: Columbia University Press, 1937)

Rindfleisch, Stefan, "Das Recht der Nacheile zur See" (Hamburg: LIT, 2001)

Roach, J. Ashley, "Proliferation Security Initiative (PSI): Countering Proliferation by Sea", in *Nordquist*, Myron H. *et al.* (eds.), "Recent Decelopments in the Law of the Sea and China" (Leiden: Nijhoff, 2006), pp. 351 *et seq.*

Robertson, Jr., H.B., "Interdiction of Iraqi Maritime Commerce in the 1990-1991 Persian Gulf Conflict", 22 Ocean Development and International Law (1991), pp. 289 *et seq.*

Rodière, René/*du Pontavice*, Emmanuel, "Droit maritime" (12th ed., Paris: Dalloz, 1997)

Roelofsen, Cornelis G., "The Claim of Some Citizens of Stettin against the Dutch Republic and its Adjudication", in *Gill*, Terry D. *et al.* (eds.), "Reflections on Principles and Practice in International Law" (The Hague: Nijhoff, 2000), pp. 175 *et seq.*

Ronzitti, Natalino (ed.), "The Law of Naval Warfare" (Dordrecht: Nijhoff, 1988)

Ronzitti, Natalino, "The Law of the Sea and the Use of Force Against Terrorist Activities", in *id.* (ed.), "Maritime Terrorism and International Law" (Dordrecht: Nijhoff, 1990), pp. 1 *et seq.*

Ronzitti, Natalino, "Coastal State Jurisdiction over Refugees and Migrants at Sea", in *Ando*, Nisuke *et al.* (eds.), "Liber amicorum Judge Shigeru Oda", Vol. 2 (The Hague, Kluwer Law International, 2002), pp. 1271 *et seq.*

Roucounas, Emmanuel, "Facteurs privés et droit international public", 299 Recueil des Cours (2002- VI), pp. 9 *et seq.*

Roucounas, Emmanuel, "*Non-State Actors: Areas of International Responsibility in Need of Further Exploration*", in *Ragazzi*, Maurizio (ed.), "International Responsibility Today – Essays in Memory of Oscar Schachter" (Leiden: Nijhoff, 2005), pp. 391 *et seq.*

Rousseau, Charles, "Droit international public" (Paris: Sirey, 1953)

Rousseau, Charles, "Cours de droit international public: La responsabilité internationale" (1959-60)

Rousseau, Charles, "Droit international public", Vol. 5 (Paris: Sirey, 1983)

Rousseau, Charles, "Le droit des conflits armés" (Paris: Pedone, 1983)

Rubin, Alfred P., "The Law of Piracy" (2nd ed., Irvington-on-Hudson: Transnational Publishers, 1998)

Salmon, Jean J.A., "Des 'Main Propres' comme condition de recevabilité des réclamations internationales", 10 Annuaire Français de Droit International (1964), pp. 225 *et seq.*

Salmon, Jean J.A., "Les accords Spaak-U Thant du 20 février 1965", 11 Annuaire Français de Droit International (1965), pp. 481 *et seq.*

Sands, Philippe/*Klein*, Pierre, "Bowett's Law of International Institutions" (London: Sweet & Maxwell, 2001)

Saunders, Phillip/*Williamson*, Hugh, "Small Islands and Archipelagic States", in *Crickard*, Fred W. (ed.), "Multinational Naval Cooperation and Foreign Policy into the 21st century" (Aldershot: Ashgate, 1998), pp. 170 *et seq.*

Schaumann, Wilfried, "Die Gleichheit der Staaten" (Wien: Springer, 1957)

Scheuner, Ulrich, "Durchsuchung von Schiffen", in *Schlochauer*, Hans-Jürgen *et al.* (eds.), "Wörterbuch des Völkerrechts", Vol. 1 (1960), pp. 407 *et seq.*

Schmalenbach, Kirsten, "Die Haftung Internationaler Organisationen" (Frankfurt am Main: Lang, 2004)

Schmidt-Radefeld, Roman, "Enduring Freedom – Antiterrorkrieg für immer?", 18 Humanitäres Völkerrecht (2005), pp. 245 *et seq.*

Schoen, Paul, "Die völkerrechtliche Haftung der Staaten aus unerlaubten Handlungen", (Breslau: Kern, 1917)

Schoenbaum, Thomas J., "Admiralty and Maritime Law", Vol. 2 (4th ed., St. Paul: Thomson West, 2004)

Scholz, Oliver, "Die Durchsetzung von Zwangsmaßnahmen nach Art. 41 der Satzung der Vereinten Nationen, insbesondere mit militärischen Mitteln" (Frankfurt am Main: Lang, 1998)

Schramm, Georg, "Das Prisenrecht in seiner neuesten Gestalt" (Berlin: Mittler, 1913)

Schreuer, Christoph, "Unjust Enrichment", in *Bernhardt*, Rudolf (ed.), "Encyclopedia of Public International Law", Vol. 4 (Amsterdam: North-Holland, 2000), pp. 1243 *et seq.*

Schröder, Meinhard, "Verantwortlichkeit, Völkerstrafrecht, Streitbeilegung und Sanktionen", in *Graf Vitzthum*, Wolfgang, "Völkerrecht" (2nd ed., Berlin: de Gruyter, 2001), pp. 545 *et seq.*.

Schwebel, Stephen M., "May Preparatory Work be Used to Correct Rather than Confirm the „Clear" Meaning of a Treaty Provision?", in *Makarczyk*, Jerzy (ed.), "Theory of International Law at the Threshold of the 21st Century" (The Hague: Kluwer Law International, 1996), pp. 541 *et seq.*

Scott, James Brown (ed.), "The Declaration of London – A Collection of Official Papers and Documents" (New York: Oxford University Press, 1919)

Segelken, Hans, "Kapitänsrecht" (2nd ed., Hamburg: Verlag Weltarchiv, 1974)

Seidl-Hohenveldern, Ignaz, "Piercing the Corporate Veil of International Organizations: The International Tin Council Case in the English Court of Appeals", 32 German Yearbook of International Law (1989), pp. 43 *et seq.*

Seidl-Hohenveldern, Ignaz, "Aliens, Property", in *Bernhardt*, Rudolf (ed.), "Encyclopedia of Public International Law", Vol. 1 (Amsterdam: North-Holland, 1992), pp. 116 *et seq.*

Seidl-Hohenveldern, Ignaz/*Loibl*, Gerhard, "Das Recht der internationalen Organisationen einschließlich der supranationalen Gemeinschaften" (7th ed., Köln: Heymanns, 2000)

Seldeni, Ioannis, "Mare clausum seu de Dominio Maris", Libri Duo (London, 1636)

Shaw, Malcolm N., "International Law" (5th ed., Cambridge: Cambridge University Press, 2003)

Shelton, Dinah, "Remedies in International Human Rights Law" (Oxford: Oxford University Press, 2000)

Sienho Yee, "The Responsibility of States Members of an International Organization for its Conduct as a Result of Membership or their Normal Conduct associated with Membership", in *Ragazzi*, Maurizio (ed.), "International Responsibility Today – Essays in Memory of Oscar Schachter" (Leiden: Nijhoff, 2005), pp. 435 *et seq.*

Siddle, John, "Anglo-American Co-Operation in the Suppression of Drug Smuggling", 31 International and Comparative Law Quarterly (1982), pp. 726 *et seq.*

Sinclair, Ian, "The Vienna Convention on the Law of Treaties" (Manchester: University Press, 1984)

Smith, Adam, "The Wealth of Nations", Vol. 1 (Rev. ed. 1937)

Sohn, Louis B./*Baxter*, R.R., "Responsibility of States for Injuries to the Economic Interests of Aliens", 55 American Journal of International Law (1961), pp. 545 *et seq.*

Sohn, Louis B., "The Human Rights Law of the Charter", 12 Texas International Law Journal (1977), pp. 129 *et seq.*

Sohn, Louis B., "International Law of the Sea and Human Rights Issues", in *Clingan*, Thomas A. (ed.), "The Law of the Sea: What lies ahead?" (Honolulu, University of Hawaii, 1988), pp. 51 *et seq.*

Soons, Alfred H.A., "Enforcing the economic embargo at sea", in *Gowlland-Debbas*, Vera (ed.), "United Nations Sanctions and International Law" (The Hague: Kluwer Law International, 2001), pp. 307 *et seq.*

Sorensen, Christina E., "Drug Trafficking on the High Seas: A Move toward Universal Jurisdiction under International Law", 4 Emory International Law Review (1990), pp. 207 *et seq.*

Sorensen, Max, "Principes de droit international public", 101 Recueil des Cours (1960-III), pp. 2 *et seq.*

Sornarajah, Muthucumaraswamy, "State Responsibility and Bilateral Investment Treaties", 20 Journal of World Trade Law (1986), pp. 79 *et seq.*

Stein, Torsten, "Proportionality revisited – Überlegungen zum Grundsatz der Verhältnismäßigkeit im internationalen Recht", in *Dicke*, Klaus *et al.* (ed.), "Weltinnenrecht – Liber amicorum Jost Delbrück" (Berlin: Duncker & Humblot), pp. 727 *et seq.*

Stern, Brigitte, "A Plea for 'Reconstruction' of International Responsibility based on the Notion of Legal Injury", in *Ragazzi*, Maurizio (ed.), "International Responsibility Today – Essays in Memory of Oscar Schachter" (Leiden: Nijhoff, 2005), pp. 93 *et seq.*

Stokke, Olav Schram, *"Introduction"*, in *id.* (ed.), "Governing High Seas Fisheries – The Interplay of Global and Regional Regimes" (Oxford: Oxford University Press, 2001), pp. 3-5

Stone, Julius, "Fictional elements in treaty interpretation – A Study in the International Judicial Process", 1 Sydney Law Review (1953-1955), pp. 344 *et seq.*

Streinz, Rudolf, Europarecht (5th ed., Heidelberg: Müller, 2001)

Strupp, Karl, "Das völkerrechtliche Delikt" (Stuttgart: Kohlhammer, 1920)

Subilia, Jean-Luc, "L'allocation d'interêts dans la jurisprudence internationale" (Lausanne, 1972)

Sunga, Lyal S., "The Emerging System of International Criminal Law" (The Hague: Kluwer Law International, 1997)

Talmon, Stefan, "The Statements by the President of the Security Council", 2 Chinese Journal of International Law (2003), pp. 419 *et seq.*

Talmon, Stefan, "Responsibility of International Organizations: Does the European Community require Special Treatment", in *Ragazzi*, Maurizio (ed.), "International Responsibility Today – Essays in Memory of Oscar Schachter" (Leiden: Nijhoff, 2005), pp. 405 *et seq.*

Tanzi, Attila, "Is Damage a distinct Condition for the Existence of a Internationally Wrongful Act?", in *Spinedi*, Marina *et al.* (eds.), "United Nations Codification of State Responsibility" (New York: Oceana Publications), pp. 1 *et seq.*

Tavernier, Paul, "L'année des Nations Unies", 37 Annaire Français de Droit International (1991), pp. 617 *et seq.*

Thirlway, Hugh, "The Law and Procedure of the International Court of Justice 1960-1989", 62 British Yearbook of International Law(1991), pp. 16 *et seq.*

Thorsen, Howard B., "U.S. Coast Guard in Review", 130 Naval Institute Proceedings (May 2004), pp. 99 *et seq.*, 100

Todd, Paul, "Private Law Aspects and Commercial Concerns associated with Emerging Issues in Maritime Security", in *Mejia*, Max (ed.), "Contemporary Issues in Maritime Security" (2005), pp. 299 *et seq.*

Treves, Tullio, "*The Rome Convention for the Suppression of Unlawful Acts Against the Safety of Maritime Navigation*", in *Ronzitti*, Natalino (ed.), "Maritime Terrorism and International Law" (Dordrecht: Nijhoff, 1990), pp. 69 *et seq.*

Treves, Tullio, "The International Law Commission's Articles on State Responsibility and the Settlement of Disputes", in *Ragazzi*, Maurizio (ed.), "International Responsibility Today – Essays in Memory of Oscar Schachter" (Leiden: Nijhoff, 2005), pp. 223 *et seq.*

Truver, Scott C., "The U.S. Navy in Review", Naval Institute Proceedings (May 1994), pp. 114 *et seq.*

Valencia, Mark J., "The Proliferation Security Initiative: Should Malaysia join?", 142 Maritime Studies (May/June 2005), pp. 14 *et seq.*

Verdross-Drossberg, Alfred, "Theorie der mittelbaren Staatenhaftung", 1 Österreichische Zeitschrift für Öffentliches Recht (Neue Folge) (1948), pp. 388 *et seq.*

Verhoeven, Joe, "Etats alliés ou nations unies ? L'O.N.U. face au conflit entre l'Irak et le Koweït", 36 Annaire Français de Droit International (1990), pp. 145 *et seq.*

Verzijl, Jan Hendrik Willem, "Le droit des prises de la Grande Guerre" (Leyde: Sijthoff, 1924)

Verzijl, Jan Hendrik Willem, "International Law in Historical Perspective", Vol. 6, (Leiden: Sijthoff, 1973)

Vialard, Antoine, "Droit maritime" (Paris: Presses universitaires de France, 1997)

De *Visscher*, Charles, "Les responsabilités des États", Bibl. Viss. 2 (1924), pp. 87 *et seq.*

Graf Vitzthum, Wolfgang, "Geschichte des Seerechts", in *Graf Vitzthum*, Wolfgang (ed.), "Handbuch des Seerechts" (München: Beck, 2006), pp. 1 *et seq.*

Voelckel, Michel, "Le Navire et les Situations Internationales de Crise", in *Société française pour le droit international* (ed.), "Le Navire en Droit international" (Paris: Pedone, 1992), pp. 183 *et seq.*

Vollmar, Sabine, "Das Durchsuchungsrecht im Frieden aus Gründen des Selbstschutzes" (Bonn, 1966)

Vukas, Budislav, "Droit de la mer et droits de l'homme", in *id.* (ed.), "The Law of the Sea: Selected Writings" (Leiden: Nijhoff, 2004), pp. 71 *et seq.*

Wagner, Gerhard, "Vor § 823", in *Rebmann*, Kurt *et al.* (eds.), "Münchener Kommentar zum Bürgerlichen Gesetzbuch" (4th ed., München: Beck, 2004), pp. 1487-1488

Watts, Arthur, "The Protection of Merchant Ships", 33 British Yearbook of International Law (1957), pp. 52 *et seq.*

Wehberg, Hans, "Das Seekriegsrecht" (Stuttgart: Kohlhammer, 1915)

Weir, Tony, "Complex Liabilities", in *Tunc*, André (ed.), "International Encyclopedia of Comparative Law", Vol. 11, Part. 2 (Tübingen: Mohr, 1986), Chapter 12, pp. 12/01 *et seq.*

Weis, Paul, "Nationality and Statelessness in International Law" (London: Stevens, 1956)

Werner, Auguste-Raynald, "Traité de droit maritime général" (Genève: Droz, 1964)

Wheaton, Henry, "Histoire des progrès du droit des gens en Europe depuis la paix de Westphalie jusqu'au congrès de Vienne" (Leipzig: Brockhaus, 1841)

Whiteman, Marjorie M., "Damages in International Law", Volumes 1-3 (Washington: U.S. Government Printing Office, 1937-1943)

Williams, Glanville L., "The Juridical Basis of Hot Pursuit", 20 British Yearbook of International Law (1939), pp. 82 *et seq.*

Williams, Malcolm J., "Bilateral Maritime Agreements enhancing International Cooperation in the Suppression of Illicit Maritime Narcotics Trafficking", in *Nordquist*, Myron H. *et al.* (eds.), "Oceans Policy – New Institutions, Challenges, Opportunities" (The Hague: Nijhoff, 1999), pp. 179 *et seq.*

Wolfrum, Rüdiger, "Die Internationalisierung staatsfreier Räume: die Entwicklung einer internationalen Verwaltung für Antarktis, Weltraum, Hohe See und Meeresboden" (Berlin: Springer, 1984)

Wolfrum, Rüdiger, "Billigflaggen – Schadensersatz – Nacheile", 3 Zeitschrift für europarechtliche Studien (2000), pp. 1 *et seq.*

Wolfrum, Rüdiger, "Hohe See und Tiefseeboden", in *Graf Vitzthum*, Wolfgang (ed.), "Handbuch des Seerechts" (München: Beck, 2006), pp. 293 *et seq.*

Wollenberg, Simon Friedrich Wilhelm, "Die Nacheile zur See – eine dogmatische Betrachtung", 42 Archiv des Völkerrechts (2004), pp. 217 *et seq.*

Woodcliffe, J.C., "The demise of unauthorized broadcasting from ships in international waters", 1 International Journal of Estuarine and Coastal Law (1986), pp. 402 *et seq.*

Yang, Haijiang, "Jurisdiction of the coastal state over foreign merchant ships in internal waters and the territorial sea" (Berlin: Springer, 2006)

Yasseen, M.K., "L'interprétation des traités d'après la Convention de Vienne sur le Droit des Traités", 151 Recueil des Cours (1976-III), pp. 20 *et seq.*

Zeigler, Richard, "Ubi Sumus? Quo vadimus?: Charting the Course of Maritime Interception Operations", 43 Naval Law Review (1996), pp. 1 *et seq.*

Zemanek, Karl, "Does the Prospect of Incurring Responsibility Improve the Observance of International Law?", in *Ragazzi*, Maurizio (ed.), "International Responsibility Today – Essays in Memory of Oscar Schachter" (Leiden: Nijhoff, 2005), pp. 125 *et seq.*

Zimmermann, Andreas/*Elberling*, Björn, "Grenzen der Legislativbefugnisse des Sicherheitsrats", 52 Vereinte Nationen (2004), pp. 71 *et seq.*

Zweigert, Konrad/*Kötz*, Hein, "Einführung in die Rechtsvergleichung" (3rd ed., Mohr: Tübingen, 1996)

Annex 3: Table of cases

I. Permanent Court of International Justice

The S.S. Wimbledon, Judgment of 17 August 1923, (1923) PCIJ Series A No. 1, pp. 15 *et seq.*

Delimitation of the Polish-Czecholovakian frontier (question of Jaworzina), Advisory Opinion of 6 December 1923, (1923) PCIJ Ser. B No. 8, pp. 5 *et seq.*

Mavrommatis Palestine Concession (Greece/United Kingdom), Judgment of 30 August 1924, (1924) PCIJ Ser. A No. 2, pp. 5 *et seq.*

Case concerning the Factory at Chorzów (Germany/Poland), *Jurisdiction*, Judgment of 26 July 1927, (1927) PCIJ Series A No. 9, pp. 1 *et seq.*

S.S. Lotus Case (France v. Turkey), Judgment of 7 September 1927, (1927) PCIJ Ser. A No. 10, pp. 4 *et seq.*

Jurisdiction of the Courts of Danzig, Advisory Opinion of 3 March 1928, (1928) PCIJ Series B, No. 15, pp. 4 *et seq.*

Factory at Chorzów (Germany/Poland), Merits, Judgment of 13 September 1928, (1928) PCIJ Series A No. 17, pp. 4 *et seq.*

Territorial Jurisdiction of the International Commission of the River Oder, Judgment of 10 September 1929, (1929) PCIJ Ser. A No. 23, pp. 4 *et seq.*

Access to, and anchorage in the Port of Danzig, of Polish war vessels, Advisory Opinion of 11 Dezember 1931, (1931) PCIJ, Ser. A/B, No. 43, pp. 128 *et seq.*

Interpretation of the Convention of 1919 concerning Employment of Women during the Night, (1932) PCIJ Series A/B No. 50, pp. 365 *et seq.*

The Oscar Chinn Case (United Kingdom/Belgium), Judgment of 12 December 1934, (1934) PCIJ Series A/B No. 63, pp. 65 *et seq.*

Diversion of Water from the River Meuse (Netherlands/Belgium), Judgment of 28 June 1937, (1937) PCIJ Series A/B No. 70, pp. 4 *et seq.*

Phosphates in Morocco, Preliminary Objections, Judgment of 14 June 1938, (1938) PCIJ Series A/B No. 72, pp. 10 *et seq.*

II. Permanent Court of Arbitration

The Carthage (France/Italy), 6 May 1913, 11 RIAA, pp. 449 et seq.

The Manouba (France/Italy), 6 May 1913, 11 RIAA, pp. 463 et seq.

Spanish Zone of Morocco, 29 May 1923, 2 RIAA, pp. 615 et seq.

Lighthouses Case (France/Greece) (15 July 1931), 12 RIAA, pp. 155et seq.

Mox Plant Arbitration (Ireland v. United Kingdom), Order Nr. 3 (24 June 2003), 42 ILM (2003), pp. 1187 et seq.

III. International Court of Justice

Conditions of Admission of a State to Membership in the United Nations (Article 4 of the Charter), Advisory Opinion of 28 May 1948, ICJ Reports 1948, pp. 57 et seq.

Corfu Channel (United Kingdom v. Albania), Judgment of 9 April 1949, ICJ Reports 1949, pp. 4 et seq.

Reparation for Injuries suffered in the Service of the United Nations, Advisory Opinion of 11 April 1949, ICJ Reports 1949, pp. 174 et seq.

Competence of the General Assembly for the Admission of a State to the United Nations, Advisory Opinion of 3 March 1950, ICJ Reports 1950, pp. 8 et seq.

Interpretation of Peace Treaties with Bulgaria, Hungary and Romania, Advisory Opinion of 18 July 1950, ICJ Reports 1950, pp. 221 et seq.

Rights of Nationals of the United States of America in Morocco (France v. United States), Judgment of 27 August 1952, ICJ Reports 1952, pp. 22 et seq.

Nottebohm (Liechtenstein v. Guatemala), Second Phase, Judgment of 6 April 1955, ICJ Reports 1955, pp. 4 et seq.

North Sea Continental Shelf Case (Denmark/Netherlands v. Germany), Judgment of 20 February 1969, ICJ Reports 1969, pp. 3 et seq.

Barcelona Traction, Light and Power Company, Limited (Belgium v. Spain), Judgment of 5 February 1970, ICJ Reports 1970, pp. 4 et seq.

Legal Consequences for States of the continued presence of South Africa in Namibia, Advisory Opinion of 21 June 1971, ICJ Reports 1971, pp. 16 et seq., at 31

Fisheries Jurisdiction Case (United Kingdom v. Iceland), Judgment of 25 July 1974, ICJ Reports 1974, pp. 4 et seq.

Aegean Sea Continental Shelf (Greece v. Turkey), Judgment of 19 December 1978, ICJ Reports 1978, pp. 3 et seq.

United States Diplomatic and Consular Staff in Tehran (United States v. Iran), Judgment of 24 May 1980, ICJ Reports 1980, pp. 3 et seq.

Military and Paramilitary Activities in and against Nicaragua (Nicaragua v. United States of America), Judgment of 27 June 1986, ICJ Reports 1986, pp. 14 et seq.

Arbitral Award of 31 July 1989 (Guinea Bissau v. Senegal), Judgment of 12 November 1991, ICJ Reports 1991, pp. 52 et seq.

Case Concerning Certain Phospate Lands in Naura (Nauru v. Australia), Judgment of 26 June 1949 on Preliminary Objections, ICJ Reports 1992, pp. 240 et seq.

Territorial Dispute (Libya/Chad), Judgment of 13 February 1994, ICJ Reports 1994, pp. 6 et seq.

Maritime Delimitation and Territorial Questions (Qatar v. Bahrain), Judgment of 15 February 1995 on Jurisdiction and Admissibility, ICJ Reports 1995, pp. 6 et seq.

Oil Platforms (Iran/USA), Judgment of 12 December 1996 on Preliminary Objections, ICJ Reports 1996/II, pp. 812 et seq.

Gabcíkovo-Nagymaros (Hungary/Slovakia), Judgment of 25 September 1997, ICJ Reports 1997, pp. 7 et seq.

Difference Relating to Immunity from Legal Process of a Special Rapporteur of the Commission on Human Rights, Advisory Opinion of 29 April 1999, ICJ Reports 1999, pp. 62 et seq.

Kasikili/Sedudu Island (Botswana/Namibia), Judgment of 13 December 1999, ICJ Reports 1999/II, pp. 1045 et seq.

LaGrand Case (Germany v. United States of America), Judgment of 27 June 2001, ICJ Reports 2001, pp. 466 et seq.

Arrest Warrant of 11 April 2000 (Democratic Republic of the Congo v. Belgium), Judgment of 14 February 2002, ICJ Reports 2002, pp. 121 et seq.

Oil Platforms (Islamic Republic of Iran v. United States of America), Judgment of 6 November 2003, ICJ Reports 2003, pp. 161 et seq.

Case Concerning Avena and Other Mexican Nationals (Mexico v. United States of America), Judgment of 31 March 2004, reprinted in 43 ILM (2004), pp. 581 et seq.

Legality of Use of Force (Serbia and Montenegro v. France), Judgment of 15 December 2004, available at <www.icj-cij.org/icjwww/idocket/iyfr/iyfrframe.htm>

IV. International Tribunal for the Law of the Sea

The M/V "Saiga" (No. 2) Case (St. Vincent and the Grenadines v. Guinea), Judgment of 1 July 1999, ITLOS Reports 1999, pp. 10 et seq.

The "Grand Prince" Case (Belize v. France), Prompt Release, Judgment of 20 April 2001, ITLOS Reports 2001, pp. 17 et seq.

The "Chaisiri Reefer 2" Case (Panama v. Yemen), Prompt Release, Order 2001/3 of 6 July 2001, ITLOS Reports 2001, pp. 76 et seq.

The "Juno Trader" Case (St. Vincent and the Grenadines v. Guinea-Bissau), Prompt Release, Judgment of 18 December 2004, ITLOS Reports 2004, pp. 17 et seq.

V. International Arbitral Tribunals

Delagoa Bay Railway (Great Britain and United States / Portugal), 29 March 1900, Martens Nouveau Recueil, 2nd series, vol. 30 (1900), pp. 329 *et seq.*

Affaire des Navires Cape Horn Pigeon, James Hamilton Lewis, C.H. White et Kate and Anna (United States/Russia) (1902), 9 RIAA, pp. 51 *et seq.*

Di Caro (Italy/Venezuela) (1903), 10 RIAA, pp. 597 *et seq.*

Topaze (Belgium/Venezuela) (1903), 9 RIAA, pp. 387 *et seq.*

Dix Case, United States-Venezuela Commission (1903), 9 RIAA, pp. 119 *et seq.*

Heirs of Jean Maninat (France/Venezuela) (31 July 1905), 10 RIAA, pp. 55 *et seq.*

Henry James Bethune (Great Britain) v. United States (1 May 1914), 6 RIAA, pp. 32 *et seq.*

Owner, Officers and Men of The Wanderer (Great Britain) v. United States (1921), 6 RIAA, pp. 68, *et seq.*

Charterers and Crew of The Kate (Great Britain) v. United States (1921), 6 RIAA, pp. 77 *et seq.*

Lusitania Cases, United States-Germany Commission (1922), 7 RIAA, pp. 23 *et seq.*

Norwegian Shipowners Case (Norway/USA) (1922), 1 RIAA, pp. 307 *et seq.*

Administrative Decision No. II, United States-Germany Mixed Claims Commission (1923), 7 RIAA pp. 23 *et seq.*

Chevreau (France v. United Kingdom) (1923), 2 RIAA, pp. 1113 *et seq.*

Union Bridge Company Claim (United States v. United Kingdom), 6 RIAA (1924), pp. 138 *et seq.*

Janes Claim (United States v. Mexico) (16 November 1925), 4 RIAA, pp. 82 *et seq.*

British Property in Spanish Morocco (United Kingdom/Spain) (1925), 2 RIAA, pp. 617 *et seq.*

Illinois Central Railroad Company Claim v. United Mexican States (6 December 1926), 4 RIAA, pp. 134 *et seq.*

The Lindisfarne, Anglo-American Arbitration Tribunal, Nielsen's Report (1926), pp. 483 *et seq.*

Walter Faulkner v. Mexico (1926), 4 RIAA, pp. 67 *et seq.*

Youmans Case (23 November 1926), 4 RIAA, pp. 110 *et seq.*

Cook Case (United States v. Mexico) (3 June 1927), 4 RIAA, pp. 213 *et seq.*

Responsibility of Germany for Damage Caused in the Portuguese Colonies in the South of Africa (Portugal/Germany) (1928), 2 RIAA, pp. 1011 *et seq.*

Caire Case, 5 RIAA (1929), pp. 516 *et seq.*

Shufeldt (USA/Guatemala) (1930), 2 RIAA, pp. 1079 *et seq.*

William McNeill (United Kingdom/Mexico) (1931), 5 RIAA, pp. 164 *et seq.*

Frederick Adams and Charles Thomas Blackmore (Great Britain) v. United Mexican States, British-Mexican Claims Commission Decision No. 64 of 3 July 1931, 5 RIAA, pp. 216 *et seq.*

The "I'm Alone" (United States/Canada) (5 January 1935), 3 RIAA, pp. 1609 *et seq.*

Trail Smelter Arbitration (United States/Canada) (16 April 1938), 3 RIAA, pp. 1905 *et seq.*

Mergé Claim, Italian-United States Conciliation Commission, 10 June 1955, 22 ILR, pp. 443 *et seq.*

Sapphire International Petroleums Ltd. v. National Iranian Oil Company (15 March 1963), 35 ILR, pp. 136 *et seq.*

American Cast Iron Pipe Company Claim (19 October 1966), 40 ILR, pp. 169 *et seq.*

Beagle Channel Arbitration, 17 ILM (1978), pp. 634 *et seq.*

US-France Air Services Arbitration (9 December 1978), 54 ILR, pp. 304 *et seq.*
Young Loan Arbitration (1980), 59 Int'l L. Reports, pp. 495 *et seq.*
Iran v. United States, Case A/1, 1 Iran-U.S.C.T.R. (1981-1982), pp. 189 *et seq.*
American International Group, Inc. v. Government of the Islamic Republic of Iran, 4 Iran-U.S.C.T.R. (1983), pp. 96 *et seq.*
Esphahanian v. Bank Tejarat, 21 Iran-U.S.C.T.R (1983), pp. 166 *et seq.*
R.J. Reynolds Tobacco Co. v. Government of the Islamic Republic of Iran, 7 Iran-U.S.C.T.R. (1984), pp. 181 *et seq.*
Tippetts, Abbett, McCarthy, Stratton v. TAMS-AFFA Consulting Engineers of Iran and Others, 6 Iran-U.S.C.T.R. (1984), pp. 219 *et seq.*
Starrett Housing Corp. v. Government of the Islamic Republic of Iran, 16 Iran-U.S.C.T.R. (1987), pp. 112 *et seq.*
Islamic Republic of Iran v. United States of America (Case No. A.19), 16 Iran-U.S.C.T.R. (1987), pp. 285 *et seq.*
Amco Asia Corp. and Others v. Republic of Indonesia, International Centre for Settlement of Investment Disputes, 1 ICSID Reports (1990), pp. 569 *et seq.*
Rainbow Warrior Arbitration (New Zealand v. France) (30 April 1990), 82 ILR, pp. 499 *et seq.*
US-UK Heathrow User Charges Arbitration (30 November 1992), 102 ILR, pp. 215 *et seq.*
Companía des Desarrollo de Santa Elena SA v. Republic of Costa Rica, International Centre for Settlement of Investment Disputes, I.C.S.I.D. Case No. ARB/96/1, final award of 1 February 2000, available at <www.worldbank.org/icsid/cases/ santaelena_award.pdf>

VI. Domestic Courts

1. Belgium

The Sirius, Belgian Court of Appeals (Antwerp), 19 July 1985, European Transport Law (1985), pp. 536-543

2. France

In re Compagnie Belge des Mines, Minerais et Métaux, Conseil des Prises (6 December 1946), 13 ILR, pp. 412 et seq.

3. Germany

Reichsgericht, RGZ 117, 284 (18 June 1927)
Supreme Court of Danzig, 4 ZaöRV (1934), pp. 947 *et seq.*
Sydney Albert, Oberprisengericht, 25 November 1915, 1 OPGE 62
Arena, Oberprisengericht, 29 June 1917, 1 OPGE 343
Bundesgerichtshof, BGHZ 17, 309 (24 May 1956)

Bundesverfassungsgericht, 46 ZaöRV (1986), pp. 289 *et seq.*
Bundesverfassungsgericht, 2 BvR 1476/03 (15 February 2006)

4. Italy

Pamuk e altri, Tribunale de Crotone (27 September 2001), 84 Rivista di diritto internazionale (2001), pp. 1155 *et seq.*

5. South Africa

In re Certification of the Constitution of RSA 1996, South African Constitutional Court, 10 Butterworths Constitutional Law Reports (1996), pp. 1253 *et seq.*

6. Switzerland

Westland Case, Swiss Federal Tribunal, 19 July 1988, 80 ILR, pp. 658 *et seq.*

7. United Kingdom

Twee Gebroeders, 3 Ch. Rob. 162 (1800)
The Anna, 5 Ch. Rob. 373 (1805)
The Milan, 167 Eng. Rep. 167 (1861)
The Cairnbahn, [1914] P. 25 (C.A.)
The Posteiro, 7 Lloyd's Reports of Prize Cases (1921), pp. 21 *et seq.*
The Valeria, 9 Lloyd's Reports of Prize Cases (1923), pp. 32 *et seq.*
The Unitas, [1948] P. 205
The Unitas, [1950] A.C. 536
The Patrai, High Court of Justice (21 May 1952), 19 ILR, pp. 634 *et seq.*
Wagon Mound [1961] A.C. 388
Maclaine Watson v. Dept of Trade, High Court, Chancery Division. 13 May 1987, 77 ILR, pp. 45 *et seq.*
Maclaine Watson & Co. Ltd. v. International Tin Council (No. 2), Court of Appeal, 27 April 1988, 80 ILR, pp. 110 *et seq.*
J.H. Rayner v. Dpt of Trade, House of Lords, 26 October 1989, 81 ILR, pp. 704 *et seq.*

8. United States of America

The Fortuna, 1 Dods. 81 (12 March 1811)
The Lively, 15 F.Cas. 631 (C.C. D.Mass. 1812)
Le Louis, 2 Dods. 210 (1816)
The Amiable Nancy, 16 U.S. 546 (1818)
Madrazo v. Willes, 3 Barn. & Ald. 353 (1820)

The Apollon, 22 U.S. 362 (1824)
The Antilope, 10 Wheaton 66 (1825)
The Marianna Flora, 1 Wheaton 1 (1826)
The Alabama & The Game-cock, 92 U.S. 695 (1875)
The Atlas, 93 U.S. 302 (1876)
U.S. v. The Nuestra Senora De Regla, 108 U.S. 92 (1883)
The Chattahoochee, 173 U.S. 540, 540 (1899)
The Nancy, 37 Ct.Cl. 401 (1902)
Starrett v. United States., 39 Ct.Cl. 34 (1903)
Aktieselskabet Cuzco v. The Sucarseco, 294 U.S. 394 (1935)
United States v. Sherwood, 312 U.S. 584 (1941)
The Wilhelmina, 78 F.Supp. 57 (W.D. Washington, 1948)
Anglo Chinese Shipping Co. v. United States, 127 F.Supp. 553 (Court of Claims) (1955)
Terry v. Ohio, 392 U.S. 1 (1968)
United States v. Reliable Transfer Co., 421 U.S. 397 (1975)
United States v. Cadena, 585 F.2d 1252 (5th Cir. 1978)
United States v. Postal, 589 F.2d 862 (5th Cir. 1979)
Drake Towing Co. v. Meisner Marine Constr. Co., 765 F.2d 1060 (11th Cir.1985)
Pascua v. Astrocielo Neptunea Armandora, S.A., 614 F.Supp. 984 (D.C.Tex.,1985)
Berkovitz v. United States, 486 U.S. 531 (1988)
B&F Trawlers, Inc. v. United States, 841 F.2d 626 (5th Cir.1988)
United States v. Gaubert, 499 U.S. 315 (1991)
Autery v. United States, 992 F.2d 1523 (11th Cir.1993)
BMW of North America, Inc. v. Gore, 517 U.S. 559 (1996)
Tew v. United States, 86 F.3d 1003 (10th Cir.1996)
Lane v. Pena, 518 U.S. 187 (1996)
Mid-South Holding Co., Inc. v. U.S., 225 F.3d 1201 (11th Cir. 2000)
Taghadomi v. Extreme Sports Maui, 257 F.Supp.2d 1262 (D.Hawai'i 2002)
McMellon v. United States, 338 F.3d 287 (4th Cir. 2003)

VII. Others

Case 41/74, *Van Duyn v. Home Office*, European Court of Justice, 1974 ECR, pp. 1337 *et seq.*
Golder v. United Kingdom, European Court of Human Rights, Judgment of 21 February 1975, 57 ILR, pp. 200 *et seq.*
Case 238/78, *Ireks-Arkady GmbH v. Council and Commission*, European Court of Justice, 1979 ECR, pp. 2955 *et seq.*
Case 64/76, *P. Dumortier Frères SA v. Council*, European Court of Justice, 1979 ECR, pp. 3091 *et seq.*
Case 8/81, *Becker ./. Finanzamt Münster*, European Court of Justice, 1982 ECR, pp. 53 *et seq.*

Matthews v. The United Kingdom, European Court of Human Rights (18 February 1999), Application 24833/94, available at <www.echr.coe.int>

The Right to Information on Consular Assistance in the Framework of the Guarantees of Due Process of Law, Inter-American Court of Human Rights, Advisory Opinion of 1 October 1999, reprinted in Human Rights Law Journal (2000), pp. 24 *et seq.*

Xhavara & others v. Italy & Albania (Application No. 39473-98), European Court of Human Rights, Decision of 11 January 2001, available at <www.echr.coe.int>

Case C-47/02, *Anker and others v. Germany*, European Court of Justice (30 September 2003), Official Journal C 275/17 (15 November 2003)

About the International Max Planck Research School for Maritime Affairs at the University of Hamburg

The International Max Planck Research School for Maritime Affairs at the University of Hamburg was established by the Max Planck Society for the Advancement of Science, in cooperation with the Max Planck Institute for Comparative and International Private Law (Hamburg), the Max Planck Institute for Comparative Foreign Public Law and International Law (Heidelberg), the Max Planck Institute for Meteorology (Hamburg) and the University of Hamburg. The School's research is focused on the legal, economic, and geophysical aspects of the use, protection, and organization of the oceans. Its researchers work in the fields of law, economics, and natural sciences. The School provides extensive research capacities as well as its own teaching curriculum. Currently, the School has 15 Directors who determine the general work of the School, act as supervisors for dissertations, elect applicants for the School's PhD-grants, and are the editors of this book series:

Prof. Dr. Dr. h.c. Jürgen Basedow is Director of the Max Planck Institute for Foreign Private Law and Private International Law; *Prof. Dr. Peter Ehlers* is the Director of the German Federal Maritime and Hydrographic Agency; *Prof. Dr. Dr. h.c. Hartmut Graßl* is Director of the Max Planck Institute for Meteorology; *Prof. Dr. Hans-Joachim Koch* is Managing Director of the Seminar of Environmental Law of the Faculty of Law at the University of Hamburg; *Prof. Dr. Rainer Lagoni* is Managing Director of the Institute of Maritime Law and the Law of the Sea at the University of Hamburg; *PD Dr. Gerhard Lammel* is Senior Scientist at the Max Planck Institute for Meteorology; *Prof. Dr. Ulrich Magnus* is Managing Director of the Seminar of Foreign Law and Private International Law at the University of Hamburg; *Prof. Dr. Peter Mankowski* is Director of the Seminar of Foreign and Private International Law at the University of Hamburg; *Prof. Dr. Marian Paschke* is Director of the Institute of Maritime Law and the Law of the Sea at the University of Hamburg; *PD. Dr. Thomas Pohlmann* is Senior Scientist at the Centre for Marine and Climate Research and Member of the Institute of Oceanography at the University of Hamburg; *Dr. Uwe Schneider* is Assistant Professor at the Research Unit Sustainability and Global Change, Centre for Marine and Climate Research, Departments of Geosciences and Economics at the University of Hamburg; *Prof. Dr. Jürgen Sündermann* is Director at the Centre for Marine and Climate Research at the University of Hamburg; *Prof. Dr. Richard Tol* is Director of the Research Unit Sustainability and Global Change at the University of Hamburg; *Prof. Dr. Dr. h.c. Rüdiger Wolfrum* is Director at the Max Planck Institute for Comparative Foreign Public Law and International Law and a judge at the International Tribunal for the Law of the Sea; *Prof. Dr. Wilfried Zahel* is professor at the Centre for Marine and Climate Research, Departments of Geosciences and Economics at the University of Hamburg.

At present, *Prof. Dr. Dr. h.c. Jürgen Basedow* and *Prof. Dr. Ulrich Magnus* serve as speakers of the International Max Planck Research School for Maritime Affairs at the University of Hamburg.